A History of Persian Literature
Volume XVIII

Volumes of *A History of Persian Literature*

I General Introduction to Persian Literature
II Persian Poetry in the Classical Era, 800–1500
    Panegyrics *(qaside)*, Short Lyrics *(ghazal)*; Quatrains *(robâ'i)*
III Persian Poetry in the Classical Era, 800–1500
    Narrative Poems in Couplet form *(mathnavis)*; Strophic Poems; Occasional Poems *(qat'e)*; Satirical and Invective poetry; *shahrâshub*
IV Heroic Epic
    The *Shahnameh* and its Legacy
V Persian Prose
VI Religious and Mystical Literature
VII Persian Poetry, 1500–1900
    From the Safavids to the Dawn of the Constitutional Movement
VIII Persian Poetry from outside Iran
    The Indian Subcontinent, Anatolia, Central Asia after Timur
IX Persian Prose from outside Iran
    The Indian Subcontinent, Anatolia, Central Asia after Timur
X Persian Historiography
XI Literature of the early Twentieth Century
    From the Constitutional Period to Reza Shah
XII Modern Persian Poetry, 1940 to the Present
    Iran, Afghanistan, Tajikistan
XIII Modern Fiction and Drama
XIV Biographies of the Poets and Writers of the Classical Period
XV Biographies of the Poets and Writers of the Modern Period; Literary Terms
XVI General Index

Companion Volumes to *A History of Persian Literature:*
XVII Companion Volume I: The Literature of Pre-Islamic Iran
XVIII Companion Volume II: Oral Literature of Iranian Languages
    Kurdish, Pashto, Balochi, Ossetic, Persian and Tajik

A HISTORY OF PERSIAN LITERATURE

General Editor—Ehsan Yarshater

Volume XVIII

Oral Literature of Iranian Languages
Kurdish, Pashto, Balochi, Ossetic, Persian and Tajik

Companion Volume II
to *A History of Persian Literature*

Edited by
Philip G. Kreyenbroek & Ulrich Marzolph

Sponsored by
Persian Heritage Foundation (New York)
&
Center for Iranian Studies, Columbia University

Published in 2010 by I.B.Tauris & Co Ltd
6 Salem Road, London W2 4BU
175 Fifth Avenue, New York NY 10010
www.ibtauris.com

Distributed in the United States and Canada
Exclusively by Palgrave Macmillan, 175 Fifth Avenue, New York NY 10010

Copyright © 2010 The Persian Heritage Foundation

The right of The Persian Heritage Foundation to be identified as the originators of this work has been asserted by The Persian Heritage Foundation in accordance with the Copyright, Designs and Patents Act 1988.

All rights reserved. Except for brief quotations in a review, this book, or any part thereof, may not be reproduced, stored in or introduced into a retrieval system, or transmitted, in any form or by any means, electronic, mechanical, photocopying, recording or otherwise, without the prior written permission of the publisher.

A History of Persian Literature: XVIII

ISBN: 978 1 84511 918 8

A full CIP record for this book is available from the British Library
A full CIP record is available from the Library of Congress

Library of Congress Catalog Card Number: available

Printed and bound in Great Britain
by TJ International Ltd, Padstow, Cornwall
from camera-ready copy edited and supplied
by The Persian Heritage Foundation

A History of Persian Literature

Editorial Board

MOHSEN ASHTIANY

J. T. P. DE BRUIJN *(Vice-Chairman)*

DICK DAVIS

WILLIAM HANAWAY, Jr.

AHMAD KARIMI-HAKKAK

FRANKLIN LEWIS

WILFERD MADELUNG

HESHMAT MOAYYAD

EHSAN YARSHATER *(Chairman)*

Late Member: ANNEMARIE SCHIMMEL

CONTENTS

CONTRIBUTORS xv

FOREWORD xxi

PREFACE xxvii

THE STUDY OF POPULAR LITERATURE
IN THE PERSIAN CONTEXT. xxxv
  1. Academic approaches to popular literature xxxvi
  2. Specifics of popular literature. xxxvii
  3. Cultural components of Persian popular literature xxxviii
  4. The relation between popular and elite literature xl
  5. The relation between the individual and the collective . . xlii
  6. Persian popular literature as defined by content. xliii
  7. The influence of printing on Persian popular literature. . xliv
  8. The study of Persian popular literature: present and future xlvi

CHAPTER 1: WRITTEN KURDISH LITERATURE (J. Blau) . 1
  1. Introduction. 1
  2. Early Kurdish literature 4
    Gurani literature. 7
    The beginning of Sorani as a literary language 9
    The Kurdish press 14
  3. Kurdish literature after World War I 15
    In Armenia, 1921–89 15
    In Turkey, 1923–57 18
    In Iraq, 1919–57 19
    Prose Literature 21
    In Iran, 1912–79 21
    In Iraq and Turkey, 1958–90 22
    In the Diaspora. 24
    In Iran since 1979 26

ORAL LITERATURE OF IRANIAN LANGUAGES

In Turkey since 1991. 27
In Iraq since 1991 28
In independent Armenia 31

CHAPTER 2: KURDISH ORAL LITERATURE (Ch. Allison) . 33
1. Oral tradition in Kurdistan 34
2. The upheavals of the late twentieth century 37
3. Studies of Kurdish oral literature 39
4. Genre 41
5. Performers 46
6. Shared traditions 48
7. Kurdish traditions 51
   Mem and Zîn 52
   Dimdim 56
8. Kurdish lyric 62
   Lyrical love songs 64
   Lamentation 67
9. The future of Kurdish oral literature 68

CHAPTER 3: ORALITY AND RELIGION IN KURDISTAN:
THE YEZIDI AND AHL-E HAQQ TRADITIONS
(Ph. G. Kreyenbroek) 70
1. The Yezidis and Ahl-e Haqq 72
   Demography 72
   Religious affiliations 73
   History 73
   Some characteristic ideas and beliefs. 74
2. Textual traditions of the Yezidis and Ahl-e Haqq. 75
   The absorption of outside influences. 75
   Storylines and sacred poems 75
   Polyvalence. 76
   Characteristic topics. 76
      Creation and the First Things 76
      *Legends explaining the community's origins
      and affiliations* 78
      Saints and Holy Men 78
      Mystical themes 79
      Philosophical themes: the implications of death 80
3. The sacred poems. 80
   Formal characteristics. 80

CONTENTS

    Music 83
    Transmitters 83
    On the discovery of the sacred texts 84
  4. Questions of orality and literacy in connection with the poems 86

CHAPTER 4: PASHTO LITERATURE: THE CLASSICAL PERIOD (S. Andreyev) 89
  1. Poetic forms and genres 89
  2. Early and classical Pashto poetry 91
    The Rowshani period 92
    Rowshani authors and their works 93
    Âkhund Darwêza 104
    Khoshhâl Khan Khattak 108
    Rahmân Bâbâ and Abd-al-Hamid 110
    Later classical poetry 110
  3. Prose writing 111
  4. Conclusion 113

CHAPTER 5: MODERN PASHTO WRITTEN LITERATURE (L. N. Bartlotti) 114
  1. Introduction. 114
  2. The development of modern Pashto literature 116
    The Afghan tradition 116
    Eastern Pashto 122
  3. Other factors affecting modern Pashto written literature .. 125
    Orality and literacy 125
    The place of poets and writers in Pashtun society 126
    Modern Pashto literature and the politics of language
      and identity 130
    Literary-cum-cultural organizations 132

CHAPTER 6: PASHTO ORAL AND POPULAR LITERATURE (W. Heston) 135
  1. Introduction. 135
  2. Before 1950 139
  3. After 1950 146
  4. Bibliographies, collections and studies 148
    Bibliographies 148
    Collections 149
    Studies 152

ORAL LITERATURE OF IRANIAN LANGUAGES

5. Mass Media 156
    Chapbooks 156
    Newspapers and periodicals 159
    Radio and TV 160
    Audiocassettes and performance 161
    Cinema and VCRs 163
6. Concluding comments 165

CHAPTER 7: BALOCHI LITERATURE (J. Elfenbein) 167

1. The classical period 168
    Script and dialect 169
    The composition by individuals of classical oral ballads . . 171
    Daptars 172
    Classical poetry 175
        The Čâkur Cycle 178
        Ballads by or about personalities of the Čâkur Cycle . 181
        The Dôdâ Bâlâč Cycle 184
        Hammal Jîhand 186
2. Literature of the post-classical period: the eighteenth century 188
    Ballads 188
        Leylâ and Majnun 188
        Širin and Farhâd 188
        Dôstên and Šîrên 189
        Šêh Murîd and Hânî 190
        The tale/ballad of 'Isâ and Barî 191
    Known poets 191
        Jâm Durrak 191
        Mullâ Fazl 192
        'Izzat Lallâ 192
3. The nineteenth century 193
    Known poets 193
        Mullâ Ibrâhîm 193
        Mullâ Bampuštî 193
        Mullâ Bahâdur 193
        Fakîr Šêr-jân 194
        Mast Tôkalî 194
        Rahm 'Alî Marî 194
4. The Modern period 195
5. Miscellaneous verse 197
    Songs 197

CONTENTS

Riddles and conundrums 198
Proverbs 198

CHAPTER 8: OSSETIC LITERATURE (F. Thordarson) 199
  1. The history of writing in Ossetic 200
  2. Named authors until 1917 201
  3. After 1917 203
  4. The Nart Epic 205

**CHAPTER 9: PERSIAN POPULAR LITERATURE
(U. Marzolph)** 208
  1. History of research 208
  2. Fields of study 212
  3. Traditional popular reading matter 215
  4. Folk- and fairy-tales 218
    Terminology 219
    Language and formulaic expression 219
    Introductory formulas 220
    Closing formulas 220
    Formulas within the tale 222
    Categories 223
    Characters 224
    Aspects of performance 226
    Dating Persian folk-tales 226
  5. Proverbs and popular sayings 230
  6. Folk humor 231
  7. Folk poetry 234
  8. Outlook 239

**CHAPTER 10: NAQQÂLI: PROFESSIONAL IRANIAN
STORYTELLING (K. Yamamoto)** 240
  1. Historical background 242
  2. Storytellers 247
  3. Training 248
  4. Tumârs 248
  5. Repertoire 250
  6. Tumârs and literary sources 251
  7. Performance 253
  8. Some specific features of oral performance 254
  9. Conclusion 256

ORAL LITERATURE OF IRANIAN LANGUAGES

CHAPTER 11: KÂSHEFI'S *ROWZAT AL-SHOHADÂ'*:
THE KARBALÂ NARRATIVE AS UNDERPINNING
OF POPULAR RELIGIOUS CULTURE AND LITERATURE
(P. Chelkowski). 258
   1. Kâshefi and the *Rowzat al-shohadâ'* 259
   2. *Rowze-kh^wâni* 264
   3. *Ta'ziye-kh^wâni* 271
   4. *Parde-kh^wâni* 276

CHAPTER 12: THE POPULAR LITERATURE
OF THE TAJIKS **(R. Rahmoni)**. 278
   1. History of the study 278
   2. Proverbs and maxims 280
   3. Riddles. 281
   4. Bayt 282
   5. Dobayti 284
   6. Robâ'i 285
   7. Songs 286
      Tarona 286
      Joyful songs 287
      Satirical songs 288
      Melancholy songs 288
      Historical songs 288
      Songs for special occasions 288
      Harvesting songs. 289
      Wedding songs 290
      Dirges (*marsia*) 292
      Improvisations (*badeha*) 293
   8. Prose stories. 295
      Afsona 295
         Tales about magic. 295
         Fables (tales about animals) 296
         Tales about the realities of life 296
         Tales about love. 296
      Edifying religious stories (*qissa*) 297
      Rivoyat 298
      Naql 298
      Fabulous tales 299
      Latifa 299
      The heroic epic 300

CONTENTS

9. Folk drama. 301
10. Local poets. 301
11. Conclusion. 302

CHAPTER 13: ORAL AND POPULAR LITERATURE
IN DARI PERSIAN OF AFGHANISTAN (M. A. Mills) 303
 1. Literacy and orality in Afghanistan. 303
 2. Chapbooks and oral storytelling 305
 3. Research on oral culture in Afghanistan 307
 4. Collections of folk literature 315
 5. Studies by Western scholars. 320

BIBLIOGRAPHIES. 323
 The study of popular literature in the Persian context. 323
 Chapter 1 324
 Chapter 2 327
  Kurdish periodicals 327
  Primary literature: texts and translations 328
  Secondary literature. 331
 Chapter 3 335
 Chapter 4 339
 Chapter 5 343
 Chapter 6 346
 Chapter 7 350
 Chapter 8 351
  Select bibliography on the Nart Epic 352
  Ossetic texts referred to. 352
  Secondary literature 352
 Chapter 9 352
 Chapter 10 365
 Chapter 11 370
 Chapter 12 371
 Chapter 13 376

CONTRIBUTORS

Christine Allison studied Kurdish at SOAS, London, after a BA in Classics and French in Oxford. Her Ph.D. thesis on oral traditions amongst the Yezidis of Iraq was submitted in 1996, followed by a British Academy Postdoctoral Fellowship at SOAS (1997–2001). She then became tenured Lecturer in Kurdish at the Institut National des Langues et Civilisations Orientales, Paris, (2001–2007) before taking up the post of Ibrahim Ahmed Professor of Kurdish Studies in Exeter in 2007. Her main areas of interest are orality, literacy, memory and popular culture across the Middle East and especially amongst the Kurds. She also has a strong interest in the literary and cultural history of the Kurds of the former Soviet Union. Her publications include *The Yezidi Oral Tradition in Iraqi Kurdistan* (2001) and numerous articles on Kurdish subjects.

Sergei Andreyev studied in St Petersburg and Oxford and received his Doctorate in Oriental Studies in Oxford in 1997. He has worked in various academic institutions in Russia and the United Kingdom, including the University of St Petersburg, the Museum of the History of Religions, St Petersburg, King's College of the University of London and the Oxford Centre for Islamic Studies. From 2000–2002, he worked for the United Nations in Afghanistan. Later he was a Visiting Fellow with The Institute of Ismaili Studies, doing research on the Ismaili communities of Central Asia and Afghanistan. In addition to his published articles in books and journals, Dr Andreyev's publications include *History of Pashto Literature* (2002), and *Sufi Illuminati: the Rawshani Movement in Muslim Mysticism, Society and Politics* (2008).

Leonard N. Bartlotti is Associate Professor of Intercultural and Islamic Studies at Biola University (La Mirada, CA). An ethnographic folklorist and anthropologist of Islam, he is a specialist on the Pashtun people, and serves as a consultant to humanitarian organizations in Afghanistan, Pakistan, and Central Asia. He lived and worked in Peshawar, Pakistan, 1985–1999, where he was founder and Executive Director of the InterLit Foundation Publishers & Consultants. He received his Ph.D. from the University of Wales (2000), and served in Oxford (UK) as a Research Tutor and Lecturer in Islamic Studies. His research interests include Pashtun language and culture; Folk Poetry and Paremiology (Proverb Studies); Pakistan-Afghanistan Area Studies; and Development in Islamic Contexts. His co-edited book, *Rohi Mataluna: Pashto Proverbs*, was published by Wipf and Stock/Resource Publications (Eugene, OR, 2006)

Joyce Blau (Cairo, 1932) received her doctorate in Kurdish Studies in 1973 and accreditation as Research Director in 1990, both from the Sorbonne (Paris). From 1970 to 2000 she held the Chair in Kurdish Studies at the Institut National des Langues et Civilisations orientales in Paris. She taught Kurdish (Kurmanji and Sorani), as well as Kurdish civilization and history. Since her retirement she has participated in the work of the Kurdish Institute of Paris Foundation. She has published on Kurdish grammar and on diverse subjects in Kurdish literature and culture.

Peter Chelkowski studied Oriental Philology at the Jagellonian University and Theater Arts at the School of Drama in Cracow, Poland. He went on to study the history and culture of the Middle East in London, England, and Persian Literature at the University of Tehran, Iran. Since 1968, he has been Professor of Middle Eastern and Islamic Studie at New York University. His research interests include Islamic and Iranian Studies in general, Islamic Mysticism, Popular Beliefs and Rituals, Persian Language and Literature, and the Performing Arts. Chelkowski's major publications include *Mirror of the Invisible World* (1975), the edited volume *Ta'ziyeh: Ritual and Drama in Iran* (1979), and *Staging a Revolution: The Art of Persuasion in the Islamic Republic or Iran* (co-authored with Hamid Dabashi, 1999).

CONTRIBUTORS

Josef Elfenbein (1927) has been Professor of Iranian Studies at several Universities, lastly at the University of Mainz; he retired in 1998. He has written widely on Balochi since 1958. esp. the 2-volume *Anthology of Classical and Modern Balochi Literature* (1990), and articles in *Encyclopedia of Islam*, and *Encyclopaedia Iranica*.

Wilma Heston received her Ph.D. from the University of Pennsylvania with a dissertation on "Selected Problems in Fifth to Tenth Century Iranian Syntax". While visiting Pakistan in 1980, she became interested in the regional folk literature collections of the library of Lok Virsa, Pakistan's National Institute of Folk Heritage, in Islamabad. After learning that oral storytelling in verse was a living tradition in Pakistan's Northwester Frontier Province, she focused on Pashto folk literature. Her fieldwork there was done in collaboration with Lok Virsa; resulting publications are cited in the References of her chapter on "Pashto Oral and Popular Literature" in this volume. She is currently affiliated with the Department of Near Eastern Languages and Civilizations of the University of Pennsylvania.

Philip G. Kreyenbroek (1948) read Oriental Languages and History of Religions in the Universities of Amsterdam, Utrecht, and London. He received his Doctorate from the University of Leiden in 1982. From 1973–88 he taught Iranian Studies in the University of Utrecht. In 1988 he was appointed Lecturer in Modern Iranian Languages (later Reader in Iranian Languages and Religions) at SOAS, London. In 1996 he was appointed to the Chair of Iranian Studies in the Georg-August University Göttingen. His research work focuses on questions of orality and History of Religions in Iranian cultures, with special reference to Zoroastrianism, Yezidism and the Ahl-e Haqq.

Ulrich Marzolph studied Oriental Philology at the universities of Mashhad and Cologne, Germany, where he received his Ph.D. with the dissertation *Typologie des persischen Volksmärchens* (1982). Since 1986, he has been employed as a senior researcher at the *Enzyklopädie des Märchens* in Göttingen, Germany. Since

1992 he is Professor in the Institute of Arabic and Islamic Studies in Göttingen. Marzolph's main research interest is the narrative culture of the Muslim Near and Middle East. Besides numerous essays and encyclopedic entries, his main monograph publications include *Arabia ridens* (1992), a comprehensive study of jocular prose in pre-modern Arabic literature, the edited volume of Persian folktales collected by L. P. Elwell-Sutton, *Qesseha-ye Mashdi Galin Khanom* (together with Azar Amirhosseini-Nithammer and Ahmad Vakiliyan, 1994), and the *Arabian Nights Encyclopedia* (co-authored with Richard van Leeuwen, 2004).

Margaret Mills received her doctoral training at Harvard University, supervised by Albert B. Lord. She taught at the Department of Folklore and Folklife at the University of Pennsylvania in Philadelphia for 13 years before moving to Ohio State University in Columbus, Ohio, where she is now Professor of Folklore and Persian in the Department of Near Eastern Languages and Cultures. Mills has pursued field research on contemporary oral tradition and folklife in Afghanistan, Pakistan and Tajikistan since 1969. Her publications include her 1978 dissertation, *Oral Narrative in Afghanistan: The Individual in Tradition* (1990), the monograph *Rhetorics and Politics in Afghan Traditional Storytelling* (1991; winner, Chicago Folklore Prize, 1993), and the co-edited volume *South Asian Folklore: An Encyclopedia* (with Sarah Diamond and Peter Claus, 2003).

Ravshan Rahmoni (Rakhmonov) studied folklore at the university of Moscow and acquired his Ph.D. in 1989 with a dissertation on contemporary oral tradition in Afghanistan, *Nazm-e shifahi-ye talifiye darizabanan-e Afghanistan-e mu'asir*. His second thesis (Habilitation), defended in 1998, is a comprehensive survey of current Iranian oral tradition. Since 1978, he works at the Tajik National University in Dushanbe, Tajikistan, currently at the rank of Professor. Rahmoni has recorded a large variety of items from the oral tradition of Tajikistan, Afghanistan, Uzbekistan, and Iran, including some 20,000 pages of fieldnotes, some 11,000 pictures, more than 1,000 sound recordings of folklore texts, and almost

CONTRIBUTORS

100 video recordings. His numerous publications include a comprehensive study of folktales in the Persian language area (*Tarikh-e girdavari, nashr va pazhuhish-e afsanahaye mardum-e farsizaban*, 2001) and, most recently, an introduction to Tajik oral tradition (*Ijadiyat-e guftari-ye mardom-e tajik*, 2008).

†**Fridrik Thordarson** (1928–2005) was born in Iceland and came to Norway in 1951 to study Classical Philology and Old Iranian at the University of Oslo. He was Lecturer in Classical Philology in the University of Oslo from 1965, and became a Professor in 1994. One of his main fields of interest was the languages of the Caucasus. In 1968–9 he spent a year in Georgia, where he worked on Georgian and Ossetian. Thordarson became one of the leading experts on this language and its culture, and published widely on these subjects.

Kumiko Yamamoto received her Ph.D. in Iranian Studies/Persian Literature from the School of Oriental and African Studies, University of London. She also studied film theory at the University of Tokyo, and has written about Abbas Kiarostami. From 2005–8 she taught English at the University of Tokyo and the University of Air. She is currently a Corresponding Fellow of the Institute of Iranian Studies, University of Göttingen. Her research interests include the *Shâhnâma* of Ferdowsi, traditional storytelling (*naqqâli*), and Iranian cinema. Her dissertation was published as *The Oral Background of Persian Epics: From Storytelling to Poetry* (2003).

FOREWORD

In the 1990s I gradually became convinced that the time had come for a new, comprehensive, and detailed history of Persian literature, given its stature and significance as the single most important accomplishment of the Iranian peoples. Hermann Ethé's pioneering survey of the subject, "Neupersische Litteratur" in *Grundriss der iranischen Philologie* II, was published in 1904 and E. G. Browne's far more extensive *A Literary History of Persia*, with ample discussion of the political and cultural background of each period, appeared in four successive volumes between 1902 and 1924. The English translation of Jan Rypka's *History of Iranian Literature*, written in collaboration with a number of other scholars, came out in 1968 under his own supervision.

Iranian scholars have also made a number of significant contributions throughout the 20th century to different aspects of Persian literary history. These include B. Foruzânfar's *Sokhan va sokhanvarân* (On poetry and poets, 1929–33), M.-T. Bahâr's *Sabk-shenâsi* (Varieties of style in prose) in three volumes (1942) and a number of monographs on individual poets and writers. The truly monumental achievement of the century in this context was Dh. Safâ's wide-ranging and meticulously researched *Târikh-e adabiyyât dar Irân* (History of Literature in Iran) in five volumes and eight parts (1953–79). It studies Persian poetry and prose in the context of their political, social, religious, and cultural background, from the rise of Islam to almost the middle of the 18th century.

Nevertheless, it cannot be said that Persian literature has received the attention it merits, bearing in mind that it has been the jewel in the crown of Persian culture in its widest sense and the standard bearer for aesthetic and cultural norms of the literature of the eastern regions of the Islamic world from about the 12th century; and that it has profoundly influenced the literatures

ORAL LITERATURE OF IRANIAN LANGUAGES

of Ottoman Turkey, Muslim India and Turkic Central Asia—a literature that could inspire Goethe, Emerson, Matthew Arnold, and Jorge Luis Borges among others, and was praised by William Jones, Tagore, E. M. Forster, and many more. Persian literature remained a model for the literatures of the above countries until the 19th century, when the European influence began effectively to challenge the Persian literary and cultural influence and succeeded in replacing it. Whereas Persian art and architecture, and more recently Persian films, have been written about extensively and at different levels for a varied audience, Persian literature has largely remained the exclusive domain of specialists: It is only in the past few years that the poems of Rumi have drawn to themselves the kind of popular attention enjoyed by Omar Khayyam in the 19th century.

A History of Persian Literature (HPL) has been conceived as a comprehensive and richly documented work, with illustrative examples and a fresh critical approach, to be written by prominent scholars in the field. An Editorial Board was selected and a meeting of the Board arranged in September 1995 in Cambridge, UK, in conjunction with the gathering that year of the Societas Europaea Iranologica, where the broad outlines of the editorial policy were drawn up.

Fourteen volumes were initially envisaged to cover the subject, including two Companion Volumes. Later, two additional volumes devoted to Persian prose from outside Iran (the Indian subcontinent, Anatolia, Central Asia) and historiography, respectively, were added.

Of the Companion Volumes, the first deals with pre-Islamic Iranian literatures and the second with the literature of Iranian languages other than Persian as well as Persian and Tajik oral folk literature.

The titles of the volumes are as follows:
Volume I: General Introduction to Persian Literature
Volume II: Persian Poetry in the Classical Era, 800–1500
            Panegyrics *(qaside)*, Short Lyrics *(ghazal)*; Quatrains *(robâ'i)*

FOREWORD

Volume III:	Persian Poetry in the Classical Era, 800–1500
	Narrative Poems in Couplet form (*mathnavi*s); Strophic Poems; Occasional Poems *(qat'e)*; Satirical and Invective poetry; *shahrâshub*
Volume IV:	Heroic Epic
	The *Shahnameh* and its Legacy
Volume V:	Persian Prose
Volume VI:	Religious and Mystical Literature
Volume VII:	Persian Poetry, 1500–1900
	From the Safavids to the Dawn of the Constitutional Movement
Volume VIII:	Persian Poetry from outside Iran
	The Indian Subcontinent, Anatolia, Central Asia after Timur
Volume IX:	Persian Prose from outside Iran
	The Indian Subcontinent, Anatolia, Central Asia after Timur
Volume X:	Persian Historiography
Volume XI:	Literature of the early Twentieth Century
	From the Constitutional Period to Reza Shah
Volume XII:	Modern Persian Poetry, 1940 to the Present
	Iran, Afghanistan, Tajikistan
Volume XIII:	Modern Fiction and Drama
Volume XIV:	Biographies of the Poets and Writers of the Classical Period
Volume XV:	Biographies of the Poets and Writers of the Modern Period; Literary Terms
Volume XVI:	General Index

Companion volumes to *A History of Persian Literature*:
Volume XVII: Companion Volume I: The Literature of Pre-Islamic Iran
Volume XVIII: Companion Volume II: Oral Literature of Iranian Languages: Kurdish, Pashto, Balochi, Ossetic, Persian and Tajik

It is hoped that the multi-volume *HPL* will provide adequate space for the analysis and treatment of all aspects of Persian literature.

The inclusion of a volume on Persian historiography can be justified by the fact that Persian histories like the biographical accounts of mystics or poets often exploit the same stylistic and literary features and the same kinds of figures of speech that one encounters in Persian poetry and belles-lettres, with skilful use of balanced cadences, rhyme, varieties of metaphor and hyperbole, and an abundance of embellishing devices. This was considered to impart a literary dimension to the prose, enhance its esthetic effect, and impress the reader with the literary prowess of the author. The study of Persian historiography should therefore be regarded as a component of any comprehensive study of Persian literary prose and the analysis of its changing styles and contours. Moreover, in pre-modern times, "literature" was defined more broadly than it is today and often included historiography.

As is evident from the title of the volumes, *A History of Persian Literature*'s approach is neither uniformly chronological nor entirely thematic. Developments occur in time and to understand a literary genre requires tracing its course chronologically. On the other hand, images, themes, and motifs have lives of their own and need to be studied not only diachronically but also synchronically, regardless of the time element. A combination of the two methods has therefore been employed to achieve a better overall treatment.

Generous space has been given to modern poetry, fiction, and drama in order to place them in the wider context of Persian literary studies and criticism.

About the present volume

The Companion Volumes to *A History of Persian Literature* treat essentially of literatures that are Iranian, but not Persian. These languages stand, however, in some relationship with Persian literature. They either serve as its historical background (Companion Volume I) or have been influenced by Persian literature (Companion Volume II).

FOREWORD

This Volume treats of Kurdish, Pashto, Baloch, and Ossetic. As the literature of these languages at least until the 20th century are basically oral, the Volume has been called *Oral Literature of Iranian Languages*. To make the Volume comprehensive, chapters on Persian and Tajik oral literatures have also been included. Since the other current Iranian dialects such as Lori, Gilaki, Mâzandarâni, Tâti, Tâleshi, Yaghnâbi, the dialects of the Zoroastrian and Jewish communities of Iran and many lesser significant dialects do not possess oral literatures comparable in size to the literature of the languages discussed in this Volume, they have not been taken into account.

It is true that most non-Persian languages figured in this Volume do possess now also written literature, composed mostly during the 19th century, and occasionally earlier, but this Volume is concerned with the traditional literature of these languages, which happen to be oral. As these languages were spoken either inside Iran or in its neighboring regions, they have all received, with the possible exception of Ossetic, the influence of Persian, which has served as the administrative and literary language of the realm. It is this aspect that justifies their inclusion in *A History of Persian Literature*.

Ehsan Yarshater
General Editor

PREFACE

Given the status and importance of Persian culture and literature, the need for a modern *History of Persian Literature* has long been felt by specialists and non-specialists alike. In the field of "elevated" Persian literature—undoubtedly one of the world's great literary traditions—a detailed, modern *History* was urgently needed to introduce a modern Western readership to the literary masterpieces of the Islamic Iranian world.

Those whose views on literature are informed by traditional definitions of the concept, may regard this Companion Volume as less of a desideratum. The fact that two only partially related fields of study—on the one hand oral and popular literature in various forms of Persian, and on the other the whole range of literary traditions of the Kurds, Pashtuns, Baloch and Ossetes—are included in one volume, may at first glance seem to strengthen the impression that these subjects are of no more than marginal relevance to those interested in the literatures and civilizations of the Middle East and Central Asia.

A closer examination, however, shows both the criss-crossing web of interrelations between the "high" and "popular" literatures discussed in this volume, and their links with the classical Persian tradition, with which this *History* is chiefly concerned. Moreover, although the study of the subjects discussed here has long occupied a relatively marginal position within the wider field of Iranian Studies, in the context of a modern approach to Oriental Studies their relevance is now increasingly understood. Not only is the information these studies offer essential for a more realistic understanding of the countries and regions in question, but research in relatively unexplored fields of study has also had the advantage of forcing academics to explore new, modern methods of study.

Much of the information contained in the contributions to this volume is published here for the first time, and the work may confidently be expected to facilitate and stimulate future research. However, the task that faced the present contributors, *viz.* systematizing, describing, and contextualizing the bewildering mass of information that had so far been left unstudied, is only a first step. In order to realize the full potential of Oral and Popular Studies and the study of "minority" literatures generally, methods must be developed to enable us to interpret the material in ways that will truly further Western society's understanding of the workings of another culture. The principal connection linking those working in fields on the margins of mainstream Persian literature is that both the nature of their material, and the insights of other disciplines touching on their field of study, force them to seek new definitions, novel methodological approaches, and above all a new understanding of what they are essentially looking for.

Perhaps inevitably, given their historical development, "Oriental" studies in the West in the past tended to be modeled upon their non-Oriental counterparts, with which they shared a preoccupation with "high" culture, such as the history of the ruling classes, the religion of the learned, and the "elevated" literature of the elite. Clearly, the study of the ways in which a cultural elite produced or was influenced by aesthetically pleasing written works of literature is a rewarding pursuit for those who are fully familiar with the cultural context of their object of study, and seek a deeper understanding of the dynamics affecting an important cultural phenomenon.

Things take on a different aspect, however, when it comes to the study and interpretation of a culture that is not one's own, and to transmitting the resulting knowledge to a society which, in these days of increasing globalization, interacts with other cultures on the basis of a very tenuous understanding of their realities. That literary studies can play a role in such a process is aptly illustrated by the other volumes of this *History*. The question remains, however, whether this is the only contribution the study of Oriental Literatures can make to the dialogue of cultures. In the course of the twentieth century, the combined findings of several disciplines concerned with the study of "culture" have led to an important change of paradigm in this field. The traditional view of culture, which is implicit in many Orientalist works as well as others, tended to understand the concept as an almost static phenomenon, resulting from the impact of such slowly-developing factors as official religion, the aesthetic values inculcated by "high" art, and a view of history that is shaped by the historical writings of the elite. This essential, underlying "culture" was held to inform all outward manifestations of the culture concerned, or at least those which formed appropriate objects of study. This implied that the study of any aspect of a culture—such as classical literature—could be expected to yield relevant information about a range of other expressions of the same culture, even if these belonged to widely different periods or dissimilar fields of endeavor. Given such premises, the traditional emphasis on the study of "high" literary works seems reasonable, as these could be seen to reflect "culture" in a way that had been approved by the society itself.

In the course of the last century, however, such definitions were given up in most disciplines. Culture came to be thought of as a complex, dynamic, ever-changing phenomenon, which scholars no longer seek to understand on the basis of diachronic analyses of "attitudes" or "ideologies," deduced from a limited number of literary texts. It may not be coincidence that, when society needs explanations about a non-Western culture, one would now hardly expect the media to turn to an Orientalist, as would have been the normal procedure some decades ago. Without intending to criticize the Orientalists' successors—who tend to be representatives of general disciplines like History or Political Science, with some expert knowledge of the region in question—it seems legitimate to wonder whether the current practice is leading to a more adequate and informed covering of aspects of "culture" which puzzle the general public in the West. While traditional Orientalists used to paint a general, diachronic picture, all too often their successors now offer an equally non-specific, synchronic one—using concepts that are no less broad, all-encompassing, and ultimately non-informative. If one is to take the current trends in the perception of culture seriously, it might seem more appropriate to move away from the deductive use of larger concepts in order to explain the reality of a given situation. It may be preferable, in other words, to begin by collecting detailed, factual information about what is going on, particularly in the minds of those whose actions have caused a given problem to arise. Clearly, "the people" play a central role in such an approach, which makes it seem imperative to develop adequate and reliable methods to gauge public perceptions on a given subject at a specific time. It is to be expected that both diachronic and analytical perspectives will prove helpful in explaining and contextualizing such findings, but an initial, objective appraisal of public perceptions, preoccupations and feelings should surely play a central role in any analysis of events or phenomena in another culture.

Furthermore, as far as the Middle East and Central Asia are concerned, the current move away from general, prescriptive analyses based on the study of large units, such as a political entities or dominant cultures, is likely to lead to a greater interest in smaller, but highly distinctive cultures such as those of the Kurds, the Pashtuns and the Baloch. These groups have a strong sense of cultural identity, which finds expression in a range of political, cultural and social manifestations. These deserve to be better known in the West, not least because their actions may ultimately affect our own society.

It is in light of such new requirements that the study of the oral and popular cultures of the Iranophone peoples may offer new opportunities within the wider field of Iranian Studies. Expressions of popular culture—whether performances, films, TV programs or written works—offer essential information about the current mood of a society, and about the "mental map" or "life-world" that gave rise to it. If, with the help of related disciplines such as Discourse Analysis and Anthropology, a field of study can be developed that uses literary culture in non-Western societies in all its forms to bring to light the range of presuppositions, past experiences, common views and ideas which together inform public perceptions in a given cultural milieu, both Oriental Studies and the Humanities generally will have gained a great deal.

During a visit to Tehran in 2000 the present writer attended a series of performances by *naqqâls* (see Chapter 10 in this vol-

PREFACE

ume) who, while retelling episodes from the *Shahname*, continually drew analogies between their heroes' experiences and those of the audience—particularly by referring to the losses and horrors of the Iran-Iraq war (1980–88). Although the war had ended over a decade earlier and was rarely alluded to in the media, the audience's reaction proved that it was still very much present in their thoughts. Thus the performance of episodes from a masterpiece of classical Persian literature was adapted to the needs of a contemporary audience, thereby yielding information both as to the state of mind of that audience, and the role of classical literature in shaping their understanding of recent experiences.

A few words of explanation may be in order to justify the expression "oral and popular culture," as it might be thought that the oral aspect is adequately subsumed by the term "popular." Against this, it may first be pointed out that not all oral culture is popular, witness e.g. the sacred traditions of the Yezidis and the Ahl-e Haqq (see Chapter 8 in this volume). Secondly, the experience of largely oral cultures suggest that distinctions such as those between "literature," "history," and the transmission of religious knowledge, which are clearly valid for "high" written culture, and to a lesser extent also for popular written culture, need fundamental reappraisal when it comes to the study of oral culture. There, religious knowledge is normally transmitted in the form of anecdotes not unlike purely literary genres, and constructs of history tend to be governed by rules that spring from the need to keep history memorable, so that the interweaving of fact, myth, and explanation results in accounts that are similar in many ways to exclusively "literary" narratives. In short, while "high," "popular," and "oral" literary traditions in the Iranophone area can be seen to be closely connected with one another, all three are to some extent governed by their own rules, whose study can add materially to our understanding of the character and functions of "Literature," both in the regions concerned and generally.

As one can see from the above, a great deal remains to be done, and the present work can be said to mark a beginning rather than an end. Still, the Editors flatter themselves that it is not a bad beginning. Probably for the first time, chapters surveying the "elevated" as well as the "popular" literature of the Pashtuns, Kurds, Baloch, and Ossetes are presented together with much needed chapters on oral and popular literature in Iran, Tajikistan, and the Dari-speaking parts of Afghanistan, and with some in-depth studies of important genres.

It is partly owing to the inherent nature of oral and popular literature, and partly to the neglect of the subject in the field of Iranian Studies, that no comprehensive survey of all forms of oral and popular literature in Iranian languages can be offered. For one thing, no collection of oral texts can ever be said to cover all that exists, nor can one realistically expect to study popular literature in all its forms. Even so, much of what could have been achieved was left undone because, until relatively recently, Iranian Studies showed little interest in these subjects. The absence of a chapter on, say, folk poetry in the various regions of Iran is due to the lack of adequate sources, and of specialists competent to handle such a vast and demanding subject. A thorough treatment of films as part of popular culture may well be possible ten years from now, but at the time of writing this was an unattainable goal. The same is true of several other topics. Nevertheless, it may be said that much has already been achieved, and it is hoped that the publication of this work will stimulate the further development of a field of study whose fascination it amply illustrates.

In a work which combines Chapters dealing with several modern Iranian languages other than Persian, it has not always been possible to adhere to the general rules of transliteration used in the *History of Persian Literature*, but these rules have been followed as far as possible. Thus, the use of diacritics for consonants has been kept to a minimum in the texts of the Chapters, but these are given in the Bibliographies and the Index. Given the nature of the languages concerned, authors of Chapters on Pashto and Balochi felt that diacritics were essential to their contributions. Their wishes have been respected as far as possible. The Chapters on Kurdish literature presented special problems. While Kurdish was originally written in an adapted version of the Arabic script, the widespread use of a standard orthography in Roman script since the early 1930s (the "Hawar" system, see Chapter 1 in this volume) made

PREFACE

it seem as undesirable to transcribe the names of early Kurdish works and authors (with their high content of Arabic and Persian words) according to the Hawar system as it was impossible to rewrite modern names and titles as if they had originally been written in Arabic. To complicate matters further, the Arabic alphabet continues to be used for Kurdish in Iran and Iraq. Being unable to devise a unified, coherent and comprehensible system of transliteration for the Chapter on Kurdish Written Literature, this Editor has taken it upon himself to take the unusual step of transliterating names and publications according to the standard transliteration system for the Arabic alphabet in passages dealing mainly with the period before 1930, and according to the *Hawar* system elsewhere. In the other Chapters on Kurdish literature, typical *Hawar* forms like ş for /sh/, c for /dj/, and x for /gh/ and /kh/ have been used in transliterating Kurdish texts and certain specific expressions, and also when referring to names as they appeared in print; in other contexts sh, j, gh, and kh have been preferred. In the transcription of a few Kurdish texts, ŕ is used for the heavy /rr/.

For Pashto, the vowel ə, and the consonants ś, ź (for the phonemes whose pronunciation varies from /kh/ and /g/ in the north-east to /sh/ and /zh/ in the south-west of the Pashto-speaking region), and ŕ, ń, ṯ, and ḏ, (for retroflex consonants, the latter two in contrast to the emphatic, "Arabic" consonants ṭ and ḍ) have been used. The letters ŕ, ṯ and ḏ represent the same values in Balochi, where, at the request of the author, ð, š, č, ĵ, ʿ are used throughout for /dh/, /sh/, /ch/, /dj/ and ʿayn. For typographic reasons, the nasalized final /e/ had to be transcribed as ê<u>n</u>.

During the editorial process Ulrich Marzolph took responsibility for the contributions on literature in forms of Persian; editing the other Chapters devolved on Philip G. Kreyenbroek, who also undertook further editorial tasks such as sub-editing, layout, and preparing the Index and Bibliographies. All chapters have been reviewed by the General Editor of the *History of Persian Literature.*

Circumstances beyond the control of the Editors have led to a delay of several years in the publication of the Volume. It has not always been possible to update the information presented in the Chapters as they were originally written.

ORAL LITERATURE OF IRANIAN LANGUAGES

As was said earlier, the Editors are grateful to Professor Ehsan Yarshater for enabling the subjects represented here to be covered in a Companion Volume to the *History*, and for his support and practical suggestions whenever these were needed. We wish to thank the Contributors for producing work of a quality that made our tasks a great deal easier than it might have been, and for dealing patiently and efficiently with our queries. Among the many who assisted us in our editorial tasks, special thanks are due to Dr. des. Antje Wendtland and Dr. Katja Föllmer, who helped in various ways, to Ms Aresu Tawafi and Mr. Luqman Turgut whose help with the sub-editing, layout, Bibliographies, and Index proved invaluable, and to Mrs. Mieke Kreyenbroek for her advice on a range of practical and theoretical questions.

Philip G. Kreyenbroek
Editor

THE STUDY OF POPULAR LITERATURE IN THE PERSIAN CONTEXT

The following remarks aim at outlining a number of theoretical questions that play a role in the study of popular literature in the Persian context. The term "Persian" is used here for more or less standard versions of this language. This means that it does not fully reflect ethnic diversity, and to some extent suggests a non-existent homogeneity of Iranian culture, a suggestion that may be strengthened further by the fact that most research on the cultures and literatures of Iran is published in the Persian language. The term "popular literature," to be defined below, is used indiscriminately besides "folk literature," as a differentiation between these two concepts has no practical value in the present context. While in the following general remarks reference will be made primarily to the Persian tradition, many of the points discussed are also relevant for the study of other Iranian popular literatures, and of popular literature generally. Some of these points will therefore be discussed again, and in greater detail, in some of the following chapters, notably those on the popular literatures of Tajikistan and Afghanistan.

After a brief glance at the history of research and the various academic approaches to popular literature, this chapter will offer a general survey of popular literary genres, and go on to focus on cultural components in the specifically Persian sphere. This will be followed by a discussion of the relations between popular and elite literature, and between the individual and the collective; furthermore, arguments will be put forward for rejecting the traditional approach of defining popular literature by way of content. After a brief reference to the influence of printing on Persian popular literature, the final passage will consider the present condition as well as future requirements of the study of popular literature in the Persian context.

1. Academic approaches to popular literature

The study of popular literature requires one to consider a variety of genres over a considerable period of time, while also taking into account different forms of tradition, of performance or documentation, and of scientific approach. In terms of academic disciplines, "popular literature" falls under the rubric of both Comparative Literature and Comparative Folk Narrative Research. Although these disciplines share the same object of study, their interest in it derives from very different preoccupations and backgrounds: Comparative Literature is mainly concerned with "elite" literature, while Comparative Folk Narrative Research deals chiefly with "folklore" or "oral tradition."

Traditionally, Comparative Literature tends to argue in dichotomies, regarding "popular" literature as a lesser offspring of acknowledged forms of literary activity that are practiced and appreciated by the elite. Accordingly, popular literature is often judged as a form of "gesunkenes Kulturgut" (literally: "sunken cultural goods") (H. Naumann; see Dow 1998), as a type of literature originating among the elite which came to "sink" to lower, popular levels. The kind of literature that can only be appreciated by those who have enjoyed a privileged education is seen as superior to literature whose imagery and wording make it accessible to large numbers of people. This view implies both decline and degeneration, and risks looking at popular literature with a heavily biased, judgmental eye.

The discipline of Comparative Folk Narrative Research originated in the age of Romanticism. In contrast to Comparative Literature it tends to regard popular literature as resulting from the creative act of an anonymous collective. This collective is held to possess the capacity to preserve ancient forms of expression essentially unaltered over long periods of time, and hence to guarantee continuity. The discipline of Comparative Folk Narrative Research was initiated by German brothers Jacob and Wilhelm Grimm with their *Kinder- und Hausmärchen* (Nursery and Household Tales) (first edition 1812–15) early in the nineteenth century, and developed into a full-fledged academic discipline through the joint efforts of predominantly Northern European scholars early in the twentieth century. Their perspective was Eurocentric. Although they were aware of, and took into consideration non-European data, they did so primarily in order to elucidate the origins of European material, rather than studying those data in their own right.

In the course of the latter half of the twentieth century, both academic disciplines have to some extent adopted each other's approaches. With its various newly developed foci of interest, such as sociological significance, adaptability to context, and interactive, performance-related aspects, popular literature has become a fascinating field of research, offering insights into the mind and perception of humanity informed by a deeply-felt historical experience.

2. Specifics of popular literature

In terms of the literary genres concerned, popular literature as it was traditionally understood covers a relatively fixed canon of literary genres, such as myths; historical, religious, and demonological legends; heroic and romantic epics; narrative songs (ballads); fables; fairy tales; jokes and anecdotes; as well as shorter forms of literature such as popular sayings and idioms; children's rhymes; lullabies; and riddles (see in detail Bolukbâshi 2000). Contemporary modern folklore research regards this restriction to a pre-defined and limited set of specific genres as unduly narrowing the products of creative and receptive popular imagination to a range of phenomena that does not adequately represent the true character and meaning of popular literature. Consequently, it seeks to define popular literature on the basis of presentation or performance rather than formal content. This approach defines "popular literature" as the sum of all creative verbal activities, whether oral (in recent research often termed "verbal art") or written (corresponding to the narrow definition of literature as a form of expression in writing). In contrast to elite literature, popular literature is defined as comprising all forms of literature that are transmitted by other than dominant elite channels of tradition, whether orally or in writing. The procedure of transmission does not exclude formal or informal education of authors or performers. Even though often illiterate, performers need to possess special skills and training. Furthermore, popular literature is appreciated and/or practiced by collective consent by a considerable number of people, conveniently termed the "folk."

Since the introduction of printing, this understanding of popular literature encompasses not only the traditional stock of narrative and non-narrative genres. It also includes the huge mass of literary production aimed at popular reception, such as editions of elite literature adapted to popular usage in content and wording; devotional and trivial entertainment literature; chapbooks and "yellow press" penny-magazines; tracts on the interpretation of dreams; booklets containing common advice of a medical, pedagogical, or otherwise practical nature; and leaflets containing preprinted charms or verses from classical literature distributed for purposes of fortune-telling. Even more recently, widespread phenomena such as urban legends have come to be regarded as forms of popular literature, as did standardized forms of expression drawing on popular models practiced within the new electronic media, such as Xerox-lore, e-mail or internet-material. This way of defining popular literature is not so much concerned with the genre aspect. Rather, it is interested in means of production and distribution on the one hand, and in the sociological and psychological implications of the reception of such texts on the other.

3. Cultural components of Persian popular literature

Persian popular literature, as indeed the popular literature of any culture, is of a hybrid character, constituting a unique amalgam of constituent elements originating from various backgrounds. When dealing with this topic, one has to keep in mind that questions of origin of specific forms of popular expression are extremely difficult to solve, and easy categorizations are both misleading and futile. The process of sifting out non-Iranian elements might possibly result in finding the "pure" constituent elements of Persian culture, but there are more interesting things to learn from the texts.

In Folk Narrative Research, Iran has long attracted international attention due to its location between Europe and India, where many European folktales were long believed to have originated. As the so-called "Indian theory" (Pfeiffer 1993), propagated above all by German Indologist Theodor Benfey (1859) had it, Indian folktales on their way to Europe would have had to pass through Iran. This implied both that they influenced the Iranian tradition and that they were shaped and remodeled by standards prevalent within the Iranian context. The diversification of Iranian popular tradition and culture in general is further related to a number of historical events.

In prehistoric times, the Indian and Iranian traditions were closely related, as is shown above all in the ancient Iranian mythological and religious traditions. Since the days of Alexander the Great, who conquered Iran in 331 BCE, the Iranian tradition comprises Greek, or rather Hellenistic influences. The Muslim conquest in the seventh century CE introduced elements from the Arabic-Islamic tradition that were later followed by various traits of Turkish, Mongol, and Western European origin. Disentangling this amalgam is a tedious task, promising results that might be of interest to nationalists rather than scholars. If, beyond considerations of genre and context, all Persian popular literature has one characteristic feature, it is its dualistic world-view of the competing forces of Good and Evil, besides the general human virtue of righteousness. Elements deriving from Islam, though dominant in both elite culture and popular expression, appear as normal features of everyday life, but have not—as might be expected—shaped popular literature in any decisive manner.

4. The relation between popular and elite literature

Traditional research has often posited a dichotomy between elite and popular literature. Today, it is commonly acknowledged that these two spheres can only be understood in relation to each other. Relevant research on this particular aspect within the Persian context is scarce. Studies in the neighboring field of Arabic literature have proposed various models, parts of which can also be applied, albeit in a modified form, to Persian literature. Karel Petráček (1987) distinguishes between three literary levels:
1. Classical literature, written in classical Arabic and intended for the educated.
2. Popular literature, originally oral and eventually fixed in classical or middle Arabic, aiming primarily at uneducated members of the urban and rural middle classes.
3. Folklore, i.e. (in Petráček's view) oral literature in dialect, mainly aimed at the uneducated rural and nomad population.

Peter Heath (1996), discussing the Arabic epic of Antar (*Sirat Antar*), has further differentiated this model by outlining the specific characteristics of elite, popular, and folk literature in several respects, such as producers, venues, texts, audiences, aesthetic goals and social as well as geographical contexts. Heath stressed that different layers of literary production are not to be regarded as separate, independent spheres, but remain in constant interaction. Moreover, he pointed out that elite culture often "draws itself out of popular culture and to a large extent identifies and defines itself against it" (Heath 1996, p. 46).

These models, developed for the field of Arabic literature, can be applied to Persian literature with only a few adaptations. This application would lead to distinguish between:
1. Persian classical literature and more recent Persian literature written in the classical language.
2. Popular literature, often fixed in writing while continuing to be performed by professional storytellers, and using motifs prevalent in oral tradition while at the same time influencing subsequent oral tradition.

POPULAR LITERATURE IN THE PERSIAN CONTEXT

3. Folk literature, rarely committed to writing before the twentieth century, showing affinities to popular literature both in terms of motifs and language, and mainly performed and transmitted orally.

Beside these general classifications, one has to take into account several characteristics that are peculiar to the Persian context. First, the Persian language does not know an exact equivalent to the diglossia of classical Arabic (*fushâ*) versus spoken (dialect) Arabic (*âmmiyya*). While this element of distance between the learned and the popular is lacking, at certain periods in history Persian elite literature employed styles heavily laden with figures of speech and other adornments as well as words and phrases borrowed from Arabic, which probably rendered them unattractive to popular taste. Yet, even this kind of literature both profited from and influenced popular literature as far as themes and motifs are concerned. To quote but one example, both Abu'l-Ma'âli Nasr-Allâh Monshi's *Kalile o Demne*, compiled in the twelfth century, and Hoseyn b. Vâ'ez Kâshefi's (d. 1504) *Anvâr-e Soheyli* constitute Persian adaptations of the famous collection of animal tales and fables originally translated into Arabic from a Pahlavi original by the Persian secretary Ebn al-Moqaffa' (executed 759). Both remained popular over the centuries and helped to popularize the compilation's tales and motifs, which resulted in their reception in popular literature and verbal art.

Secondly, particularly in the early centuries after the Islamic conquest, a large number of texts written in Arabic were conceived and compiled by Persian authors, and might therefore be regarded as Persian literature written in the lingua franca of their time. Compilers of large medieval encyclopedias of jocular and entertaining narratives such as Abu Mansur al-Âbi (d. 1030) with his *Nathr al-dorr* (The Scattering of Pearls) or al-Râgheb al-Esfahâni (d. early 10th century) with his *Mohâzarât al-odabâ'* (Lectures of the Cultivated) wrote against the background of their Persian experience and potentially also incorporated material of Persian origin into their collections. Moreover, from the earliest known sources and well into the nineteenth century, many Persian authors were bilingual, fluent in Persian and Arabic, as numerous instances in popular works of narrative literature prove beyond reasonable doubt, e.g. Jalâl-al-Din Rumi's (d. 1273) *Mathnavi*, Obeyd-e Zâkâni's (d. 1371) *Resâle-ye delgoshâ* or Fakhr-al-Din Ali Safi's (d. 1532) *Latâ'ef al-tavâ'ef*. Their works, besides many others, have introduced into Persian literature a large number of narrative texts originally compiled in Arabic.

A third point to mention concerns the interaction between elite and popular layers of literature, which to some extent correspond to written and oral traditions. In simple terms one might say that, on the one hand, Persian authors exploited themes and motifs prevalent in oral tradition; on the other hand, their literary products—including their artistic adaptations of popular themes—might at times earn such fame as to become integral parts of popular tradition in their own right. The most striking examples of this type of interaction are probably the didactic tales from Jalâl-al-Din Rumi's *Mathnavi*, many of which are taken from contemporary popular tradition, but also influenced subsequent popular tradition which they reached through various channels of reception (Mills 1994).

5. The relation between the individual and the collective

Particularly when considering the interaction between written sources and oral literature, one has to keep in mind the specific situation of Persian literature in the course of history. The Persian classics were widely read and formed a standard component of traditional education throughout the Persian-speaking world, at times also including the Ottoman and Mughal empires. Classical literature was not only—and probably not even predominantly—read individually. Rather, it was common practice to read the classics aloud, to memorize and recite the text, to retell and orally perform the text in various ways, e.g. by short quotations or allusions to commonly known passages. In Iran, as in most other Near Eastern regions, the historical role of orality was different from today. It constituted a way of codification of knowledge and instruction. If only because of the cost of its production, written literature was predominantly accessible to the rich and powerful. Oral tradition, therefore, was not necessarily equivalent to "popular" tradition, since it relied on a solid command of mnemonic devices by individually trained tradition bearers.

In any case, it must be acknowledged that the collective production of popular literature, as posited by the Romantic views of the nineteenth century, exists only in a limited sense. Every item of popular literature is in the first place created by an individual author. This author acts against the traditional background and within the context of the surrounding society, with its collectively accepted system of values. As such the author's product mirrors elements produced by, or adapted to the community's collective consciousness, while at the same time it is further molded by these very elements through a gradual process of reception. Each of these elements originates from a specific historical, cultural, social, or educational background and is subject to various influences from different levels of society. Their sum total constitutes the decisive criterion for distinguishing "popular" from any other kind of literature.

6. Persian popular literature as defined by content

To further complicate matters, any phenomenon that took place in the past can only be evaluated on the basis of extant sources. As for the "popularity" of specific items of literature, research until recently favored themes and motifs as the chief criteria to distinguish popular from elite literature. Prominent scholars of Persian popular literature such as Mohammad Ja'far Mahjub (1959 ff.) and William Hanaway, Jr. (1971) have defined popular literature by criteria relating to form and content. In accordance with his primary interest in epic literature, Hanaway has proposed a rather specific definition of popular literature as "a body of narrative prose literature derived from, or in the formal tradition of the Persian national legend" (Hanaway 1971, p. 59). Mahjub, on the other hand, was able to profit from his intimate knowledge of the wide array of "popular" reading matter available in his youth. His understanding of popular literature mirrors the factual evidence of published material, though it is still dominated by the evaluation of popular elements in relation to classical literature (see Marzolph 1994, pp. 6–9.). Both approaches share their preoccupation with themes and motifs, and only to a lesser extent take into account linguistic criteria such as formal language and vocabulary, or the repetition and standardization of stereotype passages. Moreover, neither tackles questions relating to the sociological relevance of popular literature, let alone mechanisms of production and distribution, which in recent research are regarded as decisive arguments for the popularity, or popularization, of certain kinds of literature (Marzolph 1994). The limited perspective of such approaches seems permissible given the scarcity of information about the popularity of literature in the past. Even so, Mahjub has opened up new perspectives by introducing the popular reading matter of his own youth, which in many respects corresponds to the literature popular in the nineteenth century Qajar period.

7. The influence of printing on Persian popular literature

The introduction of printing in the Qajar period contributed tremendously, if not decisively, to the present-day notion of what popular literature in the Persian context actually means. Printing from movable type was introduced to Iran during the second decade of the nineteenth century (see Marzolph 2002). As this way of printing was not particularly successful in the early years, it was soon succeeded by lithographic printing, a technique that had probably been introduced around 1830. In printing from movable type, publishers had at first restricted their production to standard texts of religious, historical or classical literature. As of 1844, and exclusively in lithographic printing, publishers gradually freed

POPULAR LITERATURE IN THE PERSIAN CONTEXT

themselves from this restriction. Soon, large amounts of narrative reading matter were made available at comparatively moderate costs, thus supplying "popular literature" in both its connotations of traditional content and general availability, for the first time in Persian history. The extent to which the production of popular reading matter since the mid-nineteenth century has influenced the Persian tradition remains to be studied, as most other aspects relevant to this field. Still, it may safely be surmised that the wide distribution of popular reading matter by way of reading, reciting, and retelling, has left its traces in popular knowledge and appreciation of numerous subjects. These include, for instance, the Persian national legend, i.e. Ferdowsi's *Shahname*, classical romantic tales such as those of *Leylâ (Leyli) and Majnun* or *Khosrow and Shirin*, or jocular narratives such as the ones focusing on popular heroes such as Mollâ Nasreddin or Bohlul. Meanwhile, the distribution of printed books also contributed to popularizing religious, moral, and educational knowledge, e.g. by transmission while common (and often illiterate) people listen to the *âkhund*'s exhortations literally *pâ-ye menbar*, 'at the foot of the pulpit.'

As to folk- and fairy-tales, or minor forms of popular literature such as lullabies or riddles, printing did not contribute to their popularity until well into the twentieth century. In Europe fairy-tales had gained prominence by means of a few standard editions only, such as Charles Perrault's *Contes de ma Mère l'Oye* (1697), or the above-mentioned tales of the brothers Grimm. In contrast, knowledge and transmission of fairy-tales in the Persian context remained an exclusively oral phenomenon until Western Orientalist scholars as well as Persian intellectuals took an interest in documenting, and consequently popularizing these components of the national Iranian heritage from the first decades of the twentieth century onwards. Details of the historical development of Persian scholarship in folk- and fairy-tales will be given in the chapter on Persian Popular Literature. The activities and publications of Fazlollâh Mohtadi 'Sobhi' in the 1940s, and Abu'l-Qâsem Enjavi Shirâzi (affectionately known as Najvâ) in the 1970s created public awareness for the richness and attractiveness of Persian folklore, and furthermore resulted in a number of widely read (and thus "popular") publications.

8. The study of Persian popular literature: present and future

It is difficult to decide whether political developments since the Islamic Revolution can be held responsible for preventing the study of Iranian popular literature from developing into directions other than the collection and documentation of oral tradition. At the beginning of the twenty-first century, Iranian scholarship in Persian popular literature predominantly remains attached to the Romantic attitude of preserving sources which otherwise are thought to be bound to disappear and be lost forever. This attitude seems justified in light of both historical experience and the present conditions. Yet it neglects the fact that popular literature as a constituent of popular or "folk" tradition has always been in a state of change, that popular tradition is neither static nor monolithic. As in most other parts of the world, popular literature in Iran has been in a constant state of growth and decay for centuries, each stage being connected with specific cultural and societal frame conditions.

If one were to aim at preserving traditional Persian popular literature, as many contemporary Iranian scholars claim, one would not just have to study the conditions in which it exists within the original context, but one would need to create or re-create, and constantly preserve those very conditions so as to enable popular tradition to live on. As any such move would be both impractical and ineffective, the present task for research lies in finding out and documenting as much as possible about the range, content, meaning, and frame conditions of popular literature. This task is imperative, not so much in order to preserve popular literature as a component of Persian culture in a fixed state, as in a museum. Rather, the serious scholarly study of Persian popular literature is a way of understanding Persian tradition by appreciating popular concern as preserved in oral and written tradition.

Ulrich Marzolph

CHAPTER 1

WRITTEN KURDISH LITERATURE

Joyce Blau

1. Introduction

Kurdish literature is more extensive than is generally realized. Kurdish is the lingua franca of between twenty-five and thirty million people, most of whom live in a crescent shaped stretch of land in the northern part of the Middle East. This vast territory was never unified politically. Until World War I, it was split between the Ottoman and Persian empires, and the Allies, despite their solemn promise to establish an independent Kurdistan after the war, instead divided the Kurdish territories among Turkey, Iran, Iraq and Syria. Thus, the Kurds found themselves divided, citizens of states dominated by other ethnic groups—Turkish, Persian or Arab—whose attitude towards them was generally hostile. Outside Kurdish territory, half a million Kurds live in the states that emerged from the former Soviet Union. Eight hundred thousand live in northeast Iran, in Khorasan province, where their ancestors were sent in the sixteenth and seventeenth centuries by the Safavid shahs to guard the empire's northeastern borderlands. Over 100,000 live in Lebanon, and large numbers of Kurds live in the major cities of the Middle East. In addition, in the last three decades, a diaspora of about 850,000 has settled in Europe, the United States and as far away as Australia.

Kurdish belongs to the Iranian group of the Indo-European family of languages. The Kurdish dialects, which are dispersed over a large area, form a homogeneous group distinct from the other Iranian languages such as Persian, Balochi, Pashto, and the Caspian

ORAL LITERATURE OF IRANIAN LANGUAGES

dialects. They have never been unified and standardized, and the degree of difference among them is in proportion to geographical distance separating them throughout a large and mountainous territory that has never been politically unified. The dialects of the northern group, generally called Kurmanji (or Badinani in Iraq) are spoken by the largest number, including the Kurds of Turkey, Syria, and the former USSR, and by some Iraqi and Iranian Kurds. The central group includes the dialects of northeast Iraq called Sorani, as well as the neighboring dialects of Iranian Kurdistan called Mokri, Kordi or Sene'i. The southern group includes the heterogeneous dialects of the Iranian provinces of Ilâm, Kermânshâh and Lorestân (MacKenzie 1961–62; Blau 1989).

While it is true that illiteracy was widespread in Kurdistan until the 1950s, there has always been a small, cultivated intellectual elite. This was noted by Prince Sharaf Khan Bedlisi (1543–1604) in his *Sharaf-nâme* (Adivar, Véliaminov-Zernof, Charmoy, Vasilieva) and by the traveler Evliya Chelebi (Sakisian 1957; cf. van Bruinessen and Boeschoten 1988). This educated elite wrote in Persian and Arabic (the dominant languages of the region). Thus, as early as the thirteenth century, Ebn al-Athir (d. 1233),[1] a historian and biographer of Kurdish origin, wrote *al-Kâmel* (the work which made him famous) in Arabic. Ebn-e Khallekân (d. 1282)[2] and Abu'l-Fedâ (d. 1331)[3] also wrote in Arabic. The high-ranking Ottoman dignitary Edris Hakem Betlisi (d. 1520), wrote the *Hasht Behesht* (The Eight Paradises), which recounted the lives of the first eight Ottoman Sultans, in Persian. Likewise, Sharaf Khan Bedlisi wrote the *Sharaf-nâme* in Persian.

This phenomenon still continues. For example, Ahmad Showqi (1868–1932) earned the title of "prince of poets" because he epitomized the Arab poets of his time. Boland al-Heydari (1926–96), along with three other talented poets, created an Iraqi school of literature well known for its creativity, which had a decisive influence on the entire Arabic literary movement. Salim Barakat (b. 1951),

---

1   Ebn al-Athir was born in Jazirat Ebn Umar and has the *nisba* of al-Jazari.
2   Ebn-e Khallekân al-Arbili was born in Irbil.
3   Abu'l-Fedâ was an Ayyubid Prince, a dynasty of Kurdish origin.

considered by his peers to be one of the most brilliant renovators of Arabic prose, evoked his childhood and the daily life of the Kurdish community in his works. Yashar Kemal (b. 1922), who stands head and shoulders above the other Turkish writers of his generation, writes in Turkish. His work, translated into over twenty languages, revives the *dâstân* (epic) tradition, and is notable for its attention to Kurdish folklore. Ali Mohammad Afghâni (b. 1925) made his reputation with *Showhar-e Âhu Khânom* (Mrs. Âhu's Husband) written in Persian, and reprinted ten times since its first publication in 1961.

The beginnings of Kurdish literature are obscure. Not only do we know nothing about pre-Islamic Kurdish culture, but we also have no way of knowing how many manuscripts were destroyed in the turmoil of the endless conflict which has taken and continues to take place on Kurdish soil. The first indisputably Kurdish texts that have come down to us are written in the Arabo-Persian alphabet. For a long time this literature was accessible only to the urban population, while the literature of the great majority of Kurds—peasants and both sedentary and nomadic pastoralists— was transmitted orally. Written texts are few and generally inaccessible. The little information we have on the lives of the poets is contradictory.

The first Western scholar to write about this literature was Alexandre-Auguste Jaba, the Russian consul in Erzurum (Anatolia), who loved the Kurds and their culture. He had the good luck to meet the educated Kurdish mullah Mahmud Bâyazidi, who offered him invaluable assistance. In his *Recueil de notices et récits kourdes servant à la connaissance de la langue, de la littérature et des tribus du Kourdistan,* Jaba devoted an introductory chapter to "poets and writers of Kurdistan who have written in the Kurdish language," and gave brief biographies of the following poets: Ali Hariri, Malâyê Jezri, Faqiyê Teyrân, Malâyê Bâte, Ahmad Khâni, Esmâ'il Bâyazidi, Sharif Khân, and Morâd Khân. The dates of the birth and death of Malâyê Jezrî and Faqiyê Teyrân have since been revised by D. N. MacKenzie (1969).

The first edition of *Anjumani Adibâni Kord* (Council of Learned Kurds) was published in 1920. Its author, Amiralay Amin Feyzi

Beg (1860–1923) was a brilliant intellectual and officer, and a poet in his own right, writing in Kurdish, Turkish and Persian. Twenty years would pass before Kemal Bapir (Ali Bapir Agha, 1887–1975) brought out *Guldestey shu'eray haw'esrim* (A Bouquet of Poets of My Time; Suleimâni 1939). Even more important is the study by the historian Rafiq Helmi (Refîq Hilmî, 1898–1960), *She'r u adabiyâti kordi* (*shi'r û edebiyatî kurdî*).[4] *Mêzhuy adabi kordi* (*Mêjûy edebî kurdî*), by Alâ-al-Din Sajjâdi (Elâ-el-Dîn Seccadî, 1910–85), was published in Baghdad in 1956. In this work the author mentions 296 deceased poets from Iraqi and Iranian Kurdistan who wrote in the Sorani dialect. He does not mention prose writers, authors from other regions of Kurdistan, or living writers or poets. This should give an idea of the scope and richness of Kurdish literature, although here it will only be possible to offer a brief description (see also Kurdo 1983; Uzun 1995).

2. Early Kurdish literature

The first known Kurdish literary masterpieces appeared at a time when the Ottoman and Safavid empires were just consolidating, whilst the princely Kurdish dynasties had failed to establish their own state. Kurdistan became the object of the greed of its powerful neighbors, who fought over it incessantly, leaving behind a trail of destruction.

However, even the earliest poetry that has come down to us shows a mastery of technique that suggests that it was based on a long tradition, whose earlier works so far remain unknown. The establishment of Kurdish dynasties led to political stability that

---

4   In the first part of this text all Kurdish names and titles are transliterated according to the system generally used for the Arabic alphabet; where necessary the equivalent in the "Hawar" alphabet, a Roman script which is now widely used for Kurmanji Kurdish, is given in brackets. In the part of the text which deals with the period when alphabets other than the Arabic came to be used for Kurdish, the transcription used is based on the "Hawar" orthography, occasionally with the "Arabic" equivalent in brackets.

in turn permitted the founding of cities in which culture and literary creativity blossomed. The princes fostered the founding of schools and colleges, supervising their work and offering scholarships to the neediest. The *madreses* (Qor'anic schools) attached to the mosques were the main educational institutions in Kurdistan until just after World War II. Through these, the Kurdish princes promoted the development of a Kurdish written literary tradition, based on shared techniques and conventions. Thus each generation of Kurdish poets could learn from their predecessors. Through poetry Kurdish became a literary language, while written prose texts emerged only much later. The poets adopted the basic forms of Arabo-Persian poetry, thus acquiring a store of genres and stylistic techniques. In their desire to trace the origins of Kurdish poetry as far back in time as possible, some Kurdish scholars have claimed that the first Kurdish poet was Bâbâ Tâher, sometimes called either Hamadâni or Lori (Sejjâdi 1956, p. 170). The argument is based on the origins of this mystic, who was born in Hamadan, claimed to have been situated in the Kurdish territory. Other specialists, such as Jaba or the Kurd Qanatê Kurdo (1909–85) considered Ali Termuki (or Termâxi), or Ali Hariri to be the first Kurdish poet (Kurdo 1985, pp. 14, 57). The most famous poet of the classical period is Sheikh Ahmad Nishâni (1570–1640), who is better known by his *takhallos* (pen name) of Malâyê Jezri (Jeziri, Cizîrî, Cizrî). Like many literate Kurds, he knew Arabic, Persian and Turkish. His *Divân* (collection of poems) includes over two thousand verses, and his *qasides* and *ghazals* remain popular and are still taught in the *madreses* of Kurdistan (see Hartmann 1904; Amêdî 1977; Sharafqandi 1982). Malâyê Jezri also composed sonnets, as did Mawlawi in the nineteenth century and as modern Kurdish poets still do. Malâyê Jezri's love poetry, which was influenced by the Persian poets, notably Hâfez, fits into the context of Sufi mysticism. The poet celebrates the wine of ecstasy, and the joy and suffering of mystical love in its ideal form. Like many mystical poets, Malâyê Jezri was considered a saint in his lifetime, and legends about his life and miraculous deeds abound. He chose to write in the dialect of the Azizan family, Princes of the principality of Bohtân/Bukhtân connected by tradition with various heroes of the early days of Islam established there in 1514—an important point—and the content of his work was inspired by the Persian poetic tradition.

With great effort, and in spite of some inevitable differences, Persian and Kurdish poets modeled their poetry on Arabic forms. They adopted rhyme and a metrical system based on Arabic prosody, in spite of significant differences between Arabic and Iranian languages in this respect.

Malâyê Jezri traveled all over Kurdistan and had many disciples. In this way his literary standards, as well as the language of the Princes of Bôtân, became core elements of classical Kurdish literature. A disciple of Malâyê Jezri's who deserves mention is the enigmatic Mohammad of Mikis, known as Feqiyê Teyran (The Birds' Jurist, 1590–1660), who composed *qasides* and *ghazals*. He may have been the first Kurdish poet to write novels in verse, using the sweeping poetic span of the *mathnavi* (rhymed couplet) form. He left several works, signed with his initials M. H. (Mim Hâ): *Hekayeta Sheikhê Senhani* (The Story of Sheikh San'ân), *Qewlê hespê resh* (The Poem of the Black Courser), *Qeseya Barsiyayi* (The Story of Bersis), and an elegy on the death of his master Malâyê Jezrî.

Ahmadê Khâni (1650–1707) was a mystical poet and philosopher, who understood the people and felt himself one of them. His greatest work, *Mem û Zîn*, a long *mathnavi* of 2,655 distiches, rich in poetic imagery and lyrical scenes, is based on the popular romance *Memê Alân*, which recounts the tale of the pure love of Prince Mem and Princess Zîn (Lescot 1999).

In composing his work Ahmadê Khâni borrowed his imagery from the stock of Persian poetry. Probably inspired by Nezâmi of Ganje's *Leyli o Majnun*, he composed his poem in the Persian *mathnavi* style, each line consisting of two hemistiches in *hazaj* meter. This is a popular meter, compact, light, musical and rapid, and very well suited to the natural genius of the Kurdish language. The sad romance of the two heroes is replete with national symbolism, and patriotic declarations of faith abound in it. The poet presents his romance as a reaction against the growing nationalism of the Ottoman and Safavid empires, proclaiming the individuality of the Kurds and their right to independence and freedom. Ahmadê

Khâni formulated the four major problems of Kurdish literature, namely: the profession of the writer; the role of poetry; the relations between language, literature, and society; and finally the status of the Kurdish language itself.

Gurani literature

At about the same time, in the far south of Kurdistan, one of the most brilliant members of the Kurdish Ardalân dynasty,[5] Halo Khan (1585–1616), reached an agreement with Shah Abbâs at Isfahan. In exchange for paying tribute and defending the Empire's western frontiers, the Kurds were granted peace and a measure of independence. Halo Khan and his successor, Khan Ahmad, rebuilt towns and patronized men of letters and poets who composed their work in Arabic, Persian, and above all in Gurâni, a language which was much more widespread then than it is today.[6] It was amongst the Gurân and the people of Hawromân (who speak a form of Gurâni) that the esoteric faith of the Ahl-e Haqq was born, a faith that was to gain a considerable following in later years (see Chapter 3 in this Volume). Gurâni became the most important language in the classical textual tradition of the Ahl-e Haqq. The Ardalân princes, who may secretly have adopted this faith, favored Gurâni, which became the language of their court. Gurâni literature was promoted, and Gurâni became the common literary language in southern Kurdistan, and at the courts of the Bâbân and Sorân dynasties, which were settled on the western slopes of the Zagros.

Gurâni developed its own lyrical, epic and religious poetry (MacKenzie 1965; Mokri 1956), using a ten-syllable meter in rhyming couplets with a caesura between the two hemistiches. This form

---

5 The Kurdish Ardalân Khans ruled over a vast territory, surrounded by high mountains, roughly equivalent to the present day Iranian province of Kordestân.
6 The term Gurâni derives from Gurân, the name of an Iranian-speaking people who today occupy regions to the north and west of Kermânshâh, in the Iraq-Iran border area. Like Kurdish, their language belongs to the north-west group of Iranian languages.

is characteristic of the folk poetry and music of the Gurân region and of Kurdish areas that used Gurâni as a literary language.

It is generally believed that one of the first poets to write *ghazals* in Gurâni was Yusuf Yaskâ (c. 1592–1636), whom some Kurdish scholars compare with the Persian Rudaki. He founded a school of poetry and had many disciples (see Soltani 1998), including Shaikh Ahmad Takhti Mardukhi (1617–92), Shaikh Mostafâ Besarâni (1641–1702), and Ahmad Bagi Komâsi (1796–1877), among many others. Khânây Qobâdi (1700–59) eulogized Mohammad and Ali in his poem *Salavât-nâme*, but he is mainly remembered for his romantic epic *Shirin o Khosrow* (Kerîm 1975), as Malâ Bulâd Khan (d. 1885) is for his beautiful poem *Leyli o Majnun*. The last and most famous poet to write in Gurâni was Sayyed Abd-al-Rahimi Malâ Sa'îdi Tawegozi (c. 1806–82). His tomb has become a place of pilgrimage. He was descended from an old family that traced its origins to Pir Khedri Shâho, who lived in the fourteenth century at Khânegâh and Pâwe in the Hawromân area. He wrote poetry under the *takhallos* of Ma'dûm or Ma'dûmi, but is better known by the name of Mawlawi (Mewlewî). He wrote religious eulogies in Persian, Arabic and Gurâni,[7] drawing his inspiration from Sufism. Following the example of the Persian Sufi poets, Jalâl-al-Din Rumi, he celebrated the mystical wine of ecstasy (*she'ri meykhʷâri*; see Kerîm 1998). He is, however, better known for his romantic poems and lyrics (*she'ri suz*) written in a language that mixes the Hawrâmi and Tawegozi dialects. He uses the characteristic rhyming couplet form of oral Gurâni poetry, with a decasyllabic meter. Mawlawi is the only Gurâni poet to have also composed stanzaic lyrics.[8] In poetry rich in unusual imagery, the poet sings of nature, and it is he who introduced the traditional image of the young Kurdish girl into the Kurdish poetic tradition. Gurâni was so in-

---

[7] His *Aqîday marziyya* (The Gratifying Belief), written in 1863, is a treatise of 244 verses, written in Tawegozi, a Gurâni dialect, on Islamic doctrine and theology. His *al-Fadila* (written in 1868–69), deals with the same subject in 2,031 Arabic verses. His *al-Fawâ'eh* is a Persian version of the same work in 525 verses written a year later.

[8] Stanzas with crossed rhymes, the first line rhyming with the third, and the second with the fourth.

fluential as a language of poetry that the word itself came to mean "song" in Sorani Kurdish.

The beginning of Sorani as a literary language

On the Western side of the Zagros, on the Shahrezur plain, a rival Kurdish dynasty, the Bâbân, reigned over a vast territory that stretched from the Lesser Zab to the Sirwân (Diyâla) River. Its territories included Koy Sanjaq, Khânaqin, and parts of Garmiyân (Kirkuk) and western Persia. In 1781 Mahmud Pâshâ took the first steps towards transferring his capital from Qarâ/Qalâ Shuwalân to a new site about twenty kilometers to the southwest, which he named Suleimâni in honor of the Pâshâ of Baghdad. His nephew, Ebrâhim Pâshâ Bêbê, who came to power in 1783, developed and strengthened the city's administration and carried out pious works.

His cousin, Abd-al-Rahmân Pâshâ Bêbê, took office in 1789 and reigned intermittently for twenty-three years. An ambitious prince, he dreamed of overthrowing Amânollâh Khân Ardalân, who reigned over Senne (Sine, Sanandaj). To mark his independence from his overlords, whether Ottoman or Persian, and to emphasize his difference from his historic rivals, the Ardalâns, Abd-al-Rahmân decided to promote the dialect of the Shahrezur region. He invited artists, men of letters and poets, and encouraged them to drop Gurâni and adopt the local dialect instead, which became known as Sorani.[9]

The first thing these poets and literati did was to "translate" into Sorani the great works of the Kurmanji oral tradition. This is the task to which Ali Bardashâni (d. 1812) devoted himself, writing the first texts in Sorani Kurdish. He also composed *qasides*, and his *ghazals* are so well adapted to Kurdish musical styles and dance rhythms that they have been set to music. His talent was

---

9   The word derives from the name of the Sorân/Sohrân (red) dynasties that dominated the region around Hewlêr/Erbil.

recognized in his lifetime and he was called "Poet of the Bâbân Principality."

In the nineteenth century, following the general growth of national movements in the area, a Kurdish national movement also developed, although it was strongly tinged with tribalism. Kurdish literature blossomed, but the majority of the literati used Arabic, Persian or Turkish. For a long time Kurdish was considered to be a sort of Persian dialect, so much so that the elite used Persian as their means of expression.

The early part of the century saw the blossoming of the "Nâli school" of poetry, or the "Bâbâni school" in Suleimâni, under the aegis of Prince Ahmad Pâshâ, grandson of Abd-al-Rahmân Pâshâ Bêbê. This school achieved the acceptance of the Kurdish of Suleimâni as a literary language, and to judge by the number of authors using this dialect, it soon gained ascendancy in the area. The founder of the Nâli school is Malâ Khedri Ahmadi Shaweysi Mikâ'ili, or Malâ Khedri Sharazur, a subtle man of letters known by his *takhallos*, Nâli. He was born in 1800 at Khâk u Khol, a village near Suleimâni, and died in Istanbul in 1856. Like Malâyê Jezri, Nâli used poetic techniques as adapted by Persian poets, at the cost of considerable effort as, until then, the poetic forms of the *qaside* and *ghazal* were unknown to the Bâbân Kurds. The poet devoted several *ghazals* to the glory of Prince Ahmad Pâshâ, his sponsor and admirer, as well as to the Bâbân dynasty. The poetry at first had religious overtones—it was the period in which the mystical brotherhoods were flourishing—but it was his lyrical poems that enjoyed the greatest success.

Another member of this "school" was Abd-al-Rahmân Beg Sâhebqerân (*c.* 1805–69), who helped to lay the foundations of this new literary language. Under the pen name of Sâlem, he wrote many lyric poems, panegyrics, satirical poems, and above all poems on historical themes, which made his reputation. In his poetry, Sâlem used the *hazaj* meter, which is best suited to the genius of Sorani Kurdish.

It was in this period that the Ottoman government reaffirmed its control over the Muslim populations of the Ottoman Empire by liquidating the Kurdish Principalities and exiling their princes

WRITTEN KURDISH LITERATURE

and traditional leaders. Kurdistan disintegrated and became the scene of indescribable chaos. When in 1851 the Bâbân dynasty was overthrown and Prince Ahmad Bêbê was exiled to Istanbul, the poets left Suleimani. Sâlem settled in Tehran, writing poems that expressed the pains of exile. He returned to die in Suleimâni in 1869

Sâlem's cousin, Mostafâ Sâhebqerân (1800–59) also belonged to the Nâli School. His poetry is distinguished by its lyricism and patriotic sentiments. At first he wrote under the pen name of Kordi, and when he left Suleimâni he chose the name of Hejri (the Emigré or Exiled). Kordi's lyrical poems, which are of exceptional beauty, are tinged with feelings of pain. Thereafter, Sorani poetry developed outside the borders of the former Bâbân principality at Garmiyân (Kirkuk), Mokriyân and Ardâlân.

Among the second (last half of the nineteenth century) and third (twentieth century) generation of poets there were those who were more talented and popular than the members of the Nâli School. Nonetheless, it was thanks to the latter that the speech of Suleimâni became a literary language, not only in the Suleimâni region itself, but throughout the whole of what the Kurds today call "Southern Kurdistan," stretching from the Great Zâb in the west to the Iranian province of Kordestân, where it eventually replaced Gurâni.

Suleimâni was the first Kurdish city to be endowed with a secular school, the "Mektebi Rüshdiye,"[10] which was established in 1893. In 1907, a Sixth Form High School the "E'dadiye" or "Malkiye." The most gifted students continued their higher education in Istanbul, where they rubbed shoulders with learned men from all the countries of the Ottoman Empire and learned European languages. New ideas broadened their horizons. On their return to Suleimâni these young men were appointed to military or administrative positions in the region. Suleimâni thus became a training ground for schoolteachers, literati and scientists.

---

10   The Mektebi Rüshdiyye/ Rüshtiyye were secondary schools opened to students who had finished the traditional *madreses* and wanted to follow an army career.

ORAL LITERATURE OF IRANIAN LANGUAGES

Two poets are of particular importance: Hâji Qâder Koyi and Shaikh Rezâ Tâlebâni. Hâji Qâder Malâ Ahmad, better known by the name of Hâji Qâder Koyi, was born around 1816 in a village near Koy Sanjaq, which at that time was an important center of Islamic studies. On completing his studies, he left for Istanbul, where he became the teacher of the children of Bedir Khan Pâshâ (Badir Xan Pasha), who had been living under house arrest since the overthrow of the Botân principality in 1847. He thus came to know the Kurmanji language and literature and, in particular, the work of the great poet Ahmadê Khâni. He came into contact with foreign intellectuals. He paid homage to his masters Nâli and Kordi, whom he described as great visionaries. His *qasides* (Se'id 1925; Muhemmed 1973–76; Kerîm 1976), written in simple language so as to be understood by all, have a distinct social content. They represent a response to the progress that science had shown him was possible. He protested against the lethargy of the mullahs, whose egotism and intellectual laziness he criticized as obstacles to freedom of thought; he objected to their inadequacy in the face of modern life. He was the first to introduce into his poetry contemporary events and modern foreign terms and names: telegraph, railway, Russians, France, Japan and China. The patriotic verses of Hâji Qâder Koyi were like music to the ears of all strata of the Kurdish population, even those in the remotest villages. Many of them have entered the everyday language and are used as proverbial maxims (Paul-Margueritte 1937). Hâji Qâder Koyî died in Istanbul in 1894.

Another popular poet is Shaikh Rezây Tâlebâni, who introduced satire into Kurdish poetry. He was born in or around 1835 at Tâlebân, a village near Garmiyân (Kirkuk), of an old influential family of Qâderi Shaikhs, who had *takiye*s in several villages in Kurdistan. Very early on, Shaikh Rezâ clashed with his family, whom he accused of stealing his property. He traveled a great deal and spent eight years in Istanbul under the patronage of the Grand Vizier, Kâmel Pâshâ. For two years he was Persian tutor to the son of the Khedive of Egypt, and then, after a pilgrimage to Mecca, he spent the rest of his life in Kirkuk with his family. Some of Shaikh Rezây Tâlebâni's poems were first published posthumously in 1921,

WRITTEN KURDISH LITERATURE

in *Anjumani Adibâni Kord* (see above), and then in the periodical *Diyâri Kordestân* (A Gift from Kurdistan; Baghdad, 1925–26). A collection of his poems finally appeared in 1946, edited by his grandson (el-Tâlibânî 1946; cf. Resûl 1979). His poems can be classified into five types: autobiography and reminiscence; love and romance; the satire of rival tribes; panegyrics or invective; and the satire of misers (Edmonds, 1935). His work is distinguished by his strong language (*zur-e kalâm*), bordering on the obscene, found particularly in poems satirizing the religious beliefs and rituals of the Ahl-e Haqq (on whom see above). He died in Baghdad in 1910.

Another poet who must be mentioned is Mahwi, the pen name of Malâ Mahmud, son of Malâ Othmâni Balkhi, whose *qasides* and *ghazals* have a lyrical-mystical tone and are distinguished by their great sweetness. Mahwi was born in a village near Suleimâni around 1830, into a Naqshbandi family. He studied at Senne (Sanandaj) and Sâblâkh (Mahâbâd), and in 1859 was ordained as a mullah by the learned Zahâwi, the famous Mufti of Baghdad. Sultan Abdulhamid II granted him a stipend and appointed him manager of the Suleimâni *khâneqâh* which became known as the Khâneqâh Mahwi, where he was buried in 1906. A central theme in his work is the (female) beloved, through whom one may attain the Truth, and ultimately the Divine. His *Divân* was published in 1922 (Âghâzâde 1922). The poetry of Hareq Malâ Sâleh (1851–1907) is also imbued with an ardent Sufi faith.

Further east, in the Mokriyân area on the eastern slope of the Zagros range, lived Abdollah Beg Ahmad Ebrâhim (d. 1916), who adopted the pen name of Adab, but is better known as Mesbâh al-Diwân (Light of the Assembly). Born in 1859 in a village near Sâblâkh into a family of Kurdish notables, he studied in Teheran. He married Nosrat Khânom with whom he was passionately in love, but she abandoned him for the governor of Sâblâkh when he was seriously ill. His poetic work is marked by a considerable aesthetic charm, inspired by his personal tragedy. His poems, describing the beauty of Nosrat Khânom, were violently criticized by the supporters of classical poetry, who saw them as going against the norm and sullying their ideal of an impersonal beloved. His work played a major role in the development of written literature in Iranian Kurdistan.

The nineteenth century also saw the beginning of a movement for women's emancipation. Mâh Sharaf Khânom Kordestâni (1805–47), better known by her pen name, Masture (lit. "covered," i.e., "chaste") Kordestâni, is certainly one of the finest female personalities of the period in the literary world of the Middle East. She was the favorite wife of Khosrow Khan, the governor (*vali*) of Ardalân (d. c. 1834) who also was a poet, writing under the pen name of Nâkâm. For a long time, it was thought that Masture wrote only in Persian, but her poems in Gurâni have recently been discovered.[11] She wrote still unpublished a theological work "aqâyed" and is also the author of a Majma' ol-odabâ (The Gathering of literati).[12] Masture's most important work is a genealogical history of the Ardalan Princes from the 12th century to 1847, "Tarix-e Ardalân," written in Persian in 1847, published for the first time by Nâser Âzâdpur, Sanandaj 1946. It was translated into Sorani by Hasan Jâf and Shukur Mostafâ "Mejuy Ardalân," Baghdad 1989, then translated into Russian by E. I. Vasil'eva with the title "Mâx Xânun Kurdistâni, Xronika doma Ardalân," Nauka, Moscow 1990. The poet Nâli was a great admirer of Masture and dedicated one of his *qasides* to her. Also worthy of mention are, among others, the female poets Mehrâbân (1858–1905), daughter of Malâ Hosni Barwâri; Sira Khânom (1814–65) of Diyarbakir; and Khâtun Khorshid, daughter of Shaikh Ma'ruf Kawlos.

The Kurdish press

The development of the press paralleled that of the Kurdish national movement, and its influence on Kurdish national life and culture was particularly important. The first Kurdish newspaper, which significantly bore the name *Kordestân*, appeared in Cairo in 1898, in both Kurdish and Turkish. Its founders were Meqdâd Medhat Beg and Abd-al-Rahmân, son of Badr Khan Pâshâ, the prince of Jezrê Bôtân who was deposed in 1847. The Kurdish exiles who gathered

---

11 Masture-ye Kordestânî Mâh Sharaf Khânom, *Divân-e Masture*, ed. Hâj Mirzâ Yahyâ Ma'refat, Tehran, 1925.
12 Bâbâ Mardux Ruhâni Shiva, *Târikh-e Mashâhir-e kord*, vol. 1, Sorush, Tehran, 1985, p. 386.

around the paper were influenced by new European ideas and culture. For example, they published a condemnation of the massacre of Armenians in 1894–96. The publishers' stand against the régime in Istanbul forced them to move the paper's office to Geneva, then to London and Folkestone, and then back to Geneva again, where the last issue (no. 31, April 1902) was published. In Istanbul, the monthly *Rôji kord* (Kurdish Day) became *Hatâwi kord* (Kurdish Sun) in 1913. In 1916, Sorayâ Badr Khan published the Turkish-language weekly *Jin* (Life), which proclaimed "Kurdistan for the Kurds." He also published the weekly *Kordestân* in 1917–18 (37 issues).

World War I and its aftermath altered the Kurds' situation. After the division of Kurdistan between the Ottoman and Persian empires came the division of the Kurdish territory among Turkey, Iran, Iraq, Syria, and the regions of the Soviet Caucasus. The fate of the Kurds and the development of their language and literature came to depend on the degree of freedom they were granted by the central governments.

3. Kurdish literature after World War I

In Armenia, 1921–89

Despite their small numbers, the Kurdish communities of Soviet Armenia occupied an important place in the life of the Kurdish people. From the early 1920s, this community was considered a "nationality," with full recognition of its language. It enjoyed state support and had its own schools, press, publishing house, and radio broadcasts. It had to develop an alphabet, and initially a modified Armenian alphabet was adopted which was used in Kurdish schools in Armenia and Georgia from 1922 on. In 1928–29, a modified Roman alphabet was officially introduced, which had been developed by the Assyrian I. Maragulov and the Kurd Erebê Shemo (Rondot 1933).[13]

---

[13] From here on Kurdish terms will be transcribed according to the "Hawar" alphabet.

Illiteracy among the Kurds—mostly Yezidis, who were traditionally illiterate—was soon overcome, and an intellectual elite began to flourish. Thanks to the dynamism of Academician Frejman and especially I. A. Orbeli, who was Professor of Kurdish Studies in Leningrad (1914–35), Kurdish Studies developed there, as well as in Moscow, Yerevan and Baku (Bennigsen 1960; Mokri 1963).

Self-taught for the most part, Kurdish poets and prose writers were strongly influenced by Armenian and Russian literature, and their works are politically committed. Emînê Evdal (1906–64), a porter who became a teacher, Heciyê Cindî (1909–90), and the poet Casimê Celîl (1908–98) published their works in the bi-weekly Kurdish periodical *Riya Taze* (The New Road), which was published in Yerevan from 1930, and in a number of pamphlets. The poets became known because their work and names were included in the "Almanacs of Kurdish Soviet writers" and other anthologies. The first play, *Qitiya du dermana* (Medicine Box, 1932), was written by Haciyê Cindî, who devoted a great part of his life to collecting and publishing texts of Kurdish folklore. Then, in 1935, the poet Wazirê Nadir (1911–47) published a play called *Reva Jin* (The Kidnapping). He also wrote a long poem in epic form, *Nado û Gulizer*, which celebrates the heroic adventures of a young Kurd and his fiancée during the war. Erebê Shemo (1897–1979), one of the most productive Kurdish novelists, published *Kurdskiĭ pastukh* (The Kurdish Shepherd) in Russian in 1931, and an autobiographical novel in Kurdish (*Shivana Kôrmanca*) in Yerevan in 1935. Later the author took it up again and expanded it, republishing it in 1958 under the title *Berbang* (Dawn). Poetically and skillfully he described the everyday details of his childhood as a shepherd and the open-air life of the nomads. He also recounts how, having become a Communist, he saw combat during the Soviet Revolution of 1917.

On the eve of World War II, the authorities' efforts to unify the Soviet Union and promote patriotism resulted in the adoption of Cyrillic instead of a number of newly created alphabets, including the Kurdish one that had been based on the Latin alphabet. The Kurdish press, publishing houses, and schools in the USSR have been using a modified Cyrillic alphabet since then.

WRITTEN KURDISH LITERATURE

The novel *Dimdim*, which Ereb Shamilov (Kurdish: Erebê Shemo) published in Yerevan in 1966, was based on a famous epic poem celebrating the heroic early seventeenth-century defense of a fortress, commanded by the "Khan of the Golden Arm," Prince of Baradost, against the Safavid aggressors. *Jiyina Bextewar* (Happy Life, 1959) came out, followed by its sequel *Hopo*. Both novels describe the life of the Kurds under the Soviet regime, and were republished in *Berevok* (Collection; Yerevan, 1969). Semand Siyabendov (1909–98) published the beautiful popular romantic epic *Siyabend û Xecê* (Siyâband and Khajê, 1959). *Bîranînêd min* (My Memories), by the novelist Ehmedê Mirazî (1899–1961), was published posthumously in Yerevan in 1966. The novel *Hawarî* (The Call) by Heciyê Cindî was published in 1967, and *Gundê Mêrxasa* (Village of the Brave) and *Sher Çiyada* (War in the Mountains) by Elî Ebderrehman (1920–94) came out in 1968 and 1989, respectively. *Keskesor* (Rainbow), a collection of poems by Usivê Beko (1909–69) appeared in 1961. In an Armenian work which translates as "Customs of the Kurds in Transcaucasia" (Yerevan, 1957), Eminê Avdal (see above) compared the position of the Kurds before and after the Soviet regime. In 1964 Ismail Duko (b. 1930) published *Zewacê bê dil* (Loveless Marriage). In *Shiyer* (Poems, 1957) Etarê Shero (1901–70) expresses his thoughts on the situation of the Kurds under the Ottomans, in short poems.

Behara Taze (New Spring; an annual literary publication, Yerevan, 1980–90) published poems, short stories and even novels by writers of the second generation: Emerîkê Serdar (b. 1935), editor-in-chief of *Riya Taze*; Wezîrê Esho (b. 1933) and Ezîzê Gerdenziyari (b. 1945), a prose writer and playwright. Women also took part in literary activities. Sima Semend (b. 1935) published *Xezal* (Gazelle) in 1961 and *Do Shayî* (Two Pieces of Good News) in 1967, and the work of the poet Hinara Tajin appeared in the fourth issue of *Behara Taze*. Tosinê Reshit (b. 1941) and Eskerê Boyik (b. 1941) published their plays *Siyabend û Xecê* (Siyâband and Khajê) and *Mem û Zîn, drama ji pênc perdan* (Mem and Zin, a Drama in Five Acts) with the Stockholm publishers Roja Nû in 1988 and 1989 respectively. Ereb Shemo's novels *Dimdim*, Stockholm, 1983), *Jiyana Bextewar* (Happy Life; Stockholm 1990); *Hopo* (id.; Stockholm), and *Berbang* (Dawn; Stockholm, 1988) were published abroad in the Hawar alphabet. Shemo's *Dimdim* was translated into Kurdish Sorani by Shikur Mistefa and published in Baghdad in 1975.

In Turkey, 1923–57

The Turkish Republic carried out an assimilationist policy towards its Kurdish subjects. In the name of national unity, the government denied the identity of the several million Kurds and ordered their language, described as archaic, to be eradicated. Kurdish schools and publications were banned. The use of the words "Kurdish" and "Kurdistan" constituted a legal offence; these terms were officially replaced by "Mountain Turk" and "Eastern Anatolia" or "the East." Turkish Kurdistan was declared off limits until the 1960s. Kurdish intellectuals went into exile, and it was in Syria, then under a French mandate, that Kurdish Kurmanji literature flourished. Kurdish intellectuals gathered in Beirut and Damascus around the brothers Celadet (1893–1961) and Kamuran (1895–1978) Bedir Khan (Badr Khan), who became the architects of a Kurmanji Kurdish cultural revival. They adapted the Latin alphabet to Kurdish in much the same way as had been done for Turkish, and introduced the new script in the periodicals *Hawar* (Call; Damascus, 1935–43), *Ronahî* (Clarity; Damascus, 1941–44), *Roja Nû* (New Day; Beirut, 1943–46) and *Stêr* (Star; Damascus, 1943–45). The Bedir Khan brothers carried out literary research, exploring the possibilities of Kurmanji as a modern literary language. Among their colleagues on these periodicals was Shêxmûs Hesen (1903–46), better known by his pen name of Cigerxwîn (Bruised Heart). His poems, classical in form but patriotically inspired, express his love for his devastated country. Using the rich tradition of Kurdish folklore, Cigerxwîn composed fables that are clearly parables calling for Kurdish unity. His first two collections, *Dîwana Cigerxwîn*, 1945; *Sewra Azadî*, 1954, came out in Syria, but he had to wait until the 1970s to publish his last collections. One may there also mention Osman Sebrî (1905–93), who was a born storyteller, and the poets Qadrîcan (1914–74), Reshîd Kurd (1910–68), and Nûredîn Zaza (1919–88).

However, after World War II, when Syria became independent, the Kurds lost their freedom and the writers again went into exile.

In Iraq, 1919–57

When, after World War I, the British decided to annex the Kurdish Vilayat (province) of Mosul to the new Arab state of Iraq, their first act was to dismiss the Turkish officials and replace them with Kurds, "assisted" by British advisers. The Kurdish language was introduced to replace Turkish in official matters and Persian in personal correspondence. The first Kurdish printing press was established in 1919 by Major Ely B. Soane (d. 1923) in the town of Suleimâni. The development of Kurdish printing promoted Sorani Kurdish, which writers and poets renewed and perfected. This dialect thus showed its potential as a modern literary language.

Having become citizens of an Arab state, the Kurds were obliged to adopt the Arabic alphabet, although technically this script was ill suited to transcribe Kurdish. Literary output developed in the late 1920s in Suleimâni, Hewlêr/Erbil and Baghdad. Contact with the West, and translations of Byron, Shelley, Lamartine, Maupassant, Schiller, Goethe and Pushkin, brought the Kurds out of their isolation and profoundly changed the character of their poetry. Exposure to modernism drew poetry away from its traditional paths. Although poems initially retained their classical form, their contents showed many innovative elements, such as expressions of love, despair and anger; traditional poetry was enriched by references to the author's inner world. Characteristic of this new tendency was the poem *Min û estêrekan* (The Stars and I) by Piramêrd (Old Man), the pen name of Hajî Tewfîq (Hâji Towfiq, 1867–1950). However, realistic, patriotic and social themes predominated and reflected current events. The poet sang of the love of their country and the glory of freedom. A characteristic example of this new tendency was the poetry of Ehmed Muxtar Jaf (1897–1935), whose poetic output oscillated between romanticism and social themes, and of Hemdî Fettah Beg Sahibqiran (Sâhebqerân, 1878–1936), who defended the common struggle of the Kurdish and Arab people, as did Ebd el-Wehîd Nûrî (1903–46) and the witty Zewar (Ebdellah Muhammad, 1875–1948). The "kurdification" of the language, stripping it of loan words and forms from the dominant languages (Arabic, Persian, and Turkish), can be credited to the writers of this period.

Later, whilst many new genres were adopted—such as the lyric-epic drama—which allowed the struggles of the Kurds to be presented in a more vivid and dramatic way, the structure of classical poetry broke down. The 1930s saw the appearance of syllabic verse, which was close to the oral tradition, and of prose poems and free verse. Shaikh Nûrî Shaikh Salih (1897–1958) was the first to break with tradition. He was quickly followed by the great Goran (Ebdellah Suleiman, 1904–62), who abandoned Arabo-Persian metrics (*aruz*), with their quantitative rhythm and single rhyme, for a syllabic rhythm and multiple rhymes, close to folk-poetry and songs. His many travels gave him a deep knowledge of Kurdish society, which is evoked in his work by means of original imagery. The majority of his poems, which sound like revolutionary anthems, have been set to music. His political ideas earned him several prison sentences, which permanently damaged his health (Kerîm 1980). *Ey Reqîb* (O Enemy) by Dildar (Yûnis Malâ Re'ûf, 1918–48) became the National Anthem of the Autonomous Republic of Kurdistan (1946), and was subsequently adopted by all Kurdish nationalists.

Poetry continued to flourish in Iraqi Kurdistan; important contemporary poets further include the musically disposed Ehmed Herdî (b. 1922), whose poetry is imbued with sadness; Salim (Shaikh Salim Shaikh Ehmed Ezebanî, 1892–1959; Dilzar (Ehmed Mistefa Heme Agha Hewezî, b. 1920), who wrote his most beautiful poems in prison; Bêkes (Feqî Ebdellah, 1905–48), whose son Shêrko (b. 1940) has become the figurehead of the new generation of poets; Kamiran Mukrî (1929–89); Kakey Fellah (b. 1928) and Muhammad Huseyn Berzincî, who used the pen name "Eyn Ha Ba."

WRITTEN KURDISH LITERATURE

Prose Literature

Prose began to blossom with the development of newspapers and magazines: *Pêshkewtin* (Progress; Suleimâni, 1919–22), *Jiyân* (Life; Suleimâni, 1926–38), *Ronakî* (Light; Erbîl, 1935–36), and above all *Gelawêj* (Sirius; Baghdad, 1939–49) and *Hîwa* (Hope; Baghdad 1957–63). One of the first short stories, *Le xewi me* (In my Dream) by Cemîl Sa'ib (1887–1950), which appeared as a serial in *Jiyanewe* (Rebirth; Suleimâni), denounced British colonial policy. *Meseley wijdan* (A Matter of Conscience), a satirical tract against corruption, was written in 1926 by Ehmed Muxtar Caf (see above), though it was not published until 1970. The social theme is even more pronounced with Huseyn Huznî Mukriyânî (1893–1947) whose *Ademîzad le sayey derebegî* (Man in Feudal Society) was banned by Iraqi censorship as soon as it came out in 1945, as was *Janî gel* (The People's Hardship) by Ibrahîm Ehmed (b. 1914), the first novel in Sorani, which came out only in 1973. Shakir Fettah (1914–88) created the Kurdish short story and published the children's stories, *Hawrêy minal* (Children's Friend; Baghdad, 1948) and *Tîshk* (Sunbeam; Baghdad, 1947), which denounced poverty and oppression. In *Afretî kurd* (Kurdish Woman; Baghdad, 1958) he called for the emancipation of women. Muherrem Mihemmed Emîn (1921–80), a talented prose writer, published *Mem Xomer* (Uncle Omar; Erbîl, 1954) and *Rêgay azadî* (Road to Freedom; Suleimâni 1959).

In Iran, 1912–79

The government of Iran carried out an assimilationist policy towards the Kurdish population. Ebd-el-Rezzaq Bedir Xan (and later Ismaîl Agha Simko) founded the periodical *Kurdistan* in Orumiye in 1912. The only literary period in this region was that of the Autonomous Republic of Kurdistan (January–December 1946), which despite its brief existence, stimulated a flourishing of Kurdish letters. The poets Hêmin (Mihemmed Emîn Sheikh el-Islâm, 1921–86) and Hejar (Ebd-el-Rehman Sherefqendî, 1920–91) were promoted as "Poets of the Nation." A number of publications were printed on a single printing press, bought in the USSR: the newspaper *Kurdistan* (organ of the Democratic Party of Kurdistan; Sablax/Mahâbâd; 113 issues starting from December 1945); *Hawarî nishtiman* (The Country's Call, 1946), *Girugalî mindalanî kurd* (Kurdish Children's Babblings, 1946); and *Helala* (Tulip; the paper of the Kurdish women's association, 1946). A play, *Daykî nishtiman* (Mother Country) was staged (the topic: "The mother country is in danger, she is in chains and is finally saved by her sons"), and enjoyed great success. Kurdish became the official language of the administration, press and schools. All these efforts to develop the Kurdish language and literature were brutally interrupted by the repression that followed the overthrow of the Republic in December 1946. The leaders were hanged on March 1947 and intellectuals forced into exile.

In Iraq and Turkey, 1958–90

Following the Iraqi military coup d'état in July 1958, a provisional Constitution was adopted, Article 3 of which for the first time specifically states that Kurds and Arabs are joint partners in the Iraqi nation. The Kurdish press enjoyed a freedom it had never experienced before. The periodical *Rojî Nö* (New Day; Suleimâni 1960) published Mihemmed Mustafa Kurdî's allegorical short stories, and Rehîm Qazî published his work *Pêshmerge* (Partisan; Baghdad, 1961), which described the birth and overthrow of the Republic of Kurdistan in 1946. After an initial period of unity, the recognized rights of the Kurds were gradually challenged and whittled away. In 1961 the five Kurdish newspapers were banned and their editors jailed. In September of that year President Qâsim (Qâsem) sent two divisions against Kurdistan, and the struggle between Kurdish nationalists and the Iraqi government, punctuated by periodic ceasefires and truces, continued until 1975.

The long drawn-out insurrection of the Iraqi Kurds strengthened Kurdish nationalism in Turkey and Iran, which then became a major factor in the region. *Ileri Yurt* (The Country Ahead), a

WRITTEN KURDISH LITERATURE

Kurdish-Turkish daily paper, was published in Diyarbakir for two years (1958–59). In September 1962 several bilingual Kurdish-Turkish magazines appeared: *Dicle-Firat* (Tigris and Euphrates; eight issues, 1962–63), *Roja Newe* (New Day; a literary and political monthly in Turkish, Kurdish and Zaza[14]); *Deng* (Voice; 1963) and *Dengê Tazo* (New Voice; four issues, 1966). The periodicals were quickly closed down and their editors arrested and sentenced to long prison terms. Mûsa Anter, born in 1918, who published the play *Birîna resh* (Festering Wound; 1965 in Kurdish and Turkish), spent several years in jail before his assassination in Diyarbakir in 1992. The poet Bucak was assassinated in 1966. The publication of a children's reader and a bilingual edition of the romantic epic *Mem û Zîn* earned Emin Bozarslan (b. 1934) a jail sentence. The following magazines were brought out: *Özgürlük Yolu* (The Road of Freedom, a monthly in Kurdish, Zaza and Turkish, ed. Faruk Aras, Ankara, 1975), *Rizgarî* (Liberation, a political and cultural monthly in Kurdish and Turkish, ed. Rushen Arslan, Ankara and Istanbul, 1976) and *Roja Welat* (Sun of the Fatherland, a bi-weekly published in Kurdish, Zaza and Turkish, ed. Mustafa Aydin, Ankara, 1977, circulation: 35–40,000). These magazines were successively banned, and their publishers and editors sentenced to prison. The persecuted intellectuals were, once again, obliged to go into exile. Many of them settled in Sweden, where they became the source of an impressive renaissance of Kurmanji Kurdish literature.

Around the same period, from 1959 to 1963, the weekly *Kurdistan* was published in Tehran under the auspices of the Iranian government, totaling 205 issues, a record compared to most previous Kurdish publications, which had been banned after only a few months. A group of brilliant intellectuals gathered around the paper and, from a literary point of view, it was a success, although it was only distributed abroad, not in Iran itself.

The truce between the Iraqi government and the Kurds (1970–74) permitted the development of a significant Kurdish literature in

---

14 Zaza or Zazaki, also called Dim(i)li, is spoken by several million people in Turkey and belongs to the Iranian family of languages.

Iraq. The following is only a brief selection of the many works that appeared during that period.

After much wandering, the Kurdish poets Hejar and Hemin (see above) sought refuge in Iraq, where they could at last publish their work. The same was true of Hesen Qizilcî (1914–85), a gifted novelist with an acute sense of observation. Poets and writers published their work in the twenty-nine periodicals that appeared in this period (of which two were based in Kirkuk, six in Hewlêr/Erbil, and four in Suleimâni). Baghdad became the most important Kurdish cultural center. A Kurdish Academy of Science was created in 1970, and the first issue of *Govarî korî zanyarî kurd* (Journal of the Kurdish Academy of Science) appeared in 1973. This 800-page bilingual (Arabic/Kurdish) volume was edited by Ihsan Shîrzad, Minister for Regional Government. An interesting phenomenon emerged, which was to be repeated in other circumstances: intellectuals from various parts of Iraq, who until then had been fairly well integrated into Arab intellectual life, began to become "Kurdicized." Journalists, historians, linguists, scientists and engineers started to write in Kurdish.

The emerging literary output suffered the repercussions of the breakdown in negotiations between the Kurds and Saddam Hussein, who had come to power in Iraq, and then from the two Gulf wars. Poets and writers had little chance of publishing their work on the small portable printing presses of the Kurdish guerrillas. Nevertheless, Mihemmed Mukrî (Mohammad Mokri, b. 1952), one of the best Kurdish novelists, brought out his attractive lyrical novel *Heres* (Avalanche; 1985) and *Tole* (Revenge; 1985) under these conditions, as did Sherko Bêkes (b. 1945), who published *Helo* (Eagle; a collection of poems in three parts, 1986).

In the Diaspora

Many Kurdish writers sought refuge in Europe, where they joined the hundreds of thousands of Kurdish immigrant workers. In Sweden, which encouraged the integration of immigrants and promoted the development of their cultural identity, there was a remarkable renaissance of Kurmanji Kurdish which, for lack of freedom, was fading away in Turkey and Syria. Young intellectuals, who were exiled in a land far from their own and who had had previously written only in Turkish, began to "Kurdicize" their writing with great courage and perseverance. Poets and writers first published their work in various periodicals: *Armanc* (Goal; Spanga (Sweden), first appeared May 1979), *Berbang* (Dawn; Stockholm, first appeared July 1982), *Roja Nû* (New Day; Stockholm, 1983), and many others. Publishing houses like Jîna Nû (New Life; Uppsala), Roja Nû (New Day), Welat (The Country), Kitêbxana Sara (Sara Bookshop), Apec, and many others, published the works of poets and writers: the collected poems of Gundî, Rojên Barnas (b. 1945), Firat Cewerî, Seydayê Kelesh (b. 1930) and Kemal Burkay (b. 1937). Mahmut Baksi (1944–2001) was the first foreign member elected to the steering committee of the Union of Swedish Writers. The talented Mehmed Uzun (b. 1953), author of a number of bestsellers translated into many languages (see Bibliography), has since replaced him in that role. Bavê Nazê published two novels (see Bibliography), Nûrî Shemdîn, Ahmet Cantekin, Shahînê B. Sorekli (b. 1946), and Ihsan Aksoy (b. 1944) published novels and short stories.

Publishers specializing in Sorani Kurdish brought out the journals *Mamostay Kurd* (The Kurdish Teacher; ed. Ferhad Shakely, Uppsala, first appeared 1988), *Ala* (Flag; Uppsala, first published 1988), and *Rabûn* (Uprising; Stockholm; first published 1992) in which Enwar Qadir Mihemmed, Cemshîd Heyderî, Heme Se'îd Hesen, Rizgar Ebdullah, Rafiq Sabir, and many other writers from Iraqi and Iranian Kurdistan published poems and short stories.

The poet, writer and linguist Malmîsanij (Mehmet Tayfun, b. 1952) is actively developing Zaza. He has many disciples who publish in *Ayre* (The Mill; Stockholm, first published early 1986), *Piya* (Together; ed. Ebûbekir Pamukcu, Skärholmen, first appeared April 1988), *Ware* (Camp; a Zaza cultural periodical published in Baiersbronn, Germany, 1992) and *Vate, kovara kulturî* (The Word, a cultural magazine; ed. Malmîsanij, Skärholmen, first published 1997). In 1993 Faruk Iremet published a collection of poems in Kurmanjî-Dimilî, *Rondikê çavên tî* (The Light of Your

Eyes), with APEC Publishers in Spanga (Sweden), and the novelist Munzur Çem (born near Dersim about 1934) published the novel *Hotay serra Usifê Qurzkizî* (The Seventy Years of Yusif Qurzkizî; Stockholm, 1992).

In Germany, Balî Xan and Rohat brought out an anthology of Kurdish poetry in 1982, and the young novelist Brîndar (b. 1963) published two novels. Darwesh M. Ferho published his poems in Belgium.

In France, Kurdish intellectuals founded the Kurdish Institute of Paris in 1983. The Institute, whose Director is the physicist Kendal Nezan, aims to promote Kurdish language, literature, and culture by bringing out the semi-annual review *Hêvî/Hîwa* (Hope; in Kurmanji, Sorani, and Zaza/Dimilî; Paris, first published September 1983)[15] and then *Etudes Kurdes* (Kurdish Studies), a semi-annual review, first published in 2000. Twice a year since 1987 it has brought together about twenty Kurdish writers and linguists to study the problems of spelling and modernization of Kurmanji Kurdish. A bulletin, *Kurmancî*, is published after each of these seminars.

Kurdish Cultural Centers—some of them short-lived—sprang up in many European and North American cities.

In Iran since 1979

The Islamic Republic of Iran, established in 1979, has not responded to the hopes of the Kurds, who demanded Kurdish language schools and publishing houses in the Kurdish provinces. A Congress of Kurdish Intellectuals was held at Mahâbâd from 25 to 27 September 1986 and, despite very strict censorship in the Islamic Republic, Ehmed Qazi (b. 1935) published the satirical short stories *Baqabên* (Bond; 1984). Hawar (Eli Heseniyani, b. 1939) published *Sharî wêran* (The Ruined City; Orumiya, 1984), which deals with social problems. The poet Fatih Sheikhelislamî (b. 1936) chose exile

---

15 The Kurdish Institute of Paris was in fact the first to encourage the development of Zaza.

in Sweden. The monthly *Sirwe* (Gentle whisper of breeze; founded by the poet Hemîn, first published in Orumiya, 1984), was published by the Salaheddin Ayyubi Publication Center and subsidized by the local authorities. Originally a quarterly, the magazine became a monthly in 1986, and published the works of Ibrâhîm Yûnisî (b. 1920s), Fettah Emîrî (b. 1946), Elî Hesenyanî (b. 1939), Celal Malikshah (b. 1955), Fatime Huseyn-Penahî, Cîle Huseynî (1964–96) and Necîbe Ehmed, a novelist and translator. Edited by Ehmed Qadî (b. 1936), *Sirwe* played a major role in the development of Kurdish language and literature in Iran, where teaching Kurdish is still discouraged. Other periodicals included the magazine *Awêne* (Mirror; ed. Seyyid Mihemmed Mûsawî, Tehran, first published 1986); *Awiyer/Adîder* (the name of a mountain; ed. Bahrâm Weledbegî, Sine/Sanandaj, first published 1996); the Persian/Kurdish review *Sirwan* (the name of a river; Meriwan), and the periodical pamphlet *Tîshk* (Sunbeam; published in Iraq by the Democratic Party of Iranian Kurdistan). These magazines have been banned and their editors put in prison or charged.

In Turkey since 1991

In Turkey, in the spring of 1991, the coalition government of President Turgut Özal recognized the existence of a Kurdish language, after half a century during which Kurdish identity had been denied; this led to a flowering of Kurdish letters. Braving the difficulties (the civil war in Turkish Kurdistan and the threats which were often carried out anywhere in Turkey—witness the over 4,500 Kurdish intellectuals who became the victims of extrajudicial executions), poets and writers published their works in Kurdish or Kurdish/Turkish reviews and magazines, brought out by publishers in Istanbul, Ankara and Diyarbakir. Kurdish works which were originally published in the Diaspora could now appear in Turkey, and Kurdish and Turkish translations of European works on Kurdish studies were published. In 1991 publication of a Kurdish magazine (*Rojname*, Journal; Istanbul) was permitted for the first time. Published in Kurdish and Zaza by Ahmet Z. Okçuoglu, it had a circulation of 45,000 in Turkey. Istanbul saw the publication of *Deng* (Voice; ed. Hikmet Çetin, 1989), *Newroz* (New Day; in Turkish, Kurdish and Zaza, published by Huseyin Alatash, 1991), *Nûbihar* (Beginnings; a cultural magazine with an Islamic slant, ed. Suleyman Çevik, 1992) and *War* (Camp; a quarterly review on Kurdish language and culture, ed. Kamber Soypak, 1997). In Diyarbakir there appeared *Govend* (Round Dance; ed. Mazhar Kara, 1991). Publications were often banned and their editors arrested, only to reappear later on with a new name and editor. Thus the Socialist Party's weekly, *Azadî* (Freedom; ed. Hikmet Çetin), appeared in Istanbul on 27 May 1992 and was banned on 13 May 1994, its editors arrested or indicted. It reappeared under the name of *Dengê azadî* (The Voice of Freedom) on 20 May 1994 under the editorship of Behram Alabey and Fevziye Perishan. Banned on 11 March 1995, it reappeared under the title *Ronahî* (Light) on 21 May 1995, ed. Shemseddîn Çelik, Burhan Erdem and Ihsan Turkmen. A new ban on 10 October 1996 led to another change of name, to *Hêvi* (Hope) and then, since 3 July 1999, to *Roja Taze* (New Day).

In Iraq since 1991

Kurdish literature flourished in the security zone created in 1992 in Iraq by the Americans following the first Gulf War to protect the three Kurdish provinces and ensure their control by Kurdish organizations. Writers and poets enjoyed a hitherto unknown freedom, adapting readily to democracy and established political parties. Intellectuals participated in the seventeen political parties and organizations that sprang up, published newspapers and reviews, and set up radio and television stations. Literature, then, reflected the outlook of the political parties which the authors belonged to. In 1991, 71 papers and magazines came out (34 in Erbil, 23 in Suleimâni, 11 in Duhok and 3 in Kirkuk), and in 1992 there were 77 (38 in Erbil, 25 in Suleimâni, 12 in Duhok and one in Kirkuk; see Pirbal 2000). Despite the relatively free elections of May 1992, no stable authority was set up in Iraqi Kurdistan; the Kurdistan Democratic Party controlled the western part of the region, and the Patriotic

Union of Kurdistan the eastern part. The number of publications diminished. By 1993 only forty-eight remained. Some literary and cultural reviews stood out: *Alternatîv* in Suleimâni; *Peyv* (Word) and *Serhildan* (Uprising) in Duhok; and *Sibêy* (Morning) in Erbil. In the same year the complete works of Me'rûf Berzencî (1921–63) were published on modern printing presses in Erbil. Mihemmed Mukrî, a talented novelist, published (or republished) *Tole* (Revenge; 3rd edition), *Heres* (Avalanche; 3rd edition) and *Ejdîha* (Dragon) in 1998.

In May 1994, fighting broke out between the Kurdistan Democratic Party and the Patriotic Union of Kurdistan, which led to the partition of this section of Kurdistan. The writers, divided between the two hostile camps, came to the sad conclusion that their tragedy was not a foreign product but was partly created by the Kurds themselves. There was no room for independent literature in this atmosphere, and the depressed writers and poets joined the long procession of intellectuals who had left for exile in Europe or the United States.

In 1996, U.S. mediation resulted in a truce between the rival camps and the establishment of two Kurdish zones, which began competing with one another. The Universities of Suleimâni, Erbil and Duhok opened their doors to several thousand students and nearly a hundred specialized reviews and magazines appeared in Iraqi Kurdistan; *Hezarmêrd* (name of a region; Suleimâni) and *Shaneder* (id., name of a region; Erbil) are periodicals devoted to archaeology; *Shakar* (Excellence; Suleimâni) and *Huner* (Art; Duhok) focus on the fine arts. Particular attention has been given to the translation of the major works of English, French and Swedish literature. The periodicals *Wergêran* (Translation; Erbil) and *Serdem* (Age; ed. Shêrk Bêkes, Suleimâni) offer high quality translations into Sorani Kurdish. There was also a theatre and cinema review (*Sînema w Shano*, Cinema and Theater; Erbil), reviews that specialized in literature for children, and satirical magazines, such as *Sîrxurme* (Poking with the Finger; Suleimâni) and *Melay meshhûr* (The Famous Mullah; Erbil). Mention should also be made of the Academic journals: *Zankoy Duhok* (University of Duhok; Duhok), *Zankoy Selahedîn* (University of Selahedîn; Erbil) and

Govarî dewlî (National Review) of the Center for Strategic Research at Suleimâni.

The economic (and intellectual) embargo imposed by the international community[16] and by Baghdad, and the division of the area into two Kurdish zones, was considered disastrous by Kurdish poets and writers. A younger generation of angry writers rejected the authorities, whom they criticized for their incapacity to solve the Kurds' political and social problems. They came together in associations and young writers' committees. In Duhok, Muhsin Quçan, Selman Kuvlî, Hizirvan, Isma'îl Badî, Fazil Amir, and Shukrî Shebaz gathered around the review *Nûxwaz* (Modernists, 3 issues). In Akrê, the writers Azad Dartash and Emîr Findî supported this group. In Suleimâni, *Yaney Çîrok* (The Club of Short Story Writers) brought together the writers Farûq Homer, Ita Mihemmed, Tako Kerîm, and others who sought to renovate the Kurdish short story. In the same city, a new wave of writers expressed themselves in the review *Gutar* (Speech; ed. Ehmed and Ramyar Mehmûd). Also active were the *Komeley Hawrêyanî shêwkarî* (The Writers' Guild Association), *Komeley Hesht* (Association of the Eight), and *Destey Tem* (The Misty Group), which were renewing the visual arts.

In Erbil, a Writers' Union which had published an important cultural manifesto in the magazine *Wêran* (Ruin) in the Spring of 1994, succeeded in livening things up, and artists like Hemdî Hesen, Cîlo Tahêr, Nîhad Camî, Sadîq Mihemmed, and others were able to stage some original plays.

Women writers also emerged: Kecal Ehmed, Shirins K., Kazîwe Salih, Erxewan, Maria Ehmed, Sara Efrasiyab, Behre Muftî, and Elham Mensûr published short stories and poems. Necîbe Ehmed Hekim, Mehabad Qeredaghi, Rewas Caf, and Nezend Begikhani who live abroad but whose work is published in Iraqi Kurdistan, should also be mentioned here.

---

16 The Kurds were under a triple embargo—from the United Nations after the Gulf War in 1991, from Baghdad, and from Iraq's neighbors, who were concerned that a successful Kurdish government in Iraq could incite Kurdish minorities in their own territories.

Even more interesting is the new trend of using Roman instead of Kurdish Arabic script, which is underway in Hewlêr/Erbil as well as in Duhok, Zakho, and Akrê in the province of Badinan. In Erbil, the reviews *Dicle* (Tigris) and *Golanî Latînî* (Golan in Roman) came out in the Kurdish-Latin alphabet generally known as the "Hawar" alphabet. Several papers and journals published in Badinan partly use Latin script: *Peyv* (Word), *Gazî* (Call), *Metîn* (name of a mountain), *Huner* (Art), *Lalish* (name of a region) and *Duhok* (name of a city). This "cultural revolution" in Iraqi Kurdistan has a dual aim: to establish closer relations with the Kurds in Turkey, Syria, and the diaspora, and to promote contacts between Kurdish writers and poets living in various countries through the use of a common alphabet. This is a most important step towards the unification of Kurdish and of Kurdistan.

Similar approaches were made towards the Arab world: the review *Peyivîn/al-Hîwar* (Dialogue; Suleimânî) and the monthly *Golan al-Arabî* (Golân in Arabic; Erbil) were published in Arabic. Significant cultural exchange was established between Kurdish intellectuals of Iraq and Iran, and regular meetings between the two have proved mutually beneficial.

In independent Armenia

In Armenia, where most of the Kurds of the former USSR live, the nationalist regime led by the Dashnak party completely transformed the lives of the Kurds. The Armenian victories in Karabagh, the occupation of Azerbaijani territories and the consequent war between the two states led to the expulsion of the Armenian Muslims, including 20,000 Kurds who had hitherto lived in peace and harmony with their neighbors. These Kurds sought asylum in Russian cities such as Krasnodar and Stavropol. Only the Yezidi Kurds continued to be tolerated in Armenia. Kurdish literature in Armenia, which had enjoyed favorable conditions since the 1930s, began to dry up. The bi-weekly *Riya Taze* (New Road) now appears only intermittently, and that only because of the devotion of a small team of three editors who publish it at their own expense.

ORAL LITERATURE OF IRANIAN LANGUAGES

Shakro Mgoi founded the *Kurdskiĭ Nauchno-prosvetitel'ski Tsentr* (Scientific and intellectual Kurdish Center; i.e., the Kurdish Cultural Center in Moscow), which publishes the works of Russian and Kurdish specialists in Kurdish studies, such as M.S. Lazarev, M.A. Hasratian, O.I. Jigalina, A.H. Bagirov, I.A. Smirnova and K.R. Eyubî. Ehmedê Mirazî's *Bîranînêd Min* (My Memories; Istanbul, 1997) was published in the Hawar alphabet.

The flourishing of Kurdish poets, writers and intellectuals, first in Iraq and the former USSR, then in Iran and today in Turkey illustrates the way national and cultural developments run parallel to each other.

CHAPTER 2

KURDISH ORAL LITERATURE

Christine Allison

Verbal artistry is much valued among the Kurds. Contests between well-known bards, vying to out-sing each other, are within living memory in the villages; audiences are still stirred by stories of battle, moved by songs of love, and entertained by the exploits of fast-talking tricksters. The creative use of the Kurdish language is a vital part of Kurdish "folklore," part of that construct of a traditional past which is essential for the development of a national consciousness (Smith 1991, p. 21). The imagery of Kurdish nationalism draws much of its emotive power from its allusions to the rich landscape of centuries of Kurdish oral literature. Popular Kurdish singers not only perform songs from Kurdish folklore, but often employ traditional musical forms and imagery in their own compositions, as in Shivan Perwer's *Hawar* (Cry for Help), about the chemical bombing of Halabja. Such images, already imbued with complex associations for those brought up in the villages, are endowed with new layers of meaning in the modern nationalist discourse, and are also resonant for the Kurdish youth of the cities and the diaspora. Languages other than Kurdish, particularly Turkish, are sometimes used for such nationalist messages, but they draw on the images of Kurdish oral literature.

To describe fully the "superabundance," as Vilchevsky termed it (in Nikitine 1956, p. 255), of Kurdish folk literature is beyond the scope of a single chapter. The aim here is to give a flavor of this distinctive literature. Accordingly I will outline the current situation of Kurdish oral literature and its relevance for the Kurds, and give samples of some of the more important works. Considerations of space preclude comprehensive listings of all the folk traditions, though the Bibliography should prove adequate for those who wish to study this literature further. There is an undue bias here towards the poetic genres rather than prose. Again, this is partly for reasons of space, but also because most of the poetry enjoys higher prestige and popularity amongst the Kurds. I have intentionally passed quickly over those oral traditions, interesting though they are, which are shared with Persians, Turks and Arabs. The poetry discussed here is distinctively Kurdish; it may contain motifs which are shared, but it embodies Kurdish concerns, and has meaning within the modern Kurdish discourse. Much of it also concerns events from Kurdish history.

1. Oral tradition in Kurdistan

Despite the long tradition of Kurdish scholars and authors, many of whom used Arabic, Persian or Turkish as well as Kurdish in their writings, the great majority of Kurds in the past were not literate enough to be able to read "literature." Today, state education in Turkey, Iran and Syria is given in Turkish, Persian and Arabic respectively. Even in Iraq, the Sorani (Southern Kurdish) dialect alone has been officially authorized for use in the education system. Within the Kurdish Autonomous Zone in Iraq, the Kurmanji dialect has only recently come to be taught at all levels in schools in the Badinan region. The former Soviet Union had sizeable minorities of literate Kurds and Georgia and Armenia in particular supported study of Kurdish language and folklore. However, in the homeland, many Kurds cannot comfortably read Kurdish, and much Kurdish literature, especially in Kurmanji (Northern Kurdish), remains oral. This is not to say that Kurdish society is at a "pre-literate" level, with a uniform "oral" world-view prevailing over all those who have no reading skills (Ong 1982). Such ideas are peddled in the Turkish context as part of anti-Kurdish propaganda and are unfortunately accepted by some Kurds who see their traditional culture as irredeemably primitive. Although there are certain aspects of oral literature, such as repetition and the use of mnemonics, which are found in almost all types of oral tradition throughout the world, we must beware of generalizing both about the nature of oral literature and the thought processes of those who produce and listen to it. A Kurd from Diyarbakir who is able to read Turkish novels is likely to have very different attitudes toward history, the supernatural and aesthetics from than, say, a Yezidi villager in Northern Iraq who has never been to school. Yet both may be equally illiterate in Kurdish, and equally appreciative of songs of past Kurdish heroes and lovers.

Not only do terms such as "literacy" and "orality" have different meanings in different contexts (Street 1984), but in Kurdistan they do not exist in isolation from each other. Literacy has been known in Kurdistan for many centuries as a skill of the elite valued by the majority. Its association with the dominant "Religions of the Book" has given it spiritual power; it has been used for protective amulets and divination. The prominence of literacy has also meant that the dividing line between "oral tradition" and written text is not at all clear-cut. For more than a century, Kurdish oral traditions have been collected and published, becoming written texts. Conversely, texts written by renowned literary poets, such as Mewlewî or Feqiyê Teyran, may be memorized and pass into oral tradition, and much spurious material may eventually be attributed to them (Kerim 1998; Celîl 1985, pp. 53–81); characters, episodes and even whole storylines from literary works may be used by the composers of oral genres. Much of the richness of Kurdistan's folklore comes, not only from the free exchange of oral traditions and their components between Kurds and their neighbors, but also from the interaction of the written with the oral.

It would be rash to generalize too much about oral literature just because it is oral, and the sheer variety of language, religion, and social structure in Kurdistan should warn against thinking in terms of one type of "oral" mind-set existing over the whole area. To delineate the effects of orality on Kurdish culture, more detailed work focusing on specific areas and communities is needed. However, there is an important point to be borne in mind when considering all Kurdish oral traditions, which comprise all sorts of material which we might categorize under such headings as popular literature, history and philosophy. It is very easy to be swayed by one's own preconceptions. Orientalists have in the past been particularly guilty of looking at native genres and finding them wanting, usually because they have not conformed to preconceptions of analogous Western genres, or of classical literary genres. Kurdish oral literature cannot be properly understood as "literature" unless its meanings for the Kurds are taken into account, the meanings for both the immediate audience which observes the performance, and also, nowadays, the wider Kurdish audience, particularly those young people in cities or the diaspora who do not attend performances but who know of the traditions and ascribe meaning to them. Divorced from its social context, this literature cannot be understood properly. A particularly important factor to be considered is performance; when and how oral literature was performed, and audiences' attitudes towards it.

It is easy to see how, in the past, the performance of various kinds of oral literature fitted into everyday rural life. One hears of folktales being told during the long winter nights when families huddled together for warmth, of epithalamia being sung at village weddings, of love-songs sung when flocks were taken to summer pastures, of men's and women's work-songs. Until relatively recently, most villages also had a *dîwankhane*, where local men would gather in the evening and guests passing through would stay. News would be exchanged, stories told and songs sung. However, oral literature was not just a homely village phenomenon. There were urban contexts too, such as teahouses and other public spaces. But perhaps the most elevated context of all was in the great houses. Many of the Kurdish emirs, who flourished up to the mid-nineteenth century, were patrons of the arts, whose courts hosted performances of both literary and oral material. Evliya Chelebi's improbable description of the skills of Abdal Khan Bitlîsî was no doubt founded on a real reputation as a patron of arts and sciences (Dankoff 1990, pp. 93–109). Literacy amongst tribal leaders at the end of the Ottoman Empire was mixed, but they also provided a venue for performance and had their own court poets to sing their praises, as befitted their status. Soane gives the Southern Kurdish example of Taha Beg, who wrote poetry and enjoyed Persian literature (1926, p. 228), but Driver (1919, p. 30) reports that Ibrahim Pasha Milli's son Mehmud Bey, whose stronghold was at Viranshehir (now in Turkey), was illiterate. It is likely that some of the "folk" poets and storytellers in these courts were literate and multilingual.

In the past, Kurdish communities lived alongside Christians, Jews and Turkmen, speakers of Armenian, neo-Aramaic, and Turkish dialects. Not only did these languages share many oral traditions with Kurdish, but many members of minority groups spoke impeccable Kurdish, and some have been recorded performing Kurdish oral literature. There are many examples in Celîl 1978. Zaza and Gurâni, Western Iranian dialects spoken by substantial communities of Kurds (van Bruinessen 1994, pp. 29–37), also have a rich oral literature; in the case of Gurâni this lies alongside an established literary tradition. These dialects share many traditions and genres with Kurmanji and Sorani. Such local linguistic and cultural variety has added to the richness of Kurdish oral literature.

2. The upheavals of the late twentieth century

As the twentieth century ends and the twenty-first begins, oral literature, like most other aspects of Kurdish culture, is in transition. Recent history has profoundly changed society. In Turkey, the guerrilla war between the government and the Kurdish Workers' Party (PKK) resulted in villages being cleared and vast shantytowns growing up around cities. The PKK's operation out of Syria prompted the Turks to secure a previously permeable border, cutting off Syria's Kurds from their relations in Turkey. Communities have also been changed, and in some cases dispersed, by the "Great Anatolian Project," a system of hydroelectric dams. In Iraq, villages were cleared during the Iran-Iraq war and later in the "Anfal" campaign (Middle East Watch 1993), and the populations deposited in "collective villages," often at some distance from their previous homes. The Gulf War of 1991, the abortive Kurdish uprising and exodus to the mountains, and the ensuing civil strife between the Iraqi Kurdish parties, resulted in more displacement. Iranian Kurds suffered from the upheavals of the Islamic Revolution and sporadic uprisings against it, and from their territory becoming a battlefield in the Iran-Iraq war. The Autonomous Zone in Iraq enjoyed more stability, apart from a brief period of civil war between the dominant Kurdish parties. Since the fall of Saddam Hussein and the American intervention in 2003, the area has retained some stability by comparison to the rest of the country, though it is not untainted by the troubles elsewhere.

Such catastrophes, which affect every aspect of Kurdish life, have obvious consequences for oral literature. Fewer and fewer Kurds are living in villages, and those forms of tradition associated with venues and activities which no longer exist are dying out. This includes work-songs associated with village-tasks which are unnecessary in town or refugee life, such as grinding with millstones. Also in decline are performances of long narrative poems and fairytales; television provides much of the entertainment for most ordinary evenings. Additionally, there is, in some communities at least, a feeling that performances of "happy" songs and stories are inappropriate in times of distress and anxiety. Nevertheless, lyrical songs and cheerful dances are still performed at weddings and other gatherings, whether political or otherwise. The *gerrelawije* of the Mahâbâd area, where listeners take turns singing, still exists (Blum and Hassanpour 1996, p. 328). Laments for the dead are still performed in the traditional way. Some of the oral traditions which are not often performed, such as the long narrative poems, are leaping the "genre barrier" and becoming the subjects of novels and plays, where they are read and appreciated by younger generations. Thus, for much oral literature, survival depends on genre.

The Kurdish diaspora continues to grow, and is already a substantial global community. The Kurds in diaspora are using the relative freedoms of Europe, North America, and Australia in particular to express their own, Kurdo-centric, perspectives, and for political organization. Using modern means of communication, such as satellite TV and the Internet, they can reach the Kurds in the homeland more easily than with printed matter (Hassanpour 1998). Many Kurdish nation-building discourses are refined and transmitted throughout the homeland by Kurds in the diaspora. These include specific perspectives on Kurdish history,[1] a rehabilitation of the concept of Kurdish culture, and a portrayal of traditional Kurdish village life as a rural idyll. Examples from Kurdish oral literature are cited in support of all these.

3. Studies of Kurdish oral literature

Few early collectors of Kurdish oral traditions presented their collections as examples of literature. Most of the early collections are evidence presented primarily for linguistic research (Lerch 1858; Prym and Socin 1887, 1890; Makas 1897–1926; Mann 1906, 1909), though a few, such as Jaba 1860, declare an intention to give information on other topics, such as Kurdish tribes and literature.

The development of folklore as a field of study affected Kurdish scholarship. Oral literature was perceived as an important part of Kurdish folklore, which is also considered to include many other items such as traditional costume, agricultural implements, etc. Early Kurdish journals such as *Hawar* (1932–45) published many oral traditions, sometimes with explanatory notes for non-Kurds. In the second half of the twentieth century it became clear that Kurdish oral traditions were in decline, as a result both of general modernizing processes found in many developing societies and of the specific proscription of Kurdish culture in Turkey and Iran. The widespread idea that folklore reflects the collective character of the people producing it in a uniquely intimate way has found expression amongst both Kurdish and foreign folklorists (Bois 1946; Nikitine 1956, p. 259ff.). Kurdish scholars in particular have seen folklore as a fund of information about the past, an expression of the people's feelings, and a repository of popular wisdom. Proverbs,

---

1   Ancient history, particularly the belief that the Kurds are descended from the Medes, has been strongly emphasized. The Kurdish satellite station MED-TV and its successors in particular screened programs about ancient history and about Kurdish folklore, placing great emphasis on symbols such as the *Newroz* festival.

for instance, are often called "sayings of the forefathers" (*gotinên pêşiyan*) and are one of the most commonly collected genres. It is widely recognized that this national treasure is in decline. As one eminent scholar has written, "not a day goes by but Kurdish oral tradition loses something of value" (Celîl 1985, pp. 5–6, 9). Kurds have responded to this crisis by making collections and publishing. These initiatives range from the large-scale works, such as *Zargotina Kurda* (Kurdish oral tradition) of the Jalîl (Celîl) brothers in the former Soviet Union (Celîl 1978), and the two-volume *Folklor, komele berhemêkî folkloriye* (Folklore, a collection of folkloric work) from Erbil (Cutyar et al. 1984–85), to the valuable smaller collections made by teachers, writers and other interested parties who devoted their spare time to visiting villages and recording folklore. Due to the political situation, most collections were made in Iraq and the former Soviet Union, with some in Iran, Syria and the diaspora and very few indeed in Turkey. Since Iraqi collections focused mainly on Sorani material, it was the Soviet folklorists who kept Kurmanji folklore studies alive through the twentieth century. They also contributed to studies of music. Kurdish folklore has regularly been featured on the radio in Iraq, Iran and the Caucasus, and, very recently, on satellite television (Hassanpour 1998). Such enterprises have in turn had an effect on the oral traditions, as a concept of "the correct version" grows among the audience, and young performers sometimes learn material from books or broadcasts. Nevertheless, Kurdish folklorists agree that only a small proportion of the available material has been preserved by collection.

Secondary literature on Kurdish oral traditions is not plentiful. With important exceptions, most of the works by Kurdish folklorists are collections rather than studies of the material. Although they provide important records of oral traditions, they were mostly produced for a public that was already familiar with local genres and performance trends, and much remains unexplained for the outsider. Performances are rarely contextualized; where performance details are noted, often little explanation is given of its wider significance in the community. As noted above, this characteristic is shared by many, though not all, of the linguistic studies which include oral literature. Exceptions which have short but useful introductions include Mann 1906 I, pp. XXVII–XXX; Blau 1975, pp. 4–7; MacKenzie 1990 II.

Although some noted Kurdologists have given broad outlines of the role played by oral literature in Kurdish life (Bois 1946, 1986; Nikitine 1956), outsiders wishing to understand this on a detailed localized basis have needed to do fieldwork, which recent history has made difficult. There have been some notable studies of Kurdish music; a vital accompaniment to much of oral literature; which include some description of social context, such as the work of Blum, Christensen and Tatsumura, but unless extensive fieldwork could be done, scholars of oral tradition have had to undertake the type of analysis which can be based mostly on collected texts (e.g. Chyet 1991a). Even these are scanty; for instance, no comprehensive typology of narratives has yet been made for Kurdish.[2] Comparison with better-documented traditions, such as Arabic, Turkish, Aramaic and Armenian, can be fruitful, and the studies of the folklore of the Kurdish Jews now living in Israel, such as Brauer and Patai 1993 and Sabar 1982, are particularly useful for the Kurdologist.

4. Genre

Although genre is a key factor in understanding Kurdish literature, there are many problems in defining and discussing the genres. Many narrative traditions are found in several genres, and it can be illuminating to consider a tradition in its various forms and the impact that a change in form has on the tradition. However, some genres, such as proverbs and fables, are highly prescriptive of both subject matter and form.

The role played by genre in the interpretation of oral literature by Kurdish audiences is crucial. For example, it may indicate whether or not traditions are to be literally believed, or it may sig-

2　Spies 1972, lists examples from a specific collection giving correspondences with Aarne and Thompson's motif-index; Jason 1962, does the same for Drushinina's collection. Marzolph 1984, has Kurdish examples.

nal a particular emotional mood. The spoken genres of Kurdish, the forms of discourse used, and questions of style, have so far been very little studied by academics. Genre is not determined only by a combination of text with style and form, but also by social context (Ben-Amos 1976; Dundes 1964). The occasion and location of a performance can have a significant impact on its evaluation by the audience and thus on its meaning. The variety of generic terms found in Kurdish is somewhat bewildering; what follows is a general description, giving some of the most common terms and their approximate meanings.

In the Kurdish context, as in many others, "emic" (local) and "etic" (outsider) genres of oral tradition do not usually match. An additional complication for both outsiders and locals is the variety and inconsistency of terminologies and classificatory systems found in different areas, and different traditions of Kurdish folklore study. Even the most commonly found Kurdish generic terms are rarely understood without ambiguity throughout the entire Kurmanji- or Sorani-speaking area. Many terms are also more general, and used by Persians, Turks, Arabs and Armenians with subtle differences of meaning. Various names of Arabic or Persian literary genres are also used for Kurdish oral genres which are quite different in form. Some generic distinctions used by Kurds, both at a local level and in scholarly collections, are indications of content, such as *stranêd tarixî*, "historical songs," and *stranêd evînî*, "songs of love." Other generic terms relate to purpose, such as *stranêd govend/raqs*, "songs for dancing"; in practice one can usually infer that these latter will be rhythmic and upbeat, and many will be about pretty girls. Still other generic terms are known by occasion, such as the *payizok*, the "autumn song," which is associated with the return from the idealized summer pastures (rarely a feature of contemporary Kurdish life) and the preparation for a grim, hard winter. This term usually denotes melancholy lyrical songs, but can in some contexts refer to a different genre, a "rhetorical riddle" whereby a pattern is set up of questions with predictable answers. Thus it is very difficult to discuss genre in Kurdish in a rigorous and systematic way; we must have some recourse to etic terms.

KURDISH ORAL LITERATURE

Certain local terms have been directly equated with etic terms. Thus, *dastan, hikaye* and *efsane* are "epic," "story," and "legend" respectively. This is useful as a general rule of thumb but does not bear detailed scrutiny; apart from the debates surrounding these terms in English, there are always Kurdish exceptions, areas and contexts where the terms have other meanings. The term *dastan/ destan*, for example, for most Kurdish scholars, means a long, elevated heroic or romantic narrative about exceptional people and events. However, in some areas the term means little more than "narrative" and does not have heroic connotations. It does not necessarily denote a specific form; the telling may be in prose, or poetry, or both. But if a tradition is described to a researcher as *dastan/ destan*, it is likely that it is prestigious and that long poems exist on the subject even if the individual performance attended by the researcher is a prose account. General terms for oral literature, both prose and poetry, are often taken from other languages, such as *qisse* from Arabic, but Kurdish terms such as *axiftin, gotin*, which strictly mean "speech," are also sometimes used.

Many terms describing form are used in Kurdish. The oral literature includes much poetry, most of which is sung, with or without musical accompaniment. There is a general distinction between the long narrative poem and the shorter lyrical song; in fact they are usually performed in different ways by different types of performer (see above). The long narrative is called *beyt* in most Sorani areas and some Kurmanji areas,[3] and *qewl* in other Kurmanji areas, but in Kurmanji at least both these terms can also mean shorter religious poems, such as the Yezidi *Qewls* and *Beyts*. There seems to be no special word distinguishing the form *cante fable*, or alternating prose and verse, from verse narrative. Other terms for the verse narratives include *shi'r*, an Arabic word meaning "poetry" in general, *bend* which can also mean a line or verse of poetry, and the Sorani *bend û baw*. The shorter, lyrical song is called *stran, meqam, kilam, goranî*, which are also general words for 'song'; the longer songs are called *lawik, qetar* or *heyran*. *Livêj /liwêj* is sometimes

---

3   *Pace* Chyet 1991, p. 80. The word is used in this sense in Badinan at least. For the use of *qewl* in this sense see Chyet *op. cit.*, p. 78.

used for lyric in general, but often indicates a song with a religious theme. *Heyran, heyranok* often denotes love songs in particular. This distinction between narrative and lyric holds good in many areas, but it is important to note that it is not absolute; there are many borderline cases where, for example, a song performed by a *stranbêj* may contain various narrative elements. Kreyenbroek (1999) has usefully suggested the term "allusive" poetry, which alludes to events or beliefs known by the audience, but which are not explained within the poem itself. A whole spectrum of material exists, from poems which recount stories to songs which are very allusive indeed, which require a great deal of background knowledge to understand them, and whose purpose is to arouse emotion rather than to inform. A great deal of the literature lies between these two extremes.

There are many less prestigious verse forms. The upbeat dance songs with strong rhythms, called *dîlan, govend, reqs* or *beste* are particularly popular, and performed at weddings and celebrations; Bedir Khan (1932, p. 11), on the other hand, defines *beste* as "les chansons plus lourdes" with melismas and repetition. Various examples of traditional lullabies or *lorî* have been collected (e.g. Nikitine 1947, p. 46). Most work songs, on which little has been written, have disappeared, but some are still remembered, such as the rhythmic songs for grinding grain and cutting crops. Laments for the dead, called *shîn, dîlok/dîrok* (a usage probably peculiar to Yezidis, since *dîrok* more usually means 'history'), *giriyan, lawarna* are the province of women and an important social duty in all Kurdish communities. They are performed on specific occasions and are to be distinguished from the lyrical eulogies performed by singers who are usually male.

The meters of Kurdish oral poetry are not well understood. Early attempts to analyze it in terms of quantitative meters (Socin 1890, pp. xxxviii–lxiii) were less productive than emphases on stress or syllabic meter (Mann 1909, p. xxxii ff.). Although these are useful for some areas, such as the syllabic Gurâni and Sorani poetry, it is clear from the collections that in other poetry line length can be very variable, making meaningful syllable-counts difficult, and that rhyme, which is a noticeable feature in most poetry, can be consistent for many lines, or for just a few.[4] The Kurdologist Basil Nikitine (1956, p. 270) goes so far as to say that Kurdish folk poetry "ignore à vrai dire le rythme et ne connaît que la rime." Chyet (1991a I, p. 144), who gives a very useful account of stanzaic structure in narrative poetry, says of Kurdish folk poetry: "Meter as we know it does not exist, syllable counts being a useful substitute." However, for some areas and genres the evidence suggests otherwise; in Badinan, for instance, many examples of narrative *beyt*s are highly rhythmic, with strong stresses in the lines, whereas the performers of lyrical *stran* deliver their long lines very fast, with some extended melismas towards the end of the (clearly marked) stanzas. Such confusions will not be resolved until broad comparative studies are undertaken which are sensitive to genre and regional differences, and which include melody types and other performance details. It is clear that melody plays an important part in Kurdish poetics; if Kurdish rhythm and meter are to be understood properly, the vital dimension of performance must not be ignored.

Kurdish prose genres are not yet well understood either. Of the narrative genres, a key distinction is that between fiction, *chîrok* (which includes *efsane* and *hikaye*) and fact; a historical narrative (*dîrok, tarix*) would rarely be called *chîrok*. It is unclear how far Kurds consciously perceive subdivisions within these broad categories. One well-defined prose genre, however, is the proverb, *pendekan, gotinên mezin, gotinên pêshiyan*, "the sayings of the ancestors." They are usually short and pithy; many use rhyme. Some are extremely blunt, others more oblique so that their meaning is obscure to outsiders.

---

4   The words that rhyme at the end of the lines usually have their stress on the penultimate syllable in both narrative and lyric. The many varieties in rhyme-scheme make it difficult to draw up fixed definitions of stanza (cf. Mann *loc. cit*).

5. Performers

There is often a distinction in Kurdish between those performers who perform with musical accompaniment and those who use only their voice. For the former, the Turkish term *ashik* is often used in the former Soviet Union and Iran; Kurdish terms include *stranbêj* (song-teller) elsewhere in Kurmanji areas and *guranbêj* in Sorani areas. The latter are often called *dengbêj* (voice-teller) in Kurmanji and *chirger* (singer) in Sorani, and are usually associated with the long narrative poems, whereas the *stranbêj* perform folk-songs, *stran* or *kilam*, which are often lyrical, and accompany themselves with instruments such as the *saz, tembur, oudh,* and *kemanche* (Celîl 1978 II, p. 26; Allison 2001, pp. 68–70). A *dengbêj* may also accompany his singing by clapping his hands or by striking other available surfaces. However, this distinction is not absolute; narrative poetry can be accompanied with musical instruments.

Becoming a *dengbêj* or *stranbêj* required considerable training. Oskar Mann has described how aspiring performers would apprentice themselves to a known singer and learn his repertoire, paying for their training by doing chores (Mann 1906, pp. xxviii-xxix). Some would build up their own repertoires by moving on to other masters. It is unclear whether "lessons" as such were given or whether the student learned by imitation and constant exposure to the master's music. However, having had an apprenticeship with a known performer was an important element in being accepted as a performer oneself. The performer who has learned from reading books (or watching videos) is a modern phenomenon and probably not yet fully acceptable as a *dengbêj* or *stranbêj*. Many children of performers, both boys and girls, have been pupils of their parents, a convenient arrangement for girls in particular, who would be less able to travel elsewhere to learn. It seems that there was also prestige for the master in being seen to have pupils. Along with the composition of new songs to be performed alongside the famous old ones, having pupils was an attribute which marked out the truly successful performer.

Nearly a century ago, Oskar Mann described traveling performers in Persia who gave performances in exchange for payments of food and money. In the modern context the wandering *ashik* who makes his entire living this way seems to have disappeared; performers tend to be semi-professionals, who may travel long distances to perform at specific events, such as weddings. People well known at the village level might perform at local celebrations, though with the decline in performance of long narratives this is more likely for *stranbêj* than *dengbêj*. In some areas being a semi-professional performer confers higher status than being fully professional; *dengbêj* and *stranbêj* are considered to be above the *mitirb*, or "common" musicians who play instruments such as the *zurna*, though this is not only a matter of the distinction between "professionalism" and "semi-professionalism," but also the type of material performed and instruments used.

For the prose genres, performers are less clearly designated than for the poetic. These genres require less specialist training to attain competence, though they do undoubtedly require skill and experience, and, until the second half of the twentieth century, a large percentage of the population must have known at least some traditional narratives well. Although the word *chîrokbêj* (storyteller) is known and used in many areas, such performers enjoy lower prestige than the *dengbêj* and are rarely known over a wide area. The wandering *chîrokbêj* who earns his living from his stories seems, like the *ashik*, to have disappeared; recent accounts of storytelling all feature performers who had other jobs. Performers of prose narratives in general are declining in number, as most are elderly and the young are relatively uninterested in learning these oral traditions (Blau 1975, p. 4). Narratives such as fairy-tales seem to enjoy less respect than historical narratives, especially eyewitness accounts of important events.

Most well-known Kurdish *dengbêj* and *stranbêj* are men, but women are also lively exponents of Kurdish oral literature. They mostly perform for other women and children. Although there is no *a priori* prohibition on women performing in mixed company, in practice their performance (especially singing) is felt in many communities to be immodest (e.g. Blum and Hassanpour 1996, p. 328). Nevertheless there have been a number of well-known female performers, though few of these have made recordings. However, given the restrictions on women's opportunities for apprenticeships, the prose genres, such as *chîrok*, are more open to them than the poetic ones. There are also genres which are exclusively the province of women: not only the improvised lament, which a woman may sing for a family member or on a professional basis for others, and which she learns from attending mournings and observing other women, but also the *lorî* (lullaby) and other traditions associated with childcare and women's work.

Most Kurdish oral poets remain anonymous, but a few are remembered by name. Some, like the mysteriously-named Feqîyê Teyran (Jurist of the Birds) and Mewlewî, are literary poets, to whom orally-transmitted poems are attributed. Others, such as Evdalê Zeynik and Ehmedê Fermanê Kikî, were folk-poets and performers.

6. Shared traditions

The Kurds share many of their traditions with other peoples of the Middle East and Central Asia. Many of the long narrative traditions, which have been termed "romantic," "epic" or "heroic," are ubiquitous, such as *Yusof and Zoleykhâ* and *Leyli and Majnun*. Others are better known in some regions than others, for obvious reasons; the collections show that traditions about the Turkic hero Koroglî (Koroghlu, Gurughlî) are better known in the Caucasus and Iran than in Iraq. As one would expect of an Iranophone people, the Kurds possess many narrative traditions also common in Persian, such as *Farhâd and Shirin, Khosrow and Shirin, Vis and Râmin, Bizhan and Manizhe*. All of these common traditions have been found in the form of long narrative poems, spoken prose alternating with sung verse, and prose tellings; many also exist in allusive lyrical songs, where the singer takes the part of a protagonist and addresses others. They are also alluded to in proverbs.

Of course, the Kurds use such common traditions for their own purposes, and there are interesting differences from the renderings of other peoples. The large body of traditions about the great warrior Rostam, for instance, portrays him as a Kurd. There is good reason to suppose that this belief predates the contemporary Kurdish nationalist discourse, as the Rostam traditions have not received the same attention from nationalists as, say, the *Newroz* (Nowruz) myth or *Mem and Zîn*. Some popular tellings of Farhâd and Shîrîn locate the action in Kurdistan and present their protagonists as distinctively Kurdish (Mokri 1964, pp. 355–73). A particularly notable example of such specifically Kurdish usage is the tradition of Kawe the blacksmith, the Kâve of the *Shahname*, and the myth of *Newroz*, the Iranian New Year. In the *Shahname* the brave blacksmith Kâve raises a banner of revolt against the tyrant Zahhâk, who has snakes growing from his shoulders which require feeding on the brains of boys. The boys are of course taken from Zahhâk's subjects, and Kâve has already lost most of his children as a result. He rallies the people around the hero Faridun, who eventually vanquishes Zahhâk and becomes king. This is a canonical myth not only for Persian national identity but also for the Kurds. The Kurdish nationalist discourse has placed great emphasis on it and on the *Newroz* or New Year festival in late March, which, for the Kurds, commemorates it. Drawing on Kurdish, rather than Persian oral traditions, Kurdish nationalists stress Kawe's role—their Kawe kills Zahhâk himself—as well as his Kurdish identity (e.g. Perwer 1990). The Kurdish Zahhâk tends to be presented as a monster rather than the corrupted hero of the *Shahname*. Kawe's contemporary appeal, as an ordinary working man who raises a banner of rebellion on behalf of an abused people, is clear. In the past, *Newroz* was celebrated with relative freedom by Kurds in Iran and Iraq, but not in Turkey and Syria. However, over the past generation or so, *Newroz* has grown in Turkey from a festival known and observed by some Kurds only, and not always connected with the Kawe myth, to a symbol of Kurdish identity and rebellion, an occasion of mass political protest and often of violence. The Turkish government has taken the political impact of *Newroz* seriously, attempting to present it as a piece of purely Turkic rather than Iranian cultural property.

The landscape of less elevated Kurdish folk literature also abounds with common Iranian, Turkic and Islamic elements. Among the supernatural figures, heroes of fairytales encounter adversaries such as the evil *dêw* (the Persian *div*), ogres, and other monsters. The mythical bird called *Sîmirkh*, the Persian *Simorgh*, is terrifying but often gives help in exchange for favors done. The *perî* or fairy is ambivalent and mischievous; it may cause harm for humans or give help, especially when services are rendered; the same may be said of the *jinn*. Heroes sometimes marry fairy princesses in the course of the story. The benign figure of Khizir or Khidr, known throughout the Islamic world, often provides help and guidance; unlike some other peoples, such as the Arabs of the Gulf, the Kurds often do not distinguish between him and Elyas. Ancient and supernatural elements may be used alongside objects from modern life such as telephones or automobiles with no apparent harm done to the audience's enjoyment (e.g. MacKenzie 1990 II, p. 11).

Less obviously "supernatural" figures occurring in Kurdish folk narratives are also shared with other peoples. These include Mullah/Hoja Nasreddin, who is also locally known as Bahluli-Zana and Mela Mezbûre, and the bald-headed trickster Kechelok. Many stories are also told about the prophets, especially Solomon; these vary in the number of supernatural elements in them. Some remote historical figures have also accumulated a great many stories. Alexander the Great and Shah Abbâs, like Solomon, are often presented as archetypal arrogant kings who are taught a lesson, often by lesser beings. They believe that they are immortal and try unsuccessfully to avoid death, or they attempt to extract tribute from all, even the animals (Celîl 1978 II, pp. 185–99). Like their neighbors, the Kurds portray Alexander as horned (a feature derived from the Qor'anic Dhu'l Qarneyn: XVIII, 84ff, "having two horns", generally believed to have been a reference to Alexander); this attribute was clearly felt to be mysterious and inspired various stories such as that of the discovery of his four horns by his barber, who told Alexander's secret to some reeds growing by a spring. When they were cut they told it to everyone (Celîl 1978 II, p. 198).

Like those of their neighbors, many Kurdish fairytales follow the common pattern of an unproved hero, often a younger brother, receiving magical help from sorcerers, jinns or animals, facing dragons, monsters, witches or evil monarchs, and overcoming them to win one (or more) princesses. Characters are stereotypical; women are portrayed as wicked stepmothers, witches, passive beauties, resourceful princesses or invincible warriors (in disguise). Kurdish folk narrative often has a degree of social comment, with many stories of cruel lords, lecherous clerics and clever peasants. Many humorous anecdotes make fun of cuckolded husbands, domineering women, and non-Kurds. The moralistic animal fable of the *Kalile and Demne* collections in various languages is also found throughout Kurdistan.

7. Kurdish traditions

Narratives of Kurdish history are, for obvious reasons, less widespread amongst the Kurds' neighbors than *chîrok*, which are often found across large areas. Some tales are strongly localized, associating certain places with a well-known character or etiology. Often several localities put forward rival claims to be the site of well-known events. Historical prose narratives of past events are still told, but knowledge is often confined to local or family events; many families preserve a body of stories of the past associated with their genealogies. Knowledge of past events is also transmitted via social, religious or political networks.[5]

However, it is the poetry which enjoys a special place in Kurdish hearts. Of the long narrative *dastan/beyt* traditions, there are several which are well-known throughout Kurdistan. Amongst these, *Zembîlfirosh* is the story of a handsome young basket-seller lusted after by an older princess; *Kerr and Kulik* is about the deeds of two noble Kurdish brothers; and *Khej and Siyabend* tells of two lovers who elope together and perish on a mountain. However, the two best-known are *Mem and Zîn* and *Dimdim*. Each is much enjoyed in performance and has been used in Kurdish nation-building.

---

5   My own informants who had lived in small Kurdish communities during their youth cited family, religious networks (such as the Naqshbandi and Qaderi brotherhoods, see van Bruinessen 1992, pp. 203–64), and members of political parties as sources of knowledge, both of news and of historical events.

Mem and Zîn

Mem and Zîn, often referred to as "the Kurdish national epic," is the title of a literary poem composed in the seventeenth century CE by Ehmedê Khanî. It is based on a traditional tale, the subject of various *beyt*s, called *Memê Alan*. The oral traditions are often referred to by members of the community (many of whom are unaware of the differences between the two) as *Mem and Zîn* rather than Memê Alan. Although there are many supernatural elements in the story, much of it is set in Jezîrê Botan (the modern Cizre in Turkish Kurdistan), and many Kurds believe that there is a kernel of truth in it—that there were once real people called Mem and Zîn who loved each other and died young.

The star-crossed young lovers of this story are both exceptionally beautiful. They live far from each other, but are magically introduced when Zîn is brought to Mem. When she is returned home, Mem seeks her on his great, magical horse "from the sea," Bor or Bozê Rewan. He becomes the guest and then the friend of the virtuous Qeretajdîn, whose brother is betrothed to Zîn. This brother renounces his claim in Mem's favor. Zîn's father (sometimes her brother) is an emir whose wicked minister Beko has a daughter, also called Zîn. Despite Qeretajdîn's attempts to protect the couple, Beko arranges matters so that Mem is imprisoned and dies. Zîn dies immediately afterwards. When their graves are opened they are found to be embracing. The emir cuts off Beko's head whilst he is peering at the two lovers; a drop of his blood falls and a thorn bush grows there, keeping Mem and Zîn apart.

Although this tradition is often described as "epic," its genre has been rightly questioned. Chyet (1991a I, pp. 64–101) examines it according to very strict criteria and makes a convincing case for it to be considered as a Kurdish equivalent of *halk hikaye*, the Turkish "folk romance," a long narrative that blends prose and poetry. It certainly lacks many common elements of heroic epic, notably long martial episodes. Mem himself is hardly a typical "epic" hero, being most often characterized by the descriptions *Memê delal* (Mem the lovely) and *Memeyê nazik* (Mem the delicate) (Chyet 1991a, p. 225). His astonishing beauty, which inspires love, is what distinguishes him. Episodes in which he proves himself as a hero by feats such as taming the wild horse Bozê Rewan are a feature of some versions only. He is disrespectful to his elders, thoughtless of the welfare of his horse, and excellent at games such as chess rather than battles and hunting. Chyet (1991a I, p. 354ff.) cites several instances of his implicit or overt effeminacy, and points out that it is the hospitable warrior Qeretajdîn who is the more satisfactory Kurdish hero and whose generosity has become proverbial among the Kurds. Although Mem is not a model to be emulated, his attraction for audiences is more likely to lie in the pathos of his situation; he is unable to marry the girl he loves because of constraints of honor, as she is betrothed to another. This is also a recurrent theme in Kurdish love lyric and a common enough dilemma in Kurdish society and beyond; for example, folk renderings of *Leyli and Majnun*, which focus on the human aspects of the story rather than religious allegory, are common throughout the Near and Middle East.

The *Mem and Zîn* traditions are set in a world of extraordinary people and supernatural interventions, of royalty and riches. Here is a developed example of a common opening motif (Celîl 1978 I, p. 65; tr. Chyet 1991a II, pp. 460–61):

Her dem, her dem, der deme,	Every time, every time among the times,
Mîrê cina gazî dike: Gelî sazbenda, ez li bextê we me,	The Emir of the jinn calls out, "O musicians, I implore you,
Kîja civat caxîya, ko ûn têda r̂ûnên, û saz û sazbenda xwe biʿedlînin, ʿewil ûn bikin ḥikayeta stîya Zîn û Meme.	When you assemble and set to tuning up your sazes, tell first the story of Lady Zîn and Mem."
Saz û sazbend bi hevça dibên.	All the musicians said together,
Ya mîrê min, dilê me lîyane,	"O my Mir, our hearts are heavy,"
Bajarê Muxurzemînê bajarekî mezine, gelekî girane,	The city of Mukhurzemîn is a great city, very weighty,
Ev bajarê hanê li ser sêsid û şest û şeş kuçane,	The city contains three hundred and sixty six masses of stone,
Her kuçekê li ser sêsid û şeşt û şeş miḥelane,	Each mass contains three hundred and sixty six town quarters,
Her miḥelakê li ser sêsid û şeşt û şeş minarane,	Each quarter contains three hundred and sixty six minarets,

Her minarekê li ser sêsid û şeşt û şeş malane,	Each minaret serves three hundred and sixty six houses,
Qesr û qonaxê Alan-paşa li ser çar lengerane,	The castle and palace of Alan-pasha is on four anchors,
Du lengerê wî li orÔa behrane,	Two of its anchors in the middle of the sea,
Du lengerê wî li serê çîyane,	Two of its anchors on the tops of mountains,
Ev qesra hane li ser çar ṭebeqane,	The castle contains four stories,
Her ṭebeqekê li ser sêsid û şeşt û şeş odane,	Each story contains three hundred and sixty-six rooms,
Her enişkê qesrê, kevirekî aqût û almast têda cîdane,	In every corner of the castle is a stone of rubies and diamonds,
Ev kevirê hanê, şewqa xwe dide orṭa behrane.	These stones shine out over the middle of the sea,
Her odakê sê katib têda rûniştîne,	In every room three scribes are seated,
Li ser kursîya destê wan ser masane,	In chairs, their hands on the table,
Qelemê wan bînanê jehra meŕane,	Their pens like the venom of snakes,
Rojê hezara digrin, davêjine hebs û singdana, û pênsid ji hebsa berdane ...	Each day they take a thousand [men] and throw them in the dungeon, and set five hundred free ...

Despite the grandeur of many parts of the story, there are also lighter moments. When Zîn is magically transported to Mem's bed by fairies or angels who want to see who is the more beautiful, several versions exploit the humor of the situation, featuring the two arguing over where they are and who is the intruder. One version collected from the Antep area in 1901 has a very developed dispute. It does not seem to be love at first sight; Mem's amazing beauty apparently does not have the usual effect on Zîn. Each demands to know what the other is doing in the bed and threatens to call the guards. They accuse each other of drunkenness, smoking hashish and general immorality. Zîn, anxious about the compromise to her good name, calls her maidens, "O maidens! What hashish-smoker is this that has come to my bed tonight? It's a disgrace! Send news of this to my cousins the Jelalîs, our butchers, so that they will send his arms to the other world for me." Mem retorts, "... as for smoking hashish, whose daughter are you ... that you are taking over my abode?" Each then gives their name and family, and describes their city. They agree to call for their respective servants to test where they are. Of course, it is Mem's servants who reply, because they are in Mem's castle. Zîn immediately changes her tune, throwing herself at Mem's feet and saying, "Don't do to me what I have threatened to do to you!" The exchange of rings as love-tokens then takes place very quickly, and receives far less attention than the conflict between the lovers (von Le Coq 1901, pp. 36–44; tr. Chyet 1991 II, pp. 68–72).

The oral versions of *Mem and Zîn* represent a tragic and moving tale set in a fantasy Kurdistan. It is easy to see how a good storyteller could make this very entertaining, but this does not explain what sets this tradition above other tragic love narratives such as *Khej and Siyabend* in Kurdish opinion. The answer seems to be the association of the *Mem and Zîn* oral traditions with the literary epic. Ehmedê Khanî's epic was not the first literary work to be written in Kurdish, but it was clearly an attempt at a new kind of Kurdish literature; it shows awareness of, and pride in, Kurdish identity. In the modern period it has also inspired Kurdish intellectuals, who have seen it as a proto-nationalist text (Şakeli 1983). Khanî's remarks in the introductory section, criticizing Persian and Turkish rule over the Kurds (Bozarslan 1990, p. 56), and the story itself has been read as an allegory, with Mem and Zîn representing the two parts of Kurdistan divided between the Ottoman and Persian empires (Hassanpour 1989, p. 84). It is also a status symbol for Kurdish culture, a work which cannot be dismissed as "folklore." The Memê Alan traditions have basked in its reflected glory and have borrowed elements from it, and have been set apart from other Kurdish oral literature. *Mem and Zîn*'s perceived significance as a nationalistic work may also account for the lack of studies of it in the former Soviet Union, where Kurdish nationalism, like other minority nationalisms, was discouraged. In the former Soviet Union, unlike Europe, there are far fewer publications on *Mem and Zîn* than on *Dimdim*.[6]

---

6   I am grateful to Professor Joyce Blau for suggesting this to me.

Dimdim

The story of *Dimdim* is well known across Kurdistan, and versions have been collected in both Sorani and Kurmanji. Armenian versions are also known. The Kurdish versions are almost all couched in the form of the long narrative poem or *beyt,* or the *cante fable* of alternating prose and poetry. The core of the story, which can have various additions, is the capture of a fort (called "Dimdim" and manned by brave and virtuous Kurds) by the armies of the Shah of Iran. The defenders die heroically. In many versions, the commander of the fort, whose name varies, is called by the title, *Khanê Lepzêrîn/Khanê Chengzêrîn* (Prince Goldenhand), and the whole story is often known by this name.

Many, if not most versions of the story, contain enough details to link them with the siege and capture of a Kurdish fort commanded by Emer Khan, ruler of Baradost, by the armies of Shah Abbâs in 1609. The Shah wished to curb the power of the Mukri and Baradost principalities, and Emer Khan had refortified a ruined fort on Dimdim Mountain, some eighteen km south of Orumiye in Iran. After capturing the fort and massacring the inhabitants, the Shah settled a Turkish tribe in the area, which further weakened the Kurdish principalities. These events are all recounted in written sources, which is most unusual for a Kurdish oral tradition.[7] However, the fact that the story is attested by written sources has been irrelevant to the vast majority of the Kurdish audience of the *beyt* of *Dimdim,* who would have believed it was true anyway. For the traditional Kurdish audience, the *beyt* of *Dimdim* is *literature,* a historical event fashioned into a romance, aesthetically pleasing and resonant with powerful themes. It is the modern Kurdish audience, literate and educated in schools, which needs the reassurance of written sources to endow *Dimdim* with historical value.

Dimdim is much more than its core story. The figure of Prince Goldenhand himself predates Shah Abbâs' capture of the Kurdish fort. This title is given to Asad-al-Din Kelabi, who had recaptured

---

[7] This is recorded by Shah Abbâs' official historian, Iskandar Monshi Torkman. See Hassanpour 1990 for details.

Hakkari from Âq-Qoyunlu control in the late fifteenth century, by Sharaf Khan Bedlisi (Sheref Khan Bitlîsî), in his history of the Kurds, the *Sharaf-nâme*, finished in 1596 (Bedlisi 1985, pp. 129–32). Interestingly, this Prince Goldenhand is also associated with the capture of a strategic fortress, though in this case he is the victor, having entered the fortress disguised as a Christian. Bedlisi, writing a little more than a century after these events, seems to have found his epithet mysterious and accounts for it by a story (which he acknowledges to be hearsay) that the Khan won favor with the Sultan for his prowess in battle. Similar explanations are found in some of the oral versions. The need to explain this epithet in a rational way indicates that its meaning had been lost; it may be far older even than Asad-al-Din Kelabi. Prince Goldenhand himself is not the only element in the *beyt*s of *Dimdim* that is demonstrably older than the siege of the Baradosti Dimdim by Shah Abbâs. The motif of the Khan tricking the Shah by asking him for a patch of land the size of an ox-hide, and then cutting the ox-hide into such narrow strips that when they were put end to end they measured out a substantial site for the fortress, is used in Virgil's *Aeneid* in connection with the founding of Carthage (I: 368).

Although these examples demonstrate that parts of the story are very old indeed, any search for an *Ur-Dimdim* will inevitably be fruitless. The story has been constructed differently in different contexts; there are several *oikotypes*, "subspecies" of the story as it were, coming from various areas, each adapted to the conditions of its own environment. Ten of the versions published since 1860 show many variations, not only in the plot, but also in style. Of these ten, one has its provenance in Turkey, another seven in Northern Iraq, and two others in Iran. The version from Turkey (Jaba 1860) is a prose account of the defense and eventual defeat of the fortress of Dimdim, in the area of Hakkari, in the time of Shah Isma'il (the early sixteenth century). It locates the action near its own area, not in the Orumiye area. The versions from Iraq, some of which were collected in the former Soviet Union,[8] describe how the Khan, with the Shah's per-

---

[8] Celil 1961, p. 120ff; Celil 1978, pp. 164ff, 177ff; they were performed by men who fought alongside the Iraqi Kurdish leader Mullâ Mustafâ Bârzâni during the brief life of the Republic of Mahâbâd (1946–47); when this fell, they followed him into exile in the former Soviet Union.

mission, builds the fortress, but as his power grows the Shah sends an army against him. They locate the action in Iranian Kurdistan, but some emphasize the role of tribes and places in Iraq; for example, the Khan is said by some to come from Amadiya. The two versions from Iran (Mann 1906, pp. 1, 12) are in the Mukri sub-dialect of Sorani, and one presents the Kurds' resistance to the Shah as a holy war.

The Mukri poem stands out from the others, not only in terms of dialect; it uses the rhyming system of most Kurdish folk narrative poetry, but whereas many of the Kurmanji versions are almost uniform in line length, the Mukri poem has an introductory section where the lines are far longer. It opens as follows (Mann 1906, p. 12):

Dilim ranawestê li ber ewê xemê, li ber ewê janê	My heart cannot withstand this pain, this sorrow,
Bangêkim we ber xudayî, ewî dî kem ber pêxemberî axirî zemanê,	I call on God, I call again on the Prophet of the end of the world,
Bangî dî kem we ber çakî germênê û le kuêstanê,	I call on the holy one of winter quarters and high summer pastures,
Bangî dî kem we ber Pîr Sulêmanî li Banê,	I call again on Pir Suleyman of Bane,
Bangî dî kem we ber Sultan Semedî malê xoî dakird li deştî Wurmê digel kewne Lacanê ...	I call again on Sultan Semed who dwelt on Urmiya plain by ancient Lajan...

This introductory section goes on to invoke various holy figures in addition to the local saints, including Hasan, Hoseyn and Ali, and Khidirelyas (see above). According to Oskar Mann (1909, p. 22 n. 1) this opening is quite popular, but it is very different from the opening of many of the Kurmanji poems, a typical one of which begins thus (Celîl 1960, p. 101):

Xurmîne xweş xurmîne	Here's a sound, a sweet, sweet murmur
Mesela Xanê Çengzêrîne,	The story of Prince Goldenhanded
Eva raste, derew nîne.	Here's the truth, there is no lying.
Xanek hebû ji muquriya,	Once there was a Mukri prince
Çol û besta digeriya	Wandering through the open country
Li cî-wara ne hêwiriya.	He never stayed long in one place.
Xan rabû li Kurdistanê	He got up and out of Kurdistan
Çû ba şahê Îranê	Went off to see the Shah of Iran
Bibê xweyiyê mal û xane.	To find himself a house and home.

KURDISH ORAL LITERATURE

This Kurmanji version and others like it move straight into the story. They do not necessarily cut straight to the siege; some chronicle the development of the relationship between the Khan and the Shah, and its breakdown, in some detail. The Khan may win favor with the Shah, and in some versions he wins a golden hand as well, by protecting the Shah's horses, or fighting a lion. Introductory formulae, if they exist at all, are short. The Kurmanji versions of this *beyt* are overall less lyrical and allusive than the Mukri poem. Much of the Mukri poem consists of soliloquies, or of listings, such as when the Khan looks out and sees first one rider, then another, from different places; each is described in succession. There is a great deal of repetition for poetic effect rather than plot advancement. Typical of this is the eulogy of *Dimdim* itself, part of which is given here (Mann 1906, p. 16–17)[9]:

Dimdimim berdî debêye	My Dimdim is a rock like a powder-flask,
Karîtey geye Kûkeye	Its beams stretch as far as Kuke.
Xan bi xezayê meşğule.	The Prince is waging holy war.
Dimdimim berdêkî xiče	My Dimdim is a round rock,
Čûar ţerefî lêwe biče,	Surrounded on all four sides,
Beheşte bi şîr bikiče	Win paradise by your sword!
Xan bi xezayê meşğule	The Prince is waging holy war.
Dimdimim berdêkî şîne	My Dimdim is a blue-green rock,
Čûar zistane, pênc hawîne	For four winters, for five summers,
Têda Xanî Lebzêrîne	Prince Goldenhand has been inside it,
Zeferiyan pê nebirdîne.	They have won no victory over it.

The Kurmanji versions have soliloquies and emotional passages too, but the Mukri poem has fewer narrative sections in between. The listener needs more background knowledge of the plot to understand the poem than s/he does for most of the Kurmanji poems. Of course, lyrical elements are not the exclusive province of Sorani narrative traditions; Kurmanji narratives sometimes have

---

[9] I have attempted to reconcile Mann's orthography with current systems of transcription; I have preferred *êy* to Mann's *êî*; ordinarily, Kurmanji conventions would have *ê*, but Mann clearly intends more than *ê*, and Sorani conventions are less clear-cut for Latin script.

them too. The point here is that even when very little performance data is available, the same narrative tradition can be seen to have a range of different treatments in different areas. Research with audiences would be needed to ascertain whether the emotions aroused by the Mukri *Dimdim* are different in nature or intensity from those aroused by the Kurmanji versions, and how this would vary in different areas.

Given the lack of "oral literary criticism," or studies of audience response to *Dimdim*, we must look elsewhere for indications of its contemporary meanings for the Kurds, and we find these in the modern accounts. It has been the subject of novels and poetry (Shemo 1966; Dost 1991). One particularly interesting version, whose emphases reveal something of patriotic Kurdish preoccupations, was "edited" and published in 1970 by Jasimê Jelîl, a poet and folklorist living in the former Soviet Union (republished in Arabic script in 1982). Like some of the oral versions, the need to explain difficult words result in rationalistic explanations; however, unlike the Mukri, Iraqi and Anatolian versions, the name Goldenhand comes from a trial in which the Khan shows a horrified Shah his bravery in holding a red-hot coal unflinchingly in his bare hand. This is one of various proofs of his heroism, and an important episode in the relationship with the Shah, which is carefully developed. The name *Dimdim* itself is also explained, as an onomatopoeic word for the noise of a stone dropped from the castle down into the valley.

Social concerns are also evident in this version. The lovely Gulbihar, the Khan's wife, is the daughter of a simple shepherd; beauty is not only found amongst the nobles, says Jalîl. The hierarchical system is also implicitly criticized; the Shah is in many ways reluctant to fight the Khan but is forced to do so by the system in which he lives. It is easy to discern the socialist focus here. When all is lost for the fortress, Gulbihar escapes with her children, having made an impassioned speech to the Khan, saying that women are as strong as men and that she will face the future and bring up their sons alone. This latter point is not merely ideological but also highly resonant; many Kurdish women are left with children, either through their husband's death or his joining resistance forces, and this is an important area of the Kurdish experience.

KURDISH ORAL LITERATURE

The keynote of this modern telling, however, is the characterization of the Khan himself as an idealized Kurdish hero. In the first section Jalîl says (Celîl 1982, p. 1; tr. Kreyenbroek):

Bejn bilind bû ew 'efat û û mêrxas,	He was tall, brave and courageous,
Hebû me'rîfet rehm bû bêqeyas,	A man of honor, of unparalleled generosity,
Alîkar bû ew piştemêr bû Kurda,	Giving help freely, offering support to the Kurds.
Hezkirî bû ew nav eşîreda,	He was much loved among the tribes.
Tunebû bende jê heznekira,	There wasn't a humble Kurd who didn't love him.
Xweyî nav hurmet bû bendara bira.	He had great dignity, but he was a brother to the ordinary people.

This type of Kurdish hero with the common touch is modern, and the community he lives in at the beginning is an idealized one set in the mountains, with blue skies and birds flying freely. His good qualities are illustrated by his actions during the story, and he is defeated only by treachery and the cunning of the enemies who surround him. An important aspect of many Kurdish discourses is the (justifiable) perception of being surrounded by enemies on all sides, and of seeking the limited refuge of the mountains, an image used by Khanî; thus *Dimdim* can easily be (and has been) read as an allegory of Kurdistan.

Dimdim contains powerful themes that inspire Kurdish nationalism; one noted Kurdish scholar (Rasul 1979, p. 52) describes it as "the greatest of the Kurdish *dastan*s." Although an early literary poem was composed about the fall of the Celali fortress, attributed to Feqiyê Teyran (Celîl 1967, pp. 67–72), it has not had the impact of Khanî's poem, and does not seem to have affected the status and content of the oral *Dimdim* traditions in the same way as Khanî's poem affected Memê Alan.

The *Mem and Zîn* tradition will remain important for the Kurds because of Khanî. However, the story of *Dimdim*, which lends itself so well to allegory, may well give Kurdish writers more creative scope than the story of the two star-crossed lovers. If folklore continues to provide inspiration for Kurdish nationalists (and there is no reason to doubt it), we can expect to see the *Dimdim* story become a potent nationalistic symbol.

8. Kurdish lyric

Events of modern history, especially of the nineteenth and early twentieth centuries, are sometimes commemorated in long narrative poems (for example the Twelve Horsemen of Merîwan, and a "Barzani *beyt*" which glorifies a clan prominent in religion and politics, exists in Northern Iraq) but more often they survive in the form of lyrical songs. Although such songs remain popular and are performed more often than the long narrative poems, many describe local events and personalities. They contain many stock elements, and often little background information within the song itself; performers sometimes contextualize them for modern audiences by a brief introduction. Many of these lyrical traditions are very conservative; the audiences expect the performers to conserve the original composition. However, it may be that the allusive nature of the songs and their need for contextualization makes them harder to preserve intact than narratives, which at least have the course of the story as a mnemonic. If they have a shorter lifespan than narratives, this may explain why the vast majority of the surviving songs refer to the last two centuries only.

The presence of stock elements in the songs and the audience's conservative expectations do not rule out creativity in performance, though it is hard to perceive this from those collections that give texts alone. For example, in the tradition of lyrical song or *stran* performed primarily by the Yezidis of Northern Iraq, which was once also widespread in Turkey (where it was usually called *lawik*), audiences respond to such devices as a speedy delivery with very little pause for breath, and extremely long melismas near the ends of lines. Comparison of different performances of the same song shows that singers can be individualistic, or even idiosyncratic in style. Audiences also have strong opinions about the strength and quality of individual singers' voices.

Many of the martial lyrics concern battles between tribes or between a tribe and Government forces. The version of a song about the two brothers Bishar and Jemîlê Cheto which was collected by Basil Nikitine (1947, p. 40–41; unfortunately, only published in its French translation) opens with a statement by Bishar:

KURDISH ORAL LITERATURE

> "... Brothers, we are at war. I am Bishar, blond Bishar. I can no longer live with the Turkish government, with its tricks and prevarications. Let it be understood for my soul and body: I will not fire on the rank and file. They are only the children of the State. I will fire on the *Kaimakam* (district governor), the *bınbashı* (colonel), the *yüzbashı* (captain), the *mülazım* (lieutenant). I will rebel openly from my fortress, like a tiger waiting behind a rock to pounce ... Misfortune falls on the world every three days." Cemîl calls out three times: "Bishar, o brother, get up, we must accomplish something great so that our name is known through the world ... Brothers, we are at war."
>
> Cemîl calls out to Bishar: "Brother, you know that one Friday the shaikh came to our house [to bless it]. Keep hold of your Martini rifle, don't move the Mauser from your shoulder, do not fire on the rank-and-file, they are the children of the State. Look at all the ones whose sword hangs by their side, whose belt is sewn with gold and silver, throw those ones down ..."

This song is typical of the martial lyrics in its direct speech, its declaration of pride and determination, its exhortatory sections, and its lack of explanation of why the fight is taking place. Sometimes it is not a protagonist but a witness who speaks, often a woman. The primary focus of such songs is often the prelude and aftermath of battle; accounts of the battle tend to be vivid and impressionistic, but not fully descriptive. Nikitine (1947, pp. 42–43) has the following song about an intertribal battle:

> In the gorge of Bernava, bare and white as a stone slab, look at him, father of Solhê, well-armed, riding an Arab horse, with his breastplate and trappings. Celal-ed-Dîn cried out to Feqî Obeyd, "Hurry, the moment has come." It is a difficult moment, beware of Osmankî Zoro. He is not reliable, like his father... The gorge is wrapped in mist. Listen to the sound of the Martini rifle, firing *kice-kice* from the shoulder of brother Osman ... Osman, killer of men. There is a pool in the gorge, look, the way to retreat is beyond it. It is time the reinforcements of Ghaydaî hill came to us ...

Protagonists in these battles are invariably heroic; confident and brave, and, if their appearance is described, beautiful. Although their names, and the sites of battles, are carefully preserved, they are described in terms appropriate to the lyrical genre. It is not the purpose of the lyrical genre to give information about the historical individuals.

Lyrical love songs

With a few exceptions, such as those songs where Mem and Zîn or Khej and Siyabend declare their love for each other, Kurdish love lyrics are about historical individuals, who lived within the last two centuries or so. In these songs we can see the interplay of true stories with the conventions of this form of oral literature. These lyrics describe heterosexual love, and often deal with the conflict between a lover's wish for union with the beloved and the conflict resulting from his/her social duty of marrying another. Sometimes there is another reason for the lovers' separation—the illness or death of the beloved, or an event that may have sent him/her far away. The songs are firmly rooted in village or tribal life, with many small and everyday details. They may contain the words of the woman or the man, or both in conversation with each other. A typical example is the song of Besna, a young woman of the Omeri tribe (near Mardin, Turkey), who complains bitterly about having been married off to an old man. (Collected from the well-known singer Ehmedê Fermanê Kîkî, Bedir Khan 1933).

... Werê kutiyê dilan vekin,	... Come, let us open the boxes in our hearts.
Ji derdê dinyayê, biqul û birîn e,	Pained and injured from the grief of the world,
Feleqa min dawî nîne, dinya derewîn e,	Alas, I have no future, the world is false,
Bavê min xêrê bike, xêrê nebîne,	Let my father do good but never get it,
Genim biçîne, zîwana reş hilîne,	Let him sow wheat and reap black weeds,
Çima ne dam torînê mala Hesen aġa	Why didn't he give me to the young man from Hesen Agha's house,
Xortê di Omerîyan, simbêlsorê ser Xanîya,	A young Omerî man with red moustache up on the flat roof,
Ez dam Brahîmê Temo, mîna gayê pîre,	But he gave me to Ibrahim Temo, who is like an old ox,
Dranê wî ketine riya wî a spî di hinarê rêyê min rabûne ...	His teeth all gone, his white beard scratches my cheek...

KURDISH ORAL LITERATURE

After some years of this marriage, Besna eloped with a young man. There is more than one tradition of lyrical songs about her (Bedir Khan 1933; Cigerxwîn 1988, pp. 151–53).

Some lyrical songs express conflicting emotions, which makes them all the more convincing. For example, there is a tradition of songs called *Xerabo!* (Bad boy!), in which a young girl rebukes her beloved, usually for marrying another. In one Omeri variant the girl says:

Xerabo, weleh, tu xerabî.	Bad boy, you really are wicked.
Tuê ji dinyayê, ji alemê xirabtir î.	You're worse than the world, worse than the universe.
Tu ji koma pismamê mi çêtir î.	You're better than my cousin's lot [i.e. her in-laws].

She curses him at various points for having married another, wishing sickness and death on him. Yet later she says:

Xwedê teyala bike, Rebî, heçi ji xerabê min re bêje "Tu xerabo"	May God grant that whoever says to my bad boy, "you are bad,"
Bila karîn û warîna zarokê nêr tu care dimala wan de nabo!	May there never be the cries of a boy-child in their house!
Bila sed olçek genimê sor li bine beriya Mêrdînê biçîne, li şwîne bila qerezîwana reş nabo!	If they sow a hundred measures of red wheat down before Mardin, let there be no black buckwheat in their plot!
Êmayî, bila kuliyê par û pêrar lê rabo!	For the rest let the locusts of last year and the year before attack it!

and:

Heçî ji Xerabê mi re bêje: "Tu baş î, tu pirî genc î,"	Whoever says to my bad boy "You are good, very handsome,"
Xwedê teyala bike, Rebî, kulmek garîsêli pişta mala biçine,	May God grant, if they sow a fistful of millet behind the house,
Li şwîne sed olçek genimê sor hilîne,	Let a hundred measures of red wheat grow up on their plot of land;
Bi ofara bînî qîza şêxkî, ağakî ji xwe re bîne...	That the grain left on the threshing-floor is enough for him to marry the daughter of a *shaikh* or *agha*...

The complexity of emotion and the forthright nature in which it is expressed in these songs give an impression that a real individual is speaking. This "realism" is itself a convention of the genre.

Another convention of the lyrical love songs which is very noticeable is the description of the beloved's desirability, which raises the issue of gender. Both men and women are said to be beautiful, tall, as imposing as a tree (or a minaret!), like a rose or the wild basil, but the descriptions of women and their bodies are much more intimate. The question of voice is important—the songs are composed by men and sung by men, but the description of women's desirability is very often put in the mouths of women. Sometimes they describe their hairstyle, make-up or jewelry, sometimes their bodies.

The breasts are a focal point of such descriptions. Besna says:

Sîng û berê min sipî ne, mîna çira şîr in,	My breasts are white as the fresh milk
Mina sêvê Melotê, şevê Qanûnan li ber serê nexweşan,	Like the apples of Malatya, on nights at the bedside of the sick,
Hem tirş, hem teḥl û hem şêrîn in ...	At once acidic, sour and sweet ...

"Xerabo's" lover compares her own nipples to juicy grapes; both Kurmanji and Sorani songs often compare breasts to fruit—not just apples and grapes, but also melons and lemons. There is clearly a fantasy element here, as few Kurdish women could be expected to list their attractions so clearly in public, but many Kurdish traditions about love, not only the lyrical songs, are fairly explicit. One of the many dance-songs about girls, *Kênê*, declares, "By day you are my mattress, by night you are my quilt."[10] There are also ribald songs in Kurdish, though they are not well represented in the collections for obvious reasons.[11]

Kurdish lyric, set in the villages and pastures, describes a way of life that has now ended for most Kurds. Part of its appeal lies in its evocation of this rural past.

---

10   *Bi rojê tu doşeka min î/ bi şevê tu lihêfa minî*; from a recording of a Sinjari singer circulating in Badinan, 1992 (the author's collection).
11   See Makas 1926, p. 95 for a rare example: a song addressing the female genitals, apparently sung by young boys to embarrass and annoy girls. Epithalamia might be another source of ribald material.

Lamentation

Lamentation after a death is a social duty for Kurds of all religions, and it is the special province of women. Such laments are extemporized and should be distinguished from the lyrical eulogies sung by male singers in ordinary performances. They are performed at specific time intervals after the death, with different performance conventions in different areas. This material lacks prestige and there have been few publications on it (Rudenko 1982; Allison 1996); it is also possible that performers might feel that recording it could bring misfortune.

Some laments, sung by a semi-professional rather than a close relative, have been collected in Tbilisi (Jelîl 1978 I, p. 490ff.). These consist of short, poignant images, and are often highly allusive. Many depict exile and desolation for the deceased or the family:

Çiya gotê çiya,	Mountain said to mountain,
Go: "Ka xelqê li van ciya?"	"Where are the people in these places?"
Me go: "Birîndarin, nexaşin,	We said, "They are wounded, sick,
tapa wan tinene, mevê şandîye bilindciya, gelo kî êlêra dagerîya?"	they cannot move, we sent him [the deceased] away to the high places, but which clan has he come down with?"

Others are of joy that turns to sadness; the motif of a wedding, the archetypal time of joy in Kurdish folk literature, is often used:

Xerîbê min pak veŕêkin,	Make my exile clean and tidy.
Deste kincê zevatîyê lêkin,	Put bridegroom's clothes on him,
Ax û berê giran şakin.	Let the dust and heavy earth rejoice.

The imagery of laments is very similar to that of other Kurdish oral poetry. The dead are described in the same terms as the beloved of the love lyrics—beautiful and desirable. The mountains, the pastures, the plains, and the plants and animals within them all have their own associations and meanings. Scholars have barely begun to map out this literary landscape, which seems to be quite consistent over large areas of Kurdistan.

9. The future of Kurdish oral literature

In the past century, Kurdish oral literature has faced many threats, apart from the upheavals mentioned above. Some scholars consider literacy to be a danger for oral poetry in general. Indeed it has been remarked that paradoxically the relative underdevelopment of Turkish Kurdistan and lack of educational opportunity there have favored the survival of Kurdish oral traditions (Chyet 1991a I, p. 414). However, in many societies, literacy can coexist with oral composition and performance. The decline in performance and composition in Kurdistan may not be due to literacy *per se* as much as to education systems which valued modernism and perceived folklore as primitive, and to the arrival of other forms of entertainment, especially radio and television.

In 1940 Roger Lescot (1940, p. vi) predicted the demise of oral literature, along with the decline of patriarchal and tribal systems. Various scholars, notably Vilchevsky, have seen folklore, with its praise-poetry and tribal heroes, as a means of consolidating the power and influence of the *agha*s and *beg*s (in Nikitine 1956, p. 258) and it is likely that some progressive Kurds find it offensive for this reason. An alternative to this is to see it as the verbal art of the common people, as opposed to urban literate elites, and it has also been promoted as a typically Kurdish and rural cultural element, in contrast to the more urbanized and centralized Persian, Turkish and Arabic cultures.

In recent years a broader spectrum of Kurdish media has arisen; its performances of traditional material and its many references to images and episodes of oral literature entertain those who are already familiar with it. It also educates the many urban Kurds in Kurdish "folklore," using the traditional imagery of the oral literature. Satellite television in particular is an important unifying factor for "Kurdishness," as it is the first medium that has the capability to reach the entire homeland. It plays an important part in the preservation of traditions and increases their prestige, but, like the other media, it encourages the notion of universally "correct" versions, threatening local oikotypes. Its language of folkloric imagery, (the mountains, flowers, the village, oppressive forces, resistance fighters), designed to reach urban as well as rural Kurds, is far simpler, in range and syntax, than the images of the oral literature. The standardization of the Kurdish experience will inevitably lose much local variety but is necessary for nationhood, and satellite TV is one of the few means at the Kurds' disposal to bring this about. Local identities can still persist, but, for nationhood to exist, a national identity would need to be created which has meaning for all Kurds; oral literature is playing a crucial role in the Kurds' attempts at its formation.

CHAPTER 3

ORALITY AND RELIGION IN KURDISTAN: THE YEZIDI AND AHL-E HAQQ TRADITIONS

PHILIP G. KREYENBROEK

Orality plays an important role in many spheres of Kurdish culture, not least that of religion. The religious traditions of the majority of Kurds, however, have so far received little attention from researchers. At the time of writing the scarcity of available sources would therefore make it impossible to offer a general survey of oral religious literature in Kurdistan. In the course of the twentieth century, however, the sacred poetic traditions of two small religious communities based in Kurdistan have come to light, and enough is now known about these to allow a tentative and provisional description.

These groups, the Yezidis and the Ahl-e Haqq (also known as Yâresân or Kâkâ'i), are minorities whose beliefs and practices are clearly distinct from those of "mainstream" Muslims. Although the two communities live relatively far apart and were probably never closely connected, their religious traditions are strikingly similar in many ways. One reason for this may be that they developed in cultural milieus of the same type—relatively isolated communities where writing did not play a prominent role, and which were too remote from centers of orthodox Islamic learning to be overawed by their authority. It is possible, moreover, that a common substratum of pre-Islamic religious views and practices played a role here.

Both traditions comprise a large corpus of sacred poetry, and prose narratives of various types. The sacred poems, the Ahl-e

ORALITY AND RELIGION IN KURDISTAN

Haqq *Kalâm* and the Yezidi *Qewl* and *Beyt*,[1] in a sense represent these communities' equivalents to the scriptural traditions of other faiths; they are regarded in that light by some Western researchers, and increasingly by members of the groups themselves (see further below). Although they were traditionally handed down orally, the poems were memorized *verbatim* by trained "reciters," and they appear to have been preserved relatively faithfully, in some cases for a very long time. When studied in isolation most of these texts are very difficult to understand, which seems to invite comparison with Zarathustra's equally perplexing *Gâthâs*. While any explanatory tradition to the *Gâthâs* is probably lost for all time, however, most of the sacred poetry of the Ahl-e Haqq and Yezidis can be understood in light of the sects' traditional religious knowledge, which at the time of writing is endangered but still in existence.

One of the great opportunities the study of these religious systems offers, in fact, is the possibility of analyzing and demonstrating the interdependence, in two non-literate cultures, between formal sacral poetry on the one hand, and the religious narrative tradition in its various forms on the other. The Ahl-e Haqq and Yezidi traditions further illustrate both the tenacity and the adaptability of these largely non-literate cultures, and their ability to shape their sacred texts in such a way as to maximize their effectiveness as religious discourse.

After some general remarks on the Yezidi and Ahl-e Haqq communities, this chapter will examine aspects of their poetic and religious traditions, with some emphasis on the sacred poems.

---

1 The transcription of Yezidi words here follows the accepted spelling of Kurmanji Kurdish (see Blau in this Volume); that of words from the Ahl-e Haqq tradition and general Islamic terms follows the conventions used for Persian.

ORAL LITERATURE OF IRANIAN LANGUAGES

1. The Yezidis and Ahl-e Haqq

Demography

Both Yezidis and Ahl-e Haqq have important centers in the area generally known as Kurdistan. The heart of the spiritual universe of Yezidism is Lalish, somewhat to the north of Mosul in Northern Iraq, which contains the great sanctuary of Shaikh Adi. Important Yezidi communities live in the Sheykhân and Jabal Senjâr areas of Northern Iraq. Some groups have settled in Armenia and Georgia, and a smaller number live in Syria. Remnants of the once large Yezidi community of Turkey are still found in southeastern parts of that country, but most Turkish Yezidis have sought refuge from religious persecution in Western Europe, notably in Germany. All Yezidis speak Kurmanji Kurdish and most of their religious texts are in that language. The Ahl-e Haqq are ethnically and linguistically more diverse. There are communities in Iraqi Kurdistan (where they are generally known as Kâkâ'i), in the Iranian provinces of Kordestân, Kermânshâh, and Western Azerbaijan, and in Tehran and some other Iranian cities. In the course of history, Persian, Kurdish, Lori, and Turkish-speaking communities have all contributed to the Ahl-e Haqq tradition (Minorsky 1953, 1954; Weightman 1964; Hamzeh'ee 1990, p. 23). From the point of view of oral religious literature,[2] however, the most important tradition is that of the Gurân area in the extreme west of Kermânshâh province in Iran, in whose language (Gurâni, see MacKenzie 1961; Blau 1996, p. 21), the largest and best known collections of *Kalâm*s are composed. Gurâni is sometimes referred to as the "sacred language" of the group.

---

[2] The theological writings of the "modernist" Ahl-e Haqq tradition founded by Hâjj Ne'matollâh Jeyhunâbâdi (on which see Mir-Hosseini 1994 and the *Encyclopaedia Iranica*, VIII, pp. 297–301, s.v. Elahi, Hajj Nur-Ali), are beyond the scope of this Chapter.

Religious affiliations

Curiously, in view of the many similarities between them, the religious affiliations and self-definition of the two groups are very different. The prevalent opinion among modern Yezidis is that their faith is independent of Islam; at a very early stage in its development the community called itself "the Sunna" and boasted of being anti-Shi'ite (Kreyenbroek 1995a, pp. 226–7), which implies that they felt part of the community of Muslims. Today, most (though not all) Ahl-e Haqq regard themselves as Shi'ites (Mir-Hosseini 1994b).

History

The founder of the mystical Order that was to give rise to Yezidism was a Sufi of Umayyad descent and strongly Sunni leanings. Shaikh Adi ebn Mosâfer (d. circa 1160 CE) settled in the Kurdish Hakkâri mountains in the early twelfth century CE, where he attracted many followers. These eventually formed a Sufi Order, the Adawiyya, whose membership extended far beyond Kurdistan. Less than a hundred years after Shaikh Adi's death we hear of aberrant views among the Adawis living in the Lalish area; as these tendencies grew stronger they led to tensions with the sect's orthodox neighbors, and eventually, it seems, to the alienation of Yezidism from Islam (Kreyenbroek 1995a, pp. 27–36).

Soltân Sahâk, whom the Ahl-e Haqq regard as the founder of their tradition and as a major incarnation of the Divine, probably flourished in the Gurân area in the fifteenth century CE (Mokri 1963; Mir-Hosseini 1996, p. 114). Since his followers regarded Ali as one of many divine manifestations they were regarded as ultra-Shi'ites (*gholât*) and their Islamic identity was not challenged.

Some characteristic ideas and beliefs

One of the most striking elements shared by the Ahl-e Haqq and Yezidi traditions is their distinctive myth of the Cosmogony. In both traditions it is said that God the Creator first fashioned a Pearl which contained the various elements that were to form the universe. He then evoked a group of seven divine beings and made a Pact with their leader, who became the Lord of this world. A bull-sacrifice, it seems, was performed.[3] After this the Pearl disintegrated and its elements formed the world we know. The world was left to the care of the Seven.

Both Ahl-e Haqq and Yezidi beliefs are based upon the view that some of the events of the Time of Creation essentially repeat themselves again and again in cycles of exoteric history, which are in fact no more than manifestations of a deeper, esoteric reality. God and the Seven, in other words, play their roles on earth during each period of history in various manifestations as human beings. The Ahl-e Haqq tradition lays greater emphasis on this cyclical aspect, whilst the Yezidi texts seem to focus more on the essentially divine nature of Shaikh Adi and the Holy Men associated with him (Kreyenbroek 1998, pp. 176–79). The fundamental idea that the same essence may surface more than once in different forms also finds expression in the belief in reincarnation, which is found in both traditions, and in the meta-historical character of their religious narratives. These may imply, for instance, that one historical figure was essentially identical with another who lived at a different time, both being manifestations of an essence which already existed at the time of Creation. This perspective informs the oral religious traditions of both sects.

---

3   This element of the myth is not attested in the Yezidi texts that have so far come to light, but see Kreyenbroek 1995, pp. 56–57.

2. Textual traditions of the Yezidis and Ahl-e Haqq

The absorption of outside influences

Kurdistan lies at a cultural crossroads. In the course of time the Kurds have been exposed to a number of different cultures, many of whose ideas and values were expressed in their religious traditions. At the same time, it seems, Kurdish tribal society was conservative and to some extent inward looking, discussing information from outside at the frequent formal and informal gatherings of group members. This procedure apparently enabled the Ahl-e Haqq and Yezidis to absorb elements from a succession of civilizations by adapting them to their traditional understanding of the nature of fundamental reality. In the largely non-literate cultural environment of these groups, knowledge, whether indigenous or foreign, was normally transmitted in the form of anecdotes. Such tales could easily be incorporated into the general framework of a mythology based on the view that the various events and personalities that seem to loom large in the history of man are all manifestations of one underlying reality (see above).

Storylines and sacred poems

A group of storylines that are felt to have religious significance forms the core of the religious knowledge of both traditions. These include what Westerners would call myths, legends, edifying tales, and stories about the great figures of the faith. The storylines may generate a range of actual narratives. They may popularly be told in prose as short and relatively simple stories (most of the stories found in Western publications on Yezidism belong to this type), while more elaborate and complex versions may be transmitted as part of a learned religious tradition.

Many sacred poems are based on such story lines, alluding to them constantly. Several of these poems would be unintelligible to those who are unfamiliar with the (elaborate) prose version of the stories in question. Although in both traditions the sacred poems have a higher status than prose narratives, the two genres are in fact interdependent. The very fact that many poems cannot be understood without the prose versions, it seems, ensures that the latter continue to be remembered in their original form.

Polyvalence

Before listing some individual topics that figure prominently in both traditions it may be relevant to point out that many such themes can be understood in more than one way. A theme that is found in both the Ahl-e Haqq and the Yezidi tradition, for example, is that of catching a falcon or a similar bird of prey. An Ahl-e Haqq text about this theme stresses that members of the Heptad have succeeded in catching this bird; a Yezidi *Qewl* describes a devotee's attempts to catch one, which appear to succeed but ultimately leave the "hunter" empty-handed (some stanzas from both texts are given below). As is well-known, in the Zoroastrian tradition the falcon is connected with *kh^w arnah*, a phenomenon whose "capture" and possession seem to have ensured well-being. From a Sufi point of view the story could symbolize the seeker's quest for a vision of God, or knowledge of ultimate reality. Both traditions may have played a role in the genesis of these poems. On the other hand, a modern Yezidi tradition has it that the coming of the falcon represents the visit of a greater Shaikh to a lesser one; the latter's preparations for this honor were insufficient and the great Shaikh is said to have departed again immediately.

Characteristic topics

Creation and the First Things

The distinctive cosmogony found in both traditions has been discussed above. The prose introduction to a collection of Ahl-e Haqq

Kalâms (Suri 1965, pp. 22–29), which to judge by its characteristics is based on oral narrative, recounts the myth as follows:

> The water of the sea was an ocean. For some time the Pearl was in the water. There was no (contrast between) ocean and dry land. The King of the Universe (i.e. God) uttered a command to the Stone,[4] the Stone disintegrated, and from the pieces of the stone smoke rose up into the air. One piece of that stone flew up into the air and became the sky; and He fashioned the stars also, and all the servants (He had) at that time are called angels, and He made the Moon, the Sun, and he made His own light enter the Stone and hurled it. And He also instituted Night and Day and the Four Seasons, and He gave supervision of the year to four Angels; sometimes (they are called) the Four Persons and sometimes the Seven Persons.

A passage from the Yezidi text *Meshefa Resh* (trsl. from Bittner 1913, pp. 36–39; on the *Meshefa Resh* see below), which probably represents an authentic Yezidi tradition, contains a similar account:

> Before earth and heaven God was on the ocean. He made himself a ship, and he was in the midst of the waters, circling around. He made the Pearl from himself and ruled over it for forty years. After that he kicked it. Oh wonder! From the tumult and uproar of this, those mountains (were created). From the dust those hills were made and that heaven from the smoke. He established it and made it solid and supported it without columns. Then he locked the earth, and took a pen in his hand and began to write down (the names of) all creatures. After that he created six[5] divinities from His essence and His light. The creation was as one lights a lamp from another lamp with fire.

In the Yezidi *Qewl* tradition a description of this sequence of events is interspersed with references to symbols deriving from the Sufi tradition, such as Love (*mihebbet*), the (Wine) Cup (*kas*), and the Mystery (*surr*). While some of these symbols are understood

---

4   Both "Pearl" and "Stone," it seems, are names for the primeval object from which the world originated. On the connection between the Pearl in the Yezidi and Ahl-e Haqq traditions, the stone Sky in early Zoroastrianism, and the Indo-Iranian image of an enclosing space of rock or stone that contained the prototypes of the constituent elements of the world, see Kreyenbroek 1995, pp. 52–59.

5   The number of these beings is generally said to be seven.

to have a well-defined meaning in modern Yezidism, others have come to seem mysterious. (On Sufi influences see further below, under Mystical themes).

Accounts such as these probably represent a learned tradition, some of whose elements may go back to pre-Islamic times. More popular Yezidi accounts of Creation and the First Things tend to be simpler, focusing on Tawusi Melek's role in bringing order to the world and on legends about Adam and Eve.

Legends explaining the community's origins and affiliations

A well-known Yezidi legend states that the Yezidis are descended from Shehîd son of Jerr, who was generated by Adam without Eve (Kreyenbroek 1995a, pp. 36–37). Whatever the remote origins of this legend, it is now recounted in the community to explain why Yezidis, being ontologically different, may not marry non-Yezidis. Some *Qewl*s deal with the relationship between the venerated Yezidi figure Êzîd (whose name presumably derives from that of the Umayyad Yazid I, r. 680–81), and his father, the caliph Mo'âwiya (r. 661–80). It is recognized that Êzîd was Mo'âwiya's son, but his mother is said to have left her husband before Êzîd was born. Such texts explain the connection between Yezidism and Islam, while at the same time implying that they are wholly distinct. Narratives whose obvious purpose is to explain the group's position *vis-à-vis* surrounding communities form part of both Yezidi and Ahl-e Haqq oral literature (see also Mir-Hosseini 1996, pp. 115–16).

Saints and Holy Men

Legends and myths concerning the life and exploits of the founders of the tradition, their companions, and other great figures of old, are prominent in both traditions; among the Yezidis the latter group includes personalities who also play a role in the Islamic tradition, e.g. Ebrâhim, Esmâ'il, and great Sufis such as al-Hallâj and Râbe'e al-Adawiyye. Both traditions make it clear that such figures are seen as manifestations of an essence that may also have appeared in different forms. This aspect tends to play a prominent role in Ahl-e Haqq narratives, while the Yezidi tradition usually focuses more on such figures' miraculous powers.

Mystical themes

Reference has already been made to the influence of the Sufi tradition on the Yezidi *Qewl*s. In fact the sacred poems of both communities contain references to concepts, insights and symbols deriving from Islamic mysticism. One such concept is that of the *nafs* or "ego-soul," which must be controlled if a person is to achieve or maintain spiritual purity. In the following passage from a *Qewl* the ego-soul is compared to a horse, which will run wild if it is not controlled.[6]

Weke te bor nedibeste	If you have not tied up your horse
Lixaf û hefsar çûn ji deste	You lose control of the bit and the reins,
Borê te li hemû mêrga dike qeste	Your horse will make for all possible pastures.
Ew şuġlê nefsê bû, xulkê xudanî ji ber şikeste.	That is the work of the ego-soul, corrupting the divine nature.
We nabî, we nasêwirî	Let this not be, it is not right!
Ne wacibê erkanêye, borê te li hemû mêrga biçerî	There is no need to let your horse feed on all pastures
Ew şuġlê nefsê bû, roja axiretê xulkê xudanî ji ber kirî.	That is the work of the ego-soul; on the Last Day your divine nature will have been lost.

A deeper understanding of mystical concepts is probably restricted, however, to a limited circle of educated community members.

---

6   The passage is from the *Qewlê Babekê Omera*, which was recited for Dr. Khalil J. Rashow by Shaikh Eli, son of Shaikh Shemo. It was transcribed by the former and translated by the present writer.

Philosophical themes: the implications of death

As in most religious literatures, many Ahl-e Haqq and Yezidi poems and narratives have philosophical implications. Several Yezidi *Qewl*s and *chîrok*s, moreover, explicitly deal with the meaning of death from various angles. There is a story line, for example, about a man who goes in search of immortality and obtains a promise from Fate that he will not die unless he gives away three apples. The story explores some of the implications of immortality on earth, and describes how the protagonist eventually gives away his apples and dies. A *Qewl* that is often recited at funerals describes an ordinary man's history from conception and birth, through the various stages of childhood and adult life, to the judgment of the soul after death. The text emphasizes that birth and death are part of a process decreed by God. On the one hand such texts are clearly intended to comfort the bereaved, but on the other they have a theodicean element, implying that death is not an evil to be blamed on a malevolent god, but rather an inevitable consequence of man's status on earth.

3. The sacred poems

Formal characteristics

From a formal point of view the sacred poems of the two groups have little in common. The Gurâni *Kalâm*s have a syllabic meter, with two half-verses of five syllables each. The first four half-verses of a poem (or sequence of poems) usually show the rhyme-scheme a a, b a or, less often, a a, a a. In older *Kalâm*s,[7] part or all of the first half-verse is usually repeated in the second. Some collections of texts consist entirely of quatrains with such a rhyme scheme (Mokri 1969). Other *Kalâm*s tend to have longer poems, which

---

[7] These *kalām*s, which are known as 'Perdiwari', are thought to go back to or precede the time of Soltān Sahāk, who lived in the fourteenth century.

may continue the end-rhyme throughout (a a, b a, c a, d a, etc., as in the Arabo-Persian *qaside*), or consist of several groups of rhyming verses. The older *Kalâm*s are said to have been uttered by a venerable, divine or legendary figure from the religion's past, who is named at the beginning of the text ("X says," see below). In other cases the poem may be attributed to a historical figure that played an important role in the community.

The Yezidi tradition comprises two main categories of long sacred poems, *Qewl* and *Beyt*. Although, with a few exceptions, Yezidis consistently classify each text as belonging to one of these categories, no clear definitions can now be offered of the characteristics distinguishing the two whose formal characteristics seem very similar; the distinction may lie in the origins of these texts; *Qewl*s are held to have been composed by Yezidis of great spiritual standing, a claim that is not made for *Beyt*s (in fact, one well-known *Beyt* can be shown to be a popular version of an old poem by a Muslim Kurd).

Both groups of texts consist of a varying number of stanzas (*sebeqe*); most have more than ten stanzas, and the maximum number attested is 117. A *sebeqe* typically consists of three or four lines, at least some of which have end-rhymes. As with much Kurdish poetry, the definition of the metrical system of the *Qewl*s is problematic: there is neither a quantitative meter as in Arabo-Persian *aruz*, a strict syllabic meter as in the *Kalâm*s, nor a clear stress meter. However, there are usually an average number of both stresses and syllables. The name or pen name of the (reputed) author is sometimes mentioned in the text, sometimes suggested by the title by which the poem is known, but often unknown.

Other genres of Yezidi religious poetry include "prayers" (*du'a*), which share most of the formal characteristics of *Qewl*s and *Beyt*s, but are generally shorter;[8] the same is true of a group of poems known as *qesîde*, most of which are short hymns of praise to holy figures.

---

8 Passages which occur in a *Qewl* may also form part of a prayer, see e.g. Kreyenbroek 1995, pp. 216–17 and pp. 258–61.

ORAL LITERATURE OF IRANIAN LANGUAGES

The following passages from Ahl-e Haqq and Yezidi sacred poems may serve to illustrate some of the differences and similarities between the two. Both texts deal with the theme of the capture of a falcon (on which see above). The following stanzas from the Ahl-e Haqq text known as *Dawra-y Dâmyârî* (The Cycle of the Hunt; Mokri 1967, p. 206), are said to have been uttered by the Holy Beings Benyâmin and Dâwud:

Benyâmin maramô: dâmim wa dastâ	Benyâmin says: I have the trap in my hand
Wa lutf-e Khwâjâm dâmim wa dastâ	By the grace of the Master I have the trap in my hand.
Dâwud-e Rahbar wa shun-e shastâ	Dâwud is the Guide follows the hunt
Khwâjâm qodrata	My Master is the Power
gholâm sarmastâ	his slave is intoxicated.
Dâwud maramô: dâmish niyâni	Dâwud says: He has set his trap,
Dâmyâr Benyâmin dâmish niyâni	Benyâmin the Hunter has set his trap.
Neynâ tananish waraw kaywâni	He has made it just now, facing Saturn,
Shahbâziš girtan Khwâjây Penhâni	He caught the noble falcon, the Lord of the Hidden.

As was noted earlier, the Yezidi *Qewlê Pîr Sheref* (Kreyenbroek 1995a, pp. 264–72), which includes the following passage, emphasizes the ephemeral nature of the protagonist's success in capturing the falcon:

Mestim sikranim	I am drunk, I am intoxicated
Nêçîrvanê bazani	I am a hunter of falcons
Aşiqê surra giranim ... [9]	I am a lover of the precious Mystery ...
Dava min ji muwe	My trap is made of hair
Derê dirba vedibuwe	Its mouth is open
Baziyek tê weribuwe	A falcon was caught in it
Min nedizanî ji min berbuwe	I did not know, it left me.

---

9   A number of stanzas have been omitted.

82

Dava mine zirave	My trap is a subtle one
Derê dirba xoyaye	Its mouth is visible
Baziyek kefte nave	A falcon fell into it
Min nedizanî, min berdave	I did not know, I let it go.
Çî baziyekî qewiye	What a strong falcon it was
Min di dava xo da diye	That I saw in my trap
Min nedizanî surra Şêxadiye	I did not know it was the Mystery of Shaikh Adi.
Çî baziyekî di cîda	What an excellent falcon it was
Min di dava xo da dîte	That I saw in my trap
Min nedizanî	I did not know,
surra Siltan Êzîde	it was the Mystery of Sultan Êzid.

Music

Music plays an important role in both the performance and transmission of the sacred poems of both sects. Every original Yezidi *Qewl* has its own melody and style of singing (*kubrî*). When, as sometimes happens, texts from several original compositions are combined to form a new *Qewl*, the original passages retain their *kubrî*, so that the music changes during the performance of the *Qewl*. Among the Ahl-e Haqq the role of sacred music is no less central (see During 1989). In both traditions it is said that the soul of the First Man would not come to his body until the sacred instruments had come down to earth from heaven. For the Ahl-e Haqq, the sacred instrument is the long-necked lute (*tambur*). Yezidism regards both the tambourine (*def*) and the flute (*shibab*) as sacred.

Transmitters

As will be shown below, the various genres constituting the religious discourse of these groups are fundamentally interconnected and interdependent. However, the sacred poems have an especially venerated place in these systems, and they are traditionally memorized, studied and performed by trained, and in the case of Yezidism professional, transmitters (Yez. *Qewwal*; AH *Kalâmkh^{w}ân*).

These figures, the scholars of their communities, recite or sing the sacred poems at religious gatherings of various types. The Ahl-e Haqq *Kalâms* are typically recited during the group's relatively frequent religious "assemblies" (*jam*). In Yezidism, *Qewl*-singing sessions form part of religious festivals and funerary rites; moreover, traditionally groups of *Qewwals* annually toured the various lands where Yezidis lived, stopping at villages to exchange news, collect taxes, and conduct religious sessions. At these sessions they displayed an effigy of a Peacock (representing Tawusî Melek, the Peacock Angel, who is believed to rule this world), preached a sermon (*mishabet*), and performed *Qewls*.

Ahl-e Haqq and Yezidi reciters and religious leaders were traditionally trained, not just to perform the sacred texts but also to understand and interpret them. The background and training of the Ahl-e Haqq *Kalâmkh^{w}ân* is generally informal, but traditionally their Yezidi counterparts were formally trained (Jindy 1998). The office of *Qewwal* is restricted to (male) members of two tribes (Hekkarî and Dumilî). Local tradition has it that a training college for *Qewwals* existed until the early decades of the twentieth century, but no trace of this now remains. At present, prospective *Qewwals* learn the requisite knowledge and skills from their fathers or from other knowledgeable men who are prepared to act as teachers. The Yezidi *Qewwal* tradition is clearly endangered by such factors as modernity, persecution and emigration. Modernity also affects the *Kalâmkh^{w}ân* tradition, not least becauses Gurâni is increasingly used for religious purposes only.

On the discovery of the sacred texts

There has been some controversy in Western academic circles about the sacred texts of the Yezidis. When, in the mid-nineteenth century, travelers' accounts first created an interest in Yezidism in the West, it seems that scholars were hoping to find written scriptures to help them interpret the nature and origin of Yezidism. The significance of the oral *Qewl* tradition was not recognized, and since only one uninformative Arabic text had been produced in response to travelers' queries, it was assumed that the Yezidis either did not have an important textual tradition (Badger 1852 I, p. 115), or that their sacred books were hidden (Layard 1853, p. 89). Occasional reference was in fact made in the community to mysterious holy texts which were referred to by the names *Meshefa Resh* (Black Book) and *Jilwe* (Ar. *jelwa*, Illumination), but for some decades no copies of these works were found. Then, in the late 1880s, a series of manuscripts began to be offered for sale to Western travelers whose contents included two short texts with the titles *Jilwe* and *Meshefa Resh*. By the early twentieth century, at least half a dozen such manuscripts had come to light. Curiously, these early versions of the "Sacred Books" were written in Arabic rather than Kurdish; later, in 1911, the Carmelite Father Anastase Marie announced his discovery of what he claimed to be the original Kurdish versions of the texts. A German translation of Anastase's text was published two years later (Bittner 1913). For a time, it was assumed that the new discoveries did indeed represent an ancient scriptural tradition. However, a few years later Alphonse Mingana, a Christian scholar from the Zakho area who claimed to know the Yezidis well, convincingly challenged the authenticity of these works as representatives of an ancient manuscript tradition. In view of later discoveries and insights, it now seems clear that these "Sacred Books" were indeed forgeries, although their contents suggest that their author had considerable knowledge of authentic Yezidi traditions.[10]

More than half a century later the question of the religious textual tradition of Yezidism surfaced again. The first step in this process was that members of the Yezidi community began to commit their sacred texts to writing. In 1978, O. and J. Jalil published some *Qewls* as part of their work on Kurdish folklore. The following year saw the publication, in Iraq, of Silêman and Jindy's *Êzdiyatî*, which focused entirely on religious poetic texts (*Qewls*, *Beyts*, and

---

10 Texts that purported to be versions or lost chapters of these putative sacred books continued to be published until the late 1970s (see Bibliography under Ahmed, Frayha); see further below.

prayers). More *Qewl*s were published in Silêman's *Gundiyatî*. Silêman and Jindy's work in particular led to a new awareness of the *Qewl*s in the Yezidi community, particularly among Yezidis living in the West. Texts which had long seemed mysterious and were felt to be the exclusive preserve of *Qewwal*s, now came to be seen as part of the religious and cultural heritage of the community as a whole. The fact that *Qewl*s could now be studied in written form, rather than listened to with reverence on religious occasions, naturally contributed to this development. This new interest in turn led some Yezidis to record and publish more sacred poems, and contributed to a renewed interest in Yezidi religious literature among Western academics.

The history of the discovery of the Ahl-e Haqq *Kalâm*s in the West is less complex. Attention was drawn to the existence of these poems in the early twentieth century, when V. Minorsky acquired a manuscript containing some Turkish *Kalâm*s (see Minorsky 1960). In the course of the century more collections of *Kalâm*s, mostly in Gurâni were published in works intended to reach a non-Ahl-e Haqq public[11] (*Kalâm*s are now also published locally for the community's own use). These publications were generally based, in part or *in toto*, on earlier written documents, none of which can be shown to have existed before the nineteenth century. These developments, it seems, are connected with an increasing tendency on the part of the Ahl-e Haqq community to commit its ancient tradition to writing.

4. Questions of orality and literacy in connection with the poems

The transition from a predominantly oral to a (partially) written tradition led some Yezidis and Ahl-e Haqq to think of their sacred literature in terms of concepts which derive from literate cultures, and may be misleading when applied to a tradition such as theirs.

---

11 See Bibliography, under Ivanow, Mokri, Surî, and Safizâde.

ORALITY AND RELIGION IN KURDISTAN

On the other hand, it cannot be assumed that the mainly oral character of a tradition implies that writing plays no role there at all.

Yezidis in the West, it seems, increasingly tend to think of the *Qewls* as parts of a Canon, a well-defined authoritative codex of sacred texts similar in status to the Scriptures of other religions. As the nature and functions of the original tradition were in reality quite different, this can lead to misunderstandings. Similarly, the editors of several collections of Ahl-e Haqq *Kalâms* (e.g. Suri 1965, pp. 16–19; Safizâde 1996, p. 20; cf. Mokri 1967, p. 3) have claimed that their works go back to the *Ketâb-e Saranjâm* (sometimes given the alternative title *Kalâm-e Khazâne*),[12] which is described as the central and most authoritative collection of *Kalâms*. The underlying assumption seems to be that such texts, whether they are known from oral tradition or from late manuscripts, are all parts or versions of a single, original, sacred book. In view of the dissimilarities between the collections themselves, and the discrepancies between the various claims about the nature and composition of the original *Ketâb-e Saranjâm*, the existence of such an original codex seems doubtful. It seems more likely that parts of a fluid oral tradition of religious poetry (which may already have been grouped into collections of texts felt to be connected with a particular stage or event of sacred history), were first committed to writing for private purposes, and later used by researchers intent on reconstituting an ancient codex which may never have existed.

On the other hand, the names *Saranjâm* and *Khazâne* are used too consistently in the Ahl-e Haqq tradition to be dismissed as fabrications. It seems likely that many community members believed in the existence of a sacred text bearing such a name, which was generally thought of as a book.

The Yezidi tradition may throw some light on this state of affairs. As was noted earlier, although the alleged "Sacred Books" known by the titles *Jilwe* and *Meshefa Resh* can safely be regarded as forgeries, the names themselves were mentioned as titles of Yezidi religious texts in what appear to be reliable sources (see Kreyenbroek

---

12 So Safizâde 1965, p. 20; Elahi 1987, p. 162. On the *Kalâm-e Khazâne* see also Mokri 1967, p. 3.

1995a, p. 14). The former title ultimately goes back, it seems, to a work entitled *Ketâb al-jelwa le-arbâb al-khalwa,* which was written by Shaikh Hasan ebn Adi (d. 1254 CE), one of the early leaders of the Yezidi community; the work is no longer extant, but was presumably in Arabic. It is now known, moreover, that some families belonging to the Adanî group of Shaikhs (hereditary religious leaders who trace their lineage to Shaikh Hasan ebn Adi), still possess a document or book which is referred to as *Jilwe* and regarded as a sacred book. Apart from being objects of veneration, such documents are typically used for purposes of divination and healing. Although they are not normally shown to outsiders and no detailed comparison has therefore been possible, it is thought that the contents of individual documents vary but that each contains texts of a religious nature, often including *Qewl*s.

In the Yezidi community of Jabal Senjâr, it seems, the title *Meshefa Resh* is sometimes used for a similar type of document (Kreyenbroek 1995a, p. 14). Given the mainly oral character of the tradition as a whole, the existence of such documents is unlikely to have affected the transmission of the *Qewl*s to any significant extent. However, it probably strengthened a tendency to think of the oral textual tradition as ultimately representing an authoritative written source. Although no evidence is currently available to confirm this, it seems possible that a similar state of affairs led the Ahl-e Haqq to think of collections of their sacred texts as a book.

In sum, what is now known about the religious textual traditions of the Ahl-e Haqq and the Yezidis naturally represents only a fraction of the oral religious literature of the Kurds. The richness and complexity of these traditions suggest that further study of these and similar traditions can be expected to add materially to our knowledge of the cultures concerned, and of oral literature in general.

CHAPTER 4

PASHTO LITERATURE: THE CLASSICAL PERIOD

Sergei Andreyev

Pashtuns reside mainly to the north and south of the Durand line that now forms the Afghan-Pakistani border. Their numbers are estimated at twenty-three million people, and their language, Pashto/Pakhto (*Paśto*) belongs to the Eastern Iranian family of languages. The Pashtuns were gradually Islamized over the period of five centuries from the tenth century CE onwards. The majority of them are Hanafi Sunnis, while there are also a few Shi'ite tribes. They are a tribal people with a complex hierarchy composed of unions of tribes, separate tribes, clans and households. Usually they are politically disunited, and even in a state of feud with each other over, as they themselves admit, "women, gold and land," or as some anthropologists argue, matters of tribal and personal honor. Despite this constant warfare, the Pashtuns possess some sense of unity based on their common language, origin, customs and concepts.

1. Poetic forms and genres

In the domain of oral culture the Pashtuns' military lifestyle, typical of many frontier societies, found its artistic expression in a form of popular poetry called *lanḓəy* or *nəmakəy*,[1] which very often focuses

[1] Given the differences between two main dialects of Pashto, *viz.* Western and Eastern or Kandahari and Peshawari, and the multitude of local variations, terms for poetical genres can vary from one place to another. Thus the *lanḓəy* (< *land* "short") in the Western dialect is called *ṭapa* or *misrəy* in the East.

on military adventure and the pursuit of tribal and personal honor (MacKenzie 1958; Girs 1984). However, the *landəy* is only one of many genres of folk poetry, albeit the most popular, since thousands of these short poems are recited throughout the Pashtun lands. Due to its prosodic peculiarities, it made little impact on the development of written Pashto poetry, which stylistically and topically was strongly influenced by classical Persian models (Kushef 2000).

However, given the peculiarities of the Pashto language (notably the lack of a clear distinction between short and long vowels, which makes a differentiation between short and long syllables almost impossible, and the fact that clusters of two or even three consonants occur, usually at the beginning of a word), the Pashto meters are not quantitative. Nevertheless, many Pashto authors tried to imitate certain aspects of *aruz*, though in a rather clumsy way. The meter of Pashtun folk songs, where the feet are marked by regular patterns of accents, fits Pashto poetry more naturally (MacKenzie 1996, I, pp. 339–40; II, pp. 59). Therefore, those authors who unabashedly adopted folklore poetical forms usually wrote the more eloquent poetry.

The most popular form of both folk and classical Pashto poetry is the *chârbeyta* (lit. 'four distiches'). This appellation is rather artificial, since the *chârbeyta* is not limited to four *beyts*, and every *band* (strophe) can consist not only of four *beyts*, but also of four hemistiches (*mesrâ'*). The number of *mesrâ's* can reach twenty-odd, while the number of *bands* is unlimited. With regard to the alteration of the rhyme the *chârbeyta* is divided into two main types: "simple" (*sâda*) and "chain" (*dzandziri*), where the penultimate line of every band rhymes with the first line of the introduction (*sar*), and the last line of the band rhymes with the second line of the *sar*. The rhyme schemes are rather diverse but there is always a refrain, with fifteen types (Rafi' 1970, pp. 226–34), the simplest being a a; b b b a; c c c a; d d d a, etc.

Another popular genre used by Pashtun poets is *bagatəy* (also *bagati* or *bugti*), which is confined exclusively to the Pashto literature and originates in oral tradition. Usually it is a short poem sung by two performers with an introduction in two lines and no more than ten strophes, normally each consisting of four lines. The rhyme is always a a; b b b a; c c c a ... etc.

Well in line with the old Iranian minstrel tradition, popular Pashto poetry is often sung, rather than read, during special events called *tang takor* (musical evening).[2]

Apart from using their own folk genres Pashtuns also adopted classical forms of Arabo-Persian literature, albeit with some modification. Thus alongside classical *ghazal* (often called *loba*) with two introductory lines and the rhyme aa-ba-ca-da, there also exists a specific Pashto *ghazal* with different rhyme-schemes (MacKenzie 1958, p. 320; Dvoriankov 1973, pp. 47–50). The most popular rhyme-schemes in Pashto are 8, 12, 14, 15 and 16-syllables with possible apocope variations (for more details on Pashto rhyme see Pelevin 2001, pp. 211–15).

2. Early and classical Pashto poetry

It seems impossible to establish exact dates for the beginning of Pashto literature. According to local tradition the oldest available poem in Pashto dates back to the eighth century CE. It is included in a compendium of Pashto popular poetry and anecdotes (*rewâyat*), entitled *Pəta Khazâna* (Hidden Treasure).[3]

Undoubtedly the oldest known Pashto work in prose, which was written down at the time of its composition, is the *Daftar* of the Yusufzay chief Shaikh Mali. This is a history of the Yusufzay tribe, its conquest of Swat and the beginning of the periodical redistribution of land (*wêsh*) in these newly acquired territories. Although Pashtun tradition claims that the *Daftar* was composed at the beginning of the fifteenth century CE, evidence from various sources suggests that the Yusufzays led by Shaikh Mali did not conquer Swat before the 1530s. Later Afghan sources also mention

---

2 Poetry in classical genres can also be sung, but less commonly, although its performance is often accompanied by music (Kaleem 1954, p. 21). For a description of the performance of Pashto poetry see Girs 1995, pp. 41–42.

3 The book's Afghan publishers claim that it was compiled in Kandahar in the early eighteenth century CE. However, it is now generally assumed that the work is a forgery made in Afghanistan in the 1940s (Gerasimova; Girs 1963, p. 30; Morgenstierne 1961, p. 220). In any case, the dating of all the texts it contains is entirely arbitrary.

a few tribal histories written in the middle of the sixteenth century. Unfortunately, none of these sources is extant now.

The Rowshani period

This ancient period in the history of Pashto literature ended when new authors, unlike their predecessors, started using Pashto consciously and developed a particular style and literary norms. This is the period of the Rowshani[4] literary activities. The conscious use of the Pashto language seems to be a distinctive watershed, as it marked the beginning of the cultural self-awareness of the Pashtuns, and of their opposition to the language of the dominant high culture, Persian. It appears that the Rowshani movement was not an isolated phenomenon. In India and adjacent regions the turn of the second Hejri millennium (16th century) witnessed the spread of popular Sufi movements, as opposed to the more intellectual and elitist Sufism of previous centuries. These movements, many of them fueled by millenarian expectations, started to use vernacular languages for preaching their eclectic doctrines to their many adepts, who often came from the lower classes. The Rowshaniyya (c. 1560–1640) was a predominantly Pashtun Sufi movement which flourished at the time of the expansion of the Mughal Empire to the Pashtun tribal area. The founder of the movement was Bâyazid Ansâri (c. 1521 or 1525 until 1572 or 1575), also called Pir-e Rawśân (Guide of Light), whose name was given to the movement, which belonged to the tradition of practical devotional Sufism. Bâyazid Ansâri was an eclectic Islamic thinker whose teaching focused on the concept of the centrality of the Perfect Guide (*pir-e kâmel*) as indispensable for spiritual perfection. Philosophically, Bâyazid Ansâri and his followers were strongly influenced by the concepts of "Unity of Existence" (*vahdat-e vojud*), and the "Perfect Man" (*ensân-e kâmel*). The Rowshani movement is the first relatively

---

4 This is *rowshâni* in Persian and *rawśâni* in Pashto. Sine both Persian and Pashto sources on the movement exist, the spellings "Rowshani" and "Rowshaniyya" will be used here.

well-documented example of the supra-tribal unification of the Pashtun tribes. Bâyazid Ansâri and his descendants were not Pashtun tribesmen but claimed to originate from a family of the prophet Mohammad's companions (*ansâr*). His ancestors acted as communal religious servants. By appealing to the individual religious feelings of their followers at the expense of their tribal identity, the Rowshani leaders diverted the Pashtuns from their tribal life, and created a new political and religious entity of their followers.

In their activities, which soon acquired a political dimension, Bâyazid Ansâri and his successors followed the pattern of "bloc building" (*gund-bâzi*), which is characteristic of Pashtun tribal politics. Initially, the founder of the Rowshani movement tried to attract as many personal followers as he could, forming with them classical Sufi master-disciple relationships. However, individual relationships resembling the organization of a traditional Sufi brotherhood turned into a new kind of institution, often described as "maraboutic Sufism." In this form of Sufism, affiliation to the spiritual guide is based on a collective adherence of a clan or tribe to a Sufi Master's family. This body of followers forms an Islamic coalition addressing a particular religious issue, which also acquires a political dimension. This Sufi-tribal alliance did not last long, as both Rowshani doctrine and political practice undermined tribal structures. The tribes, wishing to preserve their identity, eventually deserted the movement. This led to the defeat of the Rowshani movement and its eventual collapse.

The Rowshani literary period lasted for about a century from the end of the sixteenth to the second half of the seventeenth century. It was followed by the post-Rowshani period, when the religious heritage of the sectarians was suppressed but their literary techniques were imitated and further developed by a new generation of Pashtun authors.

Rowshani authors and their works

As stated above, the beginning of an independent literary tradition in Pashto is associated with the Rowshani movement, which apart from being a significant intellectual and political event in the history of the Pashtuns, made a profound impact on their literary tradition.

Among a significant number of theological treatises and mystical poetry in Pashto written during the Rowshani period, the *Kheyr al-bayân* by Bâyazid Ansâri occupies a central place. The book's title, *Kheyr al-bayân* (The Best Explanation or The Best Revelation), was suggested by its form, which is a manifesto of the Rowshani creed presented as a direct conversation between God and Bâyazid Ansâri. The latter insisted that the *Kheyr al-bayân* was a divine revelation (*elhâm*), and wanted his disciples to follow its teachings throughout their lives. The followers of the Rowshani movement regarded the *Kheyr al-bayân* as their sacred book which, like the *Qor'an*, had some mystical power. According to Ali-Mohammad Mokhles, the author of another important Rowshani work, *Hâlnâme-ye Bâyazid Rowshân*, which is predominantly in Persian, Bâyazid Ansâri is the sole author of the *Kheyr al-bayân* (Mokhles 1986, p. 388). Other sources which mention this book confirm Mokhles' statement. The only exception is Âkhund Darwêza, a bitter antagonist of the Rowshani movement, who asserts: "He did not compose it all himself, for some of it was written by the atheist poet Mollâ Arzâni [Bâyazid's *khalife* (representative or successor) and the author of a *Divân* of Rowshani poetry], and some of it this accursed one himself compiled." In the next passage Darwêza specifies Arzâni's contribution: "The poems [of Mollâ Arzâni] were inserted into Bâyazid's book" (Darwêza 1892, p. 149). This claim is supported by the modern Afghan scholar Khâdem, who writes: "According to the tradition (*naql dǝy*) Mollâ Arzâni took an active part in writing and editing the *Kheyr al-bayân*" (Khâdem 1945, p. 55). It is unclear whether the Afghan scholar relies on oral tradition or merely aims to support Âkhund Darwêza's view. However, the Berlin manuscript of the *Kheyr al-bayân* contains no poetry at all, and Mollâ Arzâni's participation is not mentioned in it. The style of the book is uniform; it is all written in rhymed prose (*saj'*). Since the *Kheyr al-bayân* was considered to be the Rowshani "Holy Scripture," it is unlikely that a disciple would have dared to add anything to this canonical text. It seems likely, therefore, that

PASHTO LITERATURE: THE CLASSICAL PERIOD

Darwêza's remarks were merely an attempt to discredit the claim of a divine origin of the *Kheyr al-bayân*.

The work is composed in the form of a dialogue between Bâyazid Ansâri and God, who is addressed as the Glory (*sobhân*). In every passage God gives the author some instructions on problems of religion, and his utterances are supported by quotations, sometimes erroneous, from the *Qor'an* and *hadith*, as well as some didactic sayings in Arabic by an unnamed guide (*hâdi*).[5] Bâyazid Ansâri answers Him with eloquent glorification and the description of his own humbleness.

The *Kheyr al-bayân* consists of three distinct parts, the first being a lengthy introduction to the second. This introduction is primarily devoted to the examination of the nature of God and the ways to know Him. The inevitability of death and the Day of Judgment are also considered. Bâyazid Ansâri describes his own importance for the religion and comments on the nature of his revelation. The second part is an account of eight "stations" (*maqâmât*) of spiritual perfection, of their essence, and of the actions prescribed for the believer at every *maqâm*. The third and shortest part is an abstract of the entire book where the main ideas of the *Kheyr al-bayân* are summarized, often in the same words as in the introductory part.

The entire Pashto text is in terse rhymed prose (*saj'*), with almost all phrases rhyming in -*ân* or -*âm*. This genre and rhyme were evidently inspired by the first verses of the *Surat al-Rahmân* of the *Qor'an*, since it is stated in the *Kheyr al-bayân* that God had ordered Bâyazid Ansâri to model his book on this *sura* (Bâyazid Ansâri 1967, p. 13). In order to keep the rhyme, Persian words with appropriate endings are introduced where Pashto does not provide the necessary rhyme. From the stylistic point of view the book is remarkable for its length, poor structure, and consistent repetition of the same ideas.

Since the publication of the first article on the Rowshani movement (Leiden 1810), there has been a general consensus that the *Kheyr al-bayân* was composed in four languages: Pashto, Persian,

---

5   The use of the word *hâdi* seems to be a narrative device enabling the author to quote popular pious sayings.

Arabic and an Indian language. It seems that this view was based on a paragraph of the famous *Dabestân-e madhâheb*, an "Encyclopedia of Religions," which states: "... and this [*Kheyr al-bayân*] is in four languages (*be chahâr zabân*): the first in Arabic, the second in Persian, the third in an Indian language (*hendi*), the fourth in Pashto... the same subject is conveyed in [the] four languages" (Mowbad Keykhosrow 1983, p. 283). Besides, Bâyazid Ansâri himself wrote "I [God] shall reveal the *Kheyr al-bayân* to you, through my power, in four languages" (Bâyazid Ansâri 1967, p. 17). However, when the Berlin Pashto manuscript dated 1061/1651 was rediscovered in 1959, it was assumed that the book as a whole was initially written in Pashto with some insertions in Arabic and Persian, whereas the first eight pages had been in Arabic, Persian, Pashto, and an Indian language, in that order (MacKenzie 1964). Indeed, only the first pages of the introductory part of this manuscript are written in four languages. The same subject is conveyed repeatedly, passage by passage, first in Arabic, then in Persian, Pashto, and an unidentified Indian language (just over a hundred words). Qor'anic quotations following each version often differ from each other. The multilingual versions continue as far as fol. 8 of the manuscript, before the second quotation of the standard formula, *besme'llâh*. Thereafter the narration is entirely in Pashto, with some Arabic quotations and their Persian translation.

However, in the early 1980s the Afghan scholar Zalmay Hêwâdmal discovered another manuscript of the *Kheyr al-bayân* in the library of the Salarjang Museum in Hyderabad. In this manuscript (dating from 1079/1668), the entire text is given in all four languages, and without an interchange of the languages. All versions except the Persian one are vocalized (Hêwâdmal 1984, pp. 9–10). Furthermore, S. A. A. Rizvi (1966–68, pp. 93, 97) reports on the existence of a Persian translation of the *Kheyr al-bayân* which is kept in the Riza Library in Rampur. It is written in simple Persian and the sentences are occasionally incomplete and unintelligible. It is not clear whether this manuscript represents the Persian portion of the book or a translation.

At first glance, the fact that the *Kheyr al-bayân* was conveyed in all four languages may contradict the Rowshani assertion that the book represents a divine revelation sent specifically to the Pashtuns in their native tongue. However, it should be noted that by the nature of his mission as a Pir, and his anti-tribal activities, Bâyazid Ansâri was bound to make some universalist claims. He therefore had to cope with the two-fold nature of a message that was specifically addressed to Pashtuns, but implicitly also to non-Pashtuns. Besides, the fact that only the Pashto version has been copied (the Berlin MS), may indicate that only this Pashto version was considered sacred.

Concerning the Pashto of the *Kheyr al-bayân*, one has to agree that the text holds few surprises apart from the spelling, and contains few unknown or uncertain words. According to Georg Morgenstierne, the first linguist who briefly studied the *Kheyr al-bayân*, Bâyazid Ansâri's language in the main corresponds to that of the ordinary "classical" Pashto literature, which is based upon the Momand-Yusufzay type of dialect, and is different from the Waziri dialect of his birthplace. Certain peculiarities can be noticed in the plurals, pronouns (Morgenstierne 1939–40, pp. 568–69), and conjugation of the link-verb (Mannanov 1970, p. 42). However, the absence of the final letter in the conjugation of the link-verb in third person *dəy/da* may be due to the general orthographic tendency to omit final vowels. The text is also characterized by awkward syntax and certain corrupted or archaic grammatical forms, especially in the ergative construction, and by its vocabulary. Therefore, the meaning of the text is sometimes obscure.

From a linguistic point of view the orthography is the most remarkable peculiarity of the *Kheyr al-bayân*, since it employs letters unfamiliar in later Pashto (cf. Morgenstierne 1939–40, pp. 567–68; Reshâd 1975; Kushev 1980, pp. 102–13). Morgenstierne argues that the fact that the same orthographic peculiarities are also found in other medieval Pashto manuscripts points to a previous literary tradition. He bases his argument on the circumstance that some of the Pashto consonants used in the *Kheyr al-bayân* are also employed by Âkhund Darwêza, and writes that "it is not conceivable that this defender of the faith should, even in matters of orthography, have borrowed from his despised opponent" (Morgenstierne 1939–40, p. 568). However, despite his hatred Âkhund Darwêza found it possible to imitate the literary style of the *Kheyr al-bayân*, as can be seen in his Pashto writings. Moreover, only four letters out of eleven specific Pashto consonants are used by both Bâyazid Ansâri and Âkhund Darwêza (see Kushev 1980).

According to popular Pashtun tradition, Bâyazid Ansâri invented the Pashto alphabet. This claim may have some foundation, since it is announced in the *Kheyr al-bayân* immediately after the introductory *besme'llâh*, that God had instructed Bâyazid in Pashto orthography and ordered him to use special diacritical marks. Then all letters of the Pashto alphabet are given. This statement appears to support the claim that the *Kheyr al-bayân* may indeed be the first work written in this graphic system, or at least it suggests that at this time the Pashto alphabet still required explanation and even "divine" legitimization. It makes Morgenstierne's argument concerning a well-established pre-Rowshani literary tradition seem more questionable.

Bâyazid Ansâri's Persian and Arabic are awkward and corrupt, even in the direct quotations from the *Qor'an*, and it was harshly ridiculed by his opponent Âkhund Darwêza.

Apart from writing *Kheyr al-bayân*, Bâyazid Ansâri also composed a number of shorter works in Pashto as well as in Persian and Arabic. Two of his Pashto *Resâles* are extant. *Də elm resâla* (Treatise on Knowledge) occupies a special place, since it does not deal with problems connected with the highest levels of mystic perfection, but with the initial stage obligatory for every neophyte (*shari'at*). Therefore, this treatise is a kind of introduction to the Rowshani creed and religious practice. Its content is arranged according to the five pillars of Islam. Observance of these "pillars" by a follower of the Rowshani doctrine does not differ from that of other Muslims. A specific Rowshani perspective becomes apparent only in the spiritual interpretation of these acts. Since *Də elm resâla* was designed for neophytes, it only briefly mentions the mystical interpretation of the pillars of Islam. Throughout the book Bâyazid Ansâri notes that this interpretation is to be revealed in full only on the higher levels of spiritual perfection of the seeker. The author also briefly mentions that on these higher levels the performance of the ritual acts is altered because of their mystical interpretation.

PASHTO LITERATURE: THE CLASSICAL PERIOD

Dǝ elm resâla was written in Pashto with some Arabic insertions. The whole text is in rhymed prose, which ends with an *-ina* rhyme, and with *mesrâ*'s and *beyt*s of different lengths. While Bâyazid Ansâri's account of ritual acts is simple and straightforward, his comments on mystical issues are difficult to translate because of the obscure language and mystic semantics. The author also makes frequent use of allusions, about which he warns in the beginning: "I speak not clearly but with implications. But they will be sufficient for those who are perspicacious" (Bâyazid Ansâri 1986, p. 3). Illegible sections in the manuscripts further add to the difficulties, as was noted by the editor.

Stylistically, the book is not uniform. The first part is devoted to general theological problems which are skillfully described, while the second part of the book contains lengthy monotonous descriptions of ritual acts. *Dǝ elm resâla* consists of an extensive introduction and twenty-four chapters. The chapters in the manuscripts are not numbered. Every chapter begins with an introductory formula written in red in the manuscripts.

Bâyazid Ansâri is known to be the author of another *resâle* entitled *Farhat al-mojtabâ* (The Joy of the Select). A copy of this treatise has been bound together with the Delhi manuscript of *Dǝ elm resâla*. There is another Rowshani treatise by Ali Mohammad Mokhles of the same *resâle* genre in the same codex chapters (Hêwâdmal 1984, 11, pp. 213–15).

Mirzâ Khan Ansâri, whom Caroe (1964, p. 229) described as "the most mystical of Pakhto poets," was probably the most prominent Rowshani author expressing the ideas of Bâyazid Ansâri in poetical form. He was admired by many Pashtun poets. The date of his birth is unknown. Probably he was a son of Nur-al-Din, the second son of Bâyazid Ansâri.[6]

---

6 The Rowshani poet Dowlat Lawâñay and the author of the *Dabestân-e Madhâheb* refer to a certain Mirzâ, son of Nur-al-Din (see Khâdem 1945, p. 50; Mowbad Keykhosrow 1983, p. 286). Raverty (1862, p. 51) reports that Qâsem Ali Afridi, a Pashtun poet from India, states in one of his odes that Mirzâ Khan was of the family of Bâyazid Ansâri. Mirzâ Khan (1976, p. 55) himself writes that he originates "from the light of pure *miyân*." This statement may imply that he is one of Bâyazid Ansâri's descendants, since the founder of the Rowshani movement was often called *Miyân-e Rawśân* (Master of Light).

According to the *Dabestân*, Mirzâ Khan lived in the time of the Emperor Khoshhâl Jahân (r. 1628–57) and was killed in the battle of Dowlatâbâd. Dowlat Lawâñay (in Habibi 1950, I, p. 81) states that he was killed in 1630–31 fighting in the Deccan. The city of Dowlatâbâd was conquered by the imperial troops in 1633 after a long military campaign in the Deccan. The "battle of Dowlatâbâd" mentioned in the *Kheyr al-bayân*, may not be the final assault of 1633. Thus, it seems reasonable to assume that Mirzâ Khân died sometime between 1630 and 1633. The year 1042/1630, which is referred to in one of his poems, is a *terminus post quem*.

There is also a view (first expressed by Raverty (1862, p. 51) and later upheld by Habibi (1950, I, pp. 80–81)), that the real name of Mirzâ Khan Ansâri was Fath Khan of the Yusufzay tribe, and Mirzâ was a pen-name (*takhallos*). However, there are strong indications that Mirzâ Khan Ansâri and Fath Khan were two different persons (cf. Blumhardt and MacKenzie 1965, p. 64).

According to popular tradition Mirzâ Khan was a great traveler and was well known from Herat to Agra. He had numerous disciples in Swat, Bajaur, Kandahar and Herat. Not participating in any Rowshani military campaigns, he lived quietly in one of the semi-independent Rajput states. He received a pension from the Mughal authorities but did not like to attend the court where he had numerous enemies. It is also said that in the latter years of his life, when married and settled in Tirah, he renounced the Rowshani creed and repented of everything he had written. On this ground he won great respect of the scholars of Peshawar, and his descendants, who lived among the Miyan Khêl in Tirah, were respected long after his death (Raverty 1862, pp. 52–55; Caroe 1964, p. 229).

In his *Divân*, Mirzâ Khan Ansâri comments on the essence of God, his oneness and man's unity with him. Altogether 202 *qasides* and *ghazals*, one *mokhammas*, and one poem entitled "Conversation of a Candle and a Butterfly," as well as a short poetical treatise on the Pashto alphabet written by Mirzâ Khan Ansâri, are known. Contrary to the general opinion of Pashtun scholars, he did not use *aruz*; the meter of his works is not quantitative (i.e., determined by the lengths of syllables). However, the number of syllables in every line is equal, and the rhythm is provided by flexible stress in

PASHTO LITERATURE: THE CLASSICAL PERIOD

the manner of popular Pashto songs. He rarely employs traditional poetical symbols (*dust, mey*), or Sufi terminology, but makes extensive use of Qor'anic vocabulary. His rhyming is very precise, and he often employs internal rhyme. Mirzâ Khan's archaic Pashto corresponds to the Eastern dialect.

A famous Rowshani poet Mollâ Arzâni Khwesgi is the author of the oldest extant *Divân*s in Pashto. Despite his dislike of the Rowshani movement, Âkhund Darwêza admits that Arzâni was a good poet and had a sharp mind. He also writes: "He turned all the tenets of the new faith into poetry, and his poems were inserted into Bâyazid's book" (Darwêza 1892, pp. 148–49). He further states that Arzâni wrote poetry in four languages: Arabic, Persian, "Indian," and Pashto, and claims that he participated in the writing of the *Kheyr al-bayân*. Later, he left Bâyazid Ansâri and went to India but his brothers remained with the founder of the Rowshani movement. Arzâni outlived Bâyazid Ansâri by a long time since in one of his poems (Arzâni, *Divân*, fol. 1b) he wrote: "Arzâni wrote these words in the year *alf tes'a* (1009 H.Q., i.e. 1600)." Arzâni's *Divân*, which is kept in the British Library, contains fifty poems with only one *qaside* and forty-nine *ghazals*[7] devoted to the examination of the central elements of the Rowshani doctrine, i.e., God's oneness with the material world, His manifestations in this world and the ways of knowing him. Stylistically, Arzâni's verses are of poor quality with awkward metaphors. None of the poems of the London *Divân* complies with the rules of *aruz*. The poems in this *Divân* are placed in alphabetical order according to the final letter of the rhyme. Only thirty letters of the Pashto alphabet are used for these final rhymes. Arzâni himself placed his poems in this order, since he testifies (*Divân*, fol. 1b): "I composed a *Divân* in the Pashto language with thirty letters." In 1977 Afghan scholars reported the discovery of unknown writings of Arzâni in the library of Afghanistan's Ministry of Culture and Information. They are Pashto quatrains (*robâ'i*, written according to the a a b a rhyme-scheme) on the eight stages of spiritual perfection as described by Bâyazid Ansâri,

---

[7] *Pace* Blumhardt and MacKenzie (1965, p. 59), who claim that it consists of 49 "odes" (*qaside*).

and on the life of the Prophet Mohammad (Hêwâdmal 1977; Rafi' 1976). In his account of Arzâni, Âkhund Darwêza also mentioned that he had written a book entitled *Chahâr *Rəmâ*, "which is full of delusions and mistakes" from the point of view of this orthodox author.[8] Nothing else is known about this book. According to the *Hâlnâme*, Arzâni is also the author of a work entitled *Mir'âth al-mohaqqeqin* (Mokhles 1986, p. 272).

Apart from being co-author and editor of *Hâlnâme-ye Bâyazid Rowshân*, Ali Mohammad Mokhles is also known as the author of Rowshani verses in Pashto. The only known eighteenth-century manuscript of his poems is kept in the British Library. The orthography is typical for the author's time. This manuscript consists of three distinct parts containing 370 *ghazal*s, 118 *robâ'i*s, and Qor'anic *sura*s. The first 28 *ghazal*s are written according to the *Alefnâme* scheme, i.e. the first word of every poem begins with the letter *alef* and the last word ends with the letter *yâ*. Beginning from the thirty-first poem, all *ghazal*s are in alphabetic order according to the final rhymes. Most of the poems have headings or introductions in Persian, written in red ink. The second section of the manuscript contains *robâ'i*s, not arranged in any particular order. The third part of the volume was written by a different scribe. It contains the Qor'anic *sura*s 67, 1–24, 73, and 12–20, followed by prayers in Arabic. In his *Divân*, Mokhles presents Bâyazid Ansâri's doctrine in a poetical form, concentrating mainly on the unity of God and the world.

Another book by Mokhles is a small theological treatise on *Haqiqat* (Truth). This work was written in prose with the insertion of some Pashto verses by Mokhles himself and other Rowshani poets. It has been identified as belonging to the *Resâle* genre (Hêwâdmal 1984, pp. 213–15).

A number of other Rowshani authors still remain relatively obscure. Little is known about their lives since they are only briefly mentioned by their admirers or opponents. Their works, apart from those published in Afghan periodicals, remain inaccessible.

---

8   Darwêza 1892, p. 149. *rəmâ is probably a mistake for *ramâ'* (excess, addition, increase, usury).

PASHTO LITERATURE: THE CLASSICAL PERIOD

Dowlat Lawâṅay (Lohâṅay) is a Rowshani author who, together with Mirzâ Khan Ansâri, was described by Khoshhâl Khan Khattak (Khaṯak 1960, pp. 861–62) as a talented Pashtun poet. Khâdem (1945, p. 55) mentions him as the tenth and last Rowshani *khalife* and writes that he died approximately one hundred years after Bâyazid Ansâri. This date seems dubious, since Khoshhâl Khan (Khaṯak 1960, pp. 861–62), who died in 1689 (i.e., approximately one hundred years after Bâyazid), refers to Dowlat in the past tense. The only date that can be established in connection with Dowlat's life is the year 1648, when Rashid Khan, Bâyazid Ansâri's grandson and the patron of Ali-Mohammad Mokhles, died. Mannanov (1983–84, p. 83) reports that Dowlat wrote an ode on Rashid Khan's death. Only a few of his poems were published.

Vâsel Rawśâni is mentioned in some sources related to the Rowshani movement. The *Dabestân-e Madhâheb* mentions him in passing as one of Bâyazid Ansâri's associates (Mowbad Keykhosrow 1983, p. 281). Khoshhâl Khan Khattak (1960, p. 78) and Mirzâ Khan Ansâri (1970, p. 63) mention Vâsel as a poet in their *Divâns*. In 1975 Vâsel's *Divân*, containing one *qaside* and fifteen *ghazals*, was published by Abd-al-Shokur Reshâd (Vâsel 1975). In his poetry, Vâsel discusses the necessity and benefits of spiritual perfection in a lapidary style.

According to the *Hâlnâme*, Mowdud, one of the *khalife*s of Bâyazid Ansâri, wrote a book entitled *Maqsud-e tâlebin* (Objectives of the Seekers; Mokhles 1986, pp. 272–89). This treatise is fully quoted in the *Hâlnâme*. It comprises pious anecdotes, admonitions (*nasâ'eḥ*) and verses in Persian and Pashto illustrating the author's points.

In emphasizing the importance of the Rowshani movement for Pashtun culture, I refer not only to the amount and significance of the texts produced by the followers of the movement and their opponents, but also to the beginning of the conscious use of the Pashto language. The fact that the sixteenth and seventeenth centuries witnessed the emergence of a Pashto literary tradition cannot be explained by the mere convenience of the use of one's native tongue. It was provoked by one of the central Rowshani ideas, *viz.* that God sends his messengers to peoples speaking their native languages. Therefore, just as the Arabic-speaking Mohammad was a prophet to the Arabs, Bâyazid Ansâri was considered an all-important spiritual guide to the Pashtuns. As was mentioned earlier, the founder of the Rowshani movement was not himself a Pashtun. He belonged to a family known as Ansâr (i.e. held to be descended from a Companion of the Prophet Mohammad), residing with the Ormur people. However, as often happens to charismatic leaders, he was not welcomed in his native community and eventually was forced to look for refuge among the Pashtuns, where he began to put his teaching into written shape.

Bâyazid Ansâri wrote in Arabic and Persian as well as Pashto. Sometimes, he wrote with his intended audience in mind, as in the case of *Serât al-towhid*, which was written especially for the Emperor Akbar. Like many other Muslim thinkers, at times he simply followed the well-established tradition of writing in Arabic and Persian, the languages of theology and high culture. However, the fact that he found it necessary to write his most important work, the *Kheyr al-bayân*, in Pashto appears to be of the utmost importance for understanding the nature of the Rowshani movement, as well as for the future development of the Pashtun culture.

After the military defeat of the movement in the 1630s, the Rowshaniyya disappeared as a political force and a significant religious factor in Pashtun life (see Andreyev 1994); its cultural heritage, however, outlived the movement's political and ideological influence.

Âkhund Darwêza

Âkhund Darwêza (1533–1638), a well-known and respected Muslim theologian, was the main ideological adversary of the Rowshani movement. He left two major accounts of it which provide a lengthy and extremely hostile view of "the Rowshani heresy," namely *Tadhkerat al-abrâr wa'l-ashrâr* in Persian, and *Makhzan al-Eslâm* in Pashto. Âkhund Darwêza originated from a distinguished family and lived a long and active life described by the Âkhund himself in his autobiography, included into his main Persian work, *Tadhkerat al-abrâr* (see above).

PASHTO LITERATURE: THE CLASSICAL PERIOD

Âkhund Darwêza is known under two *nisba*s: Nangrahâri, referring to the homeland of his ancestors; and Pêśâwari (Peshawari), referring to his place of residence. His name, Darwêza (alms), may be either his original name or an adopted *takhallos*, since his father's name was Gadây (mendicant). Among the Pashtuns he was also known under the honorific title of Khund Bâbâ (Kushev 1980, p. 39). Darwêza came from a family of mixed Turkic-Persian-Pashtun origin, which for several generations had lived among the Pashtuns. Darwêza's grandfather, Shaikh Sa'di, and his ancestors are described as having migrated from one Pashtun tribe to another and being granted extensive parcels of land by these tribes (Caroe 1964, p. 200).

From his childhood, Darwêza was interested in religious studies. He studied under the guidance of many Shaikhs, of whom the most famous was Sayyed Mir Ali Ghawwâth Termedhi, called Pir Bâbâ, a champion of Hanafi orthodoxy whose name and tomb are still venerated by the Pashtuns. Âkhund Darwêza not only became a disciple of the famous Shaikh, but his close associate and aide as well.

According to his own words, Âkhund Darwêza joined four Sufi *tariqat*s: the Kobraviyya, Chishtiyya, Sohrawardiyya and Shattariyya.[9] However, the authors of various *Tadhkere*s testify that he belonged to the Chishtiyya brotherhood (Lâhori 1902, p. 40). Having completed his studies, Darwêza started to preach among the Pashtuns and gained considerable renown.[10] The Âkhund died at an advanced age in 1638 and was buried in Peshawar.

9 In the sixteenth and seventeenth centuries, the era of the spread of popular Sufism in the region, affiliation to a particular Sufi master became more significant than membership of a brotherhood. Since Sufi guides became political figures and witch-doctors, affiliation to a number of Sufi authorities became possible. For more educated men, Sufi affiliation became a formality which was necessary for the improvement of their social status. Thus, despite his Sufi connections, Âkhund Darwêza was first and foremost a legalistic *âlem* who displayed no Sufi ideas in his writings.

10 However, the Pashtuns' attitude towards Âkhund Darwêza was not uncritical. Khoshhâl Khan Khattak, himself an orthodox Sunni Muslim, reproached the Yusufzays in his poem *Swât-nâma* for their veneration of Âkhund Darwêza, whom he regarded as a modest authority who gained fame only because of the low level of contemporary scholarship. Khoshhâl Khan also criticized Darwêza's style for lack of literary skills.

Darwêza was an industrious writer. According to Raverty (1867, p. 33) he left some fifty works, of which only a few are now known. Kushev (1980, p. 40), however, considers this an exaggeration and thinks that some chapters of Darwêza's books may have been counted as separate works. Although Âkhund Darwêza is traditionally regarded as the sole author of all his treatises, it seems that the contribution of his son Mollâ Abd-al-Karim, better known as Âkhund Karimdâd, was considerable. In the concluding part of *Tadhkerat al-abrâr wa'l-ashrâr*, Karimdâd states that the book was dictated to him by his elderly father, and that he wrote it down, later redrafted and arranged the text in the proper order, and gave it its title (Darwêza 1892, p. 220). Kushev (1969, pp. 95–98; 1980, pp. 40–43, 47) has proved that Karimdâd also wrote a third of the *Makhzan al-Eslâm*, and was a co-author of many verses ascribed to Darwêza. It is known that Karimdâd edited at least six of his father's works.

Âkhund Darwêza was a bitter antagonist of Bâyazid Ansâri. He gave him the nickname of *Pir-e Târik* (Guide of Darkness), ridiculing his title of *Pir-e Rawśân* (Guide of Light). Together with his teacher, Ali Termeèdhi, Âkhund Darwêza participated in public debates with Bâyazid Ansâri. In his books Darwêza refutes the Rowshani doctrine and describes its followers as the worst heretics. Thus, the *Makhzan al-Eslâm* is a compendium of the Muslim faith written by Âkhund Darwêza with the specific aim of refuting the teachings of Bâyazid Ansâri. It is written in Pashto with Persian insertions, so like the *Kheyr al-bayân* it is aimed at the Pashtun audience, which it nevertheless severely reproaches for their ignorance of the Muslim faith (the very ignorance that allowed the "Rowshani heresy" to flourish). The first version of the book was written in 1605 by Darwêza himself; the second, which included Karimdâd's additions (about one third of the book) was finished in 1615. The final version has further additions and supplements by Darwêza's relatives and disciples: his brother Mollâ Asghar; his grandson Mohammad Abd-al-Halim, son of Darwêza's second son Abd-Allâh; and his great-grandson Mostafâ Mohammad, son of Miyân Nur-Mohammad, son of Karimdâd. It was completed by Mostafâ Mohammad in 1700. Every contributor, including Darwêza himself, mentions his authorship in the relevant sections of the book.

Originally the *Makhzan al-Eslâm* was divided into eight sections called *bayâns*, each section consisting of a few chapters called *bâb*, *fasl*, *aqida* or *noqta*. The first seven *bayâns* are devoted to the description of various legal and ritual problems, which are expounded according to the Hanafi doctrine. The eighth section is of particular importance for the study of the Rowshani movement, as it contains a detailed account of the life of Bâyazid Ansâri and his sons until the death of Jalâl-al-Din and the accession of Ahdâd as head of the movement. This section was probably written by Darwêza himself in Pashto and Persian. It is followed by an anti-Rowshani text in Pashto by Darwêza's brother Mollâ Asghar Ghâzi. This text is called a poem, although it has neither rhyme nor meter.

In his polemics against Bâyazid Ansâri, Âkhund Darwêza used the same style of rhymed prose (*saj'*) that was employed by his opponent in his Pashto treatises, and the reader gets the impression that stylistically the author(s) consciously imitated the *Kheyr al-bayân*. The whole book is written in a poor literary style, as is recognized by Karimdâd himself in a remark towards the end of the book. In those sections of the Makhzan which were written after Darwêza, the style is somewhat better and occasionally the rules of *aruz* are applied. A considerable part of the *Makhzan al-Eslâm* is a Pashto translation of well-known Arab and Persian authors. Later, along the lines of Darwêza's book, this tradition of the Pashto translation of (mainly Persian) classical works was developed in the post-Rowshani and Durrani periods of Pashto literature.

At present there are two extant versions of the *Makhzan al-Eslâm*. They differ considerably in the arrangement of chapters and slightly in their contents. The work is very popular among the Pashtuns and a large number of manuscripts of it are available in the Pashtun lands. Thirty-five copies, the earliest from the eighteenth century, are mentioned in the academic literature (see Blumhardt and MacKenzie 1965, pp. 1–27; Kushev 1976, pp. 77–92; Kushev 1980, pp. 44–47).

Khoshhâl Khan Khattak

The Rowshani movement continued to influence Pashtun literature even after its defeat. The most illustrious and renowned Pashtun poet of the post-Rowshani period, Khoshhâl Khan Khattak (1613–89), ferociously refuted the Rowshani movement. Nevertheless, he was proud to claim that as a master of the pen he was the equal of the famous Rowshani poets. Apart from being a towering figure in Pashto literature, Khoshhâl Khan Khattak was chief of the powerful Pashtun tribe of the Khattaks, and one of the most famous men of Afghan history and culture.

During the Pashtun expansion to the South in the 14th–17th centuries, the Khattaks settled between the Indus River and Peshawar. They occupied a strategic position and controlled the vitally important Khyber Pass, which connects India with what is now Afghanistan. Thus they became one of the few Pashtun tribes to come into close contact with the Mughal Empire. In Akbar's time, Khoshhâl Khan's great-grandfather, Malik Ako or Akoray, received the *jâgir* (i.e., a piece of land given as compensation to a favorite so that he could use its product) of the plain from Kheyrâbâd to Nowshera, in return for providing protection of the road from India to Afghanistan.

As a hereditary chief of the tribe, Khoshhâl Khan at first continued to cooperate with the Great Mughals. However, as a result of the intrigues of the governor of Kabul and his own uncles, he was arrested in April 1664, after the death of the emperor Shah Jahân, and sent in chains to India where he spent more than two years in custody. When he was released from the imperial prison he joined the rebel confederacy of the Pashtun Afridi and Momand tribes. Until 1676 Khoshhâl Khan fought the powerful Mughal Empire, at times as leader of a tribal confederacy and towards the end with a mere handful of his comrades-in-arms. The Emperor Awrangzêb considered the tribal rebellion serious enough to take personal control of affairs, and remained encamped in Attock for two years. As usual in their dealings with the Pashtuns, the Mughals used the power of gold. They succeeded in bribing some clans and Khoshhâl Khan lost the tribal support. He therefore resigned the tribal chieftainship in favor of his eldest son Ashraf, and devoted himself to books and literature.

However, he could not rest in peace; his relatives, and even his own son Bahrâm, tried to kill him, as they were afraid of the elderly chief's influence on his tribesmen. Khoshhâl Khan was forced to leave his country and died in the land of the friendly tribe of Afridi.

Besides his military fame, Khoshhâl Khan is known to every Pashtun for his literary work. According to the Pashtun tradition he wrote 350 books, besides poems included in his *Divân*. The figure is no doubt an exaggeration. Nevertheless, he is the author of numerous works, both in Persian and Pashto, on a wide range of subjects such as war and statecraft, medicine, divination, falconry, house-building, childrearing, theology and ethics. He left an account of his checkered life and his family history as well as some translations from Arabic. In his poems, Khoshhâl Khan (like the Rowshani poet Mirzâ Khan Ansâri before him) adapted the natural meters of popular Pashto songs to the verse forms inherited from Persian. His meter is still syllabic, but the rhythm is created by stress, which is not fixed in Pashto. The stress usually recurs on every fourth syllable (MacKenzie 1958, pp. 319–20; 1965, p. 13). Although Khoshhâl Khan tried to imitate classical Persian poetry, he could not compete with the great Persian poets in poetical mastery and depth of thought. His poetry is courageous, harsh and straightforward. As a proud and warlike Pashtun, he is quite distinct from the sophisticated and elegant Persian poets.

Khoshhâl Khan wrote consciously as a national poet, the first to express nationalist sentiment for uniting all Pashtuns. Motivated by a strong desire to liberate his fellow countrymen from the Mughals, he used his poetical gift as a weapon in the political and military struggle. In his *Divân*, Khoshhâl Khan covers all the subjects that preoccupied him during his long and active life. He wrote about religious problems, national hopes, personal ambitions and failures, erotic experience, and everyday business.

Some of Khoshhâl Khan's verses are devoted to the refutation of the Rowshani "heresy" and praise of the "piety" of the movement's opponents, as well as to the description of the way of life of the tribes associated with the Rowshaniyya. Khoshhâl Khan's description of the social conditions of these tribes and their expulsion of traditional Muslim *ulema* constitutes unique information not found in any other source. Since Khoshhâl Khan's *Divân* is very popular among the Pashtuns, it exists in numerous manuscript copies as well as printed editions. Poems of the famous Pashtun poet have been translated into English and Russian several times; recently a comprehensive and thorough study of Khoshhâl Khan's poetical legacy (Pelevin 2001) has appeared, to which those interested in more details should refer.

Rahmân Bâbâ and Abd-al-Hamid

Two younger contemporaries of Khoshhâl Khan Khattak, Abd-al-Rahmân (better known as Rahmân Bâbâ, *c.* 1632–1708) and Abd-al-Hamid (*c.* 1660–1732), both of the Momand tribe, differed considerably from the Khattak chief. They were Sufis, little interested in politics, warfare and adventurous pursuits. Instead, Rahmân Bâbâ concentrated on the nature of divine love and its all-embracing power, whilst the more pessimistic Abd-al-Hamid saw the world as an endless combination of colors and shades that constantly and arbitrarily interchange, making man a passive observer of this perpetual game. The two poets differed not only in their mental outlook, but also in their poetical technique. Rahmân Bâbâ, who even now enjoys considerable fame among Pashtuns, achieved an admirable simplicity in his verses, which in general follow the rules of folk poetry. Abd-al-Hamid was the most enthusiastic protagonist of the Indian style of Persian poetry in Pashto literature. He even succeeded in adapting Pashto to the rules of *aruz*.

Later classical poetry

This period lasted until the establishment of the first quasi-state formations in the Pashtun lands, viz. the Ghilzay principality of Kandahar (1709–38) and the Durrani "Empire" founded in 1747. The rulers of these quasi-states tried to imitate the court life of their Persian and Mughal neighbors, and patronized court poetry which was modeled on the Persian example (and strongly influenced by the "Indian style" of Persian poetry, which not only pervaded the Persian poetry of Afghanistan, but also made a strong impact on the writing technique of some Pashtun poets). The situation was somewhat different in Kandahar, where the principality's last ruler, Shah Hoseyn (r. 1725–38), who himself wrote ballads (*badəla*) in the manner of folk Pashtun poets, patronized Pashto poetry, founded the first ever society of Pashto poets, and ordered the collection of Rahmân Bâbâ's poetry in Peshawar. Ahmad Shah (r. 1721–73), the founder of the Durrani dynasty (a talented poet who left a well-known *Divân* of contemplative lyrical poetry), also promoted the Pashto language. Due to the work of Ahmad Shah's fellow poets Sheydâ, Abd-al-Rasul, and Qâsem-Ali Apriday, Pashto literature again gained considerable momentum in the middle and second half of the eighteenth century, for the second time after the Rowshani literary activities.

However, during the reign of Ahmad Shah's son Timur Shah (paradoxically also a Pashto poet, albeit much less talented than his father), Persian gained the upper hand, which signaled the beginning of the decline of the Pashto literary tradition. Although the ruling dynasties were always Pashtun, the language was considered barbaric, and was banned from court life and marginalized. Pashto literary activities were confined to the fringes of Durrani society, where many poets nevertheless continued to write Pashto poetry mainly for a non-elite public. This situation lasted until the commencement of the modern period in the 1930s, when Pashto was proclaimed the national language of Afghanistan together with Dari (or "Fârsi-Kâboli"), and the country's cultural and political life began to be dominated by Pashtun nationalism.

3. Prose writing

Apart from poetry, Pashtun authors also produced prose works. Prose writing was not restricted to theological treatises such as those of Bâyazid Ansâri and Âkhund Darwêza. Perhaps continuing the tradition of Shaikh Mali's *Daftar*, Pashtun writers paid much attention to compiling histories. Most of these dealt with contemporary events, but some attempted to present a general picture of Pashtun tribal history, starting from early times. Some of these histories were written in verse.

Afzal Khan Khattak (c. 1661/63–1747/48), the author of a compendium of tribal histories known as *Târikh-e morassa'* (The Bejeweled History), was a son of Ashraf Khan, the eldest son of Khoshhâl Khan Khattak. After a short spell as a chief of the Khattak tribe, he left his homeland for the friendly country of the Afridis in order to avoid confrontation with his relatives contending the chieftainship. Later he became a tribal aide to Shah Âlam, a son of the Mughal Emperor Awrangzêb, who subsequently succeeded to the throne under the name of Shah Âlam Bahâdor. After the death of Awrangzêb in 1707, Afzal Khan was left in charge of his tribe's old responsibility, namely the safety of the highway to Peshawar (Caroe 1964, p. 236).

The *Târikh-e morassa'* consists of an introduction (*moqaddama*), three chapters (*bâb*), seven "journals" (*daftar*), and a conclusion (*khâtema*). The three chapters and the first three *daftars* are a Pashto translation of the Persian *Makhzan-e afghâni* by Kh^wâje Ne'mat-Allâh al-Heravi, which describes the political history of the Afghan dynasties in India, including tribal genealogy and the hagiography of some Afghan shaikhs.

The rest of *Târikh-e morassa'*, which is based on various sources, is Afzal Khan's own work with the exception of copious extracts from Khoshhâl Khan Khattak's *Bayâz* (anthology), which are given in his own words. The fourth *daftar* is omitted in all available copies of the *Târikh-e morassâ'*, but is reported to have dealt with the events in Kabul. The fifth *daftar* mainly describes the genealogy and migration of various Pashtun tribes, and the sixth is devoted to the history of the Khattaks. The seventh *daftar* deals with the lives of various Pashtun shaikhs. The Rowshani movement is briefly mentioned in the last four *daftars* of the book.

Afzal Khan is also known as the author and translator of a few other books dealing with history and ethics; he also wrote a *tafsir* (commentary on the *Qor'an*).

Later in the eighteenth century the tradition of writing tribal histories, which was initiated by the *Târikh-e morassâ'*, was continued. Thus, a history of the Durrani tribe entitled *Tadhkerat al-moluk* was compiled at the time of Ahmad Shah (Raverty 1860, pp. 4–5). Besides, there exist a number of Pashto chronicles depicting the life and reign of the founder of the Durrani dynasty, namely the *Shâh-nâme* by Hâfez (a sizeable biography of Ahmad Shah in 3,700 *beyts* in the *mathnavi* or rhymed couplet form), the *Fatâvâ-ye Ahmad-shâhi* by Abd-Allâh, and the *Soluk al-ghazât* by Mollâ Masta. Tribal histories were not only written at the Durrani court, lesser chiefs also commissioned these works. Thus a history of the Yusufzays entitled *Tavârikh-e rahmatkhâni* by Pir Mo'azzam-Shâh, based on the abridged version of a Persian/Pashto treatise *Târikh-e afâghene* by Mirdâd Motizay Khalil, was prepared for the Pashtun chief Hâfez Rahmat Khan (Kushev 1980, pp. 66–67). Apart from tribal histories and chronicles in prose, Pashto literature has a well-developed tradition of writing versified histories, which lasted until the early twentieth century (see Girs 1984, pp. 20–25).

4. Conclusion

Thus, the classical period of Pashto literature spanning, more than three hundred years, saw the introduction and accommodation of some forms of classical Arabo-Persian literature. While the classical topoi of this literature were freely adopted by Pashtun authors, the rules of Arabo-Persian prosody were more difficult to follow because of the peculiarities of the Pashto language. However, by following the rules of folk poetry many Pashtun poets instinctively found a way out of this predicament. Nevertheless, aesthetically Pashto literature did not break new ground within the colossal cultural *oikoumenê* of Iranian literatures, and in many respects remained an imitation of classical Persian models, which usually arrived from India rather than from Iran or Central Asia.

CHAPTER 5

MODERN PASHTO WRITTEN LITERATURE

Leonard N. Bartlotti

1. Introduction

The role and function of modern Pashto written literature is best understood in relation to the larger socio-political developments and historical processes affecting the Pashtun people on both sides of the Pakistan-Afghanistan border, and the symbolic significance of the Pashto language in that context. Made up of over thirty major tribes and numerous sub-tribes, Pashtuns (Pakhtun, Pathan, *Paśtun*) are spread over a broad geographically and ecologically diverse area in eastern and southern Afghanistan, and in the North West Frontier (NWFP) and Baluchistan provinces in Pakistan. Roughly split between the two countries, they are the majority ethnic group in Afghanistan, and have been that country's traditional rulers since the establishment of the Durrani dynasty in 1747. Pashtuns comprise thirteen percent of Pakistan's 140 million population. Due to their strategic location along the mountainous northwest boundary of the Indian subcontinent, the ruggedly independent Pashtun have generally lived on the margins of an empire, whether that of the Mughals in the seventeenth century, or the British and Russians in the nineteenth and twentieth centuries. Pashtun ethnic identity is marked by patrilineal descent from a common ancestor, adherence to Islam, and the tribal code of honor (*paśtunwali*, commonly called *paśto*, whose main tenets are stereotypically described as including hospitality, revenge and the law of refuge (Ahmed 1980). In addition, some consider the Pashto language to be a fourth and indispensable attribute of Pashtun identity (Caroe 1985, p. 65; Evans-Von Krbek 1977, p. 12; cf. Bartlotti 2000, pp. 67–74). Many contemporary Pashtuns would agree with the assertion that "apart from some extreme examples, Pakhtun and Pakhto [language] are inextricable" (Evans-Von Krbek 1977, p. 12). The lexical and semantic interplay of "*paśto*" as language and "*paśto*" as manner and behavior is embodied in the saying, "He is a Pathan who does Pashto, not (merely) who speaks Pashto" (Barth 1959, p. 105). Thus, in spite of any external influences the Pashto written literary tradition can be understood as an expression of the important symbolic value of the language itself in defining the identity and boundaries of the Pashtun community, both historically and in the contemporary period.

Modern Pashto written literature can be said to have started after the beginning of the twentieth century, at a time when the Indian sub-continent was under British colonial rule, and Afghanistan was emerging from a buffer state (in the "Great Game" politics between Czarist Russia and Great Britain) into a true nation state. In 1893 the Durand Line was created to demarcate the border between Afghanistan and the British-controlled North West Frontier Province. This in effect established two competing zones of influence—linguistic as well as political—over the Pashtun tribes. Thus, in the perspective of this article, "Pashto literature" is more narrow in scope than "Afghan literature," as the latter term is used for the national literature of Afghanistan, which includes literature in Pashto, Afghan Persian (Dari), and other languages (e.g. Dupree 1981; cf. Wilson 1969, p. 82). However, "Pashto Literature" comprises the two streams of Pashto literature that developed on either side of the Afghanistan-Pakistan boundary. To the east, Pashto literature developed in a colonial environment strongly influenced by English, and with the emergence of Pakistan in 1947, by an increasingly Urdu-dominated state. In Afghanistan, despite Pashtun hegemony, Pashto literature developed in a context in which Persian, with its long and venerable written tradition, was a cultural force and lingua franca, the language of government, commerce, administration, education, and the urban educated elite.

Before the modern period, people wrote in classical forms and treated classical subjects in poetry and, to a much more limited extent, in prose. (See the previous Chapter.) "Language, religion, and tradition ... combined to shape literary styles, themes, and genre" (Wilson 1969, p. 82). British colonial influence on the education system, including the founding of institutions like Edwardes College (est. 1901, Peshawar) and Islamia College (est. 1913, later giving birth to Peshawar University) under Sâhebzâda Abd-al-Qayyum, introduced English literature to a generation of writers (Caroe 1985, p. 424; cf. Dani 1995, pp. 162–65, 218–19; Bausani and Blair, 1971, pp. 64–65). Having been influenced by trends and subjects within English literature—directly and through Urdu, Persian and other translations of English novels and short-stories, the forms of modern Pashto prose are largely derivative. Modern Pashto written literature as such can therefore be said to have developed under external influences and is eclectic and largely based on non-indigenous models (Dupree 1981, p. 18).

2. The development of modern Pashto literature

The Afghan tradition

Pashto literary developments in Afghanistan are intertwined with the larger Afghan literary movement as described by Bênawâ (1961/2, 1967/8), Nancy Hatch Dupree (1981; 1985), Ghani (1988), Majrooh (1990), and Wilson (1969). In Afghanistan at the beginning of the twentieth century, a certain intellectual stagnation began to thaw as intellectuals, with traditional backgrounds in Islam and the literary sciences and deep roots in their society and culture, began to assimilate new ideas from Western works in Persian, Arabic and Turkic translations, or in English and other European languages, and to produce original works (Majrooh 1990). Literary pioneer Mahmud Tarzi (1865–1933) and his bi-weekly *Serâj al-akhbâr* (Lamp of the News; October 1911 to December 1918), was the major force behind these developments. Educated in Turkey and Damascus, and steeped in the spirit of Islamic nationalism and modernism, Tarzi viewed literature as a vehicle of cultural change and urged the adoption of a European genre of expression (Gregorian, 1967; Wilson, 1969, p. 86–87). Through the forum of Tarzi's newspaper, "the first successful news medium in modern Afghan history," the short story, novelette, novel and literary essay were introduced, and writers were urged to experiment with new literary forms such as prose and drama (Gregorian 1967, p. 345; Dupree 1981, p. 18). Tarzi and the enlightened elite who gathered around him became "proselytizers for modernism" (Gregorian 1967, p. 350) and Afghan nationalism:

> Times of poetry are bygone. It is now the time of action and effort. The era is that of motor, rail, and electricity. The times of camels, oxen, and donkeys are bygone.[1]

Impressed by Western scientific and technological achievements and ideas, Tarzi sought to show the compatibility of the values of modern civilization with the true spirit and character of Islam, and the necessity of their introduction into Afghanistan. He attacked both European imperialism and the orthodox Muslim religious leaders' resistance to change. Education was a recurring theme in progressive rhetoric (Roy 1986, p. 16; cf. Sirat 1969). To promote interest in science and learning (and in part to satisfy Amir Habibullâh's interest in science fiction), Tarzi translated European literature like Jules Verne's *Around the World in Eighty Days*, *Twenty Thousand Leagues under the Sea*, and *The Hidden Island* into Persian; these were among the first books printed in Afghanistan (Gregorian 1967, p. 358; Dupree 1980, p. 439). From the Turkish he translated Hasan Fahmi Pasha's *International Law*, which introduced concepts of international justice and legal order into Afghanistan, and a five volume *History of the Russo-Japanese War*, celebrating, with most Asians, the defeat of the Russians (Gregorian 1967, p. 358; Wilson 1969, p. 87; Dupree 1980, p. 439).

Although *Serâj al-akhbâr* was written in Afghan Persian and carried only occasional verses in Pashto, with a circulation limited

---

1 *Serâj al-akhbâr* V, No. 6, p. 9, quoted in Gregorian 1967, p. 356.

primarily to court circles and urban centers in eastern and western Afghanistan (Gregorian 1967, p. 365), its influence on the development of Pashto literature should not be underestimated. On the eve of its publication, "excluding Qurans and some imported standard religious texts, the number of all other books published in Afghanistan, including classical Persian literary anthologies, did not exceed ten" (Gregorian 1967, pp. 349, 365). Tarzi's many writings and translations, and the popular prose and style of *Serâj al-akhbâr*, stimulated the development of modern Afghan literature and journalism (Gregorian 1967, p. 366). Poets, writers and literary scholars migrated from the provinces to the capital of Kabul, took on government jobs and joined the "Official Literary Society" (est. 1930). Writers like the Pashto poet Abd-al-Ra'uf Bênawâ (1913–85) and Abd-al-Rahmân Pazhwâk (b. 1919) emerged, who were rooted in the classical Persian heritage and drew upon key symbols of Afghan history, folklore and culture in their writings. Like their progressive counterparts in the North West Frontier Province, Afghan writers began to explore themes like democracy, progress, individual freedom, socio-political reform, Islamic unity, and nationhood, leading Majrooh (1990, p. 75) to call the first half of the twentieth century a period of "genuine renaissance in arts and literature." The process, begun with Tarzi, advanced by his son-in-law, Amir Amânollâh (1919–29), and unchanged by later groups including the communists, led to the creation of "an urban space" with Western values, which reinvented traditional society as a "pole of opposition" to the state and to progress (Roy 1986, p. 16).

Amir Habibollâh's patronage of Tarzi and his newspaper led to a wider circulation of Muslim revivalist-modernist thought among the country's prominent educators, literati, religious leaders, and members of the royal family. A national press began to develop in the mid-1920s during the period of Amir Amânollâh's aggressive reforms (cf. Poullada 1969). During King Nâder Shah's reign (1929–33) certain reforms were abolished, but Nâder Shah's previously underground Pashto newspaper *Eslâḥ* (Reformation) became an official government newspaper (Dupree 1980, pp. 459–60; Wilson 1969, p. 88). As there were no private cultural institutions, the small circle of Afghan intellectuals (1,590 students enrolled in thirteen schools in 1930) were dependent upon the government for employment as bureaucrats, officials and teachers; by 1940, "the majority of the individuals devoted to intellectual pursuits were salaried functionaries of the state" (Ghani 1988, p. 442). Years later, poets and literati like Abd-al-Rahmân Pazhwâk, Abd-al-Ra'uf Bênawâ, Khalilollâh Khalili, and others were to become the ambassadors, state ministers, and presidents representing and leading the modern Afghan state (Wilson 1969, pp. 92–93). This connection between state and literati, politics and culture, is a *leitmotiv* in modern Afghan intellectual history and can be viewed as an extension of the traditional nexus between literati and the Afghan court.

A new development emerged in 1930 when King Nâder Shah established the twelve member intellectual circle called the *Anjoman-e Adabi* (Literary Society; Wilson 1969, p. 88). The Society sponsored poetry readings and started the literary *Revue de Kabul* which published the work of their leader and poet laureate, Abdollâh Khan Qâri (1871–1943), who wrote patriotic and romantic (Persian) poetry; Abd-al-Hâdi Dâwi; and Khalilollâh Khalili (b. 1909); short stories and the novel were introduced in translated (not creative) prose forms (cf. Farhadi 1985). However, in 1935 the Literary Society established a separate department for the development of Pashto language and literature; in 1937 the two sections rejoined to become the *Paśto Ṭolǝna* (Pashto Academy). The increasingly Pashtunized *Revue de Kabul* later became the Pashto literary journal *Kabul*, which was "the prime source and great stimulus to Pashtu literature in the country" (Wilson 1969, pp. 89, 95).

Though the elite traditionally spoke Dari Persian, and a number of writers wrote in both languages, the growth of Afghan nationalism, and thus of modernization, was linked to efforts to raise the status of Pashto, "the Afghan language." The *Paśto Ma'raka* (Committee for Pashto) formed in 1922, under the direction of Abd-al-Wasiya Qandahâri with a view to the promotion of Pashto (cf. Dvoryankov 1966, p. 212; Habibi 1968, p. 56). Tarzi argued that Pashto must be taught to and learned by all the non-Afghan ethnic groups: "Islam, Afghan history and Pashto," he felt were the "matrices from which the ethnic mosaic that constituted Afghanistan could grow and progress as one" (Gregorian 1967, p. 362). As Pashto became "a symbol of Afghan unity" and statehood, it became a means "to consolidate [the Pashtuns'] dominant position *vis-à-vis* the Dari-speaking Tajiks" (Rahman 1996, p. 142). By royal decree, in 1936, Pashto was made the national language, replacing Dari, though the 1964 Constitution named both as "official languages" (MacKenzie 1987, p. 547; Dupree 1980, p. 66; Dvoryankov 1966; Wilson 1969, pp. 84–85). This language policy can be contrasted with pre- and post-Partition Pakistan, where independent Pashto writers were active in the struggle for autonomy from state control and in efforts to confront state power, whether British Colonial or (in the case of Pashtunistan) Pakistani. In both countries, however, writers and literary societies have looked to the state as the primary patron of literature, and have sought to manipulate state language planning policies for socio-political ends.

When conservative fundamentalists ended the period of reform under King Amânollâh, writers like Abd-al-Ali Mostaghni (1874–1934), the former literary editor of *Serâj al-akhbâr*, who wrote in Pashto and Dari, returned to the aesthetic values, Islamic idealism and poetic forms of the Persian tradition (Dupree 1981, p. 19; Dupree 1980, p. 92). However, in the tentative democratic environment of the late 1940s and early 1950s, "sentimental socialists" like Pashto poets Abd-al-Ra'uf Bênawâ and Gul Pâchâ Ulfat (1909–78) again began to address contemporary social topics like nationalism, restrictions on women, and the struggles of the common man (Dupree 1985, pp. 77–78). After the Second World War, many Afghans were sent abroad for education in Arabic countries like Egypt (where they were inspired by the Moslem Brotherhood), in Western countries like France, West Germany, the United Kingdom, and the United States, or in the Soviet Union and Eastern Bloc countries (Majrooh 1990, p. 76). Modern writers cite the works of Balzac, Kafka, Dostoevsky, and de Maupassant as having influenced them (Wilson, 1969, p. 89).

By 1950, some within the small circle of Afghan writers and intellectuals, such as the journalist, short-story writer, and novelist Nur Mohammad Taraki (1917–79), Soleymân Lâyeq (b. 1930), and Bâreq Shâfiyi (b. 1932), were gravitating towards the emerging Marxist movement (Dupree 1985). To these writers, influenced by the social protest novels of Theodore Dreiser, John Steinbeck, and

Upton Sinclair, as well as by the forms and ideas of European existentialist and socialist literature, and that of the pro-Soviet Iranian Tudeh party, Marxism represented a theoretically coherent ideology, but more important perhaps, a mechanism for revolutionary change, a way to attain both the progress and social justice for which they yearned (Majrooh 1990, p. 78; Dupree 1981, p. 19). Pragmatically, Marxism was "the most obviously available alternative to the system in which they lived" (Bradsher 1985, p. 36). Taraki, whose stories and novels on social issues were, like other Third World writers, translated into Russian, later founded the communist People's Democratic Party of Afghanistan, and was elected President of Afghanistan in the Revolution of 27 April 1978 (Bradsher 1985, pp. 36–39, 79), while Lâyeq also played a leading role as a government leader and socialist activist. As "political luminaries," "revolutionary literati," and "poetic activists," Taraki and Lâyeq represent the writers in the 1953–78 period who co-opted literature for the interests of ideology and state (Dupree 1985, p. 80–83).

Despite experimentation with new forms in the modern period, prose writing in Afghanistan usually concerns history, social problems, culture, religion and politics (Dupree 1980, p. 92). Overall, modern intellectuals in Afghanistan have been described as a "vulnerable generation" with a "deeply split personality"; the product of foreign education or of new schools built according to Western educational systems, they emerged without foundations in the local culture or continuity with the traditional religious or Persian literary schools, and were alienated by the discourse of the religious elite (Majrooh 1990, p. 76). As Louis Dupree (1980, p. 94) noted, in spite of the efforts of several innovators, "the general state of modern Afghan literature can only be described as sterile and unimaginative. Probably the main reason relates to the mutual antagonism between Dari and Pashto writers ... modern Afghan writers sit in a cultural limbo, pens silent, as social, political, and economic reforms push ahead ..." Tragically, the political and military upheavals of the post-1980 period pushed back socio-economic reforms. Still, the tendency for Afghan writers in the *jehâd* and post-*jehâd* period, to be drawn into polemical rhetoric and political critique has continued to constrain literary development.

Eastern Pashto

Among the Pashtuns of the urban and settled areas of the NWFP in the 1920s, a "Pashto Movement" arose which emphasized Pashto as a symbol of Pakhtun identity (Rahman 1996, p. 135). The emergence of literary movements was tied to a rising sense of Pakhtun ethno-nationalism, and to the independence movement from British colonial rule in the Indian Subcontinent. One of the first literary-cum-reform societies to be formed, and a convenient historical marker of the early modern literary movement in the NWFP, was the *Anjoman-e Eslâḥ al-Afghâna* (Society for the Improvement of the Afghans), founded in 1923 in Utmanzai, Charsadda. Through this society and its writers, the new genre of essay, short story, novel and drama were introduced to eastern Pashtun areas. The movement is represented by figures like Fazl Mahmud Mâfi, Qâzi Rahimollâh, Sayyed Rasul Rasâ, Mir Hâsib Gol Kâkâkhêl (who translated Urdu novels into Pashto), Amir Hamza Khan Shinwâri, Sayyed Rahat Zakhêli, and others.[2] (Though not in the category of socially-inspired prose, also worthy of mention in this period are Monshi Ahmad Jan's collections of parables and short stories, *Də qesakhwanəy gap* [The Storyteller's Words], and *Də hagha dagha* [Odds and Ends], which reflect the traditional oral form; and the development of Pashto chapbooks, which represents a written literature for the non-elite made possible by the introduction of European printing technology; cf. Hanaway and Nasir 1996). The intellectuals and poets of the literary circle were motivated by a desire to counter social evils, superstition, backwardness, the misinterpretation of religious doctrines, etc., and sought to educate the people through literature. The socially inspired poetry of this movement was expressed in the form of *âzâd naẓm* (free verse), which in style and content was a new genre, quite in contrast with the fixed patterns of classical poetry. In subject matter, they focused on topics new to Pashto poetry, like materialism, freedom, slavery, social issues, the role of the mullah, and superstitions, sub-

---

2 For a more extensive listing of writers in this region and period, see Afridi, *Hamza Shinwari*, pp. 329–31.

jects not treated openly prior to this movement. Through the *Anjoman*, literature came to be viewed less as a romantic, individualistic (*zâti*) and metaphysical expression, and more as a purposeful (*maqsadi*) pursuit; that is, literature for the sake of life, to deal with the problems of daily life and society (e.g. communal unity), and contemporary existential or philosophical issues (e.g. patriotism, freedom).[3]

In the politically charged environment of the freedom movement, in which journalists, poets, and *literati* played a key role, Pashto journalism and writing surged. The progressive movement in the Subcontinent, inspired by socialist ends, viewed literature less as a source of entertainment for the elite, than as a tool for the depiction of evil and enlightened change among the masses. Writers protested social injustices and exploitation by the British, as well as by wealthy, landowning Khans, Maliks, Chaudhris and Waderas (feudal landlords). Humorous, satirical political dramas like Abd-al-Akbar Khan Akbar's "Three Orphans" (*Drê yatimân*), Qâzi Rahimollâh of Abdarra's "The New Light" (*Nəwê rośni*), and Amir Nawâs Khan Jalyâ's "Pain" (*Dard*), and other dramas staged between 1924 and 1930, played an important role in Khan Abd-al-Ghaffâr Khan's *Khodây Khedmatgar* (Servants of God) movement, criticizing social evils like the atrocities perpetrated by feudal landlords on their poor tenants.[4] In 1935, the first Pashto radio drama "The Cup of Blood" (*Də wino jâm*; of contested authorship), was broadcast to a rousing reception, inspiring further development of that genre by such notables as Amir Hamza Khan Shinwari, Abd-al-Karim Mazlum, Samandar Khan Samandar, and Sayyed Rasul Rasâ, and laying the foundation for later television dramas and films in Pashto.[5] Urdu newspapers (*Angar Afghân, Jâmi'at-e Sarhad, Shahbâz*) and the English *Khyber Mail* at the time began

---

3 Raj Wali Shah Khattak, personal interview with the author, March 4, 1999.
4 "Amir Hamza Khan Shinwari as a Playwright," *Frontier Post, The Weekend Post*, November 20, 1998.
5 Names associated with authorship of this groundbreaking drama include Muhammad Aslam Khan Khattak, Abd-al-Karim Mazlum, and Sayyed Bahadur Shah Zafar Kaka Khel. "Amir Hamza Khan Shinwari as a Playwright," *Frontier Post, The Weekend Post*, November 20, 1998.

to devote one to two pages to Pashto, and journalistic activists launched new publications like the Pashto daily *al-Jehâd*, and the weeklies *al-Mahrez* (1939), *al-Mojâhed* (1940), and *Hedâyat*, dedicated to the freedom movement. In the ensuing decades, other locally produced weekly or monthly journals were launched, like the *Swat Digest, Falak Sair, Koh-e Sajan, Dǝ Swat Adabi Seris, Sadâ-ye Swat*, and *Sadâ-ye Malakand*, among others from that northern region of Pakistan (Shams n.d., pp. 26–29). As with the published works of most Pashto poets and writers today, these periodicals were supported by patronage or were self-financed, and thus under-funded and short-lived.

In 1950, the *Ulasi Adabi Jirga* (National Literary Council) was established under the leadership of writers like Amir Hamza Khan Shinwari, inspiring nationalist figures like Ajmal Khattak and Dost Mohammad Kâmel, and the realist aesthetics of poets like Samandar Khan Samandar, Qalandar Mohmand, Ghâni Khan, and others.[6] Writers would present their poetry to the council, openly welcoming critiques on thought and form from the other members. The Pashto literary scene is often marked by the same kinds of social and political conventions which govern relations in Pashtun society, viz. competition and rivalry (for prestige, recognition by government and print media, support in the form of awards of merit, etc.); a concern for honor; contested notions of Islam; and relations of "exchange" in which authors, students and reviewers publicly laud or condemn (at literary events or through press reports and book reviews) the work of this or that author, usually on the basis of tribal or regional affiliation. Through the *Ulasi Adabi Jirga* and other societies that followed, the notion of literary criticism (*tanqid*) was first introduced, countering subjective notions of criticism influenced by para-literary considerations.

---

[6] Raj Wali Shah Khattak, personal interview with the author, March 4, 1999. See also Afridi, *Amir Hamza Khan Shinwari: Life and Works* (Peshawar, 1990), pp. 356–57.

3. Other factors affecting modern Pashto written literature

Orality and literacy

Although Pashto has a written poetic tradition dating back to Mughal times, the Pashtuns are a largely oral society, and thus Pashto literature was and is predominantly oral (in terms of primary sources, modes of transmission and performance contexts). Despite increases in literacy (loosely defined in the region), Ghâni's (Ghani 1988, p. 428) observation is valid for both Afghanistan and most parts of Pakistan: "Oral and *not* written literature is still the major form of cultural expression...writing has remained the preserve of a minority." Levels of Pashto literacy on both sides of the border are lower than for (Dari) Persian and Urdu, though this may vary regionally and according to age. Most of the population (90%) of pre-1979 Afghanistan has been described as "non-literate" in that they cannot read and write (Dupree 1980, p. 66). However, in the state of Swat (established in 1916, recognized by the British in 1926, and taken over by Pakistan in 1969), the Yusufzai dialect of Pashto was officially promoted as a written language (Barth 1995, pp. 112–14). The Wali (Ruler) ordered the translation and publication of new books into Pashto, and Pashto was used in the domains of power and as the medium of instruction in schools. Even after the merger with Pakistan, Pashto continued to be taught in Swati schools better and more thoroughly than in Pashto-speaking parts of the NWFP (Rahman, 6 June 1999), and there are a comparatively large number of literary societies in that area (Shams n.d.). However, overall in Pashtun areas, such factors as illiteracy; Persian- or Urdu-medium instruction from the primary level; the growing popularity of English; the failure to agree on a common script—a modified Arabic script that " 'conceals' the dialectical range" (Dvoryankov 1966, p. 217); and the absence of a generalized marketing and distribution system, combine to the effect that Pashto literature, though nominally prized, has poor market value, particularly among a younger generation who cannot read Pashto, and thus limited circulation beyond the educated elite.

The oral-written dichotomization conceals complex interrelations between forms and modes of communication in Pashto literature (Bartlotti 2000, p. 118), as it does in the literatures of other peoples. Texts are shaped by printed, written and oral media and by dynamic processes involving a series of influences and constraints (Finnegan 1992, p. 179; cf. Finnegan 1988). Pakistani literature in general is best viewed in terms of an oral-written continuum within and between language groups (Hanaway and Nasir 1996, p. 352–53). Pashtun writers stand in creative relation to their cultural tradition, drawing from a stock of religious and cultural images, traditional and contemporary forms, and subject matters common to Pashtun society and/or the Persian and South Asian regions, manipulating these in relation to social constraints and their own purposes, with a dynamic interplay between literary, textual, and performative aspects (Bartlotti 2000, pp. 115–34). For example, commonly Pashto dramas are written (under subsidy) for performance on government-controlled radio or television, more than for print distribution. Written collections of *tapa*s (Afg. *lan̠ḏəy*), a two-lined metrical genre of oral poetry (e.g. Shaheen 1984; 1994), serve as resource material for Pashtun singers and their recordings, while politically-inspired writers quote verses and proverbs (e.g. Bartlotti and Khattak 2006) in articles and letters in the press, many of which are written with poetic style and language (Bartlotti 2000, pp. 122–25). The published poems of the Pakistani Pashtun poet, Ghâni Khan, have been most widely popularized through the cassette tapes of modern singers like Takkar Ali Takkar, who have set his verses to music.

The place of poets and writers in Pashtun society

As in Arabic and many African languages, poetry—oral and written—is the privileged genre among both traditional and modern promoters of Pashto literature. The tradition of prose writing in Pashto is a rather new phenomenon compared to that of poetry, so a critique of its importance and impact is difficult. The role of the writer may be viewed as derivative of the traditional role of the poet in Islamic society, who was the wise Muslim, court counselor, and revered teacher (Wilson 1969, p. 92). In both cases, literary artistry tends to draw upon a reservoir of shared images and cultural meanings to embody or to contest traditional values, beliefs and emotions associated with religion, honor, relationships, and social problems. Not as socially liminal as, and certainly far more respected than musicians, in some ways poets and writers represent, in their persons and work, the ambiguities and irresolvable tensions which lie at the heart of tribal society between heritage and egalitarian communalism on the one hand, and autonomy (*gheyrat*) and self-defining expressiveness on the other.

This polarity is represented by two other widely respected and representative figures in modern Pashto written literature, Amir Hamza Khan Shinwari (1907–94), and Abd-al-Ghâni Khan (1913–96).[7] Each in his own way, to use Majrooh's (1980, p. 72) phrase, stands "inside the limits of sameness" regulated by Pashtun custom and tradition, while like other intellectuals, "step(s) over the boundaries of sameness" and challenges them afresh. The first is idealized as a humble *faqir*, a "Pashtun Sufi," the other an endearing renaissance iconoclast.

Amir Hamza Khan Shinwari has been given the title "Father of Pashto *ghazal*" (*Bâbâ-e Ghazal*) for having "Pashtunized" and breathed new life into classical literary forms like the *ghazal*, *robâ'i*, and *chârbeyta*.[8] The non-indigenous (Arabic, Persian) *ghazal* is traditionally written according to strict norms of rhyme and meter, and deals with subjective and aesthetic themes (*dâkhiliyat*), most notably represented in classical Pashto by Abd-al-Rahmân Bâbâ (1651–1710), and Abd-al-Hamid (1667–1732). In the view of modern Pashtun literary critics, Hamza Shinwari, however, removed the Pashto *ghazal* and other forms from the shadow of Persian and its imagery, and introduced a new style in which the terminology and symbolism, notions of beauty and life, and *Zeitgeist* were recognizably Pashtun.[9] A subjective and mystic poet in the tradition

---

7 For the life and work of Hamza Shinwari see Afridi, *Hamza Shinwari*.
8 Afridi, *Hamza Shinwari*, pp. 6, 257–67.
9 Raj Wali Shah Khattak, personal interview with the author, March 4, 1999. For a discussion of these views see Afridi, *Hamza Shinwari*, pp. 245–57, 295–99.

of the Rowshanites and Abd-al-Rahmân, Hamza Shinwari used the *ghazal* to describe Pashtun character and ideals, matters of honor (*paśtunwâli*) and problems of daily life.[10] The two strains of Sufism and Pashtun nationalism (*paśtunwâli*) that suffuse his work are captured in the following supplicatory verses (trsl. Afridi 1990, p. 4):

> Please God make my life honourable,
> To bow in front of none but you.
> Let my heart be Mussalman,
> Please make my thought Pakhtoon.
> Please God increase tenfold
> The beauty of the Laila of Pashto
> And then also increase my love
> Ten times more than Majnoon.

The same fusion is represented in a comment attributed to Hamza Shinwari that, "The name Pakhtoon represents courage, bravery, swordsmanship, manliness, hospitality, self-respect and respect for others and so on. Now these are all the divine attributes and hence it will not be in vain if God were also called a Pakhtoon" (quoted in Afridi 1990, pp. 28–56).

Following his first small book of poetry, *Də zŕə âwâz* (The Voice of the Heart; c. 1951), the publication of Hamza Shinwari's major collection, *Ghazawoone (Ghazawənê*, Yawning; 1953), inspired a generation of young poets and established his reputation as a master poet on both sides of the Durand Line. Since the 1960s *Ghazawoone* has been included in the syllabus for the M.A. course in Pashto at Peshawar University, while a follow-up collection, *Də Kheybər waźmê* (Khyber Breezes; 1968) was published by the Pashto Academy, Kabul. Hamza Shinwari's work is viewed as a bridge between classical and modern Pashto poetry. In addition to *ghazal*s, he writes *robâ'iyât* (quatrains with an a a b a rhyming scheme), *qet'at*s (stanzas having two to eight metrical lines), and *nazm* (a refrain followed by three or four rhyming lines), using distinctively Pashtun images to project a message (e.g. about freedom or Pashto) or to deal with traditional themes (e.g. pain and separa-

---

10 On the Rowshanites see Andreyev in this volume.

tion; waiting and hope; the garden and Spring; flower and nightingale). Other works include a novel, *Nəwê Chapê* (New Waves; 1957), revolving around the theme of Pashtun unity; *Nəway Paśtun* (The New Pakhtun; 1957), a controversial travelogue (*safar-nâma*) about his trip to Afghanistan; *Zhwand aw Yun* (The Cycle of Life; 1977), a *mathnawi* (a poem in couplet form) about human life; stories, essays, and a number of prose writings regarding Sufism (Afridi 1990, pp. 158–59, 331–48). In his poetry, he makes plentiful use of Pashto idiomatic vocabulary, phrases and proverbs. Hamza is also famous as a dramatist, having written the script, dialogue and songs for many plays and films, including the first Pashto film *Leylâ Majnun* (1941). His film songs became so popular that they were sung by the folk in *hojra*s (guest houses) as well as by professional musicians; the delicate love poem, *Jongara* (The Hut), has been recorded by both Pakistani and Afghan singers, and broadcast on Radio Kabul.[11]

Abd-al-Ghâni Khan, son of the famed "Frontier Ghandi" and Pashtun nationalist, Abd-al-Ghaffâr Khan (see below), is perhaps the most popular and well-known of modern Pashto poets. A writer and artist as well as a poet, who studied in America and trained in engineering, "Ghâni" is proudly represented by Pashtuns as a kind of renaissance man, and fondly nicknamed *lêwańay falsefa* (crazy philosopher). A religious and political iconoclast, he indicts hypocrisy and those who misuse religion or compromise Pashtun identity and values in the interests of power. His irreverent criticism of mullahs and panegyrics to wine, beauty and the pleasures as well as sorrows of life, made him popular with a younger generation of Pashtun Muslims and an object of criticism by pietists, particularly some Afghans who associate him with the socialist political philosophy of his father.

In 1928, Ghaffâr Khan began publishing the first journal in the Pashto language, *Paśtun*; the journal was banned in 1930, and published sporadically thereafter until permanently banned by the Pakistan Government in 1947 (Tendulkar 1967, pp. 50–55). *Paśtun*

---

11 "Amir Hamza Khan Shinwari as a Playwright," *Frontier Post, The Weekend Post*, November 20, 1998.

saw itself as the voice of the Pashtun people on both sides of the border. One aspect of this ethno-nationalistic agenda was a concerted effort to "nurture and develop the Pakhtu language" in the face of its neglect by its own people, and the criticism of "the mullahs [who] propagated that Pakhtu was the language of hell, spoken by the people in hell" (Tendulkar 1967, p. 50). *Paśtun* carried articles on social and political topics, short stories, and poems composed by readers (both male and female), and featured the poetry of the young Ghâni Khan. Ghâni's poems gave voice to the national aspirations of the Pashtuns with tender but powerful language reflecting Pashtun values and sentiments. The following verses graced the title pages of *Paśtun* (Tendulkar 1967, p. 51):

> If I, a slave, lie buried in a grave, under a resplendent tomb-stone,
> Respect it not, spit on it.
> When I die, and not lie bathed in martyr's blood,
> None should his tongue pollute, offering prayers for me.
> Mother, with what face will you wail for me,
> If I am not torn to pieces by British guns?
> Either I turn this wretched land of mine into a garden of Eden
> Or I wipe out the lanes and homes of Pakhtuns!

Writers like Ghâni Khan, Ajmal Khattak, Sayyed Rasul Rasâ, Qalandar Mohmand and others use modern style and forms to address contemporary issues. But their social realism, while influenced by new ideas from English and Urdu literature, stands in a tradition of social commentary and politico-literary leadership that may be viewed as rooted in the vigorous aesthetics of the classical Pashtun warrior-poet Khushhâl Khan Khattak.

Modern Pashto literature and the politics of language and identity

In an environment where language is a political issue, and where government language policies in pursuit of nation-building goals impact the support, funding, and publication of literature, the politics of language use has affected literary development (see Rahman

1996). For a time in Pakistan, anything published in Pashto was considered politically suspect by a government nervous lest development of Pashto language and literature foster ethnic nationalism and the rise of an independent "Pashtunistan" along its long, porous and volatile border with Afghanistan. As the Afghan government has never fully renounced its claim to influence the tribes, the Pashtun have used this very marginality in relation to or within state structures to assert a level of autonomy over their affairs; this sense of freedom, which is felt to be central to *paśtunwali*, is celebrated in Pashto poetry and literature.

Pashto language use in all domains is associated with the preservation of the Pashtuns as a distinct people. Articles in the press, letters to the editor, books, and speeches by Pashtun politicians and educators continue to express bitterness over the injustice done to Pashto in what one early leader describes as "the political battle" to advance "the Pushtu language, its literature, and education in it."[12] Writers lament the "degrading status of Pashto and the apathy of its speakers towards their own mother tongue," including "Pukhtoon leaders and government functionaries who have totally neglected to back their own language" (Shams n.d., pp. 7–10). A leading Pashto scholar asserts, "If [the] Pashto language is lost, the Pakhtun nation is also lost."[13] Such sentiments are typical. Government promotion of Urdu in Pakistan in the face of demands for mother tongue Pashto education at the primary level, and the increasing acceptance of English as an international language keyed to much needed socio-economic progress, are viewed as putting additional strains on the development of Pashto language and literature. In Afghanistan, the Taliban militia government, which arose in 1994 and by the year 2000 controlled ninety percent of the

12 Qayyâm-al-Din Khâdem (1912–82), poet and prominent member of the Pashto *Anjoman-e Adabi* (Literary Society) in Kandahar in the 1930s, quoted in Dvoryankov, "The Development of Pushtu as the National and Literary Language of Afghanistan," *Central Asian Review* 14 (1966), p. 213.
13 Rajwali Shah Khattak, Director, Pashto Academy, Peshawar University, quoted in an interview by Sher Alam Shinwari, "Future of Pakhto Language and Literature Depends upon Pakhtuns," *Frontier Post*, Cultural Panorama, 24 November 1997.

Afghan countryside, has reasserted the primacy of Pashto, along with Pashtun political hegemony, both of which have roots in the tribal values of the countryside.

Pashtun writers often compose panegyric poems to Pashto itself. This may be viewed as indicative not only of the symbolic power of language, but reflective of that near veneration of the Word, spoken or written, common to Islamic societies in general. In a sense Pashto symbolically mediates between the authoritative traditions and notions associated with Pashtun heritage and those contemporaries who, across a broad and diverse area, maintain a sense of Pashtun-ness and participation in the larger "imagined community" (Anderson 1991). Thus, for many, the language itself is a praised symbolic link between past and present.

Social and literary bilingualism in Pashtun areas remains a characteristic in the modern period (Dvoryankov 1966, pp. 211–12; Miran 1977); many Pashto writers also use Urdu or Persian as a literary medium (cf. Dupree 1980, pp. 92–93). In Pakistan, as a result of the promotion of Urdu, there has been a concurrent decline in the number of those who are also literate in Pashto. Pashto continues to be spoken in ninety percent of the homes in the NWFP and in the domains of mosque, home, council (*jirga*), and among women, though Urdu predominates in schools and bazaars (Hallberg 1992). The most widely read newspapers in the NWFP are in Urdu, compared to one Pashto daily (*Waḥdat*). As this brief sketch of Pashto illustrates, the sources, modes of transmission and performance of literature are not neutral but are constituted and constrained by social processes. The processes and constraints that have shaped Pashto literature constitute an important area for future study.

Literary-cum-cultural organizations

The formation of the *Pašto Ṭolǝna* in Kabul (1937), the Pashto Academy, Peshawar University (1955), and the Pashto Academy in Quetta (1972), marked the emergence of serious national scholarship into Pashto language and literature. In recent years, considerable creative intellectual energy has gone into the re-evaluation of older Pashto literature, the collection and publication of folk literature, and the promotion of modern Pashtun writers, with a view to defining and emphasizing the Pashtuns' literary heritage and national identity. The Pashto Academy (Peshawar) publishes a monthly research journal, *Paśto*. Among other factors, dependence on limited government funding and patronage, the absence of linkages with international scholarship, and the political realities of Pashtun society, serve as constraints on university-level literary research, training and publication. Nevertheless, the Pashto Academy may be viewed as playing an important advocacy role within the provincial and national government and education system, and providing a symbolic and institutional focal point for Pashto writers. From a government perspective, the centers represent a politically correct concern with the preservation of the "heritage" of a significant minority ethnic group. For Pashtuns, they occupy an important symbolic space in the national society, representing the contested notion of not only preserving, but promoting and developing Pashto language and literature in the interests of maintaining communal identity.

The Soviet invasion of Afghanistan in 1979, the subsequent *jehâd*, civil war and resulting flow of refugees to Pakistan and the West, including the rise of the Taliban, though disrupting Afghan literary activities on certain formal levels, resulted in the rise of *jehâdi* literature, poetry and print media whose significance and relation to earlier folkloric themes, literary forms and movements remain to be fully explored. The independent "Writers Union for a Free Afghanistan," now the "Afghanistan Study Centre," produces *WUFA*, a monthly journal that deals with both literary and political concerns. Local Peshawari newspapers like *Wahdat* (in Pashto) and the weekly "Cultural Panorama" page of the *Frontier Post* (the most widely read English newspaper in the NWFP), provide an important print medium for both recognized and aspiring writers and poets (Afghan and Pakistani), and forums for the discussion of contested issues.

Perhaps more significant for the development of modern Pashto literature are the widespread and growing number of localized, private, literary-cum-cultural organizations in Pakistan which promote Pashto. One or more "cultural councils" (*adabi jirga*) have sprung up within each city, large village or area (e.g. Peshawar, Kohat, Bannu, Landi Kotal, Swabi, Nowshera, Mardan, Islamabad, Malakand). Members of these groups pay a nominal fee and meet approximately monthly to engage in literary criticism (*tanqid*), reading and discussion of the work of a particular poet or writer, often in the presence of a visiting "chief guest," followed by a poetry recitation (*mashâyera*); other societies focus on presenting studies of classical poets like Abd-al-Rahmân or Khoshhâl Khan Khattak. Egalitarian cultural societies, many unregistered with the government and unfunded by outside agencies, provide an important performance context for both recognized and emerging, trained and unschooled, literary talent, and serve to network writers, poets and scholars within and beyond a given locale. At the same time, they link contemporary writers with the distinctive notions, forms, themes, and images associated with the Pashto literary tradition, both historical and contemporary. These grass-root literary-cum-cultural councils are the most fertile loci of literary activity, a sign of the vitality of Pashto written literature in the contemporary period.

CHAPTER 6

PASHTO ORAL AND POPULAR LITERATURE

WILMA HESTON

1. Introduction

Pashto oral and popular literature at the end of the twentieth century is the product of a culture that exists today in two countries, Pakistan and Afghanistan.[1] The current border between Afghanistan and Pakistan was demarcated only in 1893 by the Durand Line formulated in a treaty between the British, who were ruling India, and Abd-al-Rahmân, who was then ruling Afghanistan. On the British side of the Durand line, the North-West Frontier Province (NWFP) was established in 1901. Within the territories bordering Afghanistan, tribal agencies were established where tribal law prevailed, contrasting with the settled areas of Pashto speakers where British law prevailed. Pakistan has continued this separation of Pashto-speaking areas into tribal and settled areas since its independence in 1947. For the tribal areas of former British India

1   In this chapter, "Pashtun" is used for a speaker of Pashto; the spelling as Pakhto and Pakhtun for the languages and its speakers, respectively, reflects the "hard" dialects of Pashto; for other spellings and a map of dialect distributions, see Henderson 1983. Another term often used in English and Hindustani is "Pathan," which Urdu dictionaries also define as 'soldier,' a common nineteenth century occupation of Pashtuns. "Afghan" was and sometimes still is used in Pakistan for Pashto speakers, regardless of the speaker's present-day nationality. The numbers preceded by HR1, HR2, and H&N refer to entries in the two bibliographies of Rafi' (1975 and 1978/9) and the bibliography of Hanaway and Nasir (1996) included in this chapter's References; WWH refers to chapbooks in W. Heston's personal collection.

and present-day Pakistan, the international borders have been permeable boundaries for persons, goods and culture; even during the Russian occupation of Afghanistan in the 1980s, cross-border travel continued often unhindered except at major checkpoints.

Modern anthropologists as well as earlier travelers and administrators have described various aspects of Pashtun culture both within and outside the tribal areas. The importance of Islam as well as the codes of honor, hospitality, and revenge inherent in the concept known as *paśtunwali* are important to an understanding of the themes of Pashto folk literature.

This distinctive Pashtun culture exists within a complex of other cultures with which it has interacted. While cultural flows go in both directions, certain circumstances have played an important role in determining both the direction of particular flows and the kinds of evidence preserved for a particular culture. In both Afghanistan and Pakistan, for centuries the ruling dynasties and the associated elite culture were Persian-speaking. In Afghanistan, only in the twentieth century with shifts in political power did Pashto become a language promoted by the power elite. In 1936, Pashto was declared the national language, but it was co-existent with Persian; this was reaffirmed in the Constitution of 1964, but Persian continues to be a lingua franca in much of Afghanistan. Folktales are thus likely to have been at some time transmitted in Persian regardless of their origin, and collectors asking for folktales of Afghanistan are likely to obtain their tales most immediately through Persian unless they are specific about language source or have their own Pashto language skills. The *Paśto Ṭolǝna* (Pashto Academy) was established in Kabul in the mid-1920s to promote the use of Pashto (Rahman 1996, p. 142), and schooling in Pashto became possible in Afghanistan even at higher levels. Since the Russian occupation of the 1980s, the relative use of Persian and Pashto has varied according to the strength of particular political powers.

In the region that is now Pakistan, British rule gradually replaced Persian rule; the frontier area was annexed by the British after the Second Sikh War of 1849 and was part of Punjab until 1901. Although Persian had been used in addition to English in the early days of British rule on the Subcontinent, Urdu gradually replaced it in the nineteenth century in the regions that are now Pakistan (see Rahman 1966). Although not encouraging the use of Pashto for the education of Pashtuns, the British needed a certain level of fluency in local languages for their own military and civil administration; this resulted in not only grammars and dictionaries but also readers with various kinds of texts. A few British administrators had sufficient time, interest and Pashto language skill to collect folk literature, thus providing a record of oral tradition for the regions in which they were stationed. British rule also provided non-administrative travelers with a certain measure of security for travel and study in the settled areas of the frontier.

Along with British administration came British technology. This included not only the improved weaponry much prized by Pashtuns, but also the relatively inexpensive printing technology that was soon put to use for both religious and secular texts in the vernacular languages. Among the nineteenth century publications printed in Delhi, then the capital of British India, and in Lahore and Peshawar were books for British civil, military, and religious use, and also books for Peshawar shop owners, who soon saw an increase in the number of local printing presses. Among the books printed for Peshawar shop owners were chapbooks, the cheap little booklets printed on inexpensive paper with simple paper covers and contents suited to local popular tastes of non-westernized customers. The growth of non-government presses from this period thus documents the presence of an extensive popular literature in Pakistan that is not documented in Afghanistan. Furthermore, the administrative system of the British Raj plus the private collecting habits of visitors to the subcontinent led to repositories in England for both manuscripts and printed texts in Pashto. The surviving nineteenth-century written evidence of Pashto folk literature is thus more heavily weighted with materials from the regions now in Pakistan than from those of Afghanistan.

After WWI, anti-British pro-independence activities in the NWFP were tied to a strengthening of Pashto as a marker of Pathan identity. However, even in Swat, an independent princely state where Pashto was declared the official language in 1926, schools used Urdu and English as they also did in the NWFP (Rahman 1996, p. 143).

ORAL LITERATURE OF IRANIAN LANGUAGES

The patterns of language use in Pakistan remained much the same after its independence in 1947. Urdu is Pakistan's national language and the medium of instruction at government schools. At the university level English is the medium of instruction, and English is used also in the courts and the National Assembly. Thus, despite the fact that Pashto is the second most commonly spoken home language in Pakistan as a whole, the most commonly used home language in Pakistan's North-West Frontier Province, and the second most commonly used home language in Baluchistan, study of and in Pashto has been, and still is, limited mainly to academic environments where it is an optional language of specialization.[2]

During the second half of the twentieth century, a new set of technological innovations was introduced from the West. These included radio, television, film, and both audio- and videocassettes. In countries like Afghanistan and Pakistan, where non-literates are still a majority of the population, the impact of these non-written forms on folk and popular culture is readily apparent but has yet to be systematically studied.

Divisions between literary and popular works are never black and white, and by the close of the twentieth century, isolated villages whose culture might easily have been categorized as "folk" have had available a much different set of cultural products than was available even to the urban elite fifty years earlier. Literature classes of universities, however, have generally continued to study the written traditions of earlier centuries, as well as the more recent products of academies and related university faculty. These materials will be excluded from this chapter, which will focus on collected oral materials as well as materials in print or other media that are intended for the general population. The chapter will first examine collections of folk materials made prior to 1950 and will then turn to more recent collections, studies and bibliographies, and the contributions of mass media to Pashtun culture in the second half of the twentieth century.

2   In the 1980 census, 68.30% of the households in the NWFP, 25.07% of those in Baluchistan, and 99.70% of those in the Federally Administered Tribal Areas had Pashto as the language "usually spoken" (*Pakistan Statistical Yearbook* 1995, p. 66).

2. Before 1950

Among the early travelers to make use of Pashtun folktales was Charles Masson (1848), the "English deserter ... [and] long-time resident of Kabul" (Lindholm 1996, p. 8), whose poems draw on legends of specified localities. The first four and the last of his thirteen stories are from regions that are not now predominantly Pashto-speaking, but the remainder are from the Saharawân mountains in northern (Pakistani) Baluchistan, Lus (also in northern Baluchistan), Kandahar, the Turnek river valley between Kandahar and Ghazne, Kabuli Kohistân, Bâmiyân, Loghmân, the Siyâhposh hills of eastern Afghanistan, Jalâlâbâd, and the Khyber Pass. In the introduction to each poem, Masson comments on the extent to which he feels he has reproduced the original tale; although he does not specify the language in which he heard these tales, they do represent an early Western impression of folktales in the Pashto-speaking regions.

Another folktale collection made in the context of a description of the area is by S.S. Thorburn (1878) of the India Civil Service, who was stationed in Bannu District. His book includes one chapter of Popular Stories, Marwat (a Pashtun tribe) Ballads and Riddles, and another chapter with Proverbs in English translation and comments, followed by a chapter with the same Pashto proverbs in Pashto script. Thorburn (p. 172) describes briefly the professional storytellers (*ḍum*s), whether itinerant or in the service of a particular chief, as well as the latter's services as tribal genealogists and historiographers in verse. In addition, Pashtun tales include "the Akhoond's dreamy moral narratives (a Moslem cleric with teaching duties in an Islamic school) and the wandering *ḍum*'s elaborate anecdotes, gorgeous with princes and princesses, fairies and demons, down to the roaring fun of the village wit, who strings half a dozen old jokes and stories together ..." Thorburn's fifty translated and condensed tales were chosen because they were "the shortest and apparently the most original" which find favor with "the poorest and most ignorant of the peasantry." He organizes his tales into three categories: Humorous and Moral, Comic and Jocular, and Fables. Many tales have Islamic overtones involving, for example, mullahs, fakirs, and in one case King Solomon himself. When characters are named rather than anonymous, their names include the appellation *Khan* but the social structure of the tales is otherwise generally not identifiably Pashtun. The occupations, other than court-related positions such as king or vizier, include craftsmen, merchants and moneylenders, and farmers. According to Thorburn, the first of his three short ballads was written by a *ḍum*, Jarasi, "the last of all the bards...Who sung of Marwat chivalry" but no poet's name or pen name (*takhallos*) is included in it or the other two fragments.

Thorburn divides his collection of proverbs, the first of its kind in Pashto, into thirty-five categories; the number of proverbs in a category ranges from five in "Good Looks" to seventy-two in "Husbandry, Weather and Health." The final category, "Unclassed, Ethical, Didactic and Miscellaneous" includes 406 proverbs. Each category is preceded by a short paragraph with remarks on its relevance to Pashto life and customs; many of the proverbs are accompanied by an explanation and some by remarks on parallels in other languages.

Another early group of tales was written for the Reverend T. P. Hughes "by my learned Afghán friend, Moulvi Ahmad" as a textbook for the English Student of Pashto under the patronage of the Government of Punjab. These forty-nine short tales (*hekâyat*) are in prose except for occasional rhymed couplets, most often at a tale's end. Some tales are fables about animals, often paired (e.g., frog and fly; cow and camel, quail and hawk), and others are about ordinary unnamed men, often with particular characteristics (a wise man, a miser, a fool), and sometimes kings. These tales have been published separately at various times as *Ganj-e Paśto* (e.g., Ahmad 1882). A *mathnavi* version of Bahrâm and Gol-andâm by Fayyâz was also included in Hughes' volume because of its "easy and pure Pushtu" (Hughes 1893, p. ii). A later teaching text for the military by Ahmad Jan (1929) also included contributions to folk literature.

The British civil administration published settlement reports from districts that they governed; these reports sometimes included publication lists. The Hastings report (1878) for Peshawar includes an Appendix No. III: "List of works in Pakhto, and of works in Persian on the Pakhto language or History," which has entries for seventy-nine authors and includes their "Nationality." In many cases, the nationality is a tribal affiliation such as Mohmand, Khattak, or Yusufzai. The two exceptions are Fayyâz (writer of a lithographed *Shâhzâda Bahrâm* in verse) and Ghôlâm Mohammad, (author of two verse manuscripts, *Badr-e Jamâl* and *Seyf al-Moluk*, and a prose *Jang-nâma* or "war story" described as a "History of Hassan and Hussain"), whose nationality is given as "Minstrel," consistent with other reports of the late nineteenth century which view the folk poets-performers (*ḍums*) as a distinct class.

Somewhat later is a collection published by F. H. Malyon (1912) of the 21st Punjabis (the 21st Battalion of the Punjabi regiment of the Indian Army) of prose tales from the tribal areas; these ten tales were originally published with both the Pashto text and an English translation. The first four stories are Orakzai, the next four are Afridi, and the final two are Yusufzai. The notes on these stories, which were chosen to represent three major "hard" dialects of Pashto, include comments on pronunciation, grammar and lexicon. Like most of the Thorburn's tales, the stories are of unnamed persons, identified by, for example, occupation, relationship, or region: e.g., a fakir from Tirah, three brothers, or a king and his vizier; the exception is a folk figure, Nim Koni (lit. "half-made").

As in many other parts of the Islamic world, Pashto poetry is often viewed as a form to be sung. The first major collection of Pashto folk poetry was made, not by an Englishman, but by the French Orientalist James Darmesteter. His *Les chants populaires des Afghans* (Popular Songs of the Afghans, Paris 1888), includes the full scholarly apparatus of texts, translations, grammar and lexicon. Darmesteter includes a list of his sources; most of the persons from whom he collected his verses were living in what now is Pakistan. He also includes several pages on the training of the *ḍums* who sing this poetry.

Darmesteter's collection provides a useful survey in both form and content of kinds of Pashto folk poetry which continue to be popular a century later. His verse genres include three forms which, as he notes, are not found in classical Persian or Pashto poetry: the *mesrâ'*, the folk *ghazal* and the *chârbeyta* that he translates as "ballade" because of its stanzaic form; he also includes a selection in rhyming couplets (*mathnavi*) used for a description of Swat. Small samples of lullabies, funeral prayers and chants as well as riddles and sixty proverbs complete his collection.

Darmesteter divides the subject matter of his selections into historical songs, religious songs and legends, romances, and love songs, all of which continued to provide subject matter for folk poetry in the last decades of the twentieth century. In addition to the verse selections, a few passages in prose are also included, such as a short prose summary contextualizing the *ghazal* about Alexander and Loqman. The romances to which the *ghazal*s refer are Âdam Khan and Dur Khânəy, Fath Khan of Kandahar, Jalat (Jalad) and Mahbuba, Farhâd (corrupted to "faqir") and Shirin (the "princess"), 'Nimbollâ,' and a *ghazal* about wondrous sea animals. The historical songs are mainly military: a *ghazal* about the 1776 battle of Ahmad Shah with the Mahrattas; a set of five *chârbeyta*s about Sayyed Ahmad (1826–31); six *chârbeyta*s, one *ghazal*, some *mesrâ*'s and a *mathnavi* about the 1863 Ambela campaign; and eleven *chârbeyta*s and two *ghazal*s about the (Second Anglo-) Afghan war of 1879–81. The religious songs as well as the love songs include both *ghazal*s and *chârbeyta*s.

Entries in the British Museum Library and the India Office Library catalogues attest to nineteenth-century Pashto chapbook printings in Lahore and Delhi. No thorough study has yet been done in Pashto of the magnitude of chapbook publications, but the general appeal of chapbooks in the South Asian Subcontinent can perhaps be judged by Pritchett's (1985) documentation of the popularity of certain Urdu tales first printed in the late nineteenth century.

Among the nineteenth-century Pashto poets, at least four have continued to have their tales reprinted into the last decades of the twentieth century. Perhaps the most prolific of these was Ne'mat-Allâh, who has been called the Ferdowsi of Pashto (Reśtin 1946, p. 112). Three of his romances, *Fath Khân Qandahâri*, *Shirin o Farhâd*, and the *Nimbollâ* mentioned by Darmesteter, were printed in Delhi between 1883 and 1888; at least three editions of his *Hâtem*

Tâyi were printed in Lahore for Peshawar publishers. Other Pashto compositions of Ne'mat-Allâh include a romance of Akhtar Monir and Shâhzâdǝy Mâh-ru (HR2 1392), a romance of Khotan (HR2 1405), a story of the Emperor Akbar and his vizier Birbal (HR 2 1393), a *Bâgh-o bahâr* or "Tale of the Four Dervishes" (HR2 1395, three printings; see also Jatoi 1980, p. 45), a 'Cat and Rat' tale (HR2 1396), a War Story (*jang-nâma*) of Hazrat Ali (HR2 1399, three printings), of Hoseyn and Bibi Sakina (HR2 1400), of Rostam and Sohrâb (HR2 1401), and of Mir Hâtam and Moqâtel (HR2 1402, three printings), as well as a story of Mahtâb Jân and Begam Jân, or Women's Wiles (*ya'ni makr-e zanân*; HR2 1415). Bokhâri and Hamdâni (1966, p. 253–56) include other tales (such as Zarif Khân Swâti, Musâ Khân and Gol-Makǝy, Gol-Sanowbar, Bahrâm Gur, and Parrot Tales) among their extensive works.

In addition, Ne'mat-Allâh wrote chapbooks in verse on social occupations and behavior of women, and on trades and occupations, published in 1891 and 1896 respectively, both in Delhi. His translations incldued the *Qesas al-anbiyâ* (HR2 1410), a 540-page Thousand and One Nights (*Alef Leylâ*; HR2 1394), and Ferdowsi's *Shahname* in 404 pages (HR2 1407). His Pashto version of the Sindhi-Panjabi folktale 'Sohni and Mahinwal' (HR2 1406, two printings) is an unusual example of a nineteenth-century translation into Pashto from another regional language of Pakistan. On events of his own time, he wrote a *Jang-nâma-ye Chitrâl*, published in Delhi in 1897 (Blumhardt 1902, p. 5).

Many of Ne'mat-Allâh's works continued to be reprinted in the second half of the twentieth century. A 47-page edition of *Nimbollâ* was later printed in Peshawar (Jatoi 1980, p. 28); his *Fath Khan* was reprinted by three different publishers in the late twentieth century (H&N 610; WWH 8, and later H&N 611; WWH 66), as were his *Jang-nâma-ye Zaytun* (H&N 609) and *Mir Khâtam and Moqâtel* (WWH 69), along with an earlier edition (as *Hâtam*) from a Peshawar publisher using a Lahore press (HR1 112). His *Leylâ-Majnun* had a 1969 Mingora printing and two Peshawar printings (H&N 742; WWH 68, HR1 388).

Another nineteenth-century folk poet of continued popularity is Abu Ali-Shâh. His *Leylâ-Majnun* was printed in Delhi in 1882;

his tale of Bakhtiyâr, the Emperor of Persia's son, was published in Delhi in 1881 (Blumhardt 1893, p. 6), and later printed in Peshawar (Jatoi 1980, p. 45). Like Ne'mat-Allâh, he too has a version of the story of Prince Akhtar Monir and Mehr-ru (Blumhardt 1902, p. 7, published in Delhi in 1893); and a War Story of Hoseyn and Bibi Sakina (HR2 35, with three editions). His tale of Mir Hâtam is printed in a volume of war stories (HR2 40), rather than as a separate chapbook.

The works of Abu Ali-Shâh have likewise continued to be reprinted in the second half of the twentieth century. His *Âdam Khân-Dur Khânəy* was available from three Peshawar publishers (HR1 1; H&N 454, with film songs). His *Jang-nâma-ye Hasaneyn o Bibi Sakina* has had two publishers (H&N 456, 457) and his *Wafât-nâme* has been printed in both Peshawar and Mingora (H&N 458, 686).

A third nineteenth-century folk poet whose works continue to be reprinted is Mollâ Ahmad Jân, whose works are noteworthy not only for their continued reprinting, but also for their sheer length. A Delhi edition of his *Amir Hamza* was published in 1882 together with a story of the Queen of Sheba (Balqis); stories (*qesas*) of the thief and the judge (*ghal-qâzi*) in Delhi (1878) and Peshawar perhaps in 1875; of Gumbadh, Prince of Syria, in Delhi (1881), a romance of *Sayf al-Moluk* in Delhi (1882), and Parrot Tales (*Tutinâme*) in Delhi in 1883 (Blumhardt 1893, p. 9–11). He also had a Book of Dreams (*Kh^{w}âb-nâma*), and of Omens (*fâl-nâma*) printed in Delhi in 1877 with other editions in 1887 and 1883. His other works on Islamic topics included stories about Abraham (Delhi 1882) and Mansur al-Hallâj (Delhi 1878), a *Wafât-nâma* (Delhi 1888) and a *Nur-nâma* (Bombay 1890), as well as poems included in other collections (Blumhardt 1893, p. 9–11).

A century later, Molla Ahmad Jân's version of *Amir Hamza* with over six thousand couplets had two different Peshawar publishers (H&N 462 and 463, with at least one other printing, WWH 5, from the latter); his other chapbooks included a War Story of Hazrat Ali (H&N 464), and *Qesas al-anbiyâ* (H&N 465). His romance of Momtâz and Bênazir (WWH 9; HR1 391), with over six thousand couplets, is probably the longest Pashto chapbook with a named hero and heroine.

In contrast to the prolific output of the three preceding poets, the popularity of Fayyâz, an itinerant musician about whom little is known (see Bokhâri and Hamdâni 1966, p. 202), is based primarily on his version of Bahrâm and Gol-andâm; it had at least four printings in Delhi from 1867 to 1877. A century later, printings were available in the 1980s (H&N, pp. 522, 523) from at least two different Peshawar publishers of whom one had made at least three printings in the 1980s;[3] at least two other Peshawar editions of different length were printed by other publishers (HR1 360, 64 pp.; HR1 390, 40 pp.).

These folk poets whose work was first published in the nineteenth century wrote their narratives as *mathnavi*s. The tales were usually divided into sections, sometimes with a heading at the beginning of a new episode. In a couplet near the episode's end (sometimes the final couplet but sometimes several or even half a dozen couplets earlier), the poet often includes his given or pen name. At the beginning of the next section, the couplets frequently resume with a couplet such as "The narrator says..." (*râwi wâ'i*...), suggesting a storyteller's presence. If other forms of verse, such as *ghazal*s, are included, they are usually added at the end of a chapbook. Exceptions do occur in Mollâ Ahmad Jân's chapbooks in a romance (WWH 9) and a martial tale (WWH 7), where some sections are labeled as *robâ'i*s and, for the romance, *ghazal*s. The rhyme patterns in both cases are formally equivalent to a classical *ghazal* and include the poet's name in the final couplet, after which *mathnavi* sections resume. This shift between *mathnavi* and *ghazal* forms foreshadows a variation common in chapbooks and audiocassettes of Pashto narrative folk poetry in the second half of the twentieth century.

---

[3] The cover of WWH 40, purchased in 1983, is of a quite different, stylistically earlier type than WWH 41 and 42, purchased in 1986 and 1987, respectively, which have identical pictures on their covers, but the 1986 edition uses slick paper for its cover. The texts themselves, from title page with a price of Rs. 3 to end page, all seem to be printed from identical plates; they generally follow the Hughes version, but many lines differ by one or more words.

ORAL LITERATURE OF IRANIAN LANGUAGES

3. After 1950

In the Pashto-speaking areas of British India, reprintings of Pashto chapbooks from the nineteenth century into the late twentieth century attest to continued audiences for folk literature, as does anecdotal evidence of its performance in public places such as fairs and markets (e.g., Khattak 2005, pp. 31–32); major studies of folk literature for the first half of the 20th century are not yet available. The printing of pro-independence folk poetry was generally suppressed by the British; however, poetry promoting rights in Pashtun areas, especially that relating to the "Red-Shirts" led by Khan Abdul Ghaffâr Khan, circulated in oral form and when composed by major literary figures, eventually came into print.

For Afghanistan, the annotated bibliography of Nasir (2004), organized sequentially in time, can be used to document the rather sparse publication of Pashto folk literature prior to 1950 as well as more numerous publications thereafter; it includes publications from Baluchistan and others referring to particular regions within Afghanistan, thus offering starting points for comparative studies within the large Pashto-speaking area. The importance of oral but unpublished folk poetry for mid-20th century Afghanistan is the subject of a PhD dissertation by James Caron (forthcoming at the University of Pennsylvania) on "Oral Poetry as Small Media Communications, the Creation of a Pashtun Polity, and Ethno-nationalism: Eastern Afghanistan, 1930–1965."

The second half of the twentieth century saw major political and technological changes in the Pashto-speaking areas. Studies of folk literature were done by different groups of people and for different reasons; the quantity and variety of printed popular literature expanded as incomes increased; with post-WW II technology, better transportation and communications systems developed that influenced and were influenced by folk and popular culture. In Afghanistan, the *Paśto Tolǝna*, established in the 1920s, became part of the Afghan Academy established in 1967 (Rahman 1996, p. 142); this in turn was absorbed into the Academy of Sciences of Afghanistan. Most folk publications have been sponsored by the *Paśto Tolǝna*, or related sections of government organizations; the publication, *Pašto,* with articles chiefly on pre-modern history and folklore, was one of the few in which Afghan-authored articles in English, Russian and German appeared during the resistance to Soviet occupation (Magnus and Naby 1998, p. 199).

Pakistan's independence in 1947, and the departure of the British civil and military administration, was followed by the formation of organizations at both federal and provincial levels concerned with regional languages and culture. At the federal level, Lok Virsa, Pakistan's National Institute of Folk and Traditional Heritage, has sponsored research and regional collections of folktales carried out either by its own staff or through contracts with specialists in the various provinces. For the Pashto-speaking area, these included publications of translations into English of stories from various regions (e.g., Mahmud 1980) as well as Pashto stories translated or retold in Urdu and sometimes accompanied by source language texts in full or part. Its archives include tapes of tales collected in the field by Lok Virsa staff as well as by non-staff scholars working in cooperation with Lok Virsa. Given the multilingual nature of the country, tapes from one region sometimes include songs and stories in several languages, thus offering possibilities for cross-linguistic studies and folk research. Few of these tapes have yet been utilized and complete listings of them are not yet generally available.

At the provincial level in Pakistan, the Pashto Academy founded in 1955 at Peshawar University has published several collections of folk literature, as well as more literary texts and studies. However, despite the continued popularity of the nineteenth century folk poets, neither folklore nor folk literature has been considered a separate field of study in Pakistan's universities. Only a few cultural groups have included verse selections or biographical notes on particular folk poets or have reprinted an entire work in non-chapbook form.

4. Bibliographies, collections and studies

Bibliographies

In Afghanistan, the first of two bibliographies of Pashto books complied by Habibollâh Rafi was published in 1975. It includes both Afghan and Pakistani publications listed alphabetically by titles as well as brief descriptions of contents for its 500 entries; some of the entries are chapbooks by folk poets. A later volume, *Pašto Ketâb-šod*, has 1558 entries arranged alphabetically by author; it includes listings known from sources such as the British Museum and India Office library catalogues.

In Pakistan, Lok Virsa's *Bibliography of Folk Literature* by Jatoi (1980) includes over fifty books of Pashto folktales as well as books of Pashto folk songs. The titles from various languages show the commonality of certain tales, particularly those related to Islam, throughout Pakistan. These regional commonalities are more apparent between, for example, Sindhi and Punjabi tales than between Pashto and other language regions.

The bibliography of Hanaway and Nasir (1996) published jointly with Lok Virsa is devoted specifically to chapbooks; its 813 entries from various regions of Pakistan show the diversity and strength of chapbook publications in the last decades of the twentieth century. It includes over 250 chapbooks in Pashto published mainly in Peshawar, but in smaller number also from Quetta and outlying areas of the NWFP. In an earlier article, Hanaway (1995) places Pakistani chapbook publishing in a broad context geographically; the essay preceding his 1996 bibliography gives a description of 1980s chapbook printing which is probably similar to that of a century earlier, except for the shift from nineteenth-century lithography to the more recent photo-offset process. In Pakistan, it has in general not turned to typeset forms, and the chapbooks continued to be calligraphed. One easily visible change in recent years is the more colorful chapbook covers, which have replaced the earlier simple covers of colored or even plain white paper with titles and other information in black calligraphy.

PASHTO ORAL AND POPULAR LITERATURE

Collections

The prose collection, *Melli Hendâra* "National Mirror," of Mohammad Gol Nuri was originally a government publication in Kabul and later reprinted in Pakistan as a chapbook (H&N 615). This volume consists of thirteen tales in prose with occasional insertions of verses, most often *land̯ ys*, either within the tale or at its end; occasional footnotes concerning story variants or unusual words are included. Some of the stories, e.g., Âdam Khan, Fath Khan, and Qutb Khan, are known from nineteenth-century printed versions.

Later collections repeat many of these tales, sometimes reprinting part or all the *Melli Hendâra* versions. One such collection (Vejdân 1969), published with an introduction in Persian about folklore, includes three of these tales complete with the *Melli Hendâra* annotation; the volume includes other stories in Persian and proverbs in both Persian and Pashto.

The *Paśto Ṭolǝna* published two collections of Pashto folk poetry. The *Melli Sandǝre* (National Songs) of Mohammad Gol Nuri includes ten pages of plates with musical notation along with song texts; the later two-volume *Paśtani Sandǝre* (Pashto Songs), edited by Zamir and Zhwâk, is a much larger collection. It includes seven thousand *landǝys* as well as other verse forms; an appendix includes a classification of the *landǝys* by subject matter. The various kinds of verse are organized alphabetically by the initial letters of the first line of verse, rather than by the final rhyme word as in classical Pashto; the longer verse forms, i.e., folk *ghazal*, folk *robâ'i*, *chârbeyta*, *loba*, and short *qessa* or *dâstân*, typically include the poet's name. Verses of more than sixty different poets can be identified by their given or pen name; for some of these, examples of four different forms of their verse is included. Some of these poets have verses that were also included in Darmesteter's earlier volume, thus providing evidence of their continued popularity. In contrast to the poets whose verses of the nineteenth century have been reprinted in the twentieth century, these folk poets have generally not had collections of verse in printed form available for inclusion in Rafi's or Hanaway and Nasir's bibliographies. In the collection's section labeled *qessa o dâstân*, the verses themselves are always labeled *qessa*; that section's introduction (Vol. II, p. 198) comments that *qessa*s can be in either a *mathnavi* or *chârbeyta* style of verse. The last selection is in the former style; the other six each begin with a couplet or set of hemistichs concerning the subject matter which is then repeated in whole or part after each stanza.

In a chapter on *chârbeyta*s, Sho'ur (1988, pp. 108–47) uses materials from Darmesteter to present the *chârbeyta* as an oral newspaper because of its role in disseminating information about events. Caron (2007) uses a more recent *chârbeyta* by the popular poet, Malang Jan, with refrain referring to the 1953 visit of then Vice-President of the United States, Richard Nixon, illustrating again the importance of folk poetry in the social and political life of Afghanistan.

In Pakistan, an early Lok Virsa volume by Ghazanvi (1978) has a set of thirty-one romances from Pakistan's frontier retold in Urdu. Its tales are from Pashto-speaking areas including Swat, Dir (Alexander the Great and Rukhsana), Bajour, Mardan and Swabi, Peshawar and Charsadda, Kohat (a story of Bibi Eslâm from 1936) and Bannu, plus three common *(omumi)* Pashtun tales (Fath Khan-Rabiya, Momen Khan-Shirinəy, and Shâhzâda Bahrâm Gol-andâm) as well as tales from the primarily Hindko-speaking Hazara region in Abbottâbâd district. The Hazara tales include a version of Seyf al-Moluk, which is related to Pakistan's lake of that name. The adjoining frontier areas included in the book are Gilgit, Chitral, and Kafiristan; Kafiristan is linked with the tale of Âdam Khân-Dur Khanəy, well-known in both folk and literary Pashto versions. The tales are preceded by a paragraph commenting on reasons for the assignment of tales to a particular area as well as sources for the stories.

This Lok Virsa publication was followed by a set of forty-one martial tales in Urdu (Hamdani 1981); most of the tales include Pashto verse texts for part, or all, of the story. The tales begin with two stories of the early days of Islam by the nineteenth century poets, Ahmad Jân and Abu Ali-Shâh, and end with verses about fighting fronts in the 1965 India-Pakistan war by the Mardan poet, Abu'l-Wahid Têkêdâr (see Heston 1991, p. 330). Most of the Pashto texts are in rhyming couplets but some shorter selections are in verse forms with refrains; several selections are by the classical Pashto poet, Khoshhâl Khan Khattak, appropriate to the publishing institution's full name, "Institute of Folk and Traditional Heritage." Short paragraphs at the beginning of each translation include information about the text's versifier.

Lok Virsa also published translations of fourteen Pashto verse narratives collected in collaboration between a staff member and a visiting scholar (Heston and Nasir 1988). The translations were made from recordings; some were commercial cassettes purchased in Peshawar's Bazaar of the Storytellers; others were from tapes in Lok Virsa's archives or were recorded specifically for the volume. The tales include both old and new romances and martial tales; introductions and notes to the stories include the names of the singers and the circumstances of recording. Heston (1986) discusses the viewpoint and structure of one of these tales in more detail.

At the provincial level in Pakistan, the Pashto Academy at Peshawar University has devoted some of its resources to the publication of folk literature. A six hundred page, hardcover volume of over thirteen thousand *tapa*s includes an extensive introduction and colored plates with scenes of Pashtun life (Shaheen 1984). These *tapa*s are arranged in the order of the Pashto alphabet, using the letters of the beginning, rather than the final, words. The Pashto Academy has also published a small volume of children's songs (Tair 1988).

The collecting of Pashto proverbs continued in the twentieth century. In Afghanistan, a collection from the Paśto Ṭolǝna includes 1910 proverbs arranged alphabetically (Nuri 1327); a collection by Benawa (1979) of over 400 proverbs includes translations into Dari and English. The anthropologist Akbar Ahmed (1975) selected over 200 proverbs which are arranged alphabetically by initial word of the Pashto text and are accompanied by English translations and comments. A revised collection of 1350 proverbs (Tair and Edwards 2006) includes Pashto texts, English translations and comments arranged alphabetically and indexed by subject matter. Bartlotti (2000) focuses on the role of proverbs as particularly related to Islam and honor in Pashtun society. Tair (1980) also published a small collection that includes Pashto proverbs and

ORAL LITERATURE OF IRANIAN LANGUAGES

Urdu, Sindhi, Punjabi, Balochi and Brahui proverbs translated into Pashto. A collection of 100 proverbs with English translations unfortunately marred by misprints was published by Enevoldsen (c. 1990); this small volume also includes 100 Pashto *tapas* with English translations. A regional collection by Akhtar (1995) is devoted to proverbs from Swat.

As in the period prior to 1950, visitors to Pashto-speaking areas have collected and published folktales in translations. One such small volume (Parker and Javid 1970) produced through the collaboration of an American government officer and a Kabul University professor includes two dozen tales of several pages each which are often tied, like Masson's of a century earlier, to particular locations; several are noted as being in the *Melli Hendâra,* but the language sources are generally not specified. Two other collections of folktales from Afghanistan (Dhar 1982; Shah 1982) suggest, either from the content of certain stories or from acknowledgements, that Pashto speakers have been consulted. However, they include no specifics of immediate linguistic sources for particular stories. Single tales included as representative of Afghanistan are likewise not identified as to linguistic source (e.g., Forest 1996, pp. 73–77; Baltuck 1995, pp. 26–28). A collection printed in Pakistan without provincial or federal sponsorship has ten short selections (Pishinvi 1970) in Urdu with titles that generally match those in the *Melli Hendâra.*

Studies

A major contribution to the study of Pashto folk poetry was made by D. N. MacKenzie (1958), who in time-honored fashion learned Pashto in the British Army while stationed in the Subcontinent. His article on "Pashto Verse" was the first to point to the importance of stress, rather than syllable length, in Pashto poetry. Using the patterns of popular poetry, he builds a system with primary stress recurring at four-syllable intervals, and counter-stresses at intervening two-syllable intervals that fits both folk and classical Pashto verse.

PASHTO ORAL AND POPULAR LITERATURE

All but one of MacKenzie's examples of popular poetry, given in Romanized transcription with stress marked and English translation, were taken from the *Melli Sandərê* and *Paśtani Sandərê*. Despite its name, the folk *robâ'i* is not a quatrain but is similar to a literary *ghazal*. The folk *ghazal*, in turn, may have a variety of rhyme schemes rather than the simple pattern. *mm am bm cm*, etc., of the folk *robâ'i* or literary *ghazal*.[4] Both these two forms usually include the poet's name, most often in the final couplet. The *chârbeyta*, belying its name, is usually not four couplets but of longer and quite varied length and rhyme pattern; its particular characteristic is a refrain repeated after each stanza.[5] The poet's name usually appears in the last stanza rather than the final refrain line. The *loba*, like the *chârbeyta*, has a stanzaic form with a refrain. After an opening refrain line, a set of three or four nine-syllable end-rhymed lines is followed by the refrain (e.g. *r, aaar, bbbr*, etc.).

The shorter forms of folk poetry are typically anonymous, although when grouped together, a poet's name may be included. Undoubtedly the most frequently published of these is the *mesrâ'* or *ṭapa*, as it is usually called in Pakistan, or *landəy* (lit., "short") as it is often known in Afghanistan, an unrhymed couplet with nine syllables in the first hemistich and thirteen in the second. The final syllable ends in *-ina, -una, -ana* or *-ama*. MacKenzie translates nine examples, giving romanized transcriptions and indicating stress and caesura. Although each *landəy* is an independent unit, it can be grouped with others by, for example, subject matter (e.g., a particular historical event or folk romance), and sung as a sequence either by a single singer or by different people, sometimes competitively. Translations of *land ys* by the poet. Majruh (2003) provide a cultural context; translations into Persian by Manalai (2005) offer convenient comparisons with Persian for lexicon and syntax.

4　Three folk *ghazal* patterns listed by MacKenzie (1958, p. 320) are: mm aamm bbmm ccmm; mm aaam bbbm cccm; mm aabm ccdm eefm; other examples include internal rhyme.

5　A folk *chârbeyta* that is not a quatrain is also found in Hindko, the common language of Peshawar's old city. The 1978 study of Hamdâni, whose mother tongue was Hindko, includes samples of the Hindko *chârbeyta* together with Urdu translations and a discussion of the poets who write them.

Other forms of folk poetry described by MacKenzie are the "dance song" or chorus (*də atəń nâra*), which normally has three or four lines of the rhyme and syllabic patterns: (a) *m b m* and syllabic pattern: (7) 11 7 11 and the *nimakay* or *sar*, another stanzaic form, varying in length from five to fifteen syllables"; both *nimakay* examples are mixed with a *mesrâ'*. Yet another form of folk verse, the *bâbu lâla*, is "sung by the women of a bridal party to the waiting bride ... a regular tristich, rhyming *a b a*, generally with an eight-syllable line" (MacKenzie 1958, pp. 324–25). Manalai (1987) classifies folk forms by constraints (e.g, rhyme, length, strophic pattern) with examples in transcription and translation. In addition to forms described by MacKenzie, he includes the "comptine" (nursery rhyme) with its rhythmic formulations and the *sarukay*, a short form with rhythmic verses not connected to each other and usually combined with a *land̯ y*.

MacKenzie's descriptions of folk poetry forms from Afghan collections are consistent with forms found in most Peshawar chapbook poetry of the last decades of the twentieth century. When unqualified, *badəla* often refers to a verse narrative, and thus in written form it alternates with *dâstân* or *qessa*; a chapbook titled "Garland of *Badəlas*" (*də badəlo amêl*: H&N 635) has several *qessa*s in *mathnavi* form with interspersed sets of *mesrâ*'s. The *badəla* can also be qualified as a particular song category, e.g., *də wâdə badəla* 'wedding song.' In the last decades of the twentieth century, a request for a *badəla* from a Peshawar music shop or footpath vendor would result in a tape of narrative verse rather than lyric verse.

Regional differences in terminology go beyond the differing use of *land̯ y* and *t̯apa*. Bokhâri and Hamdâni's description (1966) of folk forms adds the *allâh-hu* as a category of lullaby. Bokhâri (1974, p. 137) puts the *bagat y* in a separate category, saying that it has a short meter (*mokhtasar bahr*) like the *chârbeyta*, but a completely different style of singing (*gânê kê andâz*). Momand and Sahrâ'i (1994) define the *bagat y* as a kind of *chârbeyta*. Manalai (1987, pp. 134–35) follows Zamir, who groups the *bagat y* with the *loba*. Quddus (1987, pp. 53, 56) characterizes the *loba* as "the medium of a woman" and ties the Pashto music scales to particular tunes of different *lobas*. Peshawar chapbooks have many verses labeled as *loba*s but few if any as *bagat ̣ys*. Other writers of long residence in Pashto-speaking areas use additional and sometimes overlapping terms (e.g., Dupree 1970, p. 90, n. 10). The further definition of folk poetry forms and their relationship to musical forms continues to offer possibilities for future research.

Focusing on the singing of Pashto verse, Heston (1996) uses tapes and audiocassettes of *Lok Virsa* to illustrate patterns of rhyme and repetition. The selections, given in Romanized transcription and translation, include a *chârbeyta*, four sets of *ṭapa*s, two *ghazal*s, and a sequence of narrative verse with rhyming couplets followed by end-rhymed couplets. The first set of *ṭapa*s concerns the folktale, *Shêr Âlam and Mêmunəy*, the second and third are about love and separation, and the last is a plea to *bhang* (cannabis). The two *ghazal* selections are both from classical texts, one by Khoshhâl Khan Khattak and the other by the mystic Abd-al-Rahmân, usually known as Rahmân Bâbâ.

Among the forms of folk poetry, the *ṭapa* has been given perhaps the most attention. Shpoon (1967) examines its range of subject matter, dividing it into love and beauty, social tragedies, (martial) epic, nature, and departures and exodus; he includes examples with translations. Tair wrote a lengthy introduction to Shaheen's 1984 *ṭapa* collection; in a separate book, Tair (1980) considers the *ṭapa* in relation to various aspects of Pashtun life including folk literature. The *chârbeyta*, found also in Hindko, the language of NWFP cities, and Urdu, is examined by Hamdâni (1978).

The contributions of women to Pashto folk literature are not readily apparent; folk poets are consistently male. Certain anonymous forms, particularly the *ṭapa*, are often associated with women; the impression of, for example, Boesen (1983, p. 104), working in Kunar in eastern Afghanistan, is that *landəy*s "are always sung, accompanied by the women's instrument, the tambourine (*tsamba*)," and that they are only sung when no men are present. The low status associated with professional performers and the rules of *purdah* have limited the participation of women in entertainment involving singing, except in special circumstances such as weddings. In her fieldwork among women, Grima (1992) found that the *qessa* in the sense of folktales, fairy tales and fiction from books or tradition was for outsiders, but for insiders, the *qessa* consisted "of personal experience tales or stories of local events" (p. 30). She therefore focused her research on the dominant narrative form among women, which was *qessa*s "lamenting their own experiences and life" (p. 31). In her chapter on the poetics and discourse of grief (*gham*), she looks at grief in the context of several literary folk genres. Her appendices organize three women's narratives into lines representing the unfolding of their internal cultural patterning; her lengthy bibliography provides background on Pashtun society and especially the position of Pashtun women as well as ethno-poetics of narratives. Using examples from cassettes and chapbooks, Heston (1995) points to the comparative simplicity of gendered imagery in Pashto folk poetry. Kâkar's small collection of women's songs (*cheghyân*) comes from the Pashto-speaking areas of Baluchistan; he comments that the songs are known in some dialects as *angǝy*. In the nineteenth-century tradition of collecting stories while gathering linguistic data, Septfonds (1994) includes a version of Sayf-ol-Moluk from Afghanistan and Hallberg (1992) includes Pashtuns' descriptions of recent accidents which provide possible comparison with the women's recitations documented by Grima (1992).

5. Mass Media

Chapbooks

The bibliography of Hanaway and Nasir is essentially a snapshot of a particular point in time of the folk literature continually flowing from commercial presses in Pakistan into the market for folk literature. In addition to the reprinting of nineteenth century works, a variety of other Pashto chapbooks in prose and verse were available in this market during the last decades of the twentieth century. Unlike the collections of cultural organizations, most chapbooks are by a single author, and usually consist of a single genre, a single tale or a single subject. The prose chapbooks include, for example, books of jokes (e.g., H&N 470, 478, 483), the well-traveled tales about Mollâ Nasreddin (e.g., H&N 539, 672), and tales of "Mollâ Two-onions" at the court of the Emperor Akbar (WWH 245). Other prose chapbooks include single stories, such as Aladdin's Lamp, Ali Bâbâ and the Forty Thieves, Shaikh Chelli, and Shâhzâda Shahryâr and Maleka Shâhzâd (H&N 536, 534, 543, 542), claiming on their covers to be taken from the Thousand and One Nights. Some prose chapbooks are retellings of traditional romances such as Leylâ and Majnun (WWH 247) and Shirin and Farhâd (WWH 635). Many, however, are new tales, some by writers who write only prose and others by writers who write both prose and verse. The prolific chapbook writer, Shâker-Allâh Shâker, for example, has narratives in prose: Shêrdel Dacoit, The Dacoit's Father, Two Brothers' Longing, and An Honorable Wife (H&N 653, 648 645; WWH 627), as well as in verse: The Red Litter's (i.e. bride's) Longing (*də srê ḏoləy armân*), The Unfaithful Wife, Three Girls, A Cruel King, A Killer Bride, and Salve-Bandage (*malham-patəy*), with verses including one *qessa* about Moses and one about the White Snake Prince (*spin-mâr shâhzâda*) and the Queen of Sheba (H&N 646, 650; WWH 82, 629, 410, 637).

In verse, some chapbooks consist entirely of a single verse form. A number of chapbooks consist entirely of *ṯapa*s (e.g., H&N 503, 531, 636, 676, 677; WWH 606, 612). These are usually not the anonymous, ordered *ṯapa* collections of the academies. Instead, some are arranged by a topical word (i.e., *shuńḏe*, "lips," *spoźməy* "moonlight," *qalam* "pen," and *kalêj* "college") occurring initially or elsewhere in either the first or second hemistich (WWH 624), while others are arranged in alphabetical order of first word but include the name of the author (*mosannef*) in the last *ṯapa* of each section (WWH 602), paralleling the use of a pen name in a literary *ghazal*'s final couplet. The chapbook *Felmi Tape* (WWH 621) has listings by the name of the film and the singer.

Chapbooks consisting only of *chârbeyta*s are much less common; only one (H&N 663) is included in Hanaway and Nasir's bibliography as compared to its five chapbooks of *ṯapa*s. Although a few chapbooks consist entirely of *ghazal*s in the literary style, the majority of non-narrative chapbooks have a variety of verse forms:

*ghazal*s, *robâ'i*s, *loba*s, *chârbeyta*s, *nimakəy*s, *ṭapa*s, and sometimes short *qessa*s following each other usually in no apparent order.

A major change in late twentieth century narrative verse from that of the preceding century is that instead of being composed almost entirely in *mathnavi* form, chapbooks commonly alternate between sections in rhyming couplets and sections with end rhymes. This mixed pattern usually includes the poet's name in the final couplet of the section regardless of its rhyme pattern. The name used within verses may be either a given name or a pen name or both; poets vary in their consistency and sometimes the inclusion of a pen name on the cover or title page is the only instance of its use in a particular chapbook. In addition to a personal name, the poet's village or tribe may also be included in a final couplet.

Not only do verse narratives alternate their sequences of rhyming couplets and end rhymed couplets, but they may also be interspersed with other forms of folk verse. The story of Chamnay Khan by Abd-al-Wahhâb Dasti (WWH 107), a prolific folk poet, includes, for example, *ṭapa*s (pp. 13, 30–31, 32–34) and a *robâ'i* (pp. 28–29), as well as *ghazal*s (pp. 36–37, 37–38), *robâ'i*s (pp. 41, 42), *loba*s (pp. 40, 46), a *chârbeyta* (pp. 44–45) and more *ṭapa*s (p. 38) at the narrative's end. Similarly, in the chapbook of Râmdâd Khan by Ali Heydar Joshi (WWH 110), other forms are inserted at various points in the narrative sequence.

Islam is solidly established in Pashtun culture today as it was in the nineteenth century. Chapbooks of verse usually begin with a poem praising God (*hamd*) and often one or more poems praising the Prophet or other religious figures (*na't*). A number of late twentieth century chapbooks have consisted partly or wholly of religious verse. Some can be identified by the inclusion of *na't* in the title, e.g., *Də Na'tuna Goldasta* (A Bouquet of *Na't*s, H&N 443) or by a cover picture of the Ka'ba or the mosque at Medina (H&N 601), while others are identifiable only by an examination of the contents. Particularly popular chapbooks circulate with printings and reprintings by several different publishers at the same time; Mohammad Amin's *Golzâr-e Madina*, for example, was available from three different publishers c. 1990 (H&N 596–98), with additional printings by two of those publishers by 1995 (WWH 625,

632). The most popular verse narrative in terms of current versions is *Yusof and Zoleykhâ*, which had folk versions by at least three poets, Golâb (H&N 545), Joshi (H&N 573), and Shâh Rasul Abjadi (WWH 80) in late twentieth century chapbook printings.

Like many of the non-religious chapbooks, the religiously oriented chapbooks often have a mixture of verse forms. *Də Ferây Oske* (Separation's Tears; H&N 601), for example, not only includes *na'ts* and *hamds*, but also short *qessas*, *robâ'is*, *ghazals*, *marthiyes*, and *nazm*; very occasionally, verses are labeled as *qavvâli* (H&N 540, pp. 12, 32). When *qessas* are included, they are usually about a religious figure, although exceptions occur. "Flames of Fire" (*də or lambe*; H&N 604), for example, has a series of short *qeses* including romances both local, e.g., *Âdam Khan-Dur Khânəy*, and more widely known, e.g., *Leylâ-Majnun*, as well as *qeses* about Job and Mir Hâtam, which would be the more expected heroes in this context. His chapbook also includes a series of *na'ts*, *marthiyes*, *nazm*, literary *ghazals*, *lobas*, *nimakəys*, and *ṭapas*. As with the secular chapbooks, chapbook poetry of a religious nature is not grouped by form but has various genres of verse one after another in no apparent order.

At the end of the twentieth century, the Pashto chapbook industry was thus a flourishing source of popular literature, developing in such a way that the oral folk forms transcribed for Darmesteter in the previous century were widely available in printed form in Peshawar's Bazaar of the Storytellers.

Newspapers and periodicals

In Pakistan, printed popular Pashto literature other than chapbooks is rather limited. Newspapers and periodicals in Pashto have been few; the newspapers have not included the popular supplements sometimes found in English and Urdu language papers. Sabir (1974) includes a brief chapter on Pashto reportage, noting a few writers who were also prominent literary figures. In 2003, the total circulation of Pashto daily papers was under 34,000 and smaller than the circulation of English, Urdu and Sindhi dailies; the Pashto circulation was an increase of about 50% over the preceding decade, but a decrease in the percentage of total circulation (*Pakistan Statistical Yearbook* 1995, pp. 371–72).

In Afghanistan, the press has historically been under government control and without the resources or readership for women's or film magazines. Pourhadi (1976) lists over sixty newspapers, magazines and journals together with dates of founding (1875 to 1966), place of publication (most often Kabul), language, frequency of publication, and other comments on, for example, contents and circulation. Regime changes before and during the Russian occupation, the emergence and control by the Taliban, and the U.S.-led invasion of Afghanistan in 2001 have resulted in continued shifts in newspaper publication. In the 21st century, the addition of Internet technology has provided a variety online news service related in some cases to radio broadcasts from within Afghanistan and outside (e.g., BBC and VOA). In addition, a variety of Pashto publications both current and past can be found online at sites such as http://www.benawa.com/rasanay/.

Radio and TV

In both Pakistan and Afghanistan, radio stations have been government-controlled and multilingual; in Pakistan, the radio station in Peshawar began transmitting in 1935 with an hour of Pashto per day (Abd-al-Ra'uf 1988, p. 53). The programs encouraged writers as well as singers and musicians. The personnel associated with the radio stations have been among the intellectuals of the country and music programs have accordingly given some preference to classical styles. The interest and talent of radio personnel in Afghanistan has been surprising; in 1979, the head of the music and literature department, and later Director General of Radio Afghanistan until removed by coup leaders was Dr. Mohammad Sâdeq Fetrat, who was revealed in a 1979 benefit for flood victims to be the famous singer Nâshenâs.

Telecasting has also been government-controlled in both countries. In Pakistan, the government-controlled radio and telecasting have been multilingual. Throughout the country, most of the TV broadcasting has been in English and Urdu; in the period from 1984 through 1994, there has been a steady rise in the total number of broadcasting hours with about half of them being in the Urdu broadcasts and one-sixth in English. Local language hours in Pashto from the Peshawar station have included translations of news into local languages and various educational programs, as well as dramas with a local setting and vocal music, most frequently *ghazal*s. An occasional program features a folktale or places a music performance in a village setting to simulate folk songs in a natural location. The drama serials in Pakistan are well regarded by intellectuals; several Pashto TV dramas' scriptwriters have been members of the Peshawar University faculty. Members of the Pashto Academy have also been associated with musical performances on TV, where classical *ghazal*s have been a preferred genre except during religious holidays. The arrival of the TV satellite-dish receivers has widened the viewing possibilities, as Pashto-speaking households are no longer limited to programs from stations under government control.

Audiocassettes and performance

Pashto folk poetry and songs are closely tied, as the use of *sandərê* 'songs' for collections of folk poetry indicates. Singers have been transmitters of folk poetry, whether as amateurs in men's guesthouses (*hojra*), maintained by villages or wealthy khans, or as professionals engaged for special occasions such as weddings and circumcisions. The arrival on the Subcontinent of audiocassette technology and relatively inexpensive tape players changed the means of transmission for poetry, as Manuel (1993) has described for north India. For Pashto songs, the variety of available audiocassette recordings expanded rapidly during the 1980s with the most popular verse forms being *ghazal*s and *badəla*s. Cassette players found a place in *hojra*s along with, or instead of, the traditional *rabâb*s and *mangay*s (clay water-pots used for drums).

Certain singers have been particularly popular, and their tapes have been circulated even in remote villages; the copying of existing tapes has been a common means of acquiring the songs of a favorite singer. Some tapes originated as studio recordings while others were recordings made before live audiences, sometimes on festive occasions with the usual background of other sounds including, for example, the celebratory gunfire that might be heard at a wedding. The relationship between poetry in the form of audiocassettes and printed chapbooks was a two-way flow that Heston (1991) describes; chapbooks served as texts for singers, and poetry that found success on an audiocassette was more likely to be given a chapbook printing.

Grima (1982) has translated four verse narratives from bazaar cassettes sung by three different singers popular in the 1980s: Wahid Gol singing "Shêr Âlam-Mêmunəy" by Jamâl of Sangar, and "Yusof Khan-Shêr Bânu" by Ali Heydar Joshi; Fazl-e Qayyum singing "Jalat Khan-Mahbuba" by Tâj Mohammad, and Jân Mohammmad singing "Gol and Sanowbar" by Amân Gujarâti. Grima includes Pashto and Romanized transcriptions for some tapes; the translated advertisements, announcements and interjections provide insight into the production of the tapes. In a later paper, Grima (1987) discusses issues of translation for one of these tapes.

Baily (1985) filmed an Afghan refugee musician's life in Peshawar. The scenes of singing in a musician's rooms or studio (*dâyera*), at a Pakistani wedding, and in a wealthy patron's hotel room, provide examples of performances in three settings. Like Baily's scenes of Peshawar itself, they are easily recognizable by those who have been in such places. The Pashto songs include a *ṭapa* series and a *chârbeyta*, musically both in the same melodic mode, but in different metric cycles; the film's videocassette provides English subtitles for songs and conversation (mainly in Persian). The accompanying study guide (Baily 1990) provides notes on the backgrounds of the musicians and the culture of the area as well as the filmmaking itself. As Baily (1990, p. 33, n. 6) comments in translating some *dâstân* verses, "the written history of the war in Afghanistan will have to utilize the stories recounted in epics such as this."

The amount of resistance poetry circulated on cassettes as part of Afghan resistance to the Russian occupation of Afghanistan has been considerable. Among the Afghans active in this field was

Rafiq Jân, a singer-poet whose verses on Peshawar resistance to the British in 1930 (see Heston and Nasir 1988, pp. 305–42) have already been cited in a regional history (Salim 1991, p. 116).

Computer technology has added new paths for the transmission of Pashto folk poetry as realized in performance. In Afghanistan, the effect of regime changes has been evident on the Internet; thus, a website offering Afghan "chants" (*tarânas*) performed by the Taliban in 1999 was not available in 2007. Baily (2001) traces radio and TV censorship before and during the Taliban regime and includes a CD with a Pashto chant about Taliban martyrs; Baily (2004) updates the situation for the fall of the Taliban. Since then, a wide variety of Pashto sung poetry (both classical and folk) has became available online from Afghanistan as well as from radio and TV.

Cinema and VCRs

Like radio and television, cinema in Pakistan is multilingual. It is not, however, directly under government control, although censorship and restrictions on film imports and foreign exchange have been a means of exerting political pressure. In 2001–02, Peshawar had fifteen cinema houses and Quetta had seven (*Pakistan Statistical Yearbook* 2004, pp. 468–69), showing little change over the past two decades; even in these regions of Pashto speakers, Urdu and English films are also shown. Political events, such as actual and feared bomb explosions in Peshawar cinema houses during the 1980s as well as the social disruptions with the massive influx of Afghan refugees into Pakistan, changed the composition of Pashto movie audiences from the once mixed and middle-class audiences in the 1970s to an almost exclusively male and much less-educated audiences by the end of the century.

The South Asian film industry in 1950 was centered in Bombay (Mumbai). Lahore had been actively involved in films prior to the partition of India in 1947. After Pakistan's independence, Muslim film producers, directors and stars as well as the related composers, writers, and musicians, were naturally drawn to that city. The first Pashto film, *Leylâ-Majnun*, was made not in Lahore, however, but in Bombay; the script was written by the Pashto poet, Amir Hamza Shinwari. This film was not a commercial success; possible reasons for this are discussed by Sabir (1974) in a chapter on film literature (*felmi adab*) that gives a brief background for the early years of Pashto films.

The next Pashto film was the tale of Yusof Khân-Shêr Bânu, produced in Lahore in 1970 with script and songs by the folk poet, Ali Heydar Joshi; the film's success was an encouragement for the further production of Pashto films. For two of these, *Alâqa Gheyr* (Tribal Territory; 1972) and *Pêghla* (The Maiden; 1975), the scripts and songs were again by Amir Hamza Shinwari (Qabil Khân 1990). A number of the early Pashto films drew on other folk romances or tales of local heroes. Among those listed by Gazdar (1997) are *Adam Khan*, *Ajab Khan*, and *Musa Khan Gol Makəy* in 1971; *Memoone* in 1972, *Farhâd-Shirin* and *Chirâgh-e Alladin* (Alladin's Lamp) in 1973; and *Rehim Dâd Khan* and *Momin Khan Shiriney* in 1974. For these films, the folk antecedents are easily documented in folk literature, including chapbooks. For at least two of Gazdar's film listings, *Sheytân-e Zâlem-e Jâdugar* (The Cruel Magician, 1996) and *Də Shigo Sheytân* (Sand Devil, 1996), chapbooks of similar titles (WWH 631 and 630 respectively) appeared at about the same time as the films.

In the 1980s, as film songs in Pakistani languages came to be printed in chapbook form, the term *badəla* was sometimes used for film songs in Pashto. One such chapbook (WWH 36, 253) called itself "the first book of film songs" (*də filmi badəlo r̂ombe ketâb*), and was available in Peshawar's Bazaar of the Storytellers in 1987. Like other chapbooks of film songs, it lists the titles of the movies and the names of the five included singers along with the words to the songs; although rhyming couplets predominate, many of the songs show shifts in rhyme patterns. Most books of film songs feature only one or two singers. The presence of a specialized shop such as the Parvez Felmi Stor (WWH 214), with its own publications, suggests a solid market for chapbooks of film songs.

The arrival of VCRs provided an alternative to the cinema house with the social issues and dangers (such as threats of bombing) associated with it; the popularity of VCRs flourished in the NWFP and bootleg copies of popular American films have sometimes already been available in the small towns of the NWFP while they are still showing at movie theaters in New York. Although most video stores in Pashto-speaking areas continue to keep Pashto movie videos in stock, the multitude of videos in other languages has led to less space available for them.

More difficult to evaluate is the number of videos created from recordings of TV broadcasts and private performances. Weddings in Pashto-speaking areas of Pakistan have always been an occasion to hire musicians and dancers, and video recording at weddings usually include sequences with the professional entertainers. In circles that are less strict about observing *purdah*, the women of the family, as well as any professional female musicians they have hired, may also be videotaped as they sing traditional women's wedding songs; these tapes are sent to family members abroad, providing a way for traditional songs sung on special occasions to circulate far from their original place of performance. Pashto songs from both Afghan and Pakistani television performances are also reproduced on videotape, and these also circulate internationally as well as within Pashto-speaking regions. As with audiocassette tapes, particular singers are favorites and the style of singing may be considerably influenced by western popular music, even when the song's verses are nominally a *ghazal*.

6. Concluding comments

This chapter has tried to present an overview of Pashtun oral and popular literature from the nineteenth century to the present. The civil and military administrators of the nineteenth century have been replaced by national and provincial academies as collectors of folk literature, while scholars and travelers have continued to write about Pashtuns and their culture. Popular literature printed commercially in chapbook form continued to flourish until the end of the twentieth century as tales of poets of the previous century were republished, and new writers in prose and verse contributed their works in chapbooks with more colorful covers than those of yesteryear. The introduction of audiocassettes afforded listeners a chance to enjoy a broad range of singers with oral poetry available for a wide variety of tastes. Films viewed directly or from videocassettes construct new narrative forms that interact with written folk forms; their songs circulate in both printed and recorded form. Television programs from outside Afghanistan and Pakistan supplement those of local stations. In addition, the Internet, while not yet a widely available medium in many Pashto-speaking regions, has the potential to be the vehicle for the most widespread dissemination of both songs and movies, and thus act an indispensable tool for their preservation. Changes in communication, and increasingly easier means of travel, bring a multitude of influences on popular culture that have yet to be systematically explored. A rich and varied field of study thus awaits scholars interested in Pashto oral and popular literature.

CHAPTER 7

BALOCHI LITERATURE

JOSEF ELFENBEIN[1]

It was in the early nineteenth century, as a consequence of the westwards expansion of the British in India, that the Balochi language first came to the notice of Europeans, and several brief sketches of it were written (for the most important of these see LSI X,[2] p. 335). By 1880 three good grammatical descriptions had been published (those of Pierce, Marston, and Mockler; see LSI X) and the first scientific studies of the language, by a leading Iranist Wilhelm Geiger, were written in the next few years.

It had also been noticed that a substantial amount of oral literature appeared to exist—much more than expected—and small collections of it were made and published in the early nineteenth century, mainly by English missionaries in India. As is only to be expected, however, the published grammars showed little grasp of details like dialect geography, and the literary specimens had no pretensions to anything more than curiosity value.

All of these collections were made and published by Europeans (Hittu Ram was employed in the Indian Civil Service); the sole exception known up to now is the BM Codex Oriental Additional 24048, which the present writer believes (it bears neither colophon nor date) was prepared c. 1820 in Kalat, Baluchistan, at the request of H. H. Wilson, later Boden Professor of Sanskrit in Oxford. It is well known that during his time in India Wilson was an enthusiastic collector of specimens of the exotic languages of the Subcontinent,

---

1 This article was written in 1998. At the author's request, the system of transcription normally used in academic publications is adopted in the Chapter.
2 LSI X is used throughout for Grierson 1921 (Ed.).

and it is most likely that this manuscript was prepared especially at his request (see Elfenbein 1983).

The end of the prehistory of Balochi studies and the beginning of systematic and scientific studies is marked by the appearance of M. L. Dames, whose works from the 1880s marked a watershed. In them we see for the first time a large collection of Balochi classical ballads and other poetry, as well as many prose narratives. Dames' publications superseded all previous studies, and with only a few reservations are still usable today. But there was at the time little stimulus locally for native Baloch to continue Dames' work, and Balochi was, to all intents and purposes (except for European writings), an unwritten language.

But Dames had shown concretely what had until then only been suspected, that there indeed existed a large body of oral literature, mostly in the form of ballads, as well as quite a large number of the expected little stories in prose, which only awaited collection and recording. But such an enterprise had to await, with only a few exceptions, the period after the creation of Pakistan in 1947, when a new stimulus for undertaking such labor could work upon a new generation of educated native Balochis.

Balochi literature can be fairly clearly divided into four periods: (1) The classical period from perhaps the sixteenth century to c. 1700; (2) A post-classical period to c. 1800; (3) The nineteenth century; (4) The modern period after c. 1930.

1. The classical period

Up to the modern period all Balochi literature is oral, preserved only in the memories of poets, professional reciters, or amateur enthusiasts, all of whom were, of course, illiterate. Such enthusiasts were, at least until very recently, much more numerous than might be imagined; in the 1980s most villages contained at least a few. All of our information on the oral periods of Balochi literature comes from them, and it is only thanks to the efforts of literate collectors of these traditions in the nineteenth and twentieth centuries, who patiently listened to ballad recitals and wrote down what they heard (but not necessarily understood), that we have any information at all about earlier literature.

The main written sources are collections by M. L. Dames; Mohammad Sardar Khan Baloch; Shêr Muhammad Marî; Elfenbein 1990 (mostly from written sources, but checked orally); *Mâhtâk Balôčî;* Mîr ʿĪsâ Qômî (whose unparalleled manuscript library was mainly collected by himself from oral recitations, shared with the present writer during a long visit to him in Turbat in 1961); the periodicals *Nôkên Dawr* and *Ulus* have also occasionally published short pieces; for a fuller list see Jahani (1989, pp. 25–33, 229–30).

The literature of the classical and post-classical periods consists entirely of ballads. Prose of a literary quality makes its appearance only in the modern period. Before the twentieth century, hardly any attempt was made by the Baloch themselves to write their language; but after 1947 "Balochi Academies" sprang up in Pakistan, societies whose purpose was to stimulate new writing and collect the classical, so as to make the written word play a role in Balochi society. The center of Balochi literary culture has always resided in what is now Pakistan, particularly in Quetta and Karachi; nothing of any lasting importance in this regard has ever emerged from Iran. In Afghanistan after 1978 Balochi was accorded the status of "national language" and some publications have appeared from Kabul. (sporadic publications in the Gulf States and in East Africa by emigrant Baloch communities are not included in this discussion).

Script and dialect

Only variants of the Arabic script have ever come seriously into question for native writing in Balochi. The first Balochi writing was in the Pashto script, with the usual problems of vowel representation. Dames and other Europeans used the modified Roman script usually employed by Christian missionaries (mainly British) in India; it is, in the main, quite acceptable. Geiger, of course, used the scientific script employed by Iranists. There have been official efforts in Pakistan, especially since 1960, to adopt a Roman script for Balochi, but they have come to nothing; the script used today in Pakistan for Balochi is based on Urdu, whereas that adopted in Afghanistan is based on Pashto.

There are six dialects in Balochi, of which two have long ago achieved prestige status as vehicles for classical balladry: Coastal dialect, and Eastern Hill Balochi, with some use of Kêčî.[3] These dialects have long exercised a strong influence on other dialects. Co is relatively uniform over its whole area, but EHB has a number of widely varying sub-dialects; writing in it tends to be in the variety used in the Marî-Bugṯî tribal area. Ke is without important sub-dialects.

Here a word must be said about dialects in Balochi literary composition. Oral transmission over centuries by speakers of all dialects has inevitably meant that dialects get mixed in transmission; a sort of mixed dialect is used in nearly all ballads except those in Co dialect, and balladry in EHB is strongly influenced by the Co dialect as well. By general consent, Co is the proper dialect for classical and post-classical ballads, with EHB coming second. A tradition exists in which speakers of other dialects (now also) often try to imitate the Co dialect in literary composition, even when they do not know it well. The result is a peculiar mishmash, with false Co dialect forms popping up in writings by speakers of other dialects. Similarly, Ke is often the preferred dialect for literary prose, with the same sorts of mixtures. Rakhšânî is by far the most widely spoken dialect, but it is only in the modern period that it is used at all for literary composition.

Eastern Hill Balochi is the dialect of all the publications of Dames, since all of his reciters came from the territory in the extreme east, British Baluchistan. It is also the native dialect of both Shêr Muhammad Marî and of Muhammad Sardar Khan Baloch. Mîr ʿĪsâ Qômî (hereafter Qômî) lived in Turbat and spoke Kêčî.

---

[3] On dialects see Elfenbein, "Baluchistan III," "Baločî"; for fuller notes on dialect characteristics see Elfenbein, *Anthology*, vol. 2, pp. vii–xviii. The following abbreviations will be used here: Ra = Raxšânî; Co = Coastal; EHB = Eastern Hill Balochi; Ke = Kêčî; Sar = Sarawânî; La = Lâškârî. For a full description of dialect characteristics, see Elfenbein 2003.

BALOCHI LITERATURE

The composition by individuals of classical oral ballads

The tradition that many ballads were composed by important chiefs, themselves the individuals named in the short prose prefaces to them, or by (anonymous) professional bards who were attached to the various tribes, is worth taking seriously. In fact, most of the ballads are prefaced by a short introduction of fairly standard form, giving the authorship; it runs "X son of Y sings; of the fight at Z he sings"; or "X son of Y sings; he challenges/replies to Z and sings." The word used for "sings" (and so translated by e.g. Dames) is *gušît*, the ordinary word for "says, speaks." But Dames was certainly right in supposing that classical ballads were in fact "sung," though perhaps "chanted" would be a better word. It was not customary for a chief or other important person to recite his own poetry; the custom was rather for him to teach it, line by line, to a professional reciter called often *pahlawân* (as in Persian), or more commonly *ḍômb*, *lôrî*, or *lângaw*. These latter were professional reciters and musicians of much lower social status than the *pahlawân*, usually belonging to a special caste. It was usual to accompany the recital by music on an important occasion, in which the music followed the poetry in a fixed canon using one or more instruments such as the *tabla* (drum), *surnâ* (double-reed pipe), *surôd* (short-necked fiddle), *dambûrô* (long-necked fiddle), *giraw* (nose flute), or *nar* (flute). Recitals could also take place without music, and very popular from earliest time was the *mušâ'îra*, a sort of concert of poetry, in which several recitals took place. The occasions for composing a ballad are countless: any important event, such as a birth, death, wedding, harvest, battle, migration, etc. Once the reciter had learned the poem he could add it to his professional repertoire, and recite it elsewhere on any appropriate occasion, naming (or not) the true author. This, of course, greatly contributed to the tendency of ballads to become anonymous with the passage of time.

Daptars

A good claim to being some of the oldest poetry handed down can be made for the *daptar šā'irî* "ballad of genealogy, register ballad." Although not many of these ballads have been preserved, they have such a similarity of form and content, as well as the occasional linguistic archaism, that they are particularly interesting. Only six of them are known to me, all rather short; four of them have been published:

i. LSI X, pp. 370–73, of sixty lines. It is basically in Coastal dialect, but very mixed with both Raxšānî and Persian (see below).
ii. Barker and Mengal 1969 II, pp. 273–77, also in Coastal dialect, of seventy-two lines, of which only lines 22–64 are a *daptar*: a Mullâ Šôrân (otherwise unknown) names himself in the poem as the author.
iii. Barker and Mengal 1969 II, pp. 266–67, of only nineteen lines, basically Coastal, but recited by a Raxšānî speaker.
iv. Dames 1907 I, pp. 1–3, of seventy-six lines in Eastern Hill Balochi, of which only lines 11–52 are a *daptar*. The last lines 53–76 concern the thirty-year War (see below). I have seen two others in Qômî's collection, unpublished; both are in Coastal dialect and their content does not differ greatly from these.

The content of all these *daptar*s is basically the same—the oldest migrations of the Baloch tribes, which runs as follows. The Baloch tribes rise up from their original home in Aleppo, all sons of "Mîr Hamza" (generally taken to refer to the uncle of the prophet Muhammad) to fight against the second Umayyad Caliph Yazid I at Karbalâ' in 680. After Hoseyn is slain, the angered Balochi tribes wander away eastwards. It is clear that there is no real history in this narrative: nothing is said about the journey from Aleppo to Karbalâ, and there are no details of a Balochi battle engagement there. It seems clear that the point is to assure the Baloch a good Islamic pedigree.

Thence the Baloch tribes continue their migration eastwards. The first places mentioned are Lâr and Rôdbâr: Lâr is, of course, in southern Iran, but "Rôdbâr" can be anywhere. The next places, which can be historical, are Pahra (= Fahraĵ) and Bampûr. Thence no places at all are mentioned until they arrive in Makrân, at Kêč. The mention of Kêč is common to all *daptar*s: it was a place of central importance from very early times. From this point on the *daptar*s suddenly become very much more detailed, with differing particulars. In all of them migration is steadily from west to east, identified places are named, in the right order, and real history can be contained in them. But this history, whilst containing a grain of truth, must in any case be of fairly late invention, for it really only begins with the arrival of the Baloch in south-east Iran, and details only appear with their arrival in Kêč. It seems clear that the lack of real memory of (or lack of interest in) events prior to their arrival in the eastern part of Baluchistan is because the real purpose of the *daptar*s is not to recount early history but to furnish a background to the Rind-Lašârî Wars (see below). These migrations could have taken place at any time between the eighth and twelfth centuries, and at least a kernel of the ballads could be genuinely old, from perhaps the sixteenth century, when the wars took place. It is now generally agreed, mainly from linguistic evidence, that the real original Baloch home was somewhere to the southeast of the Caspian Sea, and that the Baloch migrations to the southeast of Iran began in late Sasanian times probably caused by the disorders attendant on Sasanian disintegration and the first Arab invasions in the seventh century. Whatever the details may be, it is certain that Baloch migrations from their original home did not take place all at once, but were rather spread over several centuries, probably in independent groups. Also to be borne in mind is that there were many reverse migrations, when tribes wandered back to previous dwellings or stations. It seems very likely that much of the Balochi population of Iran has migrated back from more easterly abodes; this is demonstrated by the fact that dialects of Balochi spoken mainly in Iran (Sarawânî, Lâšârî) contain the same Indo-Aryan loanwords as the other dialects, retaining their Indian phonology with the retroflex stops $\underline{t}$, $\underline{d}$, and $\acute{r}$, hardly loanwords from the east, and which could hardly have developed their phonology spontaneously on Iranian soil.

Mîr Jalâl Khan features in all ballads as the overall chief, before the division into the traditional *bôlak*s (tribes), but nothing is otherwise known of him. There are traditionally five tribes: Rind, Lâšârî, Hôt, Kôraî, and Jatôî, but the only two mentioned in the early parts of the *daptar*s are the Rind and Lâšârî, the largest. The leaders mentioned are Jalâl Khân, Šayhak, Nôdbandag, and Čâkur. All of these except perhaps the first are anachronisms, interpolated from the sixteenth century. (Many individual lines from the *daptar*s are known to practically everybody, and it is easy to see how famous names from a famous era could be inserted in what is in effect a cultural heritage: a reciting bard simply put in a name well-known to his audience.)

A quotation from part of a typical *daptar* may make these points clearer. Here is a possible reconstruction of the badly bowdlerized text given in LSI X. The text is based in part on the two other similar versions I have seen (but detailed commentary cannot be given here):

1. *râjâ ač halab zahr bîtant* The tribes from Aleppo became angry
   â rôč ki yazîd sar zîtant On the day that their heads were attacked by Yazid
2. *sultân šâh husayn kušta* Sultan Shah Hoseyn was killed
   râjân purr hasad bad burta The tribes, full of jealousy, bore it badly.
3. *lâšâr mizzilê pêš kaptant* The Lâšârî s advanced one stage (farther)
   nôdbandag saxîên rapta Nôdbandag the Generous (went with them)
4. *šahaykk pa padâ-ê gôn kapta* Šahayk went along after him
   rôdbârê darâ êr-kaptan They descended beyond Rôdbâr
5. *gwastant ač gîyâbên lârâ* They passed by grassy Lar
   dêm pa pahraî bâzârâ Facing the bazaar of Pahra
6. *bampûrê darâ ganjênân* Beyond the boundaries of Bampûr ...

The following three couplets mention no new names or places; then:

9. ... ...
   lâšâr ništa mân lâšârâ The Lâšâri settled in Lâšâr
10. *rind mân pahraî bâzârâ* The Rind in Fahraj town

The next places mentioned are:

14. *gurrânâ šutant čô râdâ*   In roaring they went like thunder
    kêč o makurân tâ sindâ   (To) Kêč and Makrân up to Sind

The meter is a steady eight-syllable line in three feet, with the stress on the first syllable; the apparent extra syllable in couplet four is eliminated by reading *padâ-ê* as two syllables. Rhyme is very irregular, as expected in early verse. Archaisms are: *râd*; *Makurân*; *bâzâr* 'settlement with a market.' In other *daptar*s we have *Sêîstân* as three syllables, *nîðârây* 'resting place' (now 'stage in a theater'), the phrase *kêč râstên pallawâ-int*, 'Kêč is on the right side,' i.e. to the east, for marchers from Sistan.

It is not to be denied that, in the long transmission of these early ballads, the principle of *lectio facilior* has played an important role, making it very difficult to know how the ballads, if they are really old, originally looked. Balochi is by nature an extremely conservative language, and a thousand years ago it cannot have looked very different from what it is today: it is, for example, phonologically older than the Pahlavi of the third century inscriptions.

Classical poetry

Balochi classical poetry is most conveniently divided into several cycles of what may be called "heroic balladry," and the main subject is tribal conflict. Most ballads, as mentioned above, begin with a short prose statement in which the composer names himself, usually as the main protagonist of the events of the ballad. But in the total lack of any details of the oral transmission, it is impossible to be sure.

Dealt with are exclusively the (likely) historical events of the eastern parts of Baluchistan, in present-day Pakistan, from about 1500 CE onwards. There are, indeed, passing references to places in Iran, but none of them seem convincing. It is also impossible to say how old the originals of the ballads are, but the tradition that many of them are contemporaneous with the events they describe seems in many cases credible.

ORAL LITERATURE OF IRANIAN LANGUAGES

A brief description of the kind of society mirrored in the oldest ballads is a necessary preliminary. It is a "heroic" one, entirely tribal, hierarchical and male-dominated, in which the individual is entirely subordinated to his tribe. Women, however secondary, have a marked influence on many events: a principal cause of conflict was rivalry for their favors. Women's purview is, however in principle the family, both before and after marriage, and only rarely do they take an active part in public life.

In classical times Baloch tribes were only loosely organized, with a chief, usually hereditary, at their head, assisted by his closest friends and advisors in council. The powers of a chief are, however, limited, and derive from the consent of his "subjects" and his Council, and an especially able or ambitious member of the tribe can always be a source of conflict. The chief's principal functions are to uphold *riwâj* (see below) and to decide disputes both inside and outside the tribe. Here the Council of Elders plays a major role. This Council, or *jirga* of *kamâš* (graybeards), was in classical times not permanent but chosen by general consent for each occasion as it arose, but from the time of Nasîr Khan I of Kalat (r. 1749–95) members of the Great Council were appointed on a permanent basis.

Baloch existence was at least until the fourteenth century—and thereafter also to a large extent—in the main nomadic, as is to be expected, given the barren and inhospitable nature of their territory. Only after this time did tribes begin to settle and acquire recognized lands, mainly for grazing sheep, goats, and camels, of which large herds were not uncommon. Grazing rights were also always a potential source of conflict. Agriculture and commerce of any sort were alien to the Balochi mentality until fairly recently. The main activities were stockbreeding, in which women could own their own herds independently, and fighting. For many tribes, even into the nineteenth century, fighting was the main purpose of life.

Thus for men, life meant self-assertion over other men, usually with violence. But only in special cases did an individual actually engage in an act of violence, a raid, for example. The standard picture is one of a "group of heroes" acting for their tribe; probably the most serious punishment that could be meted out was to expel a man from his tribe and make him an outlaw. This is a fruitful source of much tragic balladry, for then a man must lose his grip on his own identity and be lost forever. The origins of many tribes are to be ascribed to criminal expulsions: the eponymous founder of the tribe was expelled from another tribe.

Life is thus entirely conditioned by tribal law (*riwâj*), unwritten until Nasîr Khan had it written down (in Persian) in the eighteenth century, but still all-powerful in classical times before then. The customs described above, together with the following specific duties prescribed by *riwâj* had always been deeply embedded in Balochi society. These three main duties, "pillars of Balochi tribal life" were:

i. *bâhôṯdâri* "(custom of) asylum." It is required to offer to any person *bâhôṯ* (asylum) upon request, with no questions asked. The person affording *bâhôṯ* is the *bâhôṯdâr* and may expose himself to considerable personal risk; but in principle he may not refuse it, and must aid and succor his *bâhôṯ*.

ii. *mihmândârî* (hospitality), offered to guests, mainly travelers, and lasts three days in principle. The *mihmândâr* (host) is often the tribal chief or his deputy.

iii. *bêrgirî* (revenge-seeking) is mainly inter-tribal, but can also be inter-familial. It is incumbent on all male tribal members, and in its working it illustrates very clearly the "impersonal" status of an individual member of a tribe. He is duty-bound to seek revenge for slights, insults, or wrongs done to him, his family, or even his tribe. As object of his revenge, anyone of an "equivalent status" may serve, any "equivalent member" i.e., a person of equivalent social status, of a family or tribe. The duty of revenge-seeking may neither be questioned nor avoided, and of course is the cause of many a tragedy when individual needs and desires conflict with the impersonal duty of a tribesman. The rule is thus "an eye for an eye, a tooth for a tooth." Adultery required the murder of both guilty parties; forgiveness was not allowed.

A man who cares strictly for these things is "honorable" (*nangdâr*) and "honor" (*nang*) is what makes life meaningful—without it nothing is possible. One's honor must be defended with one's life, if necessary. Of such stuff were Balochi heroes made, and often the Balochi hero is a tragic hero.

All collections of these "heroic cycles" are in the Pakistani Coastal, Eastern Hill, or Kêčî dialects. As far as can be ascertained, nothing in this category has been published in Afghanistan or elsewhere except for the brief specimens in Zarubin 1930, which are in Raxšânî.[4] The original dialect of this poetry was undoubtedly Coastal ("Rindî"), and it is to be noted that Eastern Hill Balochi is most closely related to that dialect.

Historical confirmation of the events described has proved very difficult, but it has been possible to identify some proper names (though not of the Baloch) and some places; the locations are all to the east of Kêč in Pakistani Makrân, through Sibî and into West Panjab. None of the events take place in Iran or Afghanistan.

The Čâkur Cycle

This most important and extensive cycle concerns the events of the Rind-Lâšârî Wars of perhaps 1475–1525, or possibly a bit later. A large amount of balladry about these wars has been composed, some of it likely to be contemporary or near-contemporary with the events described. Some of the older compositions have survived either as individual ballads ascribed to their authors or incorporated into other ballads. With the passage of time, different whole ballads got worked together, so that today it is difficult to identify the original components of a composition.

During the eastwards migrations of the Baloch, two major tribes began to separate out, the Rind under Šayhak and his son Čâkur, and the Lâšârî under Gwahârâm (Eastern Hill Balochi: Gwâharâm). Relations, at first friendly, began steadily to worsen, especially after the death of Šayhak, and at last peace could no longer be maintained between them.

---

[4] In Afghanistan, Raxšânî is the officially approved dialect. For its early use see Zarubin, "K izucheniu Beludzhskogo ïazyka i fol'klora." Sarawânî and Lâškârî are only spoken in Iran, and are not written.

BALOCHI LITERATURE

There was a rich young woman named Gôhar, of the Mahêrî subtribe of the Lâšârî, and who perhaps lived near Bampûr (according to one version; this cannot be right). She was courted by Gwaharâm, whose suit she spurned. There is a fair amount of unpublished poetry containing an exchange of messages between the two; Gwaharâm sends love-messages, and Gôhar spurns them, apparently because of consanguinity (not usually a hindrance in Balochi society, where first-cousin marriage is quite usual). But in one unpublished version of the affair, Gwaharâm already has four wives and refuses to divorce one of them to make a place for Gôhar.

Gôhar, together with her camel herds, seeks refuge (*bâhôṯdârî*) with Čâkur, who accepts her and undertakes her protection. In most versions, Čâkur lives near Sibî. He himself begins to court Gôhar, who for her part prefers him. There is a colorful exchange of insults between Gwaharâm and Čâkur, the (unpublished) ballads purporting to be the original compositions of each. It is finally agreed to settle the matter by a horse race, to be run by Rêhân Rind and Râmên Lâšâr, who also happened to be good friends. Both are said to have composed ballads about the race, which turned out to be a neck-and-neck affair. The Rind judges however award the winner's prize to Rêhân Rind, leaving Râmên furious. In his rage he secretly organizes a few young Rind hotheads to raid and kill some of Gôhar's young camels.

Čâkur comes to know about the deaths of Gôhar's camels and is in his turn very angry. Gôhar tries to pacify him by telling him that her young camels died a natural death, but Čâkur will have none of it and determines on an all-out fight with Gwaharâm and the Lâšârî. The likely outcome of such a struggle is foreseen by Čâkur's best friend and chief lieutenant Bîbarg, who seizes the rein of Čâkur's horse to restrain him. "We will not strike down the whole realm for the sake of a woman's camels." Bîbarg is taunted as a coward and lawbreaker by several young Rind heroes, and no one listens to him.

The first battle is joined at the Nalî Defile (near Sibî). After heavy losses on both sides (all descriptions of the actual fighting are very brief) the Lâšârî are victorious, and Čâkur finds himself standing alone, sword in hand, on the field of battle. He is saved by the generosity of the Lâšârî Nôdbandag (Gwaharâm's father) who rescues him on his horse Pull. For this act Nôdbandag is reviled and insulted by Gwaharâm. But Čâkur lived to fight another day.[5] Thus the first and most important encounter of the entire thirty-years' war. Some other short episodes have been published in the periodical *Mâhtâk* and elsewhere:

i. The Rind regroup and there is another battle; the outcome is undecided, but many named heroes are killed.
ii. The Nuhânî, another Baloch tribe, join the Lâšârî, and there follows another defeat of the Rind (unpublished).
iii. A very large battle is joined in North Baluchistan near Nuškî, where the Lâšârî suffer a decisive defeat (unpublished).
iv. Some years later, Čâkur tries to form an alliance with the "Turks" of Herat. This episode is described in Dames 1907 IV: The "Turks" in question may be troops under Dhu'l-Nûn Beg Arghun, of Kandahar and Herat, c. 1500. They are disposed to help Čâkur and the Rinds, but are bribed not to do so by Gwaharâm. Three times Gwaharâm bribes them to summon Čâkur and to set him a hero's task. Čâkur successfully accomplishes all of the tasks, whereupon the "Turks" assemble an army and together with the Rind fight a successful battle against the Lâšârî below the Bôlân Pass, between Quetta and Sibî.
v. Another battle takes place "much later"; the outcome is undecided, but there are heavy losses on both sides (unpublished).
vi. The "Turks" again agree to fight with Čâkur, and there is a final decisive battle in which the Lâšârî are virtually exterminated, and they play no part in subsequent Baloch history. Gwaharâm escapes with a few followers to the plains of Sind, and Čâkur settles near Sibî, where he builds a palace (some ruins of which are still to be seen). Čâkur sings a lament for the great destruction of the wars: *Sêwî, môkal-ên* (Sibi, Farewell!); a widely-quoted poem of twelve lines, one version of which is given in Elfenbein 1990, p. 332, no. 1. The text is partly unpublished.

5   The most complete versions of this story are in Dames 1907, II–VIII. A shortened version is given in Baluch 1977, pp. 87–95, of fifty-six couplets. The unpublished versions I have seen do not add any new details. Perhaps all, up to this point, stem from one original.

Ballads by or about personalities of the Čākur Cycle

i. Bîbarg (EHB: Bîwaragh, also Bîwragh; Dames 1907: Bîbrak; Arabic Abu Bakr), a Rind, son of Mîr Bahâr Khan, nephew of Čākur, proverbially brave and wise, a hero of many martial and romantic adventures. There are several ballads about his exploits in Dames 1907, no. XX; in Marri 1970, with titles by the author (*Lal Saδô*, p. 29f., 70 lines; *Syâlî Ghussawa*, p. 34f., 22 lines; *Grânnâz*, p. 40f., 136 lines (= no. 67 in Elfenbein 1990, pp. 390–98); *Ô Warnâî*, p. 47f., 62 lines); and in Baluch 1977 (p. 115f., 50 couplets; p. 157f., 9 couplets; p. 168, 10 couplets; p. 172f., 19 couplets; p. 178, 30 couplets). Many of these ballads are said to have been composed by Bîbarg himself; there are many unpublished versions as well.

The most interesting of these ballads is titled *Grânnâz* by Shêr Mohammad, said to be composed by Bîbarg himself. Part of the story of the Rind-Arghun alliance in the thirty years' War, it deals with the romance between Bîbarg and Grânnâz, who is called "The King of Kandahar's Daughter." Bîbarg abducts her from her home in Kandahar and brings her to Sibî. Because of the Rind-Arghun alliance, he cannot expect any sympathy from Čākur, and so he seeks refuge with Gwaharâm. There is at least one unpublished ballad, purportedly from Bîbarg to Čākur explaining his actions and asking for forgiveness. Čākur approves and obtains the retirement of the Arghun army which had arrived in Sibî to take Grânnâz back, and Bîbarg and Grânnâz are married. Marri's (1970) *Ô Warnâî* (above) is a marriage song, perhaps original.

ii. Haybat(ân) (EHB: *Haywatân*; Dames 1907: *Haibat, Haivtân*), a Rind, Bîbarg's son. Four (or five) heroes come together and make vows. The episode is also known as the "Oaths of the Rinds" (*Rindânî Kawl/Kôl*),[6] and there are many versions, of which two are given in Elfenbein 1990 (no. 60, pp. 354–59; no. 61, pp. 360–61); Dames 1907 (nos. XII, XIII, XIV); Dames

---

6   *Qôl* is a commonly used etymological spelling of *kôl* 'oath'; most Arabic loanwords in Balochi are spelt as in Arabic, as is the case in Persian.

1909 (Part II no. X); Marri 1970 (*Qôl Haywatâne*, p. 7f. 52 lines [Elfenbein 1990, no. 62]; Baluch 1977, p. 321f., 23 lines). The actors are variously named, but the oldest versions name Čâkur, Haybat, Jârô, and Nôdbandag. Haybat and Jârô are common to all versions known to the present writer. Haybat swears not to return any camels that stray into his herds from elsewhere. Some camels from Čâkur's herd stray into Haybat's. Čâkur prepares to fight, but a conciliation is effected, and Čâkur allows Haybat to keep the camels. (The clearest published version is in Dames 1907, no. XII).

iii. Jârô, a Rind. One of the "oath-takers" (see above). His part in this episode is given in Dames 1907, no. XIII; Elfenbein 1990 no. 60; ŠMM (*Qôl Jârôê*, p. 15f., 36 lines); Baluch 1977 (pp. 314–18, 11 couplets). Jârô, known as "the one of the sour answer" (*jawr jawâb*), swears that he will kill anyone who touches his beard, or who kills his friend Haddê. Čâkur induces Jârô's child's nurse to get the child to touch his father's beard; the child is duly killed by his father. Čâkur later organizes a horse race, when Haddê touches Jârô's beard; Haddê is killed by Šâhô, Jârô's nephew. Finally, Jârô kills Šâhô and buries him together with Haddê in one grave. There are several unpublished ballads relating all or parts of this story.

iv. Nôdbandag, a Lâšârî, one of the "oath-takers." Known as "the generous" (*saxî*) or the "gold scatterer" (*zar zuwal*), he was a greatly admired personality, and there is a large ballad literature about him, a good part unpublished. Since his father was a Lâšârî and his mother a Rind, he was to some extent plagued by divided loyalties in the Rind-Lâšârî Wars. He rescues the Rind chief Čâkur at the end of the first battle (see above) and has to suffer taunts for his deed (one unpublished ballad of 50 lines gives more details of this incident than others do). Dames 1907, nos. XIII and XIV describe his oath to give all he possessed to anyone who asked for it, and never to touch money with his hands. (Cf. also Elfenbein 1990, nos. 60 and 61). There are also versions in ŠMM (*Lôlî* p. 92f., 110 lines) and Baluch 1977 (p. 224f., 31 couplets). Čâkur makes a hole in Nôdbandag's moneybag, and the coin in it falls out, but is not collected by

Nôdbandag. (An unpublished ballad describes how the coins were collected by a troop of poor women who were gathering tamarisk branches for kindling; there is an interesting debate on "stealing by finding"). In another ballad Čâkur gets a minstrel (*ḍomb*) to demand Nôdbandag's property, and Nôdbandag gives him everything, even the shirt off his back. Several other unpublished ballads describe in detail how a musk-camel (a camel whose mouth has been sweetened with musk) arrives at Nôdbandag's house in the middle of the night, laden with rich clothes and other goods.

v. Rêhân Rind, "the Bard" (*lângaw*). Besides the ballad mentioned above for the Čâkur Cycle (1.3, above) there are ballads given in ŠMM (*Kûnje mahδaw*, p. 20f., 49 lines), and in Baluch 1977 (pp. 305–13, 31 couplets), which tell the story of his love for Sangî, and the accident in which he wounds his own horse, and the animal later dies. There are also several unpublished ballads (supposedly composed by him) in which he (a) swears revenge for the slaughter of Gôhar's little camels; (b) laments the death of Sâlô, a mistress; (c) describes in a battle poem a skirmish with the Arghuns.

vi. Râmên Lâšârî, said to be the author of several unpublished ballads, in which (a) he swears that he was the winner of the horse race with Rêhân Rind; (b) he encourages Gwahârâm to continue fighting the Rinds after his severe defeat near Nushkî (see above 1.3, iii); (c) his death in battle is also sung, by an unnamed bard, in an unpublished ballad.

vii. Bîbarî, the wife of Umar, chief of the Hôt tribe. In a famous incident of the Thirty Years' War, the "Episode of the Lizard," a lizard runs into her house, pursued by two boys from the Kalmatî tribe. Bîbarî bars the way to them, saying that the lizard is her refugee and under her protection. The boys do not listen and kill the lizard. Bîbarî complains to her husband upon his return home, and, furious, he organizes a bloody attack on the whole Kalmatî tribe. An inter-tribal feud develops out of this fighting, lasting several generations until both sides are exhausted. There is reason to date the poem to the eighteenth century.

There are several ballads describing Čâkur's fighting as a freebooter for the Mughal Emperor Homâyûn when he marched on Delhi in 1555 to recover his throne from Šêr Šâh. There is a tradition that Homâyûn was a refugee amongst the Baloch after 1540, when Šêr Šâh drove him out. In Dames 1907, no. XVI, there is a ballad on this subject, ascribed to Šâhzâd, a son of Čâkur. Other campaigns by Čâkur in Panjab and Multan are described in a ballad printed in Dames (1909, pp. 10–11), under the heading "Legendary History of the Baloches." However, this episode, as well as Čâkur's fighting for Homâyûn, has genuine historical credentials. I have attempted a reconstruction of Dames' ballad XI (Elfenbein 1985).

The Dôdâ Bâlâč Cycle

The next most important cycle is certainly the Dôdâ Bâlâch Cycle, which is probably to be dated in the eighteenth century, perhaps 1750 or later. The cycle is important for several reasons. Whilst none of it can be assigned a definite historical niche, it is impressive for its realism, and its often personal styles of narration make it come very much alive. Some of the ballads are probably contemporary with the events described in them. The same transmission problems obtain as in the Čâkur Cycle.

The lady Sammî and her husband, members of the Bulêdî tribe, come as refugees to Dôdâ, overall chief of the Gôrgêj tribe, in the Rind confederation. Sammî's husband dies and, as often happens, there is a disputed inheritance. Sammî withholds from her dead husband's heirs the part of the herds which are her own property, which by *riwâj* she is entitled to do. Most versions then describe a raid on her cattle by Mîr Bîbarg, a Bulêdî chief, which he dares to do in broad daylight. While this takes place, Dôdâ lies asleep in the sun and does nothing.

Dôdâ is rudely awakened by two women relatives, who tell him what has happened. Dôdâ is very reluctant to undertake countermeasures, but after taunts and jibes by a whole group of women, who accuse him of cowardice and law-breaking, Dôdâ reluctantly gathers together a small band of men and sallies forth to meet Bîbarg

BALOCHI LITERATURE

at the Garmâp Pass near Sangsilâ in Bugṭî country (south-east of Sibî), and after a short and bloody encounter he is killed. There is a rather extensive ballad literature about Dôdâ, mostly unpublished. Many accounts describe subsequent long-continued fighting between the Gôrgêj and the Bulêdî, in which explicit comparison is made with the Rind Lāŝārî Wars of long before, and Dôdâ is often compared in them with Čâkur. But the Gôrgêj are always on the defensive against the Bulêdî, who are superior both in numbers and in strength. At last the Gôrgêj are virtually exterminated; only Dôdâ's family is left, together with his brother Bâlâč and his half-brother Nakîb.

Nakîb, whose mother was a black slave-girl, is the more mettlesome of the two, whilst Bâlâč hesitates to take action, like Dôdâ. Years pass (in some versions three) in which Nakîb continually exhorts his brother to action, but without success. At last, after a dream (impressively described in one unpublished ballad), Bâlâč decides to act; and together with Nakîb the two alone proceed to harry the Bulêdî over their whole territory, said to extend from Sibî as far as the Indus, the two of them slaying three-score-and-one warriors in one oft-described encounter. In a later battle, when Bâlâč and Nakîb gain reinforcements, Bîbarg himself is slain, and the remaining Bulêdî migrate to southern Sind.

Many of the ballads (published and unpublished) narrate in great detail the initial incident, where women taunt Dôdâ, and later Bâlâč, for indecision and evasion of duty. There are also several ballads in which the shame and doubt of Bâlâč feature prominently; all versions have rousing urgings to action by Nakîb.

Nearly all of the dialects of Balochi spoken in Pakistan are used in the written transcriptions of the oral recitals of this cycle. Especially notable is an Afghan Raxšânî version of the *Bâlâč-Nakîb* exchanges collected by Zarubin (1930, pp. 664–68), which gives 155 lines of a version of the *Bâlâč-Nakîb* story (with a Russian translation). None of the sources I have seen or heard carries the whole story. Besides that of Zarubin, the following publications contain parts of it:

i. Baluch 1977, pp. 401–10, in EHB 29 couplets; Bâlâch is said to be the author.

ii. ŠMM in EHB (pp. 149, *Bâhôṭ*, 45 lines; p. 151f., *Huðâ čôn a-kant*, 103 lines; p. 157f., *Gôn baðân*, 66 lines; p. 163, *Bašârat*, 107 lines; p. 172f., *Kôlanî balâ*, 74 lines; p. 176f., *Abêd ža*, 29 lines).
iii. Dames 1907, no. XVIII, in which Bâlâč himself appears to be the poet ("Bâlâč sings"), three ballads are given, all in EHB (no. 1, 45 lines; no. 2, 56 lines; no. 3, 48 lines).
iv. Elfenbein 1990, (no. 57, 27 lines; no. 58, 47 lines; no. 59, 67 lines, mainly in Ra; but no. 59 in Ke).
v. Barker and Mengal 1969, II, (pp. 288–92, 65 lines, in Ke from a Ra reciter. For the content, see Elfenbein 1990, no. 59).

Hammal Jîhand

The many ballads about the struggles of Hammal Jîhand with the Portuguese in the sixteenth century also form a cycle. Hammal Jîhand, "Sultan of Kalmat" on the Makrân coast, was chief of the Hôt tribe. Most of the ballads about him concern a final naval battle with the Portuguese, which most likely took place some time after 1550. Nowhere is the Portuguese commander named, but if there is a connection with the torching of the Makrân seaports Gwâdar and Pasnî in 1581,[7] Hammal might also have been concerned. Portuguese archives have not been consulted, so that at present nothing more definite can be said. The ballads describe land skirmishes and naval engagements between the Portuguese and Baloch forces under Hammal, during many years. In a final battle (the central event of most ballads) Hammal was defeated and taken prisoner, and then deported captive either to Goa or to Portugal (ballads differ). Efforts to ransom him failed, and the Portuguese tried to persuade him to settle and take a European wife. Hammal refused, finally dying in prison. There is said to be a local custom in Kalmat of women mourning for Hammal by not washing their hair on Saturdays.

Some ballads describe in colorful detail the reasons for Hammal's refusal to take a European wife: it was mainly the "unclean" customs of non-Muslim Europeans which revolted him. There is a short extract about this cycle in Elfenbein 1990 (p. 272), but it

7 In some versions Tîz is given for Pasnî.

probably dates from the nineteenth century. Other texts are to be found in:
i. Baluch 1977 (pp. 353–60, in EHB, 27 couplets); other ballads of the cycle are to be found *ibid.*, pp. 360–83; some are said to have been written by Hammal himself and sent as letters to Kalmat (this seems very unlikely, since such letters must have been written in Persian, always the written language of the Baloch).
ii. ŠMM, p. 75f., *Hammal o Šêr*, about an encounter with a lion (one example of several ballads on this theme, 99 couplets).
iii. Elfenbein 1990 (no. 561, of 60 lines), in the form of a dialogue with Čâkur, a challenge to combat. Quoted in Sarawânî dialect, it is the only example of the sort I know, but this may not be significant.
iv. Barker and Mengal 1969 (II, pp. 306–13, 28 lines), in a Raxšânî greatly mixed with Coastal dialect. It is certain that Hammal's dialect was the Coastal dialect of Kalmat, and the Coastal dialect forms of this ballad were probably injected by a Raxšânî reciter to increase its credibility.

Only passing note can be taken of other classical balladry by other bards/actors of the years before the eighteenth century. The events described, mainly martial, seem likely to be authentic, but it is difficult to vouch for the authorship or the contemporaneity of the ballads. In Baluch 1977 (Ch. 4), a (weak) case is made for such warrior-balladeers as Šâhdâd, Hârîn, Mîrhân Rind, Šêh Isâ Kahêrî, to name only the best known, and Baluch gives some specimens of poetry perhaps written by some of them, all in Eastern Hill Balochi.

Some mention should be made of the fairly large amount of extant verse, some published, most not, concerning the "War of the Rinds and the Dôdâîs." Dames 1907 has no less than eight ballads about this war, in no. XVIII, with a grand total of 236 lines. Gul Khan had a high opinion of these pieces. Baluch (1977) has also printed three ballads of this group, with a total of 48 couplets. The main content is as follows: When Mîr Čâkur and many Rinds advanced on Delhi *c.* 1555 as part of the army of Humâyûn, other Rinds deserted him and returned under Bijjar westwards back towards the Indus, where they met the Baloch Dôdâîs, who had long been settled in the Indus Valley. The latter were allied with Čâkur, and an armed struggle ensued. The (unpublished) ballads narrate a long and pitiless struggle, which only ended with a division of the country, with Bijjar's Rinds settling in the Derâjât, and the Dôdâîs the area around Dera Ghazi Khan, where they were Nawabs until the end of the eighteenth century.

2. Literature of the post-classical period: the eighteenth century

Ballads

There exists a number of long ballads which could date from the eighteenth century, mostly based on well-known Persian or Arabic tales, such as *Leylâ and Majnun*, or *Širin and Farhâd:* these two have been especially widely imitated in Balochi.

Leylâ and Majnun

There is a selection from the Leylâ story in Balochi in Baluch 1977 (pp. 496–508, 44 couplets, author unknown). But in Dames 1907, no. XXXVII, there is a much longer selection of 101 lines (given also in Dames 1909 II, pp. 3–4). The version in Baluch 1977 is more pedestrian, being mainly a bare outline of the tale, whereas that given in Dames has been transformed into a local Balochi tale of tragic love set in Eastern Hill territory and largely re-written. A prose version of this tale as well as a local variant is to be found in Elfenbein 1983.

Širin and Farhâd

Extracts of a Balochi version of the tale *Širin and Farhâd* have been published in Baluch 1977 (pp. 508–15; 23 couplets), and assigned by him to an anonymous poet of the seventeenth century, on unstated grounds. Dames 1907 (no. XL) gives a slightly longer version of 52 lines. No doubt Dames is right in supposing that the Pârât of the Balochi poem is Farhâd, and in assigning the poem to the eighteenth century or later.

Dôstên and Šîrên

Of greater interest is the purely Balochi verse tale of *Dôstên o Šîrên*, of which a shortened version of 44 couplets has been given in Baluch 1977, pp. 484–90. The author assigns the story to the seventeenth century, mainly on grounds of its content, naively not considering that any poet might compose a poem about the days of yore. All others, including Gul Khân, assign the original ballad to the eighteenth century. It seems that the style of the ballad fits better with the uncomplicated eighteenth century style, and that references to earlier events are anachronisms. The version in Dames 1907 (no. XLI) is composite and in essence cannot be old (e.g. the "Arghun" capital Herat is given as "Arand", a small village in EHB territory, certainly a corruption of Balochi *Harêw*, even if genuine). ŠMM (p. 135f.) gives a version of 112 lines, which he calls *Šîrên*. The leading poet of the modern period, Gul Khan Nasîr, has used the story as the basis for an impressive modern epic in seven parts, which he published as a book in Quetta in 1964. There are long extracts from it in Elfenbein 1990, pp. 203–55. The story in outline runs as follows:

> The Rind Dôstên is betrothed to the lady Šîrên. One day the "Arghun Turks" make an attack on their village, killing a few of its inhabitants, and carry off Dôstên as a prisoner to the town of "Arand" (Gul Khân writes resp. Mughals, and Herat). Dôstên is held captive for years, and in the early part of his captivity he and Šîrên are allowed to pass written messages, which later gradually cease. Šîrên is betrothed by her parents to another, also called Dôstên. Meanwhile the captive Dôstên is made a groom of the governor's horses, which function he fulfills so successfully that in a few years he is made head groom.
> But he never forgets Šîrên, and later by means of a ruse he makes his escape and rides home to his village, just in time to hear that

Šîrên is about to be married to the other Dôstên. Disguising himself and his companions as minstrels, Dôstên sings a wedding song, one which had been written and sent to him long before by Šîrên (so Šîrên is a poet, and both are literate: in which language?) Šîrên recognizes both the singer and the song, and requests to be released by the other Dôstên, who gallantly consents; the first Dôstên and Šîrên are wedded amid general rejoicing.

Šêh Murîd and Hânî

This also appears to be a purely Balochi tale (šêh < Arabic *shaykh*). This is a very popular story, dating from the eighteenth century, about which many ballads have been composed. (There are also many modern versions.) Many of the older ballads have been published, e.g. in Dames 1907, no. XXII; in ŠMM (pp. 59–63, 103 lines, *Durrdânayên Hânî*; pp. 64–66, 60 lines, *Ašiqê ganôx*). Baluch 1977 gives an especially good selection of five specimens (pp. 244–56, 26 couplets; pp. 257–65, 30 couplets; pp. 266–67, 9 couplets; pp. 269–70, 6 couplets; pp. 271–99, 113 couplets). Many shorter specimens have been published in *Mâhtâk Balôčî* and *Nôkên Dawr*, and there are countless unpublished examples, mostly shorter episodes from the tale.

Šêh Murîd is said in several ballads to be a "follower of Čâkur," and is confused in at least one ballad version of the "Four Vows" story (see above) with Nôdbandag (see also Elfenbein 1990, pp. 360–61). Great generosity is admired as the highest of virtues amongst the Baloch. The story goes as follows:

> Murîd is affianced to Hânî, but Čâkur demands her for himself. Murîd generously gives her up and then, overwhelmed with regret, goes away on Hajj to Mecca. He becomes a wandering faqîr and in his wanderings returns several times to his home in disguise, to steal glances at Hânî—his love gives him no peace. On one such visit he is recognized and a Great Jirga is convened. Čâkur agrees to give Hânî up to him, but Murîd refuses, saying that his many years as a wandering beggar have made him unfit for her. He departs, riding his camel and singing love songs in the desert.

BALOCHI LITERATURE

The tale/ballad of 'Isâ and Barî

This is probably of Sindhi origin. The 35-line version in Dames 1907(no. LIII) is fairly typical, although it is in Eastern Hill Balochi. Several other versions in Kêčî, Raxšânî, and Coastal dialect—the Coastal versions are the only ones without admixtures—have been published in *Mâhtâk Balôčî*. The story is well known. 'Isâ is a wanderer, but Barî sits alone in the desert. 'Isâ inquires of Barî how he lives, and Barî answers and shows him the power of God, who then makes a tree sprout from the ground in the forenoon, put forth buds at noon, bear fruit in the early afternoon, and ripe fruit by the afternoon prayers.

Known poets

Here we come to identified poets, about whom there is some information, albeit little. There is space here for only the most important.

Jâm Durrak

The most notable, and also the earliest of these is Jâm Durrak, chief poet at the court of Nasîr Khân I of Kalat. His exact dates are not known. It seems quite likely that his oeuvre was written down in his lifetime, but no written remains have been preserved. He was a very popular poet, composing mostly short lyrical pieces in Co dialect. His best work is very individual, characterized by very short lines of e.g. five syllables with an irregular rhyme. A sample of his poetry is given in Elfenbein 1990 (pp. 257–71), in which an attempt is made to give a critical text. The same cannot be said of Dames' examples (1907, nos. XLII–XLVI), transposed into Eastern Hill Balochi as if Durrak's work were that of an anonymous folk poet. There are also many ballads attributed to him because of his fame, on most doubtful authority. The first attempt to collect his poetry in booklet form, *Durr-čîn* by Ahmad Bashir Balôch (1963), is not a critical edition and many of the poems are of doubtful attribution. A poor specimen of four couplets attributed to him is given in Baluch 1977 (p. 75), and several issues of *Mâhtâk Balôčî* contain examples.

A notion of the verse of Durrak can be obtained from the following short love lyric, hitherto unpublished. It is untitled.[8]

1. *tau-ê girdagên bagg*	Thou art a wandering string of camels
man godaw-ân;	I am (thy) troop of horse
2. *tau-ê rôč nêmrôč*	Thou art the day at midday
man arnaw-ân;	I am (thy) evening
3. *tau hâkân lêflê*	Thou liest on the ground
man čittir-ân;	I am (thy) mat
4. *tau pâdân šapâd-ê*	Thou art barefoot
man littir-ân;	I am (thy) shoe
5. *tau-ê syâhên syâhmâr*	Thou art a black snake
man jôgsar-ân;	I am a snake-charmer
6. *mândrân janânâ*	In chanting charms
dast-it girân	I seize thy hand

Mullâ Fazl

Mullâ Fazl of Mand, a village just to the east of the Iranian border in the Kêč valley (but whose dialect is Coastal), is reputed to be the author of many fine ballads, of which one is given in Elfenbein 1990, p. 272. Several of his longer works have been printed in *Mâhtâk Balôčî*, and much unpublished work has been collected.

'Izzat Lallâ

'Izzat Lallâ of Panjgûr in east Makran probably lived into the early nineteenth century. He composed his work in Raxšânî, his native dialect, perhaps the first to do so. A short specimen of his poetry

---

8   Taken from a badly copied Ms. in Qômî's possession, the text given here is a reconstruction in Durrak's original Coastal dialect. The rhyme is suddenly broken in the last couplet. The rhythm is syllabic, with 5-syllable lines alternating with 4-syllable ones.

is given in Elfenbein 1990, p. 274, and a longer poem on pp. 302–5. Not much of his work has been preserved; what has survived has been published mainly in *Mâhtâk Balôčî*.

3. The nineteenth century

Known poets

Many poets of the nineteenth century are known, and a fair amount of their work has been preserved. The following, in particular, are worthy of note.

Mullâ Ibrâhîm

Mullâ Ibrâhîm of Sarâwân in Persian Baluchistan. An example of his poetry is given in Elfenbein 1990, pp. 274–81. Some other specimens of his verse have been collected and printed in *Mâhtâk Balôčî*, often with errors. His dialect was Sarawânî.

Mullâ Bampuštî

Mullâ Bampuštî, who lived near Bahô Kalât, also in Persian Baluchistan, was a prolific poet. ʿIsâ Qômî had collected much of his work, which was published in *Mâhtâk Balôčî*. An example is given in Elfenbein 1990, pp. 282–86. The dialect is Coastal.

Mullâ Bahâdur

Mullâ Bahâdur from Mand, was a more important poet than the above. He is noted mainly for the technical accomplishment of his verse, which employs an exceptionally long line, sometimes of fifteen syllables, in strict rhythm. An example of his work is given in Elfenbein 1990, pp. 286–88. Much of his work was collected by Gul Khan, but it unfortunately remains unpublished. His dialect is Coastal.

Fakîr Šêr-jân

Fakîr Šêr-jân of Nushkî (Balochi Nôškê) composed his verse in Raxšânî, like 'Izzat Lallâ. His style is difficult, characterized as it is by the over-use of elliptical expressions, as well as other obscurities. Two examples of his work are given in Elfenbein 1990, pp. 286–97. Much of his poetry has been collected by Abdullâ-jân Jamâldînî and published in *Mâhtâk Balôčî*. The mixture of dialects, Raxšânî with occasional Coastal forms (not always correct) is characteristic of his poetry.

Mast Tôkalî

Mast Tôkalî, also known as Tôkalî Mast (Tawq 'Alî Mast) was a very well-known poet of the nineteenth century who composed in Eastern Hill Balochi. The specimen given in Elfenbein 1990, pp. 298–300 was collected by the late Mithâ Khan Marî, the leading authority on Eastern Hill Balochi poets. Tokali's style was more "learned" than most, with many Persianisms.

Rahm 'Alî Marî

Rahm 'Alî Marî was a Marî poet (in Eastern Hill Balochi) of the late nineteenth century, who composed mainly occasional poetry. Mithâ Khan Marî collected most of his work from local Marî ḍ ômbs. His "Song of the Battle of Gumbad" is one of his best works, a long ballad of 810 lines, about half of which is printed in Elfenbein 1990, as no. 53 (the remaining lines are in Elfenbein 1994).

The nineteenth century did not see any production of prose that can be called literature. There was of course much narrative prose in the form of stories and tales, and a representative collection of some of it is to be found in Dames 1909, and in Lewis (1855). Geiger (1889, 1893) also published some short specimens. All of these texts are in Eastern Hill Balochi.

4. The Modern period

Writers in Balochi began to proliferate in the 1930s, magazines and other journals were started in India, and in British Baluchistan some of them found occasional space for snippets of Balochi literature, both classical and contemporary. Most of these publications had a rather short life, with a very small readership and exiguous finances. Academies were also founded after 1947 in Pakistan to promote Balochi culture. Outside Pakistan very little was done.

Prose composition also began to play a part, especially as essays and short stories. Some drama was also produced, and even a novel or two written. Folktales were retold more self-consciously, and attention was paid to develop a more sophisticated narrative style, often influenced by English and American writing. In the space available, no more than a sketchy outline of this modern writing can be given here.

The two volumes of "Balochi Tales" published by Zarubin in 1932 and 1949, collected in Marv (Turkmenistan) in the Afghan Raxšânî dialect, hardly merit the name of literature, baldly narrated as the tales are, without either style or talent. They thus contrast notably with the tales in Dames 1909.

There is no doubt that the political environment in the 1930s had a marked effect on establishing the written word as a force in Baloch life for the first time. This led to the founding of one of the first newspapers of the 1930s: Mohammed Hoseyn Unqa (Anqâ) published a weekly newspaper from Mach, *Bôlân*, mainly in Urdu, but now and again there was something in Balochi too. Unqa was one of the first to interest himself in written Balochi, and did much to establish its written form, using the script conventions of Urdu.

('Abd-al-Wahid) Âzât Jamâldînî (1912–81) and his younger brother Abdullâ-jân (b. 1922) devoted their lives to the service of Balochi literature, the former being the founding editor of the "monthly" *Mâhtâk Balôčî* from 1956 (published irregularly for more than twenty years). The latter was the first Professor of Balochi in Pakistan (at the University of Baluchistan, Quetta), and both brothers were ardent collectors of classical Balochi ballads as well.

ORAL LITERATURE OF IRANIAN LANGUAGES

The *Balôčî Zubânê Dîwân* (Balochi Language Group) was founded in Quetta in 1951, the first institution of its kind, by a small group of enthusiasts as a publishing house. It lasted until 1953, and can be regarded as a forerunner of the later Balochi Academies. The *Balôčî Zubânê Dîwân*'s most important publication was probably Gul Khan Nasir's *Gulbâng*. Gul Khan (1914–83) was perhaps the most important Balochi poet of his time. He published some five volumes of verse. He was, for most of his life, ardently engaged in politics, and both in British times and especially after the creation of Pakistan he saw the inside of jails, sometimes for prolonged periods. He felt it as his principal task to further Balochi national sentiments, and to that end he wrote a great deal of verse including the powerful ballad *Byâ, ô Balôč!* (Come, Ye Baloch!), in the 1940s, which became a sort of national anthem. He was appointed Minister of Education in the provincial government of Baluchistan after the elections of 1971, but that government lasted only nine months before being dismissed, and Gul Khan, together with other leading members of the government, was sent to jail for many years.

The first Balochi Academy was founded in Karachi in 1958, and lasted until 1964. Of major importance, amongst much other publishing activity, was their publication in 1959 of *Mistâg*, an anthology of the poetry of twenty-one modern poets, each poet being represented by several of his shorter works. But permanence had to await the foundation of the Balochi Academy of Quetta in 1961: this institution has survived up to the time of writing (1998) and has published more than seventy-five books, mostly in Balochi.

In Elfenbein 1990 there is to be found a necessarily limited but useful choice of the works of some well-known writers: there are seventeen short stories and twenty-one poems of authors who were living at the time of writing, including Unqa, Âzât Jamâldînî, 'Isâ-Qômî, and several others, with ten poems by Gul Khan, including a long extract from his *Dôstên o Šîrên*. Also included are four essays and a radio drama.

It is, of course, invidious to single authors out for mention or omission in any short list of living writers, but as a guide to some of the best known, the following may serve, in addition to those mentioned above: ʿAbbâs ʿAlî Zîmî, short stories, poems; Abdul Qâdîr Nûrî, short stories; Ahmad Zahîr, poems, essays, b. 1944; Atâ Šâd, poems, b. 1939; Sayyed Hâšemî, essays, poems, novels, 1926–80; Mohammad Ashâq Samîm, poems, b. 1923; Murâd Sâhir, poems, b. 1927; Ne'mat-Allâh Gičkî, essays, short stories; Sûrat Khan Marî, short stories, essays. For a much more complete list, see Jahani 1989.

5. Miscellaneous verse

This category of poetry does not strictly qualify as literature, but it is worth presenting a short list and description of what has been published:

Songs

- *Hâlô*, a marriage song sung during the three days of preparation of the bride for the ceremony, usually sung by one woman singer, and interspersed with choruses by other women.
- *Laylarî (laylô)*, a girls' song.
- *Nâzînk*, a girls' love song.
- *Môrô*, a love song sung by men or women, sometimes with accompaniment
- *Lîkô*, perhaps the best known, a work or travel song.
- *Zahirôk*, a song of separation, yearning and homesickness.
- *Môdag*, an elegy, sung by women mourners (*modakašš*) at a wake. (Examples of all these are to be found in Barker and Mengal 1969 II, pp. 328–49; all are in Raxšânî.)
- *Dastânag*, a short song sung with the accompaniment of the *nar* flute (see Dames 1907, no. LXIII, with remarks in Vol I, pp. 184–85).

Riddles and conundrums

Examples are given in Dames 1907, no. LXIV; cf. Vol. I, pp. 195–96. All in Eastern Hill Balochi, called *Buj(h)ârat*. Elfenbein 1983 (pp. 112–17) contains a collection of thirty-six, in Co dialect; they are here called *habr/pahêlî*.

Proverbs

See Elfenbein 1989, where thirty-two proverbs are given, in various dialects. Ṣabir (n. d.) also has a large collection.

CHAPTER 8

OSSETIC LITERATURE

†Fridrik Thordarson

Ossetic[1] is an Iranian language spoken by about half a million people in the central regions of the Caucasus, mainly in the North Ossetic Republic ("Alania") of the Russian Federation, but also in the South Ossetic (until 1990 autonomous) Region of Georgia. Ossetic belongs to the eastern branch of the Iranian languages, and is closely related to the literary Sogdian and Khotanese languages of Central Asia and to Scythian and Sarmatian, which in antiquity were spoken in large areas of present-day Russia and Ukraine. The linguistic ancestors of the Ossetes are the Alan tribes, who migrated from Central Asia to the lands north and east of the Black Sea around the beginning of the Christian era. The Alans were a predominant force in the northwest Caucasus in the early Middle Ages, but they were gradually ousted by Turkic and Cherkes immigrants from the north and west. Today their language is limited to a relatively small area. The former presence of Alanic in modern Turkic- and Cherkes-speaking areas is borne out by place names of Iranian origin, and also attested by historical sources. There is some evidence that the present-day Ossetic territory was formerly inhabited by Nakh-speaking (Chechen-Ingush) tribes. Today Ossetic is flanked on all sides by non-Iranian (Turkic, Caucasian) languages. Knowledge of Russian is widespread; bilingualism is common, and in many places it is even the norm.

1 Ossetic proper names consist of the name of the family or clan, in the gen. pl. (-*ty*), followed by the personal name. Xetægkaty K'osta: Kosta of the Xetægkatæ family. An apostrophe (') after a stop indicates that it is accompanied by a glottal stop; *æ, y* are short vowels pronounced approximately as those in English *cat, bit*.

ORAL LITERATURE OF IRANIAN LANGUAGES

The Ossetes can be said to constitute a part of a cultural area, together with their neighbors of the northern Caucasus; the cultural relations with the Ingush and the mountaineers of eastern Georgia (the Pshavs, Khevsurs, Tush) are to all appearances especially close.

Ossetic has two dialects, which are hardly mutually intelligible: Iron (east Oss.) and Digor (west Oss.). The idiom of southern Ossetia (Georgia) is a variant of Iron; the literary language is based on Iron; very few literary works have been published in Digor.

No Alanic medieval literature is known to have existed. Three short Alanic texts have so far been identified (Bielmeier 1989, pp. 236–45; Thordarson, forthc.). None of these texts have any literary interest, but an epitaph written in Greek letters, found in the 1880s on the upper reaches of the Zelenchuk River, on modern Cherkes territory, date from the 11th–12th centuries (Zgusta 1987), and may be an indication that the Greek alphabet was occasionally employed to write Alanic.

1. The history of writing in Ossetic

The first documentary evidence of Christianity in Alania dates from the early tenth century; earlier Byzantine Christian missions seem likely, but are not verifiable (Thordarson 2000, pp. 213–24; Kouznetsov and Lebedynsky 1997). Christian liturgical books are not known to have existed. The Mass was probably celebrated in Greek (or perhaps partly in Georgian). Willem van Ruysbroeck, a Franciscan friar who visited the North Caucasus in the thirteenth century, says that the Alan priests used Greek books (Thordarson forthc.).

The Christian faith probably never had deep roots among the Alan population. From a cross-breed of Christianity and traditional pagan ideas, a syncretistic religion came into existence, which has subsisted down to modern times. Later Islam had its proselytes, but it hardly exerted any influence until the latter half of the 18th century. As a matter of fact, Islam never became a powerful force among the Ossetes.

OSSETIC LITERATURE

The first Ossetic book to appear in print was a small Catechism by the Archimandrite Tak'aty Gai; it was published in Moscow in 1798, and was printed in the Cyrillic alphabet with some modifications (Thordarson 1989b, pp. 457–58). At the beginning of the nineteenth century, Ivane Ialghuzidze (1775–1830) published three religious texts translated from Georgian, and an ABZ. He used the Georgian *xucuri* (clerical) alphabet, with some adaptations and additions. He also wrote epic poetry in Georgian (Alguziani 1885).

In 1844 the Russian scholar A. J. Sjögren from St. Petersburg published the first exhaustive Ossetic grammar (*Ossetische Sprachlehre*). He created a writing system on the basis of the Russian alphabet. Sjögren's alphabet was used with some minor modifications by Vs. F. Miller (1848–1913), the pioneer of Ossetic philology, and in a few books that appeared in the latter half of the nineteenth century.

This alphabet was in common use until the 1920s. In 1923, the Latin script was introduced; in 1938 it was replaced in North Ossetia by a variant of the Russian alphabet; in 1939 the Georgian *mxedruli* script, with a few additions, was adopted in South Ossetia; it was abandoned in 1954 in favor of the North Ossetic Cyrillic script.

2. Named authors until 1917

The first Ossetic poet whose name is known is Mamsyraty Temyrbolat (1843–98). He emigrated to Turkey around 1860, together with other Muslims who left their native countries after the final Russian conquest of the North Caucasus. Little is known about his life and poetry, but in a few poems he gives a tragic picture of the emigration and the destiny of the refugees in their new country. Qanyquaty Inal (1851–99) was another Ossetic poet who fled to Turkey around 1860; he later returned to Russia. He wrote poems, sketches and essays in Russian. None of these played any role of importance in the literary life of Ossetia.

Their younger contemporary Xetægkaty K'osta (1859–1906) is traditionally regarded as the "father" of Ossetic literature and the creator of the modern literary language. His *Iron fændyr* (The Harp of Ossetia, 1899) is mainly a collection of lyric poems; their tone is personal and as a rule tragic, the poet is abroad and feels nostalgia for his native country, his village and the mountains. But his themes are often also drawn from the Caucasian nature or inspired by epic traditions or folklore and mythology. The poem *Uælmærdty* (In the burial place) has its background in the traditional burial rites called *Bæx fældisyn* (Horse Consecration), where a description of the journey of the dead to the underworld is given in traditional terms (Thordarson 1989a, pp. 876–77). K'osta also wrote a great deal in Russian, both poetry and prose, e.g. the tragic poem *Fatima*, which has been filmed, with the text spoken in Ossetic translation, so far the only Ossetic film.

Gædiaty Sek'a (1855–1915) is chiefly known as a prose writer, but he also wrote lyrical poetry. He was born in South Ossetia and particularly chose the life of the mountaineers of east Georgia as themes for his short stories. His stories reveal with harsh realism and tragic beauty their unrelenting struggle for existence. For the development of social realism and for Ossetic prose writing in general his stories have been of great significance. Among his short stories *Azaw* is especially worth mentioning.

Other writers who made their debut before 1917 were K'ubalty Alyksandr (1872–1937), mainly known for his social-historical epic poem *Æfxærdty Xæsanæ* (a proper name), Kocoity Arsen (1872–1944), who as a publicist and short story writer exerted considerable influence upon the new literature; he also had a reputation as cartoonist.

Bryt'iaty Elbyzdyqo (1881–1923) is the first Ossetic dramatist of importance; he wrote seven dramas altogether; in *Amyran* he treats a subject from ancient Caucasian mythology (Georg. *Amirani*). Kochysaty Rozæ (1888–1910) owes her literary name to three comedies with folklorist themes; as a woman writer she has a place apart in the Ossetic literature of this period.

3. After 1917

For the Ossetes, as for the other nations of the Caucasus, the twentieth century was an era of cultural awakening that was not least reflected in the creation of a written language, and the growth of literary production. Most genres of modern European literature found their native representation; foreign literary works were translated, as a rule from Russian. The impact of the new cultural currents brought about a profound change in the spiritual life of the nation. The break with the old traditions of the tribal society became a frequent theme in the new literature.

The revolution of 1917 completely altered the conditions informing Ossetic literature. Most men of letters joined, or at least approved of, the new regime and remained in their native country. Some few, however, kept aloof from Bolshevism and emigrated to the West. Among these was Baiaty Gappo (Russ. Gappo Baiev, 1869–1939), who had been one of the pioneers of the literary movement around the turn of the century and a prominent figure in the cultural and political life of the Ossetes. Among his poetic publications one may mention *Gælabu* (Butterfly, 1900), a collection of poems, including some of his own, and *Iron Arghæutæ* (Ossetic folktales, 1901). After the establishment of the Bolshevik regime he settled in Berlin, where he taught Ossetic at various academic institutions and dedicated himself to the propagation of the knowledge of Ossetic and Caucasian culture.

The Bolshevik cultural policy brought about a gradual abolishment of illiteracy, which entailed a great extension of the reading public. Literary interest was aroused, and literature obtained a strong position in the national life. This demanded new types of literature. In the biggest towns, theaters were built and thus working conditions were created for dramatists. The foundation of research institutes and, after the Second World War, a university in Dzæudzhyqæu (Vladikavkaz) was not only of significance to the scholastic world, but also proved a vigorous incentive to cultural activities in general. An Ossetic scholar who has won international fame in the humanities, and particularly in Iranian studies is Abaity Vaso (Russ. Vasiliy Abaev, 1900–2000).

In general, modern Ossetic literature has followed the pattern of the literature of the Russians and other Soviet peoples. The political and economic changes that followed in the wake of the Bolshevik revolution, as well as the Second World War, made demands on literary creativity. At the same time, national history and scenes from traditional oral poetry have been a vitalizing force, no doubt often to be understood allegorically, with allusions to contemporary events.

In the interwar period, a number of new writers made their appearance. Only a few names can be mentioned here. One of the most prominent writers of this generation was Gædiaty Comaq (1883–1931), son of the above-mentioned Gædiaty Sek'a, who wrote drama, prose and poetry in addition to essays and literary criticism. Bedzhyzaty Chermen (1898–1937), Epxity Tætæri (1911–58), and Dzanaty Ivan (pseudonym Niger, 1896–1947) also were all-round writers and poets. Mamsyraty Dæbe (1909–66) was a prolific poet and prose writer; he wrote short stories, drama, novels, e.g. *Qæbatyrty kadæg* (The saga of the heroes).

Maliti Geuærgi (1886–1937) wrote poems and prose sketches in the Digor dialect, with themes from his native Digoria; his small collection of prose and poetry, *Iræf* (a Digor river name, Russ. Urukh), appeared in 1935.

The post-war period has seen a continuous increase in the literary activity of the Ossetes. Thanks to periods of improved material conditions, the demands for didactic political literature have become less appropriate. Lyrical poetry is evidently much in vogue, and personal problems have got a more prominent place. The national-romantic vein and the interest in historical and traditional epic subjects have become even more vigorous in the post-war period than before. As a representative of the last two generations we may mention Dzhusoity Nafi (b. 1925), a literary historian who has written both novels (e.g. *Fydælty tug*, The ancestors' blood), and lyrical poetry, besides translating both Pushkin and Greek drama into his native tongue.

4. The Nart Epic

The Ossetes possess a rich folklore and a traditional oral poetry which apparently derives to a large extent from Ancient Aryan, and even Indo-European epic and mythological sources. The recording and study of Ossetic oral poetry began around the middle of the nineteenth century, and is today carried out with increasing zeal by native as well foreign scholars. This has been of great importance for the development of Ossetic literature. Particularly significant is the cycle of heroic legends about the Narts (*Narty kaddzhytæ*). The Narts are a heroic race, who lived prior to human beings in the country north of the Caucasian mountains, in the age of the giants whom they defeated. This epic cycle is widespread among all the peoples of the North Caucasus. The geographical scenery and the cultural atmosphere are those of the North Caucasus, but it can hardly be doubted that the cycle is largely of Iranian origin. The etymology of the name of the race, *Nart* (collective singular) is controversial, but most likely it derives from Aryan **nar-* "man, hero, warrior," cf. **narthra-* "valor." According to the traditions of the North Ossetes, the Nart community consists of three families or clans (*mygkægtæ*): *ærtæ* (i.e., three) *Narty* (gen. sg.): the Æxsærtægkatæ, the Alægatæ, and the Boratæ (*-tæ* marks the nominative plural). The first is primarily a clan of warriors, and the most vigorous heroes belong to it. Their grand lady and clever adviser in their great exertions is Satana. The Boratæ are rich in sheep and cattle; they do not distinguish themselves by warlike exploits. The Alægatæ owe their strength to their intelligence; in their house are celebrated the common religious feasts and the great drinking bouts of the Narts. They have in their keeping the big magical bowl, *Nart-amongæ* or *Uac-amongæ* (*amongæ* an agent noun of the verb *amonyn* "to reveal"; *nart* means "valor"; *uac* "holy"). Its main function is to verify the feats of the heroes; in its presence the heroes narrate their exploits; if they tell the truth, the liquid it contains swells up and flows over; if they lie, it remains immobile.

The Nart village is situated on a mountain, where it is divided into three quarters. At the top live the Æxsærtægkatæ, in the middle the Alægatæ, at the foot of the mountain the Boratæ. The

Iranian etymologies of the names of the two first clans are clear: the Æxsærtægkatæ derive their name from *æxsar*, "power, force," also the eponymous ancestor of the clan (Ir. *xshathra-* "power, supremacy," O.Ind. *kshatrá*. The word Alægatæ is apparently derives from *arya-*, the ancient ethnic name of the Indo-Iranian peoples, *âryaka-. The name Boratæ is enigmatic.

The Æxsærtægkatæ and the Boratæ are continually waging war against each other. Batraz, whose body is made of steel, is the typical warrior; he is the defender of the Nart people against their enemies; he has the thunderbolt as his sword. Batraz cannot die until his sword has been thrown into the sea. Finally the Narts succeed in drawing the sword to the coast, thus fulfilling his own request.

Another central hero is Soslan (or Sosyryko). He excels through his intelligence as well as bravery. His solar character seems clear; he is married for instance to the daughter of the sun (Wac-Ruxs, Acy-). He is "rock-born," i.e. originated from a rock, a qualification he seems to share with Mithra, the Aryan god of the (social) contract, who is also associated with the sun. A young shepherd falls in love with Satana as she is washing her laundry on a riverbank. He cannot retain his sperm, which falls on a stone. Satana takes care of the stone, and in due time it gives birth to a boy. The Narts' blacksmith, Kuyrdalægon, grasps the newborn with his tongs and puts him in water to cool him down and makes him invulnerable. But the parts of the body where the blacksmith holds him with the tongs remain sore and vulnerable: a knee (or both knees), or his hip. Soslan grows up with the Nart youth, his only enemy being Syrdon, the diabolic rogue of the Narts. Through a stratagem of his, Soslan is hit in his vulnerable part by the wheel of Balsæg, which rolls in flames down from heaven towards the west, until it falls into the sea. The wheel is somehow connected with the myths and rites of the solstice. Soslan's nephew avenges his uncle, and splits the wheel in two; the two halves are placed on Soslan's grave. But Soslan is not dead, he lives on in his grave, where he is worshipped at certain dates in June. The grave is shown at various places in the N. Caucasus.

There are certain traits of shamanism in the character of Soslan. He descends to the underworld to seek the advice of his dead wife, as he wants to marry again. The description of his journey is in part identical with that of the sermon recited at the traditional Horse Consecration burial rites, and the formulaic phraseology is the same (Thordarson 1989a). This suggests that the story of Soslan's visit in the land of the dead reflects shamanistic ideas, and that the Nart legend and the burial traditions derive from the same source, a kind of an oral shamanistic narrative.

As a rule the Ossetic legends are in prose, the style is partly formulaic, and the language is to a certain degree archaic. Among the neighboring peoples, on the other hand, the legends are metrical, and this may originally have been the case in Ossetic also.

The Nart myths and legends are found in innumerable variants among the Ossetes as well as their neighbors; so, e.g., in South Ossetia and among the neighboring peoples of the North, the Alægatæ have almost disappeared, and the other two clans have merged.

According to G. Dumézil, who has dedicated numerous studies to the Caucasian Nart cycle, the scheme of the three clans and their functions corresponds with the tripartite structure of Aryan (and Indo-European) society: warriors; possessors of divine knowledge; and cattle-breeders or farmers.

In the rich folklore of the Ossetes we also find superhuman beings distant from the three Nart clans: Uastyrdzhi (St. George, divinity of manliness); Uacilla (St. Elias, divinity of thunder); Safa (divinity of the hearth-chain), and many others.

CHAPTER 9

PERSIAN POPULAR LITERATURE

Ulrich Marzolph

Iran is, and has always been a multi-ethnic nation. Besides the various Iranian ethnic groups—such as, to name only the largest, the Bakhtiyâris, Lors, Kurds, or Baloch—the population of Iran in its present boundaries comprises comparatively large ethnic groups of Turko-Mongolian and Arab origin. The folklore and popular literature of each of these groups naturally have their own specific characteristics, but they have been studied only to a minor extent. The present survey, while aiming to present the main characteristics of Persian popular literature, will focus on available sources, most of which have been published in the Persian language regardless of the original language of performance. The only comprehensive survey of Persian folk-literature previously published in English (Cejpek 1968) is still highly informative today. Due to its frequent pro-Iranian bias it should, however, be read with a critical distance.

1. History of research

Early preoccupation with Persian folklore appears to go back as far as the Safavid period, when Âqâ Jamâl Khʷânsâri (d. *c.* 1703) compiled his booklet *Kolthum Nane*, a treatise on women's customs (Katirâ'i 1970). The beginning of Persian folklore studies coincided with the keen interest early Western travelers took in Iran since the seventeenth century (Burnikel 1992; Osterhammel 1998). Apart from their curiosity, the main impetus for the developing field of Persian studies resulted from the strategic interest of the European powers. In India, where the British ruled since the mid-eighteenth century, the Persian language maintained its position as the language of court and intellectual lingua franca. The Russian empire, Iran's northern neighbor, also had a strategic interest in the region (see Shvarts 1974, pp. 8–21). At first, since the discovery and translation of the *Avesta*, Western scholars had focused on religious studies. This in turn prompted a linguistic interest in dialects, which soon turned to collecting items of folklorist relevance, such as folk-tales, riddles, songs, or narratives of everyday life. Pioneers in the field include the Polish diplomat A. Chodzko (1804–91), Russian scholar V. Zhukovski (1858–1918), British consuls D.C. Phillot (1860–1930) and D.L.R. Lorimer (1876–1962), Danish scholar A. Christensen (1875–1945), and French scholar Henri Massé (1886–1969). For most of these authors, folklore and popular literature constituted a pleasant distraction from their "serious" linguistic, religious, or historical concerns, and folklore data were rarely valued in their own right. Exceptions include B. A. Donaldson's study of Muslim magic, which is based on information collected mainly from women in the holy city of Mashhad (Donaldson 1938), and H. Massé's two-volume publication *Croyances et coutumes persanes* (1938), a highly meritorious survey of the field of Persian folklore, whose information derived from close cooperation with a number of renowned Persian intellectuals. Later comparative studies in Persian popular literature, such as those by F. Meier (1967, 1974), are also of prime importance.

The nineteenth century witnessed a strong orientation on the part of the Iranian elite towards the scientific achievements of the West. Folklore, with its associations of maintaining tradition, was regarded as anti-progressive and hence as undeserving of serious study. It was not until the Constitutional period in the 1920s that Persian scholars began to devote themselves to the study of folklore. At this time, strong patriotic feelings were combined with a growing awareness of the "common people," mingled with a romantic urge for unspoiled tradition. Iranian intellectuals such as Mohammad Ali Jamâlzâdeh, Ali-Akbar Dehkhodâ, Sâdeq Hedâyat, and later Samad Behrangi or Jalâl Âl-e Ahmad began to prefer plain colloquial Persian to the refined and highly artificial language that was previously used. In 1922–29 Dehkhodâ published his comprehensive collection of proverbs and proverbial phrases, *Amthâl o hekam*, while Hedâyat was the "first Iranian to study folklore and outline the methods of scholarship" (Radhayrapetian 1990, p. 94). In his *Neyrangestân* (1933), Hedâyat published a survey of superstitions and customs. Following French ethnographer Pierre Saintyves, he supplied general guidelines as to how to collect and document folklore in his essay "Folklor yâ farhang-e tude" (1945). Hedâyat's agenda, though highly influential in the subsequent Iranian attitude towards folklore, was first put in practice by Sâdeq Homâyuni in his fieldwork study on the folklore of Sarvestân in the Fârs province (1970).

As official institutions became interested in the preservation and study of folklore, the Iranian Academy, the *Farhangestân*, in 1938 publicized its intention to collect "regional (*velâyati*) words, expressions, poetry, proverbs, tales, stories, songs and melodies" (see Jamâlzâdeh 1962, pp. 92ff.). Meanwhile, in the 1940s Fazlollâh Mohtadi (known as Sobhi), probably imitating a method first attempted by L.P. Elwell-Sutton (1980), initiated a radio program of folktales, asking his listeners to send in their tales; he eventually published a series of booklets of Persian folktales (Rahgozar 1994). Sobhi's primary aim, however, was to entertain. Accordingly, although his publications are pleasant to read, they do not match modern academic standards. On the other hand, journals such as *Payâm-e now*, founded in 1944 by Sa'id Nafisi and later edited by Bozorg Alavi, started to publish many short articles on various genres of popular literature. In 1958 the *Edâre-ye Farhang-e Âmme* (Office of Popular Culture), under the direction of the Ministry of Culture and Arts, was founded; it was reorganized in 1970 and renamed *Markaz-e Melli-ye Pazhuheshhâ-ye Mardom-shenâsi va Farhang-e Âmme* (National Center for Studies in Ethnography and Popular Culture); until the Revolution of 1979 it continued to work under the name of *Markaz-e Mardom-shenâsi-ye Irân* (Center for the Ethnography of Iran). This institution and its team of researchers played a leading role in folklore research, above all through their series of monographs (for folktales see Honari 1973;

Mihandust 1973; Sâdât-e Eshkevari 1973) as well as the journal *Mardom-shenâsi va farhang-e âmme* (Ethnography and Popular Culture; founded in 1976). Between 1968 and 1974, field investigations conducted by researchers from the institution resulted in the survey of almost 400 villages and the publication of more than 20 monograph studies (see Radhayrapetian 1990, pp. 106ff).

Since the early 1960s, Sobhi's method of utilizing radio broadcasts for the purpose of collecting and propagating folktales has been successfully taken up by Abu'l-Qâsem Enjavi (d. 1993), a friend of the late Hedâyat. Enjavi initiated the weekly program *Safine-ye farhang-e mardom* (Ship of Popular Culture), educated a considerable staff of assistants and founded an institution named *Markaz-e Farhang-e Mardom* (Center of Popular Culture) within the National Broadcasting Company. In order to publish the collected texts, he established the series *Ganjine-ye farhang-e mardom* (Treasury of Popular Culture), to which he himself contributed ten volumes of annotated texts. Three volumes contain folktales (Enjavi 1973, 1974, 1977), and another three, later published together under the title *Ferdowsi-nâme*, contain popular tales connected with Ferdowsi, his *Shahname*, or the latter's heroes (Enjavi 1990). Enjavi was not only a captivating orator but also had great talents of organization. His nationwide contributors received not only pencil, preprinted paper, and envelope, but also his booklet *Tarz-e neveshtan-e farhang-e âmiyâne* (How to Document Popular Culture; 1967), containing general guidelines. Until the early 1980s, when his radio program was discontinued, Enjavi succeeded in collecting an archive of several hundred thousand manuscript texts on numerous aspects of folklore, everyday life and popular literature in Iran. His archive is a mine of information on traditional language, customs, beliefs, tales, oral history, and the like, unparalleled in any other Middle Eastern country.

Resulting from the strong national interest and considerable support by both official institutions and the royal family, folklore studies in Iran were thriving in the mid-1970s. The International Congress of Iranian Popular Culture (*Majma'-e beynolmellali-ye farhang-e âmme-ye Irân*), held in Isfahan in the summer of 1977, was attended by many qualified scholars from Iran and various

Western countries. The Revolution of 1979 caused contacts with Western scholars to be broken off, and Iranian publications on folklore to be discontinued. It took many years for folklore and popular literature to attract significant interest again (see Marzolph 1994b).

In 1986, as a result of the re-evaluation of cultural values in the Islamic Republic, the *Sâzmân-e Mirâth-e Farhangi-ye Keshvar* (Organization for the Country's Cultural Heritage) was founded. Today, the responsibility of this centralized institution includes supervising all kinds of cultural activities, encompassing archaeology, anthropology, and folklore. Its Ethnographic Department, for many years headed by Mohammad Mir-Shokrâ'i, has educated junior folklorists (up to M.A. level), and conducted various fieldwork research projects, including one on popular literature in 1994–95. The first monographs to result from this research project recently came out (Vakiliyân 2000; Jaktâji 2001). The *Markaz-e Farhang-e Mardom*, founded by Enjavi, is at present associated with the research department of the national radio institution *Sedâ va Simâ-ye Jomhuri-ye Eslâmi-ye Irân* (Islamic Republic of Iran Broadcasting [IRIB]). The few major publications from the archive's materials after the Revolution deal with popular sayings and proverbs (Vakiliyân 1987), and popular customs in the month of Ramadan (Vakiliyân 1991). In spring 2002, the first ever scholarly Iranian journal of folklore, the quarterly *Farhang-e mardom*, was published on the initiative of the leading Iranian folklorist Sayyed Ahmad Vakiliyân.

2. Fields of study

Resulting from its historical development, Folklore Studies in Iran have always been, and still are, deeply concerned with popular language and verbal expression (Katirâ'i 1978). Milestones of this branch of Folklore Studies include Jamâlzâdeh's dictionary of popular language (1962) and Dehkhodâ's comprehensive collection of proverbs (1922–29). Proverb Studies have remained a major field of research, from Amir-Qoli Amini's pioneer study on the stories connected with proverbs (1945) to the two-volume publication of texts drawn from the archives of the *Markaz-e Farhang-e Mardom* (Enjavi 1973; Vakiliyân 1987) and other recent publications (Partovi Âmoli 1990; Shahri 1991; Afifi 1992; Shakurzâdeh 1993; Abrishami 1996, 1997).

Probably the best researched category of Iranian folklore is that of folk narrative (Radhayrapetian 1990; Marzolph 1993; Rahmoni 2001). Early publications of folktales include the ones by Hoseyn Kuhi Kermâni (1935), Amir-Qoli Amini (1960) and Abolqâsem Faqiri (1970). The major collection of Persian folktales is still the one published by Enjavi (1973, 1974, 1977). It is in this branch of Folklore Studies that the impact of cooperation with foreign researchers is most productive (see Boulvin 1971, 1975; Marzolph 1984). The first major collection of Persian folktales published after the Revolution presents the tales originally collected in the 1940s by Elwell-Sutton from the oral performance of the Persian maid Mashdi Galin. Besides the tales collected at the beginning of the twentieth century from the Persian language teacher Sayyed Feyzollâh Adib, this collection constitutes the largest available corpus of any Iranian storyteller's repertoire (Elwell-Sutton 1980; Marzolph et al. 1995). Other recent scholarly publications of folktales are either republished (Homâyuni 1993 [Shirâz 1972]) or comparatively small (see, e.g., Moharrer 1986; Mir-Kâzemi 1988, 1994, 1995; Ravânipur 1990; Mihandust 1991–2001). The projected multi-volume *Dictionary of Persian Folktales* (*Farhang-e afsânehâ-ye mardom-e Irân*) by A. A. Darvishiyân and R. Khandân (1998ff.) contains no more than an alphabetically arranged comprehensive selection of previously published material.

The comparatively low standard of Iranian publications on popular literature may to some extent be caused by the difficulties Iranians have in reproducing their data. Verbatim quotations of texts collected during fieldwork often clash with literary standards, and may further contain passages liable to offend current moral standards. Before publication all folklore texts are therefore made to undergo various stages of editing, a process which tends to alter the authentic form of the texts. Moreover, important Western studies have only recently been made available in Persian translation, including Vladimir Propp's structuralist approach (Propp 1989, 1992); the international classification system for folktales developed by Antti Aarne and Stith Thompson (Marzolph 1992); and Mircea Eliade's mythological studies (1983, 1995). F. Sajjâdpur (1999) recently published a study of a limited corpus of Persian folktales analyzed according to a modern psychoanalytical approach.

As to the connection between popular and classical literature, Foruzânfar's admirable study on the sources of the tales in Jalâl-al-Din Rumi's *Mathnavi* (Foruzânfar 1954, 1991) has been paralleled by a similar study treating Farid-al-Din Attâr's *mathnavi*s (San'atiniyâ 1990). While Rumi's impact on subsequent popular tradition has been studied (Mills 1994; Marzolph 1995), the popular reception of other classical authors still awaits adequate treatment. Enjavi's three-volume collection of popular renderings of tales from, or relating to the *Shahname* or Ferdowsi is still in print (Enjavi 1990). The narrative literature of the Qajar period, of which several items were popular reading matter until well into the second half of the twentieth century, has been studied to some extent by M. J. Mahjub (1959ff.). Meanwhile, the "chapbook" literature based on classical works has been documented for the Qajar period (Marzolph 2001b), and for the mid-twentieth century (Marzolph 1994a).

Comprehensive folkloristic and/or ethnographic studies of specific localities or regions often contain authentic samples of popular literature collected during fieldwork. This branch of Folklore Studies, inaugurated by Âl-e Ahmad's three small studies (1954, 1958, 1960), and its follow-ups by Kh. Khosravi (1963) and S. Tâhbâz (1963), was pursued on a larger scale by E. Shakurzâdeh (1967, 1984), and Homâyuni (1970, 1992). While many minor ethnographic studies on various localities exist, even today only a few regions have been explored more thoroughly, notably Fârs (Homâyuni 1974; Faqiri 1978; Habibi-Âzâd 1993), Gil and Dailam (Pâyande 1973, 1976; Asadiyân-Khorramâbâdi, Bâjelân-Farroki, Kiyâ'i 1979), Boir Ahmadi and Kohgiluye (Lama'e 1970). Recent major studies were prepared by A. Lahsâ'izâdeh and A. Salâmi (1991), H. Habibi Fahlyâbi (1992), A. Shari'atzâdeh (1992) and S. Atâbak-zâdeh (1994).

Since the establishment of the Islamic Republic, all cultural activity in the country is screened by the powerful ministry of Islamic Guidance for its compatibility with the prescribed set of values. As a result some topics, especially those with religious associations, are obviously qualified as particularly desirable, e.g. the popular drama *ta'ziye* (Homâyuni 1989, 1976, 1992; Shahidi 2001), a work on popular customs during Ramadan (Vakiliyân 1991), or popular tales about the first imam, Ali (Vakiliyân/Sâlehi 2001). Other areas of popular culture, on the other hand, risk being qualified as undesirable, either because of their pre-Islamic origins, or because they are regarded as superstitions simply because they lack any obvious educational value (see Marzolph 1994b, 1994c).

3. Traditional popular reading matter

The great epics of Persian literature, such as Ferdowsi's *Shahname*, the anonymous *Eskandar-nâme* and *Romuz-e Hamze*, have been appreciated by both elite and popular strata of Persian society for centuries. Before the nineteenth century, and well into the twentieth, they were presented to the illiterate by professional storytellers (Omidsalar 1999; see also K. Yamamoto in this volume). When printing was introduced in Iran in the first decades of the nineteenth century, the reception of this type of popular literature gained an altogether new quality, as epic literature was gradually adapted to popular reading. It is particularly interesting to note that some of the shorter epical tales published in the nineteenth century, such as *Hoseyn-e Kord*, were comparatively young and had first been committed to writing not much before their first printed editions were published (Marzolph 1999b). Probably some of the later publishers even had direct recourse to manuscript collections of popular narratives, such as the comprehensive *Jâme' al-hekâyât* (Haag-Higuchi 1984). At any rate, publication of this type of literature in print decisively increased its distribution, and hence popular knowledge of tales and motifs as well as embedded social and moral concepts.

ORAL LITERATURE OF IRANIAN LANGUAGES

Thanks to a carefully drawn-up list published in 1865, we have access to the traditional popular reading matter of the Qajar period (Marzolph 2001b). The list is appended to the 1864-65 edition of the *Ketâb-e Ganjine*, a collection of writings by Mirzâ Abd al-Wahhâb Mo'tamed al-Dowle Neshât (d. 1828). Compiled by the book's publisher, a certain Hâji Musâ, the catalogue lists a total of 320 Persian and fourteen Arabic items. After listing books relating to the basic fields of Islamic law (*feqh, osul, tafsir*) and a large variety of profane sciences (dictionaries, history, medicine, philosophy, grammar etc.), the catalogue's final sections are concerned with non-scientific moralistic, educative and entertaining literature. These sections list *kotob-e ahâdith va akhbâr* (books on persons or events considered to be historical), *kotob-e ad'iye o kotob-e mosibat* (books on prayers and on the tragedy of Karbalâ), *divânât* (collections of poetry), *qese o hekâyât* (tales and stories), and *bachchekh^{w}âni* (reading matter for children). The categories dealing with (pseudo-)historical or religious literature are treated to some extent by P. Chelkowski in this volume, and do not concern us here. It is the two final sections that are of particular interest to the study of popular literature in the Qajar period.

The first section lists such well-known items as the *Anvâr-e Soheyli* (by Kâshefi), *Jâme' al-tamthil* (by Mohammad-Ali Hablerudi), and *Ajâ'eb al-makhluqât* (by Mohammad b. Zakariyâ Qazvini, thirteenth century), besides the anonymous *Eskandar-nâme, Alf leyle, Romuz-e Hamze,* and *Rostam-nâme*. The compiler of the list obviously grouped these items together because of their common narrative character. As to the narratives found there, the first is a collection of fables, actually the most widely read Persian adaptation of the famous collection *Kalile o Demne*; the second is a collection of proverbs and related stories (Marzolph 1999a); the third is the Persian translation of an Arabic classic of *mirabilia*-literature; besides *Alf leyle*, the nineteenth-century Persian translation by Abd-al-Latif Tasuji and Mirzâ Sorush of the Arabic *Thousand and one Nights* (following the Bulâq edition of 1835), the remaining three items are lengthy epics on Alexander, Hamza b. Abd-al-Mottaleb, and Rostam, respectively.

The second section lists more than thirty items, the majority of which belong to the standard stock of traditional narrative literature: *Hoseyn-e Kord* (Marzolph 1999b); *Nush-Âfarin; Bahrâm o Golandâm; Leyli o Majnun; Shirin o Farhâd; Dalle-ye Mokhtâr; Dozd o Qâzi; Rend o Zâhed; Chehel tuti* (Marzolph 1979); *Heydar-Beg; Kolthum Nane* (Katirâ'i 1970); *Yusef o Zoleykhâ; Javâher al-oqul; Shiruye; Qahramân-e qâtel; Hormoz o Gol; Chahâr darvish*, to name but the most popular. It is difficult to evaluate the compiler's intention in labeling this section "reading matter for children." It is hard to imagine that the items listed were indeed read by children themselves, as children in those days would rarely be literate. Presumably he intended to point out the entertaining and educative character of the listed works, most of which convey social and moral standards of the time in the garb of a narrative.

As to the question of readership no contemporary evidence is available. On the other hand, Mahjub's survey (1959ff.) of his own reading experience in Persian popular narratives (*dâstân-hâ-ye âmmiyâne-ye fârsi*) lists pretty much the same titles, grouped into the following categories:
1. purely fictitious stories, such as *Amir Arsalân; Malek Bahman; Badi' al-molk*; and *Nush-Âfarin*;
2. stories vaguely connected with history, such as *Romuz-e Hamze; Eskandar-nâme; Rostam-nâme*; and *Hoseyn-e Kord*;
3. stories about religious figures, such as the *Khâvar-nâme*;
4. stories embellishing the historical role of religious characters, such as the *Mokhtâr-nâme*;
5. stories about amorous or other adventures, such as *Haft peykar-e Bahrâm Gur; Chahâr darvish; Salim-e javâheri; Dalle-ye Mokhtâr*; this category also includes collections of stories such as *Alf leyle*;
6. (collections of) stories focusing on animal actors, such as *Chehel tuti; Khâle Suske; Âqâ Mushe; Mush o gorbe*;
7. minor works by classical Persian poets in popular editions.

Mahjub was born in 1923, and when he was writing in the 1950s about his reading experience as a youth, he must have had in mind the popular literature available in the 1930s. The evidence supplied by Mahjub's studies is further corroborated by a list published in the recent *History of Children's Literature in Iran*. The list is a statistical survey aimed at naming the reading matter that was popular at the beginning of the twentieth century. Its data result from recent interviews with (male) senior citizens aged over sixty (Mohammadi and Qâ'eni 2001, vol. 3, pp. 140–54). Besides their age, level of education, and place of origin, those interviewed were asked to specify the persons who promoted their interest in reading, the books they read, and the influence reading had on them. In addition to European literature in translation (such as the novels by Alexandre Dumas), we again find many of the items already listed in Hâji Musâ's list, the most frequently named ones being *Amir Arsalân* (first published in 1899; see Marzolph 2001a, p. 232), *Hoseyn-e Kord*, and *Amir Hamze*. In the middle of the twentieth century, many of these items were still produced and sold nationwide in Iran by itinerant booksellers and sidewalk peddlers. The most active publishers in this field were Sherkat-e nesbi-ye kânun-e ketâb, Mo'assese-ye châp va enteshârât-e Elmi, Mohammad-Hasan Elmi, Rajabi, and Atâ'i (Marzolph 1994a, pp. 18–20).

The stock of popular reading matter did not of course remain unaltered in the period concerned. Some items, such as *Hoseyn-e Kord*, remained "evergreens" until the twentieth century; others, such as the voluminous *Eskandar-nâme* and *Romuz-e Hamze*, were gradually reduced in size; while yet others vanished completely. At the same time, new items were produced such as versified adaptations of Persian folktales (*Shangul o Mangul, Khâle Suske, Khâle Qurbâghe, Khorus o rubâh*). Moreover, an increasing amount of pedagogical and entertaining literature for children, including schoolbooks, conveyed traditional narrative material to its young readers (Marzolph 1995b; Mohammadi and Qâ'eni 2001).

4. Folk- and fairy-tales

Judging by the number of publications on this genre of popular literature, folk- and fairy-tales were highly appreciated in the original setting in which they were recorded, and are no less popular with contemporary readers. Given the impact of modern media and the ensuing changes in society, it is difficult to ascertain the degree to which folk- and fairy-tales are still alive in the modern times. They were very popular until quite recently, and still are in rural areas. Beside nostalgia, the current popularity of folk- and fairy-tale collections may also reflect a continuous human need for this genre of tales.

Terminology

Folk- and fairy-tales are usually denoted by one of the three terms *qesse*, *afsâne* (with such variants as *afsân*, *fasân*, *fasâne*, or the dialect variants *owsun*, *owsâne*, see Honari 1973; Mihandust 1999a–d), or *matal*. The word *qesse* retains a somewhat vague relation to historical or personal realities; even characters within a given tale will relate their *qesse*, i.e., their personal history. In recent terminology, *qesse* has come to denote the literary genre of the short tale. Fictitious tales of wonder and imagination, and particularly tales relating to sorcery and magic, are usually labeled *afsâne*. This term shows an obvious etymological and semantic link with terms such as *fasâ'idan* (*fasânidan*), 'to charm, fascinate, enchant,' or *fosun*, *afsun*, 'incantation, fascination.' The term *matal*, indiscriminately used to denote popular stories (Vakiliyân 1999), is not to be confused with *mathal*, which denotes a popular saying or proverb.

Language and formulaic expression

Even though folk- and fairy-tales are usually narrated in plain language without refined embellishment, narrators may draw on a large stock of formulaic expressions. Tales of a realistic or historical background, particularly romantic or epic tales in writing, usually begin with the rhymed formula *râviyân-e akhbâr va nâqelân-e âsâr (va tutiyân-e shekar-shekan-e shirin-goftâr) chenin revâyat karde'and ke* ..., "The tellers of stories and the transmitters of ancient legends (and the sugar-cracking and sweet-talking parrots) have related that ..." (Marzolph et al. 1994, vol. 2, p. 25).

This formula, by taking recourse to previous authorities, makes the listeners expect a tale whose grounding in reality is at least formally acknowledged.

Introductory formulas

In contrast, the standard formula for fairy-tales—more or less equivalent to the English "Once upon a time"—introduces the readers and/or listeners to a world of fantasy and imagination. It is: *yeki bud, yeki nabud,* "There was a one, and there was not a one"; at times the formula *gheir az khodâ hichkas nabud,* "There was nobody but God" is added to this. In oral performance, the story-teller may then say: *har ke bande-ye khodâ be-ge "yâ khodâ,"* "All true believers (lit. all bondsmen of God) now say 'O God!,'" to which the audience replies: *Yâ khodâ,* "O God!" Another, less common formula for the introduction of fairy-tales is *ruzi (bud), ruzgâri (bud),* "(There was) a day, (there was) a time." Only after either one of these formulas does the actual tale begin, most commonly by a sentence like *yek pâdeshâhi (mardi, rubâhi etc.) bud,* "There was a king (man, fox etc.)." Sometimes the latter is further introduced by specifying *dar zamân-e qadim,* "in the old days."

The introductory formula *yeki bud, yeki nabud* finds an exact equivalent in the Turkish *bir varmish, bir yokmush* and in several other Near Eastern languages; all are related to the Arabic *kân mâ kân* (Asmussen 1968, p. 14ff.). While there are various ways to translate the formula—the Arabic can also mean "There was what there was"—it is most probably meant to introduce the readers/listeners to the never-never-land of the fairy-tale.

Closing formulas

Likewise, when the tale is over, closing formulas point out the unreal character of the preceding tale and make it clear that the action took place in an imaginary world, even though there might have been parallels to the social and historical reality of the narrator's context (Motaref 1979, 43 ff.). Closing formulas in fairytales, while also structured by means of simple rhymes, show a greater variety than introductory formulas. Most include nonsense rhymes, bringing the readers/listeners back to the real world. One of the more common formulas is *qesse-ye mâ be-sar resid, kalâghe be-khân(e)ash naresid*, "Our tale has come to an end, the crow has not reached its home" (Enjavi 1973, pp. 55, 205, 270 etc.). There are several variations to this formula, such as: *vaqti resid, ghazâhâsh gandide bud, aruse londide bud*, "When it arrived, its food was rotten, the bride had complained" (ibid., p. 311). A jocular variation is given in a variant from Isfahan: *qesse-ye mâ be-sar raft, kalâghe guzid o dar raft*, "our tale has come to an end, the crow farted and flew away." (Faqiri 1963, p. 91).

Less ambiguous than the previous formula is another one, which clearly shows the fictitious character of the tale: *bâlâ raftim, mâst bud—qesse-ye mâ râst bud; pâyin âmadim dugh bud, qesse-ye mâ dorugh bud*, "We went up, there was yoghurt—our tale was true; we went down, there was *dugh* (a drink prepared from yoghurt)—our tale was a lie." (Enjavi 1973, pp. 278, 321, etc.). A more pragmatic version of this formula includes the following variants: *raftim bâlâ, ârd bud, âmadim pâyin khamir/panir bud—qesse-ye/ hekâyat-e/sar-gozasht-e mâ hamin bud*, "We went up, there was flour, we came down, there was dough/cheese—this was our tale." (Marzolph et al. 1994, vol. 2, p, 28).

Other, less common closing formulas are: *qesse-ye mâ kh^{w}osh bud, daste-ye goli jâsh bud*, "Our tale was nice, a flower bouquet was in its place" (Enjavi 1973, pp. 259, 308); *qesse-ye mâ tamum shod, khâk be-sar-e hamum [= hammâm] shod*, "Our tale is finished, there is dust on the head of the bath house" (ibid., p. 34); *qesse-ye mâ be-resht, be-resht—morde-ye mâ konj-e behesht*, "Spin, spin our tale—our deceased one [has a] corner in paradise" (Faqiri 1963, p. 91).

In romantic tales, particularly those about lovers who are finally united after overcoming a number of obstacles, we find yet another common type of closing formula: *enshâllâh hamân-towr ke ânhâ be-morâd-e del-e-shân residand, shomâ ham be-morâd-e del-e-tân be-resid*, "God willing, you will attain your heart's desires in the same way, as they [= the characters of the tale] have attained their hearts' desires." (Enjavi 1973, pp. 115, 119, 133, etc.). The gifted Persian narrator Mashdi Galin, who narrated the documented repertoire of her tales during World War II, even amended the formulas several times to include direct references to the political party of her English listener: ... *hame-ye mottafeqin beresand*, "... may all the Allies attain"; *dustân-e mottafeqin be-maqsudeshân beresand*, "may the friends of the Allies attain their goal"; *doshmanân-e mottafeqin nâbud shavand*, "may the enemies of the Allies be annihilated." (Marzolph et al. 1994, vol. 2, p. 29).

Formulas within the tale

While both introductory and closing formulas are fairly standardized, narrators can draw on a large stock of formulas within a given tale. These formulas often relate to the tale's content and are employed according to the narrator's skill. The repertoire of Mashdi Galin (see above), which has been analyzed in detail, contains a large number of formulas within the tales (for the following see ibid., pp. 25–27). Besides short words such as *al-qesse* or *al-gharaz*, both meaning "in short," the formula most commonly used to structure a tale goes as follows: *XY dâshte bâsh, biyâ/borow (berim/berid) sar-e YZ (az YZ beshnow/begir)*, "(Now) leave XY (here), go/come (let us go/come) to YZ (listen about YZ)." In addition, there are several formulas for special occasions:
- Departure: *posht be-shahr, ru be-dasht-e biyâbun*, "The back (turned) to the city, the face (turned) to the open plains."
- Travel: *manzel be-manzel tey-ye manâzel*, "Station after station, across the stations."
- Threatening an enemy who tries to escape: *in mâhi nist be-daryâ be-re, kaftar nist be-havâ be-re*, "He is not a fish that could dive into the water, nor a bird that could fly in the air."
- Beauty: *ânqadr khoshgel o vajih [bud] ke engâr [kardi] mâh tolu' karde*, "She was so beautiful and handsome that you thought the moon had risen"; *javâheri bude dar zir-e khâkestar*, "She was (like) a jewel under the ashes."

In romantic stories a particularly extensive formula is used by Mashdi Galin at various occasions to picture the process of falling in love: *yek tir-e khadang-e softe, sufâl-e âq-par, az kânun-e sine-ye dokhtar jastan kard dar sine-ye pesar tâ par neshast—pesar yek del na, sad del âsheq-e in shod*, "A pointed arrow made of poplar [or: a straight arrow], its shaft [lit.: notch] adorned with white feathers, sprang from the young woman's breast and settled deep down in the young man's breast—the young man fell in love with her, not with one, but with a hundred hearts."

Finally, the despair that lovers experience when longing for their beloved or when separated from them, is expressed in the formula *sukhtam o sukhtam, az ravesh-e eshq-e-to âmukhtam, khâm budam, pokhte shodam, ey bi-hayâ-ye bi-ensâf, sukhtam*, "I am completely set on fire, I learned from your love; I was raw and became cooked; oh you shameless and unjust one—I am on fire!"

Categories

As has convincingly been demonstrated by the application of the international system of tale-types (Aarne/Thompson [AT] 1963) to the Persian data, Persian folk and fairy-tales fit into the general concept of the Indo-European tradition with only minor adaptations (Marzolph 1984). By the early 1980s, a total of 351 different tales from the Persian tradition of the twentieth century was available for analysis, including 50 animal tales (AT 1–299; see now Taqvâ 1997), 81 tales of magic (AT 300–749), 19 religious tales (AT 750–849), 50 romantic tales (AT 850–999), 16 tales of the stupid ogre (AT 1000–1199), 126 jokes and anecdotes (AT 1200–1999), and 9 formula tales (AT 2000–2199). According to the available data, the three most frequently published tales were AT 408: *The Orange Princess* (23 texts); AT 894: *The Patient Stone* (22 texts); and AT 20 D*: *The Fox on Pilgrimage*. Other frequently encountered tales include AT 123: *The Wolf and the Goat Kids*; AT *314: *The Magic Horse*; AT 311A: *Namaki and the Div*; AT 325: *The Magician's Apprentice*; AT 613: *Good and Evil*; and AT 2032: *The Mouse That Lost Its Tail*.

Characters

Like the folk- and fairy-tales of many other areas, Persian tales rely on a standard set of protagonists with their stereotype functions, of requisites and of actions (for the following, see Marzolph 1984, pp. 24–31).

The most common hero character is the prince, often referred to merely as *javân* (young man). Frequently, the prince is the youngest of three brothers who has to make up for the faults or incompetence of his brothers. The hero experiences dangerous adventures, fights with demons and monsters, and accomplishes difficult tasks. In the end, he receives his beloved princess and inherits the kingdom.

A typically Near Eastern heroic character is the *kachal* (baldheaded, scald-headed), often a shepherd (Elwell-Sutton 1965). At the beginning of the tale, the *kachal* is an outcast, a sluggard or a coward, and always a pauper. During the action and when he is challenged, the *kachal* proves to be clever and witty, courageous and reckless. With these qualities, he masters the most difficult tasks, often wins the favors of the princess, and becomes king. Sometimes, as in the tale of the magic horse, a prince disguises himself as a *kachal*. Another typical hero is the gatherer of thornbushes for fuel (*khâr-kan, khâr-kesh*), corresponding to the poorest level of society. Although very poor, the thorn-bush gatherer is generally a true believer, which helps him to overcome his fate and eventually to acquire wealth and happiness.

While the hero's only standard helper (besides his horse) is the thin-beard (*kuse*), his range of adversaries usually comprises the female members of his larger family. His mother-in-law, stepmother or aunt, in particular, tend to be motivated by envy, trying to destroy the hero by calumny. Other relatives, including his father and elder brothers, also agitate against him, and the only close relative who is described in a positive way is his mother. Another major adversary is the king, who is often depicted as a powerless object of his scheming advisers.

The role of women in Persian folk-tales is of a marked ambivalence. As active characters, women are wily, deceitful, and often simply evil. Only when counseling the hero, do active women—often in subordinate function—have positive traits. As passive characters, women are seldom more than objects which the hero strives to acquire, often motivated by perfunctory external matters: The hero falls in love with an unseen beauty by seeing one of her hairs floating in the water, or by hearing someone mention her name.

Secondary characters in Persian folk-tales fall into two groups. The first comprises characters from the real world, such as the above-mentioned shepherd and the thorn-bush gatherer, or a merchant, who usually has negative traits. Ethnic or linguistic minorities are usually depicted with the arrogance of the dominant culture: Jewish merchants, black slaves, and gypsy girls are malevolent characters, while members of the Kurdish or Lor populations are at best portrayed as fools. The second group comprises characters from the world of the unseen. Here one encounters a strict dichotomy. The demon (*div*), most often male, is usually both malevolent and stupid. His standard role, besides fighting with the hero, is to abduct human women in order to force them into marriage. The *div* usually possesses an external soul which he keeps in a secret hiding place. He can only be vanquished when this soul is discovered and destroyed. On the other hand, the fairy (*pari*), who is often (but not necessarily) female in folk-tales, is a perfectly positive character (Omidsalar 2002). She uses her supernatural powers, such as sorcery and the ability to fly, to help the hero achieve his tasks. Marriage between a *pari* and a human male is not infrequent. However, although the world of the *pari*s appears to be organized like the human world, these marriages rarely end happily, as the man is bound to succumb to his human foibles and to lose his fairy wife.

The action in Persian folk-tales is driven by two forces. The most powerful force in the story itself is fate. The pauper trusts in fate and is redeemed. The king challenges fate and is punished. Religion in its official form does not play any important role. If religious sentiments are voiced at all, they are concerned with popular admiration of venerated saints such as Imam Ali or Khezr, often asking for their intercession to be saved from misfortune or to achieve a particular goal. The other force, which is to some extent external, is the wishful thinking of both narrator and audience. As folk- and fairy-tales are *Wunschdichtung*, human wishes transformed into narrative, they both require and have a happy ending, thus enabling participants to have some hope of an ultimate happiness not suggested by their experiences in real life.

Aspects of performance

Romantic scholars were convinced that narrators memorize their tales *verbatim* and are capable of reproducing their repertoire word for word without the slightest change. Field research all over the world has proven that this notion generally does not correspond with the actual performance. In fact, rather the opposite is correct. Gifted narrators shape their narrative in the course of narration. In a process of constant interaction with their listeners, they may present short or lengthy versions, intersperse their narration with personal remarks, mingle versions of different tales, and so on. So far, in Iran no research has yet been undertaken on questions of context and contextual variations of narration. However, the tales collected by Elwell-Sutton from the oral performance of Mashdi Galin contain one particular tale that has been narrated three times (Marzolph 2000). Although the tale's essential structure is preserved, the three versions were clearly narrated on three different occasions, as both their content and wording differ considerably. In one case the tale was narrated in an extremely short and rather rudimentary version of some 350 words; there is a version of medium length (470 words), and an extended version (1200 words). These versions demonstrate the skillful creativity practiced by the narrator in the way she perceived and gave meaning to the tale by textualizing it in contrasting ways, each of which was presumably conditioned by a different mood and context.

Dating Persian folk-tales

Judging the age of folk-tales is a difficult affair. As soon as scholars are tempted to rely on internal data, such as the tale's psychological constitution, any kind of historical evaluation becomes hypothetical. The only way to arrive at a sound judgment is the pragmatic comparison of available external data. As data about the oral tradition of the past are almost completely lacking in Iran, the number of Persian folk-tales that can be reliably dated is extremely small.

A rare case in tracing the origin and dating of a Persian folk-tale is represented by the Persian versions of AT 123: *The Wolf and the Goat Kids*. A rudimentary version of this tale, in which a mother goat advises her children to heed the wolf, is already included in the so-called *Romulus* corpus of fables from late antiquity. This version apparently gave rise to both Oriental and Western versions of the later folk-tale, Western versions being attested since the twelfth century. Long before the first folk-tales were recorded from Persian oral tradition (Marzolph 1984, Type 123), in the late nineteenth century a rhymed chapbook version containing all major elements proves the tale to be known, if not current, in Iran (Mohammad and Qâ'eni 2001, vol. 3, pp. 51f., 55–60). Up to the present day the tale, with its simple educative message, is popular throughout Iran. Apart from the content, its structure and the fact that part of the action is narrated in verse, probably added to its appeal. The following specimen is taken from the oral performance of Ghazanfar Mahandi, a boy of about 16 from Gurchân. It was recorded by L. P. Elwell-Sutton in 1958, and lasts about four minutes in performance.

yek boz bud. in se bachche dâsht. yeki Shangul, Mangul, Daste-Gol. In har ruz miraft dar biyâbân micharid, barâ-ye bozghâlehâsh shir miyâvord o sedâ mi-kesh[id]: "Shangul, Mangul, Daste-gol."

inhâ dar miyâmadand o shireshâno mikhordand, ba'd be khâneshân miraftand.

yek ruz gorg as in kâr bâ-ettelâ' shod. gorg ham âmad o sedâ kard ke: "Shangul, Mangul, Daste-gol."

Shangul o Mangul ke dar âmadand, in gorg ishunrâ gereft o khord. Daste-gol raft tu-ye kure.

There was a goat. It had three children, [named] Shangul, Mangul, and Daste-gol. Every day it went out to graze in the pasture, brought milk for its kids and shouted: "Shangul, Mangul, Daste-gol."

They came out, drank their milk and went back into the house again.

One day the wolf got news about this. The wolf also came and shouted: "Shangul, Mangul, Daste-gol."

As Shangul and Mangul came out, the wolf grabbed and ate them. Daste-gol went into the oven.

Boz az sar âmad. do daf'e sedâ kesh[id]: "*Shangul, Mangul, Daste-gol.*" *did ke javâbi nayâmad. daf'e-ye sevvom sedâ kard, faqat did Daste-gol dar-âmad o goft ke ... bale:* "*gorg âmad o rafiqhâ-ye mârâ khord o man tanhâ mândam.*
boz raft sar-e lâne-ye khargush. yey in taraf raft o yeki un taraf raft o khargush goft: "*kist dar bâm-e mâ taraq o toruq mikonad, kâse-ye âb dar jâm-e mâ cherk-e khun mikonad?*" *goft:* "*manam, manam, boz bozake. do shâkh dâram dar falake. Shangul-o Mangul-o to khordi?*" *goft:* "*na va-llâh, be-llâh!*"
raft dar bâm-e rubâh. yey in taraf raft o yeki un taraf raft o rubâh goft: "*kist dar bâm-e mâ shalaq o sholuq mikonad, kâse-ye âb dar jâm-e mâ cherk-e khun mikonad?*" *goft:* "*manam, manam, boz bozake. do shâkh dâram dar falake. Shangul-o Mangul-o to khordi?*" *goft:* "*na va-llâh, be-llâh!*"
raft khâne-ye khuk. yey in taraf raft o yeki un taraf raft o [khuk] goft ke: "*kist dar bâm-e mâ taraq o toruq mikonad, kâse-ye âb dar jâm-e mâ cherk-e khun mikonad?*" *goft:* "*manam, manam, boz bozake. do shâkh dâram dar falake. Shangul-o Mangul-o to khordi?*" *goft:* "*na!*"
raft khâne-ye gorg. raft in taraf o un taraf o gorg goft: "*kist dar bâm-e mâ taraq o toruq mi-konad, Shangul o Mangul dar kâse-ye*

When the goat came back, it shouted twice: "Shangul, Mangul, Daste-gol." As there was no answer, it shouted a third time. Only then did Daste-gol come out, and said ... well: "The wolf came and ate my siblings. I am the only one left."

The goat went to the rabbit's nest. It walked here and there [until] the rabbit said: "Who is that stamping about on my roof, spilling dirt into my water-glass?" [The goat] said: "It's me, it's me, the goat. I've got two horns [pointing] to the sky. Did you eat Shangul and Mangul?" [The rabbit] said: "No, by God!"

[The goat] went to the roof of [the house of] the fox. It walked here and there [until] the fox said: "Who is that trampling about on my roof, spilling dirt into my water-glass?" [The goat] said: "It's me, it's me, the goat. I've got two horns [pointing] to the sky. Did you eat Shangul and Mangul?" [The fox] said: "No, by God!"

[The goat] went to the house of the wild boar. It walked here and there [until the boar] said: "Who is that stamping about on my roof, spilling dirt into my water-glass?" [The goat] said: "It's me, it's me, the goat. I've got two horns [pointing] to the sky. Did you eat Shangul and Mangul?" [The rabbit] said: "No!"

[The goat] went to the house of the wolf. It walked here and there [until] the wolf said: "Who is that stamping about on my roof, spilling *mâ cherk-e khun mikonad?"* goft: *"manam, manam, boz bozake. do shâkh dâram dar falake. Shangul-o Mangul-o to khordi?"* avval goft: *"na!"* o do-bâre goft: *"âre, man khordam."*

boz goft ke: *"pas fardâ mâ da'vâ dârim."* in boz âmad o az shir-e khodesh dushid o ye kerre-y o mâst o khâme-v o fatir dorost kard o barâ-ye ostâd najjâri bord. gorg ham pâ shod o [...] gohhâ-ye bachehâshro, ostokhânhâ-ye khorde-y o ... jam' kard o barâ-ye ostâ bord. ostâd goft ke: *"bebin boz chi âvorde."* zan-e ostâ var-khâst o did ke fatir o kerre-y o khâme-v o roughan âvorde. goft: *"bebin gorg chi âvorde."* negâh kard o goft: *"savâ az goh-e bachehâsh chizi nayâvorde."* goft: *"pas bemânad."* goft: *"yey sowhân biyâr!"* sowhân o âvord o shâkh-e boz râ tiz kard. goft: *"gâz biyâvar!"* gâz âvord o dandânhâ-ye gorgo keshid o pambe-dâne dar jâsh gozâsh[t].

mowqe'i ke raftand be-meidân-e da'vâ, gorg hey in taraf ân taraf jast o pambe-dâne bud, dige rikht o boz bâ shâkh-e tizesh zadesh, shekam-e gorgrâ darid. bachehâsho dar-âvord o gorgo dar gushe-i khâk kard.
va-s-salâm.

dirt onto Shangul and Mangul in my water-glass?" [The goat] said: "It's me, it's me, the goat. I've got two horns [pointing] to the sky. Did you eat Shangul and Mangul?" First [the wolf] said: "No!" but then it said: "Yes, I ate them!"

The goat said: "Let us fight tomorrow." The goat went, milked some of its milk and prepared some butter, yoghurt, cream, and dough, which it brought to the carpenter. The wolf also got up, [...] gathered some of his children's excrements, chewed bones and ... brought it to the carpenter. The master said [to his wife]: "Look what the goat brought." The master's wife got up and saw that [the goat] had brought dough, butter, cream and oil. [The master] said: "Look what the wolf brought." She looked and said: "He brought nothing but his children's excrements." The master said: "Bring a file." She brought the file and he sharpened the goat's horns. Then he said: "Bring me the tongs." She brought the tongs, and he pulled the wolf's teeth and put cotton-seeds in their place.

When they went to fight, the wolf jumped here and there and the cotton-seeds fell out. The goat hit him with her horns and slit open the wolf's belly. She took out her kids and buried the wolf in a corner.

That's it.

5. Proverbs and popular sayings

Maxims, popular sayings, and proverbs form an essential component of spoken Persian. While maxims are often quoted from the Persian classics, notably Sa'di's *Golestân*, proverbs and proverbial expressions rarely derive from classical literature. The Persian proverb (*mathal, tamthil*) often alludes to a condensed form of a narrative, and thus represents a common form of popular literature. Stories connected with Persian proverbs have been collected and documented as early as the seventeenth century. Mohammad-Ali Hablerudi, a Persian living in the Deccan kingdom of Golkonda during the reign of Abd-Allâh Qotbshâh (r. 1626–74), is credited with compiling the first major classical collection of Persian proverbs, and thus with inaugurating the discipline of Persian paremiological research. By providing illustrations for several proverbs, nineteenth-century lithographed editions of his famous and oft-reprinted collection *Jâme' al-tamthil* (Collection of Proverbs), added the further level of visual reception to the combination of proverb-*cum*-tale (Marzolph 1999a). These proverbs, all of which are supplemented by a corresponding tale, include counsels such as *avval rafiq, âkhar tariq*, "First a friend (to keep you company), then the (travel on your) way," proverbial hemistiches such as *pashshe cho por shod, bezanad pilrâ*, "Gnats, when great in numbers, (even) beat the elephant," and elementary wisdom such as *herfat-e mard zinat-e mard ast*, "A man's profession is his adornment" (referring to AT 888A*: *The Basket-maker*). The stories connected with proverbs have further been studied in Amir-Qoli Amini's modern folklore study (1945), and more recently in the two-volume publication of texts drawn from the archives of the Markaz-e Farhang-e Mardom (Enjavi 1973; Vakiliyân 1987). The latter collection contains narrative versions related to such widely known proverbs as *khar-e mâ az korregi dom nadâsht*, "Our donkey never had a tail, even from the time it was a foal" (Enjavi 1973, pp. 74–84; a version of AT 1534: *Series of Clever Unjust Decisions*); *shotor didi? nadidi!* (ibid., pp. 120f.; a version of AT 655 A: *The Strayed Camel and the Clever Deductions*); or *na shir-e shotor, na didâr-e arab*, "Neither camel's milk, nor a meeting with the Arab" (ibid., pp. 159–63; a version of AT 285 D: *Serpent Refuses Reconciliation*).

6. Folk humor

It is extremely difficult to assess the role of Persian folk humor. Humor is by definition aggressive, as it offers a jocular treatment of conflicts, be they political, social, economic, moral, or individual. As for style, humorous verbal expression is usually short (as in jokes and anecdotes), sometimes interactive (as in humorous riddles or jocular questions), and often arises spontaneously. Both the subversive quality of humor and its spontaneity imply severe restrictions on the availability of documentation.

Persian literature preserves several outstanding examples of humor and satire, and although these specimens were produced by members of the literate elite, they may contain elements of folklore. Even a literary collection of anecdotes such as Obeyd-e Zâkâni's (d. 1371) *Resâle-ye delgoshâ* may to some extent represent contemporary folk humor. On the other hand, the very popularity which a collection gained through the process of retelling may result in its jokes and anecdotes becoming elements of folk humor, even though they originate to a large extent from Arabic and Persian literature (see Halabi 1980; Marzolph 1992, vol. 2, index). In fact, the publication and popularization of humorous texts from literary works is a continuous phenomenon.

When the British colonial officer, Francis Gladwin, published his Persian grammar, *The Persian Moonshee* (1795), he appended a section of short humorous texts entitled *Hekâyât-e latif dar ebârat-e salis* (Marzolph 1995c). The anecdotes were apparently compiled by his Persian secretary from various works of Persian and European literature, the latter being translated in the peculiar style of Indo-Persian idiom. Gladwin's selection, originally intended as reading material for further practice, became extremely popular in the Indian subcontinent. Soon it came to be published independently; later it was translated and adapted in chapbooks in India and other areas, such as in the Pashto *Hagha Dagha* (1930). Before long some of the anecdotes it contained were collected in fieldwork from "living oral tradition" (Marzolph 1992, vol. 1, pp. 126–29). However, it was only recently presented to the Iranian public (Javâdi 1996).

ORAL LITERATURE OF IRANIAN LANGUAGES

The nineteenth century saw the publication of what was probably the most influential book in terms of Persian folk humor, the *Motâyebât-e Mollâ Nasreddin* (first Persian edition 1886; see Marzolph 1995d). The protagonist of its humorous stories is known in the Turkish cultural sphere as Nasreddin Hoja (Greek: Nastratin), and in the Arab world as Juha (Berber: Si Djeh'a; Italian: Giufà). This figure was introduced into Persian literature, by way of Arabic literature, around the eleventh century (under the adapted name of Johi or Juhi), when Persian authors began referring to him in their works, and quoting a number of anecdotes about him. A remark by the editor of the first printed Persian booklet containing anecdotes on Mollâ Nasreddin suggests that by the nineteenth century, probably through interaction with the Turkic population in Iran, the character of Mollâ Nasreddin had become popular in Persian oral tradition. To be exact, the *Motâyebât-e Mollâ Nasreddin* did not contain folk humor; rather, they constitute an adapted and enlarged translation of an Arabic booklet, which itself constitutes an Arabicized version of a Turkish original (Marzolph 1999c). Mollâ Nasreddin superseded, and in fact replaced Johi, and eventually became one of the most popular characters of Persian humor until the 1970s. When Mohammad Ramazâni published the standard Persian collection of anecdotes on Mollâ Nasreddin in 1936, he was able to include some 600 items. Most anecdotes in this volume are translated from either Turkish or Arabic sources. As its illustrations prove, it is closely connected to the standard Turkish collection compiled by Veled Chelebi Izbudak "Bahâ'i," which was first published in 1907. Ramazâni, moreover, announced the publication of a second volume containing the same number of anecdotes documented from oral tradition, a volume that unfortunately never materialized. Mollâ Nasreddin is a simple folk philosopher, who in his naiveté mirrors the limited capacity of human intellectual understanding. He wonders why melons do not grow on trees—until a nut falls on his head (AT 774 P: *The Melon and the Walnut-tree*); he forgets to count the donkey he himself is sitting on (AT 1288 A: *Numskull Cannot find the Ass He Is Sitting on*); he pretends that a pot can give birth and die (AT 1592 B: *The Pot Has a Child and Dies*). Many of his anecdotes have become proverbial in the form of compounds such as *lehâf-e Mollâ Nasreddin,* 'Mollâ Nasreddin's quilt,' denoting a dispute whose apparent cause is not the real one (Dehkhodâ 1922–29, vol. 2, pp. 816f.; Amini 1972, pp. 230f.; Shahri 1991, p. 366):

> One night, Mollâ heard a noisy quarrel in the streets. He got up, wrapped his quilt about his body and went out to see what had happened. When he got there, one of the persons involved grabbed his quilt and ran away. When Mollâ went back into the house, his wife asked him about the reason for the quarrel. He answered: "Nothing in particular! It must have been about my quilt, because as soon as they had it, the trouble stopped!"

After the Revolution of 1979, it appears as though the telling of anecdotes about Mollâ Nasreddin is officially regarded as an undesirable element of folk humor. In contrast to the dwindling number of popular booklets on Mollâ Nasreddin, there is now a growing amount of popular literature on Bohlul, the wise fool and alleged half-brother of Abbasid caliph Hârun al-Rashid. In the Shi'ite tradition Bohlul is regarded as a faithful disciple of the sixth Imam Ja'far al-Sâdeq, and he is therefore linked directly to a venerated representative of the Shi'ite creed (Marzolph 1983, 1987; Nurbakhsh 2003).

Jocular chapbooks that were widespread since the Qajar period and until the first half of the twentieth century further include *Mahbub al-qolub* (compiled about 1700) by Momtâz, and the anonymous *Latâ'ef o zarâ'ef,* or *Reyâz al-hekâyât* by Mollâ Habibollâh Kâshâni (d. 1921). The latter enjoyed great popularity at least up to the late 1970s (Marzolph 1994a, no. 81) and may well be responsible, therefore, for transmitting older humorous notions to the contemporary tradition.

Towards the middle of the twentieth century the available methods of printing permitted the production of cheap booklets in large quantities. These booklets, distributed by sidewalk peddlers, bazaar bookstalls, and itinerant merchants, are decidedly popular in character, while others present jocular tales compiled more or less from the Persian literary tradition. Comparing books of jokes published at various dates over the past fifty years, a change in jocular focus as well as moral limitations can be noticed. Earlier books of jokes, while drawing heavily on European models, possessed a strong misogynous tendency. Since the Revolution, however, such books similarly exploit foreign tradition, but they show a tendency to curb their aggression and stress verbal artistry and a refined mental appreciation of jokes.

As for the dimension of folk humor in living oral tradition and performance, there are few clues at hand. None of the published collections contain jokes collected from unrestrained oral performance. Rare specimens found in dialect studies and anthropological surveys (see, e.g., Lama'e 1970, pp. 125–27) support the claim that Iranian folk humor in its unrestricted form focuses on topics which are also popular in other regions, such as scatology, sexuality, (political) power and injustice, and the uncertainties and absurdities of life in general. The closest one might come to a general survey of folk humor in living tradition at the beginning of the twentieth century is the relevant section on *latifehâ* in the *Markaz-e Farhang-e Mardom*. Towards the end of the twentieth century, the Internet became an ideal medium for jocular expression. One of the most popular sites is the California-based *Jokestân*, to which Persian youngsters from all over the world, but presumably predominantly expatriates residing in the US, contribute individually. The site is divided into various sections, some of which represent traditional areas of Persian folk humor, such as ethnic jokes on Rashtis, Kurds, or Turks (Marzolph 2008).

7. Folk poetry

In relation to its high frequency in everyday life, folk poetry is probably the most under-researched field of Persian popular literature (Cejpek 1968, pp. 694–700; Kreyenbroek 1999). Various reasons account for this apparent neglect. Foreign Iranist scholars have often concentrated on elite literature or published mere specimen collections of popular poetry (Chodzko 1842). The growing number of Iranian publications on the subject (see e.g. Panâhi Semnâni 1997, 2000) has not yet been taken into account by Western research. On the other hand, popular poetry is characterized more strongly than popular prose genres by a high degree of spontaneity, and hence flexibility, which makes it difficult to document data for research. Probably the largest existing collection, taped from fieldwork in 1969–71 in the province of Fârs, still awaits publication (Neubauer 1983). Given the sparse amount of research available, the following remarks aim at a fairly general outline of this field of popular literature.

J.S. Meisami has pointed out that poetry, the key form of Persian literature until the nineteenth century, has remained "the central genre, to which all others are in some sense poor relations" (Meisami 1997, p. 296). Accordingly, most popular poetry is related to popular versions of elite or "polite" literature. Many passages from classical Persian literature, particularly from Sa'di's *Golestân* and Rumi's *Mathnavi*, have become widely known by means of recitation, reading, or inclusion in school-books, and are so generally acknowledged by all sections of society that they can be called "popular." Some poems, moreover, such as those by Bâbâ Tâher Oryân (fl. eleventh century; see Arberry 1937), are still so widely appreciated today that "the simplest Iranian sings his verses to this very day" (Rypka 1968, p. 234). Since the introduction of printing, the *Robâ'iyât-e Bâbâ Tâher* has been further popularized by the distribution of numerous editions of popular booklets. Similar criteria apply to the *Robâ'iyât-e Fâ'ez-e Dashtestâni* or the anonymous *Ash'âr-e kaffâsh-e Khorâsâni*. Many religious works, particularly those belonging to the genres *rowze-kh^{w}âni* or *marthiye* which deal with Imam Hoseyn's martyrdom in Karbalâ, are compiled in verse. Their frequent recitation during the mourning ceremonies in the month of Moharram clearly popularized both their content and form. Established as a genre by Kâshefi's eponymous *Rowzat al-shohadâ'* (see Chelkowski in this volume), the genre was particularly popular in the Qajar period, when many works were compiled and distributed in (often illustrated) lithographed editions (Marzolph 2001, pp. 25f.). The best known of these works are Mollâ Bemun-Ali's *Hamle-ye Heydariyye*, Sarbâz Borujerdi's *Asrâr al-shahâda*, and above all Mirzâ Ebrâhim Jowhari's *Tufân* *al-bokâ'*. This category further includes works that gained wide appreciation because of their appeal or entertaining character, such as the poems on food and cookery in Jamâl-al-Din Abu Eshâq (Boshâq) Shirâzi's (d. 1423) *Kanz al-eshtehâ'* or his *Divân-e Boshâq-e at'eme*.

The above examples represent products of elite literature that are "popular" only so far as their reception is concerned. The opposite, the inclusion of popular poetry or "oral poetry" in works of elite literature (de Bruijn 1990, pp. 469–72) is also documented. Persian epics, though predominantly a prose genre, are often interspersed with short fragments of poetry, which may be connected with their "oral background" (Yamamoto 2000; see also Panâhi Semnâni 1997, pp. 37 ff.). Some of the more recent romantic epics, such as *Najmâ-ye Shirâzi* or *Heydar-Beg*, are completely composed in poetry.

Folk quatrains (*robâ'i, dobeyti*), often performed as "local songs" (*tarânehâ-ye mahalli*), are the most frequent form of popular poetry (Ivanow 1925; Weryho 1961–62; Eilers 1969). Both in terms of linguistic and musical quality they share certain characteristics with both elite and popular literature (see Neubauer 1983, pp. xi-iff). Though based on elite standards of literature, folk quatrains often employ colloquial terms, and are popular because of their simple style and content. In terms of formal characteristics, they are composed in the *hazaj* meter in its catalectic form. The rhyme is most often composed as a a b a, with the exceptional forms a a a a or a a b b. Departures from the rules of both meter and rhyme are quite frequent. Folk quatrains used to be sung on many different occasions, at work in the house or in the fields, while traveling, or when herding the cattle. Particularly at weddings or other social meetings performers would alternate, each singer responding to the quatrain performed before him. At times the verbal performance might be accompanied by either the flute (*ney*) or the drum. The melodies to which these quatrains are performed are quite simple. While the oldest specimens of folk quatrains are those of Bâbâ Tâher, mentioned above, their tradition can be traced to the nineteenth century. Early European collectors such as A. Chodzko (1842) and V.A. Zhukovsky (1888–1922, 1902) did not recognize these quatrains as a specific poetic genre. As the quatrains are often sung one after the other, they saw the individual poems as stanzas of larger complex songs. The topics treated in folk quatrains comprise all aspects of life, including social and religious themes as well as historical and heroic ones. Love is a particularly prominent theme.

alä dokhtar to ke az Qâziyâni	O young girl from the tribe of Qâziyân
chenân Torki ke Fârsi hich nadâni	You are so Turkish that you do not understand Persian
barâhat sisad o shas buse dâdam	I gave you three hundred and sixty kisses
miyân-e busehâ jân misetânam	Between the kisses I took your soul.

(Neubauer 1983, p. 69)

agar khʷâhi man az eshqat nemiram	If you don't want me to die from loving you,
bedeh qowli ke man torâ migiram	Give me your word that I will get you.
biyâ busi bedeh az un labunet	Come, give me a kiss with your lips,
nagu râz-e khodet [râ] bâ kasunet.	And don't tell your secret to your relatives.

(Homâyuni 2000, p. 333)

Lullabies have always been, and remain, extremely popular. In their simplest form they consist of two rhyming lines, or accumulations thereof in the form of a *mathnavi*. They usually begin with the alliterating syllables *lâlâ, lâlâ* or *alâ lâlâ*. This is often followed by the name of a flower or plant (*gol-e* ...), and short narrative passages (Tazhibi and Shojâ'atdust 2000).

lâlâ, lâlâ, gol-e lâle	Hushaby baby, tulip flower,
palang dar kuche minâle	The panther wails in the street
lâlâ, lâlâ, gol-e na'nâ	Hushaby baby, peppermint flower,
bâbât rafte be kuh tanhâ	Your father has gone alone to the mountain.

(Javâd 2001, p. 15)

Longer lullabies often narrate complex stories, such as the lament of a mother who was brought to India, which is extant in a variety of versions:

lâlâ, lâlâ, bouám hassi	Hushaby baby, you are my father
dárom kerdi kolun bassi	You turned me out and closed the bolt
talab kerdam be-yak nuni	When I asked for some bread
âjor pâre várom dâdi	You gave me a piece of brick
sabu dâdi be-ow raftam	You gave me a jug, I went to the water
sar-e chashme be-khow raftam	Next to the spring I fell asleep
do tâ Torki ze-Torkessun	Two Turks from Turkistan
márâ bordan be-Hendossun	Took me to India
bozorg karda be-sad nâzi	They brought me up with tenderness
show(h)ar dâdan be-sad jâzi	And married me with a rich dowry
do tâ owlâd Khodâ dâde	God gave me two sons:
Malek Ahmad, Malek Jamshid	Malek Ahmad, Malek Jamshid,
Malek Jamshid ketow rafte	Malek Jamshid has gone to school
Malek Ahmad be-khow rafte ...	Malek Ahmad has fallen asleep ...

(Homâyuni 1969, p. 223f.)

Riddles encountered in classical literature have given rise to a complex theoretical system (Anwari Alhosseyni 1986). Their popular offspring, the *chistân* (from *chist ân*, 'What is that?'), often occurs in rhyme, sometimes in the traditional form of a *dobeyti*:

chist ân ke az har dari dâkhel mishavad	What is it? It enters through every door
az har shekâfi birun miravad	It leaves through every crack
gerd mishavad o bâlâ o pâyin miravad	It becomes round and moves up and down
jâ-ye pâyash ham nemimânad?	And never stays at rest?

(Vakiliyân 1996, p. 11. Answer: *bâd*, 'the wind')

bolbol-e in bâgham o in bâgh golzâr-e man ast	I am this garden's nightingale and this orchard is my garden
morgh-e âtesh-bâram o âtesh par o bâl-e man ast	I am a fire-bearing bird, fire is my feathers and wings
ostokhânam noqre o andar jegaram dâram talâ	My bones are silver, and in my liver I have gold
har ke in ma'ni bedânad pir-ostâd-e man ast	Whoever knows this meaning will be my teacher

(Vakiliyân 1996, p. 16. Answer: *sham'*, a candle).

8. Outlook

As for future research in Persian popular literature, much remains to be done. First and foremost, documentation of Persian popular literature from an authentic oral context of performance must continue. It is imperative both to collect and document Persian popular literature in forms as close to their original context as possible. Whether or not the published form will have to be edited owing to societal conditions, is not of prime importance as long as extensive and detailed scientific documentation is available to the researcher. In order to arrive at an adequate understanding of the meaning of popular literature for those who perform or read it or listen to it, the earlier emphasis on textual documentation is insufficient. The recorded texts need to be supplemented by as much contextual data as possible. Not much is known, for instance, about storytelling in contemporary Iranian society. Many of the texts recorded during fieldwork were apparently produced in artificially induced settings, and tell us next to nothing about what stories narrators originally tell, and why.

Moreover, in Iran expressions of the popular mind such as folklore and popular literature have often been regarded as threatening to the social and political order, and have frequently been suppressed or restricted. It is hoped that the official attitude will in the future acknowledge folklore and popular literature as essential components of national heritage. If a pessimistic view laments the disappearance of traditional folklore, the optimistic view should counter by having confidence in the people who, if traditional forms disappear, will eventually create and practice new forms of popular expression.

CHAPTER 10

NAQQÂLI: PROFESSIONAL IRANIAN STORYTELLING

Kumiko Yamamoto

The present chapter discusses *naqqâli*, or professional Iranian storytelling. It will consider the historical background of *naqqâli*; the storytellers' social status; their training; *tumârs* (scrolls of texts); repertoire; the relationship between *tumârs* and literary sources; performance; and specific features of oral performance.

Naqqâli is an Iranian storytelling tradition in which heroic and religious narratives are transmitted in spoken and written form. As it comprises both written and oral versions of a story, it provides an invaluable example of how the story is transformed according to different modes of delivery. This allows us clearly to distinguish features typically associated with oral literature from those with written. *Naqqâli* thus provides a solid basis for oral studies, which often tend to be speculative because of the lack of empirical data on oral performance. Furthermore it has played an important role in transmitting Persian epics and popular romances. While reworking such classical works as *Shahname* and *Eskandar-nâme,* the storytellers interpret and evaluate them for their audiences in the idiom shared by both. Their works, whether oral or written, can therefore be taken as "popular" commentaries on the Persian classical works in narrative form. *Naqqâli* has had an important social function, moreover, in promoting and reinforcing popular ideology and faith, in conjunction with other Persian traditional arts (e.g. *Shahname-kh{w}âni, rowze-kh{w}âni, maddâhi,* and *sokhanvari,* etc.) Study of *naqqâli* may shed light on pre-modern urban life in Iran.

NAQQÂLI: PROFESSIONAL IRANIAN STORYTELLING

Naqqâli has been studied by both Iranian and Western scholars. From the 1960s, Iranian scholars began to focus on *naqqâli* as part of the Iranian heritage, with the acute awareness that this age-old oral tradition was rapidly disappearing. They endeavored to establish *naqqâli* as a serious object of study by publishing a series of articles on its history, specific features, and its role in Persian literature (Mahjub 1958, 1961, 1970; Beyzâ'i 1962; Dustkhʷâh 1966, 1967; Sâdât-e Eshkevari 1973; Shirâzi 1973; Lesân 1976). Accordingly they focused on the continuity of the tradition, and on the role of writing in the transmission of narratives. After an interval in the wake of the political and social upheavals in the late 1970s, Iranian scholars have taken a renewed interest in the tradition, and published *tumârs*—texts written by storytellers (Zariri, ed. Dustkhʷâh 1990; Dustkhʷâh 1992; Sadâqat-Nezhâd 1995; Afshâri and Madâyeni, eds. 1998). From the 1970s onwards, Western scholars approached *naqqâli* implicitly or explicitly on the basis of theories about oral literature (e.g., Parry 1971; Lord 1960). William L. Hanaway Jr. showed that *naqqâli* played a role in the genesis of Persian popular literature (Hanaway 1970, p. 16; 1971a, pp. 143–45; 1971b, p. 60; 1974, pp. 1–24; 1996b). In the late 1970s Mary Ellen Page conducted fieldwork on *naqqâli* in Shiraz and closely studied differences between oral, written and literary versions of the Persian national legend (Page 1977; 1979). While acknowledging that the oral and written traditions interact in a complex way in *naqqâli*, she nevertheless attempted to play down the role of writing and to emphasize the creativity of individual storytellers in performance (Page 1977, pp. 150–51; 1979, pp. 200–201). This was further developed by Olga M. Davidson in her thesis on the *Shahname* of Ferdowsi or the Persian national epic (Mohl 1838–68; Bertels et al., 1960–71; critical edition by Khaleghi-Motlagh 1988-). Davidson argues that the epic was essentially composed as part of the oral tradition, and that the concept of book is a symbol for "expressing the authority and authenticity of oral poetic traditions that are being performed" (Davidson 1994, p. 48; cf. also idem 1985, pp. 131–42). This may be taken as an effort to adjust the Persian oral tradition to a preconceived idea of oral literature.[1] We shall here attempt to consider the tradition as it has been practiced in Iran.

1. Historical background

Storytelling has a long history. Some of the ancient hymns in the *Avesta* suggest that heroic tales were transmitted orally long before the time of Zarathustra. Such tales were indirectly handed down

[1] Davidson's book sparked a controversy over Ferdowsi's sources. Claiming that the poet used only written sources, notably Abu Mansur's *Shâh-nâme* of which only the preface has survived, Mahmoud Omidsalar (1995, 1996) entirely rejected the oral origin of the *Shahname*. (See also Davidson's rebuttal to Omidsalar 1996: Davidson 1998, reprinted in Idem 2000, pp. 9–28). Dick Davis (1996), for his part, called into question Ferdowsi's use of Abu Mansur's *Shâh-nâme*. By indicating that both Ferdowsi and medieval English chroniclers present the authentic and traditional nature of their works in a similar manner, Davis suggests that Ferdowsi depends on literary topoi, rather than states the truth, in referring to his sources (Idem, pp. 48–53). He thus refutes the literary basis of the *Shahname* and discusses its oral genesis, drawing on the Oral-Formulaic theory (Idem, pp. 53–56). His analysis is, however, cursory and simplified, and exhibits typical characteristics of the premature application of the theory, the most conspicuous of which is the naive division between oral tradition and the literary counterpart (cf. Yamamoto 2003, pp. 8–19). Nevertheless, this rekindled the controversy and triggered criticism among Iranian scholars: e.g. Jalal Matini (1998); Djalal Khaleghi-Motlagh (1998, 2002); Omidsalar (1999); Omidsalar and Omidsalar (1999, esp. pp. 326, 329). Their contentions, though concerned with wide-ranging topics, can be summarized as follows: oral tradition which they seem to take as archetypical vulgarity (esp. Khaleghi-Motlagh 1998, pp. 514–15; 529), conflicts with a sense of reverence with which the Iranians have held the national epic over centuries. It is therefore expedient to argue its exclusively literary basis and nature. What emerges from the controversy is the fact that whichever position one might take, the interpretation of textual evidence is ideologically predetermined and cannot yield decisive results.

and reached the Parthian minstrels called *gôsân* (Boyce 1957), who are likely to have played an instrumental role in collecting and fusing different strata of narratives such as traditions about kings and the Rostam cycle (Boyce 1954, pp. 47–51; 1955, pp. 473–77). The Sasanians (224–651) probably used storytelling for pedagogical and entertainment purposes (Boyce 1957, pp. 34–35). This practice seems to have continued after the Arab conquest. The tenth-century Arab bibliographer, Ebn-al-Nadim, tells us that the Persians were fond of listening to stories at night (Dodge 1970, II, pp. 712–17).

The historian Abu'l-Fazl Mohammad Beyhaqi provides more concrete information on oral tradition in Ghaznavid times (977–1186). Storytellers (*mohaddeth*, *qavvâl*) and poets were among the courtiers of kings and princes. While the poets were always present on ceremonious occasions and recited their poems with musical accompaniment, storytellers seem to have been confined to the private quarters of the court (cf. de Bruijn 1987, pp. 15–16). They were ready at a king's command to narrate evening stories (Beyhaqi, ed. Fayyâz 1971, pp. 153–54), and to deliver messages as emissaries (ibid., p. 162). Beyhaqi also implies that storytelling was popular entertainment among commoners (ibid., p. 905). Apart from these storytellers, we also know that *Shahname-kh^{w}âns* (reciters of *Shahname*) existed in this period, among which the name of Kârâsi has come down to us (Dehkhodâ, *Loghat-nâme*, s.v. "Kârâsi"). Kârâsi was a courtier-poet of the Buyid princes before he found a way to Sultan Mahmud's court (ibid.; Bahâr 1940, pp. 395–97). In a group of *Shahname* manuscripts Sultan Mahmud is said to have preferred listening to Kârâsi's narration to that of the poet Onsori.[2] It should be mentioned, however, that what *Shahname-kh^{w}âns* such as Kârâsi narrated in the early Islamic period was probably not Ferdowsi's text. As Hoseyn Lesân pointed out, Ferdowsi's work is not mentioned in any major anthologies of that period (Lesân 1976, p. 7; Minovi 1976, pp. 129–35). Although Beyhaqi cites a number of verses in his chronicle, he is silent about

---

[2] This episode has some variants in which Kârâsi is called a poet, *nadim* (boon companion), or teller of *Hezâr Afsâne* (Wallenbourg 1810, p. 52). J. Mohl cites yet another version where Onsori, as opposed to Kârâsi, is said to have told evening stories (Mohl 1838, I, p. XX).

ORAL LITERATURE OF IRANIAN LANGUAGES

Ferdowsi (cf. Waldman 1980, pp. 68–69). Nor does Manuchehri Dâmghâni include Ferdowsi in his list of Arab and Persian poets (ed. Dabirsiyâqi 2000, pp. 79–85; Clinton 1972, pp. 34–38). The author of the *Qâbus-nâme*, which was composed about fifty years after the completion of the *Shahname*, does not allude to Ferdowsi either (Yusefi 1966; Levy 1951). It seems likely that in early Islamic times "Shahname" was a generic term for kingly and heroic tales; we don't know whether those tales were related in verse or prose.

While there is little evidence for the storytelling tradition in the subsequent periods, the available sources suggest that storytellers continued to entertain the people. The author of *Ketâb-e naqz* (The Book of Annihilation) reproaches storytellers for leading the people astray by telling pagan stories about "Rostam, Sorkhâb, Esfandiyâr, Kâ'us, Zâl and others" in marketplaces (Qazvini-Râzi, ed. Mohaddeth 1979–80, p. 47). Such contempt for storytellers is not uncommon among intellectuals and religious authorities, and serves to confirm the popularity of storytelling. The famous fourteenth-century satirist Obeyd Zâkâni relates in *Akhlâq al-ashrâf* (The ethics of the nobles) that, after conquering Baghdad, Hulâgu Khan (r. 1256–65) ordered poets (*shâ'er*, pl. *sho'arâ'*), storytellers (*qesse-kh^{w}ânân*), Sufis, etc. to be drowned in the Tigris River in order to clear the earth from their malice (ed. Atâbeyki 1964–65, pp. 172–73). Hâfez, a contemporary of Zâkâni, implies in his *ghazal*s that despite such fierce and scornful treatment of storytellers in Mongol times, stories were told at night as they had been before: e.g. *tark-e afsâne begu Hâfez o mey nush dami; ke nakhoftim shab o sham' be afsâne besukht* (Stop telling fables, Hâfez, and have a drink for a while. We've stayed awake all night, and the candle is burned up with storytelling; ed. Khânlari 1980, I, p. 53).

It would seem that *naqqâli* was institutionalized in the Timurid period (1370–1507). The *Fotovvat-nâme-ye soltani* of Hoseyn Vâ'ez Kâshefi-Sabzevâri describes the role of storytellers in popular entertainment, with detailed prescriptions for storytelling (Kâshefi-Sabzevâri pp. 302–5, tr. pp. 296–98). Although Kâshefi does not list any specific works, his exposition of storytelling suggests that tales about historical personages and marvels were common themes (ibid., p. 302; p. 296). His prescriptions on storytelling are also instructive. As in the case of modern *naqqâli*, prose narration was interspersed with verse citations, which according to the author must be added in moderation and in good timing. The storytellers adapted their "programs" to their audiences, and spoke in plain language without much hyperbole and metaphor. They asked for voluntary contributions at the end of performances, which seem to have lasted for a fixed time period (ibid., pp. 304–5; pp. 297–98).

Present-day *naqqâls* unequivocally claim, however, that *naqqâli* originated in Safavid times (1507–1736). According to a prominent *naqqâl*, Morshed Abbâs Zariri, Shah Esmâ'il I (1501–24) appointed dervishes to propagate Twelver Shi'ism. These dervishes were divided into seventeen groups, and each developed a specific manner of narration, specializing in certain types of narrative, or addressed to a specific audience. Some praised Imams, and some recited poems at *zurkhânes* (traditional gymnasiums). Still others related heroic tales for military personnel. In order to attract their audiences more effectively the dervishes began to add heroic tales to the praise of Imam Ali (Dustkh^{w}âh 1966, pp. 73–74).

If Twelver Shi'ism helped to bind practitioners of various oral traditions together, coffeehouses, which were established in Isfahan and Qazvin under Shah Abbâs I (1588–1629), provided a common infrastructure for popular entertainers (Falsafi 1954, p. 261). In the Safavid period the coffee houses functioned as a literary salon where kings, aristocrats, notables, poets and artists were assembled to pass the time, to engage in literary discussions or to listen to poems and stories (ibid., pp. 261–64). Owners of coffeehouses were eager to employ skillful entertainers in order to attract more clientele. Famous storytellers and *Shahname-kh^{w}âns* were much sought after since they tended to form a loyal and stable audience by telling a long story in serial form (Dustkh^{w}âh 1966, p. 75).

The Qajar period (1779–1925) was the golden age of oral tradition. According to Eugène Aubin (Aubin 1908, pp. 239–40), about 6,000 to 10,000 dervishes practiced storytelling, *maddâhi* (eulogizing the family of the Prophet), and other verbal art forms. Some were itinerant performers and entertained farmers with marvelous tales on festive occasions. Others were sedentary, mostly living in big cities like Tehran and Isfahan. They performed in mosques, bazaars, squares and coffeehouses (ibid., pp. 241–42). Leaders of such storytellers were part of the court establishment. Qajar princes had *naqqâl-bâshi*s (chief storytellers) narrate evening stories; among these, Mirzâ Mohammad Ali Naqib-al-Mamâlek is well-known for his *Amir Arsalân* (Mahjub 1961, pp. XVII-XXI; Hanaway 1985). This period, it seems, also saw *naqqâli* spread among a wider audience, notably women and children who were traditionally excluded from the coffeehouses. Many stories which had been narrated at coffeehouses appeared in chapbooks (Hanaway 1974, p. 9; cf. Marzolph 1994). A literate member of a family read such books aloud to the others in the evenings and in winter.[3]

It seems likely that the Pahlavi régime (1925–79) was partly responsible for the decline of *naqqâli*. In the late 1920s *naqqâl*s were accused of instigating members of guild organizations (whose members formed the main part of their audiences) to rioting, and were forbidden to perform in coffeehouses (Zariri, p. XXVIII-XXXII; Sadâqat-Nezhâd, p. 7). Around 1935 coffeehouses were temporarily closed down to improve their conditions and to license a few capable *naqqâl*s to recite Ferdowsi's *Shahname*, which was actively promoted by the régime (Shirazi 1973, p. 99). Since then *naqqâli* has come to be identified with the *Shahname* of Ferdowsi.

A still more powerful threat to the *naqqâli* tradition, however, was the mass media which penetrated into society. In the 1940s radio broadcasting began in Iran. In the wake of World War II, this rapidly took coffeehouse patrons away from *naqqâli*. From the late 1950s, television, cinema and theater became so prevalent that many storytellers were forced out of their jobs (Âl-e Dâvud 1993, p. 3). At the time of writing the future of *naqqâli* depends on a few willing storytellers who strive to keep the tradition going.

---

[3] Morshed Vali-Allâh Torâbi told the present writer that his mother used to tell him *Shahname* stories when he was young.

NAQQÂLI: PROFESSIONAL IRANIAN STORYTELLING

2. Storytellers

Although no systematic research has been done on the social status of the storytellers in pre-modern Iran, professional storytellers seem to have been associated with popular entertainers (*ma'reke-girân*) in general, and with practitioners of verbal arts in particular. By the Timurid period storytellers belonged to a corporation of popular entertainers, which were divided into *ahl-e sokhan* (orators), *ahl-e zur* (athletes), and *ahl-e bâzi* (players; Kâshefi-Sabzevâri, pp. 275, 279). The first of these were subdivided into two: *maddâhân* and *qesse-kh^{w}ânân*. The *maddâhân* (lit. eulogizers) praised the Prophet and Imams and told religious stories in verse form (ibid., pp. 277–79, 281–82), while *qesse-kh^{w}ânân* (storytellers) told stories about historical personages and about wonders and marvels (ibid., pp. 296, 302). This last group was apparently distinguished by its narrative genre and form from *afsâne-kh^{w}ânân* (fabulists) and *nazm-kh^{w}ânân* (reciters of poetry). In the Safavid period also storytellers were part of a professional organization which included: *qesse-guyân* (storytellers), *shahname-kh^{w}ânân* (reciters of *Shahname*), dervishes, wrestlers, acrobats, rope-dancers, jugglers, puppeteers, etc. (Keyvani 1982, p. 53). They were also dervishes and belonged to Sufi Orders (notably the Qalandars in the Safavid period, and the Ajams and Khâksârs under the Qajars). They engaged in *rowze-kh^{w}âni* (reciting of the martydom of Imams) and told hagiographies (Afshâri 1990, p. 479). A seventeenth-century *shahname-kh^{w}ân*, Hoseynâ Sabuhi, was originally a vagabond dervish who came to perform the *Shahname* and *Qesse-ye Hamze* after entering into a Khan's service (Nasrâbâdi, ed. Dastgerdi 1939, p. 357). Mirzâ Mohammad also excelled in verse recitation and storytelling (*sokhan-sarâ'i*; ibid., p. 401). A nineteenth-century storyteller, Hâji Ahmad, learned snake-charming and juggling from his uncles when he was young. He later became a dervish and joined the Ajams, introduced by his Sufi mentor who also taught him the recitation of the *Eskandar-nâme*. When he came back from pilgrimage he began telling *Shahname* stories and the *Eskandar-nâme* at coffeehouses, mosques and private houses in Tehran (Aubin 1908, pp. 246–48). The internal divisions among popular entertainers were thus relatively loose, and each was constantly influenced by others through all-round performers.

3. Training

The craft of storytelling is not necessarily passed down from father to son, and the storytellers have diverse backgrounds. A seventeenth-century storyteller had a Sayyed family background and studied Islamic theology. Later in his life he became an alcoholic and ended up telling stories in opium dens (Nasrâbâdi, p. 414). A legendary storyteller in Tehran, Morshed Gholâm-Hoseyn Ghowl-Bachche, was a merchant before he became a storyteller in his thirties (Mahjub 1970–71, p. 48, n. 1). Morshed Vali-Allâh Torâbi was born into a family of *ta'ziye-khʷâns* (performers of passion plays), and had been one before he became a *naqqâl* (private communication; cf. Torâbi, p. 14). On the whole it is a matter of personal preference that someone goes into storytelling. In modern times there seems to have been no formal training system for storytellers (Mahjub 1970–71, p. 48; Page 1979, p. 198). If someone wishes to become one he first seeks out a worthy teacher by attending many different performances. This is a part of the learning process in the course of which he picks up stories and declamatory skills. Once he is admitted by the chosen teacher, he learns the relevant stories and classical poems by heart, besides listening to the teacher's performances every day. After some time he is asked to perform stories before his master and fellow students (if any), who check his voice, intonation, phraseology, or structuring of the stories, and his timing of verse recitations. When he has sufficiently mastered the craft he is introduced to one of the coffeehouses with which the master is associated.

4. Tumârs

The training of a novice storyteller would not, however, be completed until he acquires story texts known as *tumârs* (scrolls). According to Torâbi, "One would not be a *naqqâl* if one did not have a *tumâr*" (Torâbi 1990, p. 14). A novice copies his master's *tumârs*, or memorizes them in the course of his training. In general the *tumâr*

NAQQÂLI: PROFESSIONAL IRANIAN STORYTELLING

is a synopsis of a story, which is fleshed out by the storyteller in performance. Some *tumârs* can be prepared in book format if the stories are of considerable size (Afshâri 1990, p. 476; Sadâqat-Nezhâd, p. 6). *Tumârs* of this type were often composed by talented storytellers on the basis of their experiences in oral performance, their study of classical works, and of the *tumârs* they collected over the years at the later stage of their career.[4] Such works were naturally much sought after, but were rarely made available except for the author/storyteller's pupils (Sadâqat-Nezhâd, p. 6). They contain the essence of the storyteller's craft, indicating for instance where to insert verses, how to structure plots, and how to expand stories with anecdotes and proverbs. Some went as far as to write *tumârs* in coded language in order to protect their trade secrets (ibid., p. 5).

While most of the present-day storytellers write or transcribe *tumârs*, their predecessors apparently had scribes transcribe their performances or compile *tumârs* for them (Zariri, p. XVIII). The earliest known example of such a *tumâr* is the twelfth-century prose romance, *Samak-e Ayyâr* by Farâmarz b. Khodâdâd b. Abd-Allâh al-Kâteb Arrajâni (Khânlari 1968–74). The author calls himself the "compiler," "editor," or "author," etc. (*jam'-konande, mo'allef, mosannef*, etc.; I, pp. 1, 75; III, p. 63), of the story, and refers to Sadâqat b. al-Qâsem Shirâzi as the "storyteller" (*râvi-ye qesse*; I, p. 92; IV, p. 3; but cf. Gaillard 1987, pp. 10–11). The *Dârâb-nâme* of Mowlânâ Hâji Mohammad Tâheri Bighami, otherwise known as *Firuz-shâh-nâme* (Safâ 1960–62; Hanaway 1974), was also compiled by a scribe in 1483 (Hanaway 1974, p. 20). *Amir Arsalân* was reportedly written down by a daughter of Nâser-al-Din Shâh Qâjâr (r. 1848–96) during live performances by the king's chief storyteller, Mirzâ Mohammad Ali Naqib-al-Mamâlek (Mahjub 1961, pp. XII-XVII). While most of the *tumârs* were thus composed or compiled by storytellers or scribes, some were prepared by devotees of storytelling, and were sold to novice storytellers (Mahjub 1970, p. 49).

---

4   Zariri's Rostam and Sohrâb is an excerpt from such a *tumâr*.

ORAL LITERATURE OF IRANIAN LANGUAGES

5. Repertoire

By the end of the Qajar period, the repertoire of storytellers was more or less fixed to the following works (Mahjub 1958, p. 531; 1961–62, p. II; 1970–71, p. 42; Beyzâ'i 1962–63, p. 21; Dustkhʷâh 1966, p. 74; Page 1977, p. 37): *Samak-e Ayyâr*; *Qesse-ye Hamze* (a biography of Mohammad's uncle, Hamze b. Abd-al-Mottaleb; She'âr 1968–69); *Abu-Moslem-nâme* (Tarsusi; Yaghmâ'i n.d.; Mélikoff 1962); the *Dârâb-nâme* of Tarsusi (a Persian version of the Alexander Romance; Safâ 1965–68; Hanaway 1996a); the *Dârâb-nâme* of Bighami (see above); *Eskandar-nâme* (reworked in Safavid times; Afshâr 1964; Southgate 1978); *Khâvar-nâme* (or *Khâvarân-nâme*) of Mowlânâ Mohammad b. Hosâm-al-Din (d. 1470; an adventurous biography of Ali b. Abi-Tâleb; Safâ 1970, pp. 377–79); *Mokhtâr-nâme* by Abd-al-Razzâq Beyg b. Najafqoli Khan Donbali, known as Maftun (Safâ 1970, p. 383; Tauer 1968, pp. 450–51); and the *"Greater Shahname"*: i.e., Ferdowsi's *Shahname* with the later epics, *Garshâsp-nâme* (by Asadi of Tus; Yaghmâ'i 1938–39; Huart and Massé 1926–51), *Bahman-nâme* (Irânshâh b. Abi'l-Kheyr, ed. Afifi 1991), *Borzu-nâme*, *Farâmarz-nâme*, *Bânu-Goshasp-nâme*, *Shahriyâr-nâme*, *Jahângir-nâme*, and *Âzarborzin-nâme* (Mohl 1838, I, pp. LIV-LXXIII; Massé 1935, pp. 263–68; Molé 1951, 1952, 1953). While these are ultimately based on medieval epics and romances, a few works were newly created in those periods: *Hoseyn-e Kord* (Mahjub 1958, pp. 533–34; Marzolph 2000a, 2000b; Afshâr and Afshâri 2006, pp. 9–40) and *Amir Arsalân* (see above). These works have two main features in common: emphasis on Shi'ite Islam and on marvels. Many focus on Shi'ite religious figures (*Hamze-nâme, Abu-Moslem-nâme, Khâvar-nâme, Mokhtâr-nâme* and *Hoseyn-e Kord*), and even in heroic narratives heroes often punish infidels or make them convert to Islam. A well-known example of this is the *Eskandar-nâme*, where Alexander the Great is represented as the instrument of God. A less well-known example is perhaps the *Jahângir-nâme*, in which Rostam converts pagans to Islam in much the same way as Alexander does (Safâ 1970–71, pp. 327–29; Soroudi 1980). Even in stories from the *Shahname*, heroes pray to God for help in times of trouble, and thereby remind the audience of God's omnipotence. Another characteristic of storytelling material is its focus on marvels of foreign lands. The heroes travel into foreign countries, notably India, experience a number of adventures and encounter fantastic creatures. These themes were already recommended by Kâshefi in the fifteenth century for the edification of audiences (Kâshefi, p. 302).

6. Tumârs and literary sources

Although most of the *naqqâli* stories probably derive from earlier written sources, they are so strikingly modified that they can therefore be regarded as a different genre. *Tumâr* versions of the *Shahname* cover the periods between the Creation and the conquest of Persia by Alexander the Great (Dustkhᵂâh 1966, p. 74; Zariri, p. XXVIII; Afshâri et al. 1998), as opposed to that of Ferdowsi, which includes the Sasanian dynasty. The *tumârs*, moreover, comprise the *Greater Shahname*, in which the later epics are incorporated into Ferdowsi's *Shahname*.[5]

The *Greater Shahname* further presents a complex but interesting relationship with the Persian epics. Although it involves many different accounts and its realities are far from clear at this stage, it can be said on the whole that this group of *tumârs* follow the basic storylines of the epics, and in Zariri's version Ferdowsi's verses are directly quoted at decisive points in the narrative. What is noteworthy is that storytellers—as if dreading to leave anything unexplained—fill up ellipses and omissions in the original texts with fresh narrative elements composed from their stock-in-trade. They describe in detail how a young hero, Sohrâb, for example, experiences many adventures until he becomes a fully-fledged champion; such a process is generally omitted in the epics where the baby hero

---

5 *Haft Lashkar*, ed. Afshâri et al. 1998 includes the following epics beside the *Shahname* of Ferdowsi: the *Garshâsp-nâme* (pp. 40–52); *Sâm-nâme* (pp. 57–143); *Bânu-Goshasp-nâme* (pp. 197–204); *Jahângir-nâme* (pp. 205–16); *Borzu-nâme* (pp. 246–325); and *Bahman-nâme* (pp. 492–570).

matures in a matter of a few lines.[6] Such additions do not fundamentally alter the story precisely because they fill out what has been left out.

Extraneous elements which storytellers add to the epics seem to serve two purposes: expansion and interpretation of the epics. The one is self-evident: the more elements are added the longer the session becomes, which is their ultimate aim. The other point brings us back to the relationship between the *tumârs* and the epics. Interpolations are made to shed light on what is vaguely implied by the authors of the epics so that the audience can appreciate the meaning and significance of the epics. At times the storytellers repeat similar episodes many times over in order to establish a hero's strengths or weaknesses, and at times they insert a sequence of apparently unrelated events into a story to explain, for instance, why Tahmine seduces Rostam in *Rostam o Sohrâb*. The *Greater Shahname* can be regarded as a comprehensive narrative commentary on the Persian epics.

The *tumârs* thus play an important role in the *naqqâli* tradition. They serve to preserve and transmit story material, ranging from the plot structure to the names of secondary characters. Most of all, by providing formal guidance to novice and average storytellers as to how a familiar story is developed into a series of oral performances, they guarantee a minimum level of consistency among individual performances, as well as that of enjoyment for audiences. Nevertheless, the mere existence of *tumârs* does little to uphold the *naqqâli* tradition unless those are performed by the storytellers for their audiences. The *tumârs* are meant for oral performance and generally circulate only among the storytellers. When they cease to be narrated they are effectively lost. It can be said therefore that *naqqâli* is an oral tradition, though highly text-dominant.

---

6   In Zariri's account Sohrâb has many adventures before he recognizes Rostam as his father (Zariri, pp. 49–161). This phase is completely omitted in the *Shahname* of Ferdowsi, where Sohrâb becomes a youth in six lines (Khaleghi-Motlagh 1990, II, p. 125, ll. 96–101).

7. Performance

In *naqqâli* stories are told in installments, each of which last for about ninety minutes. Some storytellers give two sessions a day (in the morning and the evening), and continue the same story over six months (cf. Page 1979, p. 197). Others, like Torâbi, give one session a day and complete the *Greater Shahname* in about six months. Oral performance is conducted according to a set procedure, as illustrated in the following description of Torâbi's typical session.[7]

When arriving at a coffeehouse Morshed Vali-Allâh Torâbi prepares what he calls a *sardam* (platform) by piling up tables and chairs on which he places a *tumâr*. About four o'clock in the afternoon he hands his pupil a stick and tells him to strike a gong that hangs from the ceiling. The pupil calls for a *salavât* prayer ("*Allâhomma sallâ alâ Mohammad va âl-e Mohammad*," May God bless Mohammad and his family; Dustkhʷâh 1966, p. 78), and recites verses, concluding with another *salavât*. When the stick is returned, Torâbi, for his part, recites a *salavât* and a few poems. He calls for another *salavât* before moving on to the day's session. Typically, he tells a prose story at the center of the coffeehouse, while reading verses at the *sardam*. As he concentrates on the narration he frequently gesticulates with the stick (which sometimes represents a horse and sometimes a sword) and raises his voice. About half an hour later, he returns to the platform to say a prayer to Mohammed and to recite poetry. After repeating this once again, he strikes the gong and calls for a *salavât*. With this he picks up the story from where he left off. About thirty minutes later he exchanges a *salavât* with his audience and goes on to read verse passages. Once again he calls for a *salavât* and continues the story for about a quarter of an hour. Approximately fifteen minutes before the ending he makes a round to collect money from the audience, while calling for prayers for the Prophet.

A typical session may consist of three parts of about half an hour each, with an introduction. The beginning and end of each part are

---

7 This is based on the present writer's observations on Torâbi's performances given at a coffeehouse and a private house in Tehran.

marked by a combination of *salavâts* and recitations of classical poems, which may not be related to the story proper; they are generally used to get the audience focused on his performance. *Salavât* prayers in particular appear to be helpful for this purpose, since they demand the audience's active participation.

8. Some specific features of oral performance

Although the storyteller essentially follows the storyline given in the *tumâr*, he does not necessarily reproduce it. In order to facilitate the audience's comprehension, and to secure its return, he "reworks" the story in performance as appropriate. This reworking may involve a change of style, shifts of emphasis, and the addition of descriptive and evaluative comments. By way of illustration, a brief comparison of Morshed Abbâs Zariri's performance text (Dustkʷâh 1966, pp. 78–88), and the corresponding part of his *tumâr* (Zariri, pp. 34–42), is given below.

While Zariri uses a great deal of subordination in the *tumâr*, he performs in a paratactic or "additive" style (Ong 1982, pp. 37–38), in which simple sentences are juxtaposed and are often repeated. These features are often associated with "purely oral art form" (ibid., p. 14), and assumed to be lost when the performer acquires a knowledge of writing (Lord 1960, p. 129). Zariri's evidence, however, suggests that this is not necessarily the case; Zariri learned how to read and write only after he had become a well-known storyteller (Zariri, pp. XVII–XVIII). Evidently, his oral "additive" style has not been affected by his later acquisition of literacy and is primarily determined by the oral mode of delivery.

It is a universal feature of a *naqqâli* performance that it closes with a "cliff-hanger," or an unresolved situation (cf. Page 1979, p. 211). The storyteller stops at a point where the protagonist is laid at the gallows, so that his life is literally in suspense till the next performance. The storyteller thereby ensures that his audience returns the next day, promising at the same time that "the story will become more and more interesting day by day"

(Dustkh^wâh 1966, p. 88). Even in the middle of the performance the storyteller artificially creates suspense by interrupting an episode with *salavâts*. This happens twice, first when a quarrel takes place between two characters (ibid., p. 85), and second when one kills the other (ibid., p. 86). In the *tumâr* this episode is only a link in the chain of numerous events and actions, and does not have any distinctive features *per se*. In other words, with a little planning and careful attention to the audience (whose concentration span is limited), almost any episodes in the *tumâr* can be made into highlights of a performance. Although the narrative structure of the *tumâr* largely determines the course of the story, the storyteller has a great deal of latitude in emphasizing an episode or two in accordance with his overall design of a given performance.

Improvised elements in the performance text mostly fall into the category of descriptive and evaluative passages. When the storyteller refers to well-known characters such as Rostam, Pirân or Tahmine, he enumerates their attributes almost in a formulaic manner. Near the beginning of the performance the storyteller recites Rostam's epithets: "World champion of Iran, son of Zâl-e Zar, grandson of Sâm the cavalier, he who singularly dedicates his life to Iran, he who has protected the country of Iran from nations in the world with his sword and power for six hundred years ..." (ibid., p. 79). Such a list of attributes may be used as a "filler" to gain time for planning the narration ahead. On another occasion, however, it is used to edify the audience. When referring to Pirân (who plays a central role in the performance) as the second greatest politician in the world, the storyteller enumerates a few others, including Zahhâk (a tyrannical king of Persian myth) and Afrâsiyâb (the great enemy of Iran; ibid., p. 81). At the end of this list he does not fail to add that Pirân was such an important vizier that his death led to the fall of Afrâsiyâb (ibid., p. 81). By commenting on Pirân, the storyteller drops the audience a hint as to who will be playing a central role in the performance.

Secondary characters are also commented on if their experience is comparable to that of spectators and of the storyteller himself. When a messenger of Pirân, Yamuti, is killed and his followers return to Balkh, the capital of Turân, the storyteller speaks to the audience, full of sympathy for these figures:

> Âqâ! ba'zi kârhâ ke dar âlam jur mishe, bebin mâ age bekh^{w}â'im jur-esh konim, mitunim? Be va-llâh nemitunim. Mâ mitunim shâhrâ, soltan-e mamlekatrâ, dar yeh sâ'ati-ke delkh^{w}âh-e mâ'st az sar-e jâsh harakatesh bedim, bâ tamâm-e arkân-e dowlat va biyârimesh bâlâtar ke mikh^{w}âim ye vâqe'râ neshunesh bedim? (ibid., pp. 86–87)

Gentlemen! There are certain things that happen in the world by themselves. Look, if we should want to make them happen, could we? By God, we cannot. Can we move from his place the king or the sultan of the country and bring him high up, together with the dignitaries of his government, at a time that we want, because we want to show him an event?

Although—or rather because—Yamuti and his followers are expendable characters, the reference to them points to the presence of a power that willfully manipulates their fate and elicits the audience's empathy. By temporarily identifying with Yamuti and his followers, and distancing himself from the story whose structure requires hundreds of expendable characters like Yamuti, the storyteller poses an unanswerable question as to the character of the world, and why the majority have to submit to a few privileged people. Such rhetorical questions by the storyteller encourage the audience to reflect on their position in the real world, and to connect this to their reception of the story. In this way the storyteller links the narrative universe with the real one, and lends a sense of verisimilitude to the ancient story of *Rostam o Sohrâb*.

9. Conclusion

In *naqqâli* we can observe how a written text is adapted to oral performance, and what changes are made in the process. Nearly all sentences found in the *tumâr* are paraphrased in performance. Linguistic changes are evidently caused by the exigencies of oral performance, the text being adapted to the spoken language. By contrast, thematic changes are limited to shifts in emphasis and focus, and the storyline presented in the *tumâr* is kept virtually intact. The storyteller makes an episode into the centerpiece of the day's performance by interrupting it with *salavâts*. He highlights a character that plays a leading role in the performance by means of descriptive and evaluative comments. Thematic changes that occur in oral performance are mostly subtle and relate to the way the story is presented.

Improvised elements are ultimately concerned with the form of a story and the arrangement of each performance. Every shift of focus brings to the surface some episodes in the story that might otherwise go unnoticed. The storyteller's apt and timely comments on narrative events and characters give an old story new details and meaning, and place it in new, contemporary contexts. These and other elements which the storytellers impart to the story in oral performance help the audience view it in a different light, and to make new discoveries every time it is told. The more the story is told, the more discoveries are made because retelling always involves interpretation. By continually interpreting and reinterpreting the same stories, the *naqqâls* keep them alive in the minds of their audience.

CHAPTER 11

KÂSHEFI'S *ROWZAT AL-SHOHADÂ*: THE KARBALÂ NARRATIVE AS UNDER-PINNING OF POPULAR RELIGIOUS CULTURE AND LITERATURE

Peter Chelkowski

For almost five hundred years the *Rowzat al-shohadâ'* (Garden of the Martyrs) by Kâshefi has been the source of ever-growing and multiplying rituals, performing arts and sermons in Iran. It has nourished a countless number of poets, writers and bards. Although the book as such may be unknown to the majority of those who have been inspired by it, no other book has had a comparable impact on the Iranian masses. The indirect acquaintance of ordinary Iranians with *Rowzat al-shohadâ'*, especially those who come from the working class, peasantry and the disenfranchised poor urban population, has been through *rowze-kh*ʷ*âni, ta'ziye-kh*ʷ*âni, parde-kh*ʷ*âni*, and other rites devoted to the martyrs of Karbalâ. Even the 1979 Islamic Revolution was fueled by this book. Ayatollah Khomeini said: "If it were not for Moharram, we wouldn't have been victorious" (*Majalle-ye Sorush* 166 Oct./Nov. 1982, p. 5; *Keyhân-e havâ'i* 28 Oct. 1982, p. 7).

The Moharram observances in Iran have to a great degree been shaped by *Rowzat al-shohadâ'*. In order to achieve victory, Ayatollah Khomeini converted many popular Shi'ite beliefs and rituals into sources of mass mobilization for revolution and against the "Imposed [Iran-Iraq] War" (Chelkowski 1989a, pp. 7–11).

KÂSHEFI'S *ROWZAT AL-SHOHADÂ'*

1. Kâshefi and the *Rowzat al-shohadâ'*

Kamâl-al-Din-Hoseyn b. Ali Vâ'ez Kâshefi was born in the first half of the fifteenth century in Sabzevâr, and died in 1504 in Herat. His early life was spent in his native city, his ancestral home. His father was a respected *âlem* there. From Sabzevâr he went to Nishâpur and Mashad. Finally he settled down in Herat, where he was initiated into the Naqshbandi Sufi brotherhood, and became a prolific writer. He was under the patronage of the great benefactor of arts and sciences, Sultan Hoseyn Bâyqarâ, and his famous vizier, Nezâm-al-Din Amir Ali-Shir Navâ'i. As his fame grew he became the main *khatib* (preacher) at Friday prayers in Herat. His major thirty-three works, written in Arabic and in Persian, cover philosophy, mysticism and theology (Kâshefi 1962, pp. 6–8). Toward the end of his life he was commissioned by Sayyed Mirzâ, the son-in-law of Sultan Hoseyn Bâyqarâ, to write a *maqtal-nâme* about the passion and death of Imam Hoseyn at Karbalâ. Kâshefi writes that when he finished the book, 847 years had passed since that tragic event (Kâshefi 1962, pp. 6–8). Since the Karbalâ tragedy took place in the year 680–81, the book must have been completed in 1502–03, which almost coincided with the establishment of Twelver Shi'ism as the state religion of Iran by the Safavid Shah Esmâ'il, who ascended the throne of Persia in 1501. Since the majority of Iranians were at that time Sunnites, the *Rowzat al-shohadâ'* became a very important tool in the propagation of the Shi'ite faith, and it has been regarded as a masterpiece of the martyrology genre for almost five hundred years.

The causes and stages of development of the *maqtal* have been very well researched and described by M.-J. Mahjub in *Az fazâ'el-va manâqeb-kh{{w}}âni tâ rowze-kh{{w}}âni* (From the Praising of virtues [of the Imams] to *rowze-kh{{w}}âni*) and by F. Nâzerzâde-Kermâni in "*Hamle-kh{{w}}âni gune-ye mohemmi az naqqâli-ye mazhabi dar Irân*" (*Hamle-kh{{w}}âni*, an Important Form of Religious Storytelling in Iran).

The best known printed edition of *Rowzat al-shohadâ'* is that published by the Ketâbforushi-ye Eslâmiyye in 1962, edited by M. Ramazâni, in 420 tightly printed pages, 30 lines to a page of small script, with an additional 20-page Index. It is divided into ten chapters. The first chapter is devoted to the prophets before the mission of the Prophet Mohammad. All the misfortunes, afflictions and miseries of Adam, Noah, Abraham, Jacob, Joseph, Job, Zacharias, and John are juxtaposed in the chapter with that of the tragedy of Hoseyn at Karbalâ. This juxtaposition makes the agonies of the preceding prophets seem minimal in comparison with those of Hoseyn. The tragedy of Karbalâ is viewed by Kâshefi as the greatest of its kind in history. Indeed it transcends history and transforms it into meta-history, with cosmic dimensions. It gives the martyrdom of Imam Hoseyn a timeless and space-less quality, placing the Karbalâ tragedy in a time beyond time and a space beyond space. The misfortunes of the *Ahl-e Beyt* (the prophet Mohammad's family) are thus woven into the warp of Qor'anic stories devoted to the ancient prophets. In this fashion, Adam weeps because of his separation from Eve:

> ... the tears from the eyes of Adam were pouring down like a flood. The tears from his right eye were forming the Tigris and those from his left eye the Euphrates (Kâshefi 1962, p. 19).

Soon, however, Adam learns that his crying is nothing compared to the intensity of weeping by 70,000 angels at the tomb of Hoseyn at every Friday vigil.

The suffering of Hoseyn and its commemoration became the very core of the Shi'ite popular faith, which, as Elias Canetti writes:

> ... is a religion of lament more concentrated and more extreme than any to be found elsewhere ... No faith has ever laid greater emphasis on lament. It is the highest religious duty, and many times more meritorious than any other good work (*Crowds and Power*, 1978, p. 146).

In the story of Noah, his ship stops sailing when it finds itself above the future Karbalâ battlefield, and Noah learns that this is the place where "... the ship of the Ahl-e Beyt will sink in the whirlpool of blood" (Kâshefi 1962, p. 23). This affords Kâshefi an opportunity to make a transition from the story of Noah to the tragedy of Karbalâ. Kâshefi employs *goriz* (lit. a running away, in the sense of deviating from the main story; a transition, a digression) which is still a favorite mechanism in today's many Karbalâ rituals. Actually, in the first chapter the author often employs a double *goriz*: the first is a digression from the story of the ancient prophets to the story of the *Ahl-e Beyt*; and the second is a digression from the childhood of Hoseyn to his tragic death. In the story of Cain and Abel there is a *goriz* to Fâteme Zahrâ, the daughter of the Prophet and the mother of Hoseyn and his elder brother Hasan. She made shirts for Hasan and Hoseyn. Wearing these shirts, the boys go to the Prophet to play with him. Hoseyn's shirt is a bit tight, and the Prophet opens the collar and notices that there is a line around the neck of his grandchild. As the Prophet ponders the meaning of this line the Angel Gabriel appears and explains that at this line the head of Hoseyn is going to be severed on the plain of Karbalâ (Kâshefi 1962, p. 21). This is the second *goriz*, and the most effective one. Even in contemporary spoken Persian, when a conversant constantly returns to the one topic, the other conversant may say: *Bâz zadi be sahrâ-ye Karbalâ'* (Again you mention the plain of Karbalâ). Once the *goriz* story is finished, Kâshefi returns to the story of Cain and Abel.

Chapter two of *The Garden of Martyrs* provides the background for the story of Ahl-e Beyt. Chapters three, four, six and seven are devoted to the lives of the Prophet Mohammad, his daughter Fâteme Zahrâ, and his grandchildren Hasan and Hoseyn. They are laudatory, in praise of the protagonists of the chapters. If written separately, these chapters would fall into the category of *fazâ'el* and *manâqeb* literature (more or less corresponding to hagiography). Chapter five is devoted to Ali, the Prophet's cousin and son-in-law, the first Imam of the Shi'ites. This prose chapter, which describes Ali's life in an epic style, is similar to the poems that delineate Ali's attacks on the enemies of Islam, such as desribed in Râji Kermâni's *Hamle-ye Heydari* (lit. Heydar's = Ali's attack), compiled in the early Qajar period.

It should be noted that *naqqâli*, or storytelling, is an ancient and very refined art in Iran (see Chapter 10 by Yamamoto). Its roots are to be found in pre-Islamic traditions. The *manâqeb* and *fazâ'el-khʷâni* are forms of religious storytelling, singing the virtues of the Shi'ite saints by professional storytellers in some public space.

These are a happy fusion of the Iranian national epic with the religious Shi'ite epic. The main hero in these stories is the first Imam, Ali. His physical and spiritual strength is prodigious. He appears as a new refined Rostam, the national Iranian hero. According to Hoseyn Behzâdi-Anduhjerdi, Râji Kermâni's *Hamle-ye Heydari* is "the greatest religious epic" (Behzâdi-Anduhjerdi 1991, title page). No doubt this book is a very fine epic, but to call it "the greatest religious epic" is an exaggeration. However, it had a tremendous impact on many Iranian Shi'ite rituals such as *rowze-kh"âni* and *ta'ziye-kh"âni*. The book is written in a beautiful poetic and dramatic language. The author, it seems, wanted his *Hamle-ye Heydari* to be chanted or recited and performed in public, so he wrote it in a flowing narrative style. Indeed, the performance came to be known as *hamle-kh"âni*.

There is another *Hamle-ye Heydari* composed in part by an Iranian who lived in India, called Mirzâ Mohammad Rafi' Khan Bâzel (d. 1124). Since his book was not finished before his death, it was completed by Mirzâ Abu'l-Talab Mirfendereski. It is not as lucid as Râji Kermâni's book, but both authors had in mind the performing aspect of the book, and there they succeeded.

Other works of the Qajar period devoted to the suffering and martyrdom of the Shi'ite Imams are Jowhari's *Tufân al-bokâ'* (Deluge of Weeping), and Borujerdi's *Asrâr al-shahâdat* (Mysteries of Martyrdom). There is no doubt that these works, too, had an impact on the development of popular beliefs and rituals in Iran.

The tragedy of Imam Hoseyn starts with chapter eight. It is devoted to the martyrdom of Moslem b. Aqil. In the printed edition of the book, this chapter starts on page 210, that is, exactly in the middle. Moslem was Imam Hoseyn's envoy to Kufe. The chapter describes his short but tumultuous career: How in Kufe he won over twenty thousand people to Hoseyn's cause, and how those people, out of their love for the Imam, pledged and signed an oath of allegiance to Hoseyn, which prompted Hoseyn to leave Mecca for Kufe on his ill-fated journey which ended in his martyrdom at Karbalâ. This chapter has all the characteristics of a tragic drama in which the heroes face treachery and deception. It is vivid, full of action and very emotional. The chapter ends with the bloody murder

KÂSHEFI'S *ROWZAT AL-SHOHADÂ'*

of Moslem and his two sons, one seven years old, the other eight. This story remains one of the most beloved in today's repertory of *ta'ziye*, having even become topical in view of so many young boys who died on the Iraqi front. The cowardice of the Kufans, who for fear of the Umayyad authorities' retaliation betrayed Hoseyn, has become proverbial among the Shi'ites. During the eight-year Iran-Iraq War (1980–88), the posters and billboards across Iran that were meant to reinforce the morale of the Iranians, declared: *Mâ ahl-e Kufe nistim*! (We are not like the people of Kufe, meaning: we will fight to the end.) The courage, suffering and the brutal death of the two boys of Moslem especially move the women in the audiences of *ta'ziye-khʷâni, rowze-khʷâni* and other public accounts of their bravery and martyrdom (Chelkowski and Dabashi 1999, p. 95).

The ninth chapter is devoted exclusively to the Karbalâ tragedy, and is 112 pages long, i.e., more than one fourth of the printed version of the book. The passion, courage, and cruel death of Imam Hoseyn, and his male relatives and followers, constitute a literary genre known in Arabic as *maqtal* literature that has flourished in the Muslim world during the last thirteen centuries, first in Arabic, then Persian, followed by Turkish and Urdu. Underscoring the Arabic contribution to *maqtal* literature, the *Rowzat al-shohadâ'* bears an Arabic title, but is written in flowing, unadulterated Persian.

The first half of the book is a long introduction to the genre (*maqtal-nâme*). It is Kâshefi's dramatic exposition of the tragic events, in the straightforward, moving, yet simple language that has helped the book's tremendous popular success. In the eyes of the Shi'ites, Hoseyn did not fight for wealth, power, or political ambition, but for the Islamic ideal of social and political justice. He fought and sacrificed his life for the unprivileged, the oppressed and the humiliated. The engaging prose narration, illustrated with occasional lines of poetry (mainly *dobeyti*s, consisting of two distiches), and the vibrant description of the causes for which Hoseyn fought, makes it the master *maqtal-nâme* that has dominated popular Shi'ite literature for the last five hundred years. It introduces and preserves the timeless quality of this tragedy that allows Shi'ite communities to measure themselves against Hoseyn's principles and paradigms.

The Garden of Martyrs and its derivatives have inspired the Shi'ites to fight against injustice, tyranny, and oppression in the past and the present. Although we know from historic sources that the siege at Karbalâ lasted for nine days and ended on Âshurâ' day, the 10th of Moharram, with a swift and brutal attack by Yazid's overwhelming forces, Kâshefi gives almost every one of the seventy-two martyr companions of Hoseyn a chance to show his devotion to Hoseyn, his bravery and chivalry, as each, separately or in small groups, fights the whole enemy army. The drama is sharpened by the fact that Hoseyn and his women are witnesses to all of this, and to the savagery and brutality of Yazid's forces. It is only after he has seen the cruelty of the enemy and the death of his sons, brothers and followers with his own eyes that Hoseyn's turn comes to fight and die. His death has been deferred so that he could witness and feel the suffering of his people, the incredible thirst on the scorched plain of Karbalâ, and the bloody encounter of his fighters with the enemy forces who are a thousand times stronger. Hoseyn's determination to fight to the end despite his mental and physical agony makes him the Prince of Martyrs.

The book ends with a chapter devoted to the survivors of Karbalâ: the women and the fourth Imam, the surviving son of Hoseyn. This includes a gory depiction of the cut-off-heads of the martyrs being carried on spikes, and the caravan of chained women being led to Caliph Yazid in Damascus, with the mistreatment of the survivors vividly depicted. These scenes became the favorite subject for the painters of the Karbalâ tragedy (see Chelkowski 1989b).

2. *Rowze-kh^{w}âni*

The most important from among the religious rituals that are derived from the *Rowzat al-shohadâ'* is the *rowze-kh^{w}âni*, that is, 'recitation, reading, or chanting from the *Rowzat al-shohadâ'*.' The success of *rowze-kh^{w}âni* was preceded by the popularity of *fazâ'el-* and *manâqeb-kh^{w}âni*, which trail-blazed the public performance of religious stories by professional storytellers. The *manâqeb-* and

KÂSHEFI'S *ROWZAT AL-SHOHADÂ'*

*fazâ'el-kh^wân*s chanted their stories in the marketplace. In order to draw greater attention from the public, they would wear other than ordinary dress, and carry ancient weapons. This ritual is popularly called by its shortened form, *rowze*. Originally, in Safavid times, it was customary to read a chapter from, or a part of *The Garden of Martyrs* in public each day during the first ten days of the mourning month of Moharram. Soon it was done throughout Moharram and the following month of Safar, and eventually it came to be staged all year round. As Gustav Thaiss (1995, III, pp. 412–13) reports:

> In the period preceding the Iranian Revolution of 1979, religious gatherings (*hey'at-e mazhabi*) were organized daily within the quarters of the city by neighborhood groups and associations or by the guilds within the bazaar. Although they were intended to fulfill various religious goals, they almost always ended in *rowzakhvani*, the not-so-latent message of which was opposition to the government.

Many performances of *rowze-kh^wâni* are the result of vows taken by the sponsors upon completion of a pilgrimage, return to health, a granted wish, or even the successful passing of an examination.

All classes of society participate in *rowze-kh^wâni*. It takes place in especially erected black tents in the public square of a town or village, or in mosques, or in the courtyards of private homes, as well as in special buildings known as *hoseyniyye* or *tekye*. Usually the place where the *rowze-kh^wâni* is performed is well-carpeted and decorated with black mourning standards and flags, as well with a variety of traditional weapons such as swords, helmets, daggers, shields, bows and arrows, lances, reminiscent of the battle of Karbalâ. The Karbalâ mourning rituals are the strongest manifestations of community cooperation. The stress on common brotherhood is reflected in preparations for the Moharram/Safar observances. Both temporary and permanent *tekye*s must be decorated, not only with banners and weapons but also with cherished objects like crystal lamps, china, mirrors, and tapestry which are lent to *tekye*s for the duration of the celebrations (see Chelkowski 1986, p. 216). G.E. von Grunebaum, describing the Shi'ite ritual of Moharram writes (1958, p. 87):

ORAL LITERATURE OF IRANIAN LANGUAGES

Toward the end of the Muslim year, black tents are pitched in the streets. These tents are adorned with draperies, arms, and candelabra. Here and there wooden pulpits are erected. On the first of Muharram, when the festival proper begins, mourning clothes are donned; people refrain from shaving and bathing, and a simple diet is adopted. From the pulpit the beginning of Husain's story is narrated with as much detail and elaboration of episodes as possible. The listeners are deeply affected. Their cries of "O, Husain, o, Husain!" are accompanied by groans and tears. This kind of recitation continues throughout the day, the mullahs taking turns on the several pulpits.

Rowze-kh^wâni belongs to the category of stationary Shi'ite commemorative rituals. The size and length of a *rowze-kh^wâni* depends on the occasion on which it is performed, and on who sponsors the event. A well-rounded *rowze-kh^wâni* requires a number of *rowze-kh^wân*s; a simple *rowze-kh^wâni* could be a one-man show. The performers address the audience from a *menbar* (pulpit), or an elevated chair, so that a large assembly is able to see and hear them clearly.

The more elaborate *rowze-kh^wâni* starts with a *maddâh* (eulogist) who invokes the Prophet Mohammad and then sings praises of the Prophet and the Imams. He does it in a low vocal register and at a slow pace as he elicits audience response. The *maddâh* is followed by a *vâ'ez* (preacher/exhorter) who introduces a variety of religious and philosophical subjects; then he digresses to the Shi'ite tragedies, chanting the *mosibat* (mourning poems). The *maddâh* and *vâ'ez* warm up the audience. Then comes the main performer, the *rowze-kh^wân*, the master storyteller who recites and chants the story of Hoseyn, his family, and followers at the bloody battle of Karbalâ. His rapid chanting in a high-pitched voice often alternates with sobbing and crying intended to arouse the audience to an intense emotional state. Then enters a chorus, usually of boys, who engage in rapid exchanges with the *rowze-kh^wân*. The audience responds with weeping, chest-beating and self-flagellation. Many people in the audience go into a trance-like state. Towards the end of the performance, when the audience has been deeply aroused, the *rowze-kh^wâni* ends with congregational singing of dirges called *nowhe*. The performance of *nowhe* may last for hours, and even go on into the night.

KÂSHEFI'S *ROWZAT AL-SHOHADÂ'*

The art of the *rowze-khʷâni* depends on the ability of the *rowze-khʷân* to manipulate the assembled crowd, using his (or her, if the gathering is entirely female) choice of episodes of the tragedy as well as his or her use of body language and tonality. A successful *rowze-khʷân* can bring the members of the audience to a state of frenzy, identifying themselves with the suffering of Hoseyn and other martyrs.

Rowze-khʷâni is characterized by intermittent bursts of singing, so its success also depends on the vocal skills of the *rowze-khʷan*s. Since *rowze-khʷâni* can bring the audience to an altered state, it can be exploited for political purposes. Its religious chants, symbols and poetry can be used for social or political demonstrations on a massive scale. The *rowze-khʷâni* technique was successfully employed during the Islamic Revolution in Iran and during the war against Iraq (Chelkowski 1980, pp. 30–45).

The *Rowzat al-shohadâ'* still serves as a framework and a springboard for professional narrators who improvise creatively upon the sufferings and deeds of many Shi'ite heroes. Habitually, the *rowze-khʷân*s make digressions to the events of Karbalâ, and comparisons of the contemporary political, moral, and social situation with them. According to popular belief, participation in *rowze-khʷâni* ensures Hoseyn's intercession for the participants on the Day of Judgment. Rumor has it that an old preacher may collect the tears of the participants in a bottle, to be used as an unction for the dying.

There is a special *rowze-khʷâni* sponsored by and participated in by women, which is called *Sofre-ye Hazrat-e Abbâs*. It is performed by a professional female *rowze-khʷân*. This mourning ritual is not directly devoted to Imam Hoseyn, but to Abbâs, his half-brother and standard-bearer at the battle of Karbalâ. Thanks to his extraordinary courage, gallantry and chivalry, Abbâs enjoys a special place in Shi'ite communities, particularly among women. A *sofre* is a serving cloth upon which food is spread. A *Sofre-ye Abbâs* may be offered by a woman to fulfill a vow, permitting invited women friends to listen to the story of Abbâs's bravery, recounted by a woman. Upon the completion of this ritual, the food is distributed among the members of the community. Both in *rowze-khʷâni* and in *ta'ziye-khʷâni*, the story of Abbâs is well known for its moving literary passages in poetry and prose.

The backdrop of the saga of Hoseyn is the desolate, sun-scorched desert of Karbalâ. In the unbearable heat the plaintive cry of thirsty children can be heard. Hoseyn's encampment is surrounded by the steel of the enemy's weapons. The enemy has cut off and guards the passage to the Euphrates. Abbâs was not only Hoseyn's standard-bearer, but also his water carrier. He was killed while trying to get water from the Euphrates for Hoseyn and his family, and is therefore called *sâqi* (water-carrier). In the *ta'ziye* play entitled *The Martyrdom of the Luminous Leader of the Bani Hâshem, Hazrat Abu'l-Fazl al-Abbâs,* the scene which gave him this honorific title reads as follows (Sakine is a daughter of Hoseyn; Shemr is the most hated of the enemy leaders and the one who cuts off Hoseyn's head):

> ABBÂS who managed to fight through a passage across the enemy forces to the embankment of the river: "O Euphrates, thou art pleasant but unfaithful. Why art thou distant from the thirsty lips of Hoseyn?"
>
> SAKINE at the encampment: "Come, uncle, hurry up! Fill your water pouch with water! Help us! Come, uncle! Bring water!"
>
> SHEMR addressing the enemy soldiers: "O soldiers, do not allow Abbâs to take water to the tents of the King of the Universe! They attack and fight."
>
> SHEMR: "O Hoseyn, I have cut off your standard-bearer's hand. O Hoseyn, I have finished him on the battleground."
>
> ABBÂS addressing the audience: "When you are powerless then invoke Ali!" The audience shouts: "Yâ Ali!" Abbâs continues: "My right hand has fallen from my body. O God, let my left hand be at Hoseyn's service; I have yet a left hand. What a pity, one hand can not clap."
>
> In Hoseyn's encampment, IMAM: "I hear a thunderous wailing, 'I lost my hand.' It comes from my water-carrier."
>
> SHEMR at the battlefield: "Weep and mourn in Karbalâ, for I have cut off Abbâs's left hand! Come, o infidel army, gather around the standard-bearer of the lonely king. I shall smash his brain with my club. Abbâs, profess your faith before I cut off your head and separate it from your body."
>
> ABBÂS: "Alas, my two hands fell from my body; they were my wings. Alas, Hoseyn has lost his standard-bearer. Alas, Zeynab will be humiliated by scornful people. She'll be tormented by my death. Alas, my mother does not know that my two hands have been

severed from my body. No one could equal me in strength if my hands were still on my arms. In the midst of this tumult and confusion I hope to get a glimpse of Hoseyn's face once more. O Hoseyn, lonely am I. May I be sacrificed for you, you are so kind and generous." (Chelkowski 1986, pp. 262–63).

In the old quarters of Iranian towns, in the bazaars or in small alleys, one can still find a little *saqqâkhâne* or a 'house of the water-carrier,' dedicated to Abbâs. Usually it is a niche with a brass receptacle with a tap. Several brass drinking-cups are attached to the container by a string or chain. The niche is decorated with tiles or wall paintings showing scenes from the Karbalâ battle. On Thursday evenings the niche is lit by candles. A man who is responsible for keeping the container filled during the rest of the week sings dirges, and people slake their thirst and listen to the bard.

If Hoseyn is the supreme martyr, Abbâs is regarded as the supreme fighter. Abbâs's strong personality is very much admired in Iran. In daily life, swearing by Abbâs is the only dependable oath. In signing commercial or other contracts, people add Abbâs's name as a partner *in absentia* who will guard against the violation of anyone's rights.

The most common Shi'ite ritual among the Iranian masses is the *daste*, or procession/parade. The most spectacular *daste* takes place on Âshurâ', the day of Hoseyn's death, and on the twentieth of the month of Safar, known as *arba'in* or *chelle*, i.e., the fortieth day after Hoseyn's murder. Parades lamenting the sudden and unjust death of heroes have been performed almost from time immemorial. The mourning procession for Adonis/Tammuz in Mesopotamia, and for Siyâvosh in Transoxania are only two of many examples. The *daste* of Hoseyn developed from simple parades into a complex ambulatory ritual. The most salient feature of the *daste* is the self-mortifiers. The participants, men of twelve years of age and upwards, are arranged according to height, with the shortest up front. Some strip to their waists and strike their chests with the palms of their hands; these are called *sine-zan*, or chest beaters. Others wear black shirts, often cut away in the back. They beat their backs with chains either directly on their flesh or on the fabric of their shirts, and they are called *zanjir-zan*, or beaters with chains. The *shamshir-zan*, also known as *qâme-zan*, are those who beat their foreheads with swords or knives. The latter practice is now forbidden, but does take place secretly from time to time. All these acts of self-mortification are performed along the streets of towns and villages that are lined with mourners-spectators. The music of drums and cymbals is an integral part of the *daste*.

The leading chanter of each subgroup in the *daste* intones dirges, which are repeated by the entire subgroup. In contrast to the violent self-mortification, the lyrics of the dirges are very poetic. Even these dirges are based on the *Rowzat al-shohadâ'*. The entire *daste* halts from time to time before the tomb of a local saint or a religious edifice, where the chest-pounding of one group becomes the rhythm of a chant of another.

> The monotonous song with its strong rhythm intoxicates them. They beat themselves as hard as they can; the sound is hollow, deep, regular and unceasing, but this is not enough to satisfy all of them (Canetti 1978, p. 151).

The tempo of the chest-beating and the responding chanting quickens till it reaches an uncontrollable pitch; only then does the *daste* resume moving on. Elias Canetti (1978, p. 151) defines this parade thus:

> ...(they) might be described as an orchestra of grief; and their effect is that of a crowd crystal. The pain they inflict on themselves is the pain of Husain, which, by being exhibited, becomes the pain of the whole community. Their beating on their chests, which is taken up by the spectators, gives rise to a rhythmic crowd sustained by the emotion of the lament. Husain has been torn away from all of them, and belongs to all of them together.

Foreign residents, envoys, merchants, missionaries and travelers, who either resided in or passed through Iran in the seventeenth and eighteenth centuries have left a very rich record of what they saw there during the months of Moharram and Safar. These accounts provide a chronology of the development of the pageantry of the *daste*. As time passed, the number of participants costumed to represent various personalities in the battle of Karbalâ increased. Various episodes from the tragedy of Karbalâ were also enacted. There were costumed riders on camels and horses, followed by floats on wheels with living tableaux.

3. Ta'ziye-kh^wâni

In the mid-eighteenth century the fusion of the ambulatory *daste* and the stationary *rowze-kh^wâni* took place, producing the only form of serious drama ever developed in the Islamic world before the early modern period. The performance of the resulting theatrical form is known as *ta'ziye-kh^wâni* or simply as *ta'ziye*. The *ta'ziye* is, *mutatis mutandis*, the Shi'ite passion play. To start with, personalities of the static living tableaux were given body movements, and made to recite lyrics from the *rowze-kh^wâni*. Such lyrics were also given to the costumed characters on foot or horseback. For a time, this new form of religious performing art continued to move along the *daste* as an ambulatory performance, and then became stationary (Chelkowski 1979, p. 4). In this form, it was staged at crossroads, in town squares and market places; later it was performed in private courtyards and those of caravansaries. Eventually, special structures called *hoseyniyye* or *tekye* were built for the staging of *ta'ziye*s. Some of these were built as pious endowments by the well-to-do, others with contributions from the citizens of a city quarter. Some were private structures, large enough to accommodate the family and friends, while others were huge, seating thousands of spectators. Many *tekye*s were temporary structures built especially for the months of Moharram and Safar by local guilds, or members of the *zurkhâne* (traditional Iranian athletic houses).

The most famous *ta'ziye* theater in Tehran was the *Tekye-ye Dowlat*, the Royal Theater, built in the 1870s. Many foreign visitors to the Qajar court were extremely impressed with this building, and with the splendor of the performance of the *ta'ziye* in that theater. Although many *tekye*s were built in towns across the country, no characteristic *tekye* architecture ever developed. Still, there are features common to all *tekye*s that enhance the dramatic action and the interplay between performers and the audience; this is basically theater-in-the-round. The main performing space is a platform in the middle of the building or a courtyard. The stage, of various shapes but ideally round, is stark and un-curtained. It is surrounded by a broad circular strip that is covered with sand that is used for battles on foot and horseback, to mark subplots or to indicate journeys, the passage of time, and changes of scenes. To show a change of scene, a performer jumps from the stage and circles it. He may announce that he is going to such-and-such a place. When he climbs back on stage, it means that he has arrived there. The action follows the centrifugal force, extending from the central stage through the sand-covered circle to auxiliary small stages located in the midst of the audience (auxiliary stages are not the norm), and into the audience itself. In un-walled *tekyes*, skirmishes often take place behind the audience. This centrifugal movement of the dramatic action, from the center-stage to the periphery, and then back following a centripetal direction, envelops the spectators and draws them into the action of the play. Thus the audience becomes an actor in its own right. In many situations, the audience actually physically participates in the play.

There is almost no stage decor, as the minimalist setting is meant to evoke the desolate, bleak desert of Karbalâ. Most of the props are symbolic as well: a basin of water, for example, represents the Euphrates, and a branch of a tree a palm grove.

During the reign of Nâser-al-Din Shah (r. 1848–96), the costumes in the *Tekye-ye Dowlat* Theater were rich and splendid, though no attention was paid to their historicity. Even today the costumes are intended to help the audience recognize the characters. The protagonists dress predominantly in green, while the villains wear red. Green symbolizes Paradise, the family of the Prophet, and therefore Islam. Red stands for blood, suffering, and cruelty. Actors playing women are dressed in baggy black garments covering them from head to toe, and their faces are veiled. Thanks to this, even mustached and bearded men can play female roles as long as their voices do not give them away. When a protagonist puts a white sheet of cloth, representing a shroud, on his shoulders this indicates that he is ready to sacrifice his life and will shortly be killed. This, in turn, creates a cathartic state in the audience.

In addition to the colors, there is another clear division in the *ta'ziye* between protagonists and antagonists. The protagonists sing their parts, while the antagonists recite theirs. In the past the actors were chosen according to their physical suitability for a role. The right physical appearance was not enough, however, since a good singing voice had to complement the physical appropriateness of a protagonist. The actors (who do not like to be called actors) read their lines from little folded scripts which they hold in the palms of their hands, although the professional actors know their lines by heart. Holding a script in one's hand indicates that the actor is only a role-carrier, and that he is not assuming the character he portrays. The antagonists declaim their lines, often in violent, shrieking voices. Frequently the antagonists are made to seem like ridiculous buffoons, overplayed and overacted. All traditional attempts to distance the actors from the characters they portray are often swept away in modern productions of the *ta'ziye*. Under the influence of movies and television, the actors identify with the personages they represent to such a degree that they are carried away by the situation. The emotions of the actors are increased by the receptiveness of the audience as it meets the actors halfway. The influence of movies and television is also noticeable among contemporary audiences.

A *ta'ziye* director is at the same time a producer, music director, stage director, public relations coordinator, and prompter. He is responsible not only for the play's direction and production, music and mise-en-scene, but also all props, arrangements with the local authorities, and financial returns. The director is always on hand during the performance. He is like a traffic policeman, regulating the movement of actors, musicians, and audience. He remains constantly on the playing ground, giving actors their cues. His presence on the stage, however, is not disturbing to the audience, as he is an integral part of the *ta'ziye* production (Riggio 1988).

The core of the *ta'ziye* repertory is the plays devoted to the Karbalâ tragedy and the events surrounding it. It is within the framework of *Rowzat al-shohadâ'*, and the *ta'ziye*'s storyline follows Kâshefi's narrative. The Karbalâ massacre is divided into many separate episodes, performed on separate days. The passage of Hoseyn from Medina via Mecca to his death at Karbalâ is represented in some ten plays in as many days. In these plays, a hero single-handedly fights the entire enemy army, allowing the rest of the protagonists, grouped on the central stage, to contemplate their condition and make comments of a philosophical and religious nature. There is only one play in the Moharram repertory that is performed on a fixed day, namely Hoseyn's martyrdom on the tenth. The others can be performed in varying order. Usually the sequence starts on the first day of Moharram with a play dedicated to the death of Hoseyn's envoy to Kufe, Moslem b. Aqil. This is followed in a daily sequence by the martyrdom of two of Moslem's children, and then by the plays about the martyrdom of various members of Hoseyn's family and companions. Most commonly, on the sixth of Moharram, the Martyrdom of Horr, a faithful follower of Hoseyn, is performed; on the seventh, that of Qâsem, the bridegroom; on the eighth, that of Ali-Akbar, Hoseyn's oldest and favorite son; and on the ninth, that of Abbâs (see above). Sometimes the sequence follows *Rowzat al-shohadâ'* to the letter, and the Martyrdom of Abbâs is performed before that of Ali-Akbar. The basic repertory of the *ta'ziye* does not necessarily end with Hoseyn's death. The performances following the *Rowzat al-shohadâ*'s line may continue after the day of Âshurâ' to show the tragic lot of Hoseyn's womenfolk who were taken as captives to Damascus.

The *Rowzat al-shohadâ'* stories about the ancient prophets were also brought into the fold of the *ta'ziye*, and many plays about them have been written and performed. At the Royal Theater in Tehran the *ta'ziye* of Joseph and his Brethren was performed regularly during one of the first five days of Moharram (Pelly 1879, pp. 1–18). This type of *ta'ziye* play is connected with the Karbalâ tragedy through the employment of *goriz*, either as a direct verbal reference or as a staged short scene from Hoseyn's passion. The expansion of the repertory was followed by the expansion of performing time from the month of Moharram to the whole duration of the year.

The corpus of the *ta'ziye* plays is enormous. The *ta'ziye* is a living tradition, new plays and local variations on the traditional themes are still being composed. However, they still follow the *Rowzat al-shohadâ'* line. The best proof of this is a collection of 1,055 *ta'ziye* manuscripts housed at the Vatican Library (see Rossi and Bombaci 1969).

In the 1930s, Rezâ Shah's government, considering the *ta'ziye* a backward ritual, imposed restrictions on its performance in urban areas. Subsequently, the *ta'ziye* retreated to the rural areas. In the recent past, during the eight years of war with Iraq, the heroism depicted in the *ta'ziye* was employed to stimulate the fighting spirit of the Iranian combatants and to bring solace to those who had lost their loved ones in the fighting.

Sir Lewis Pelly (1879, p. iii), the author of *The Miracle Play of Hasan and Husain*, a collection of thirty-seven *ta'ziye* plays translated into beautifully ornate Victorian English, writes in his Introduction:

> If the success of a drama is to be measured by the effects which it produces upon the people for whom it is composed, or upon the audience before whom it is represented, no play has ever surpassed the tragedy known in the Mussulman world as that of Hasan and Husain.

On the title page of the book, the author writes that the plays were "collected from oral tradition." Here Pelly is referring to the *ta'ziye* style of writing which could be called anti-literary. The *ta'ziye* scripts are almost never intended for reading, but for performing. They are written as separate parts for each of the *dramatis personae* on loose narrow sheets of paper that the actors can hold in the palms of their hands. The value of these scripts must, therefore, be measured in their theatrical context, taking into consideration setting, costumes, movement, delivery, voice, music, and even choreography. Peter Brook (1979), the famous contemporary theater innovator who witnessed a *ta'ziye* in the 1970s, says:

> I saw in a remote Iranian village one of the strongest things I have ever seen in theater; a group of four hundred villagers, the entire population of the place, sitting under the tree and passing from roars of laughter to outright sobbing—although they knew perfectly well the end of the story—as they saw Hossein in danger of being killed, and then fooling his enemies, and then being martyred. And when he was martyred the theater form became truth.

4. *Parde-khwâni*

Yet another performance/ritual that grew out of the *rowze-khwâni* and *ta'ziye-khwâni* tradition is *parde-khwâni*, also known as *parde-dâri* or *shamâyel-khwâni*. The *parde-khwân* tells the story of Karbalâ in a very emotional and dramatic style with the help of a large painting in the background. This narrative painting, some eight feet by four, is an artistic reflection of the *ta'ziye* production. The *parde-khwân* is an itinerant painting-narrator who follows the story on the canvas from start to finish. He goes from one locality to another, hangs the painting and partially sings and partially recites the story, using a pointer to elucidate the scenes. He is like a *rowze-khwân* to whose histrionics a visual element has been added.

Parwiz Mamnoun (1967, p. 19) describes the painting-recitation scene as he remembers it from his childhood:

> ... a painting on a large cloth was nailed to a wall in an open space by the storyteller (*parde-dâr*). In front of this [wall] a crowd of observers gathered, some squatting on the ground, others standing behind them. ... The story of the *parde-dâr* proceeded somewhat in this fashion: he first sang in praise of the Prophet and his family. Thereafter he invited the public to send a salutation to the Prophet Mohammad. In this fashion he created a dramatic bridge between his song and the story. In the introduction to an episode he presented the characters [who would appear in the story] and then he would point to various people [in the painting] with his stick as he hoarsely described the battle on the painting. Naturally the *parde-dâr* utilized the art of declamation while he told the story. He knows the importance of changes in tonality in his speech, of imitation, and of gestures. During the following battle scenes he described the proceedings with a rough voice and a much faster rhythm. In order to stir up his public to the tragic fate of the Hussein family, he would march up and down clapping his hands and twirling his stick in the air. If it were necessary, he would even weep.

According to Samuel Peterson (1981, pp. 111–12):

> Once it was publicly accepted, to the general dismay of the orthodox, that the roles of the martyrs and their adversaries were enacted by devout Muslims, the step toward the public's acceptance of paintings

depicting the same narratives was not a major one. To illustrate that the Qajar genre of Karbalâ painting was essentially a translation of *ta'ziyeh* production into the visual arts, one need only compare the paintings with productions and texts of the dramas.

The verbal narrative, however, is based on a *tumâr*, a story outline in prose, which is derived from *Rowzat al-shohadâ'* or another *maqtal-nâme*. Very realistic scenes from the Karbalâ battle and other Shi'ite martyrology are painted in oils on canvas. The *parde* painting can easily be rolled up and carried from village to village. *Ta'ziye* was usually performed in an urban environment, and required a great deal of time and funds. The outlying villages in the countryside could not therefore participate in them. In those regions the substitute for the professional *ta'ziye* was *parde-kh^{w}âni* (Chelkowski 1998, pp. 90–97).

However, the antecedents of this narrative painting and painting-recitation could be found in Safavid times. Michele Membré (1539–42), a Venetian envoy to the Safavid court writes (Membré 1993, p. 52):

> ... the Sophians (i.e., the Safavids) paint figures, such as the figure of 'Ali, riding on a horse with a sword ... In their squares there are many Persian mountebanks sitting on carpets on the ground; and they have certain long cards with figures; and the said mountebanks hold a little stick and point to one figure after another, and preach and tell stories over each figure.

Out of the performance/rituals discussed in this chapter, the only one that is losing its vigor is the *parde-kh^{w}âni*; the others are not only alive, but are undergoing a renaissance. This is a relatively unusual state of affairs, given that they have to compete with radio, television and the movies.

In conclusion, it must be said that the Karbalâ narrative has not lost its popularity or vigor, considering the tremendous changes that have taken place in Iran since 1979. Moreover, although illiteracy has been largely eradicated in the country, oral religious literature still reigns supreme.

CHAPTER 12

THE POPULAR LITERATURE OF THE TAJIKS

RAVSHAN RAHMONI[1]

The popular literature of the Tajiks is now accessible to all who speak Persian. In the course of time many popular texts have found their way into the works of classical Persian authors (see Braginskiĭ 1956). The present article will discuss popular literature in the framework of popular culture generally.

1. History of the study

Russian scholars have played a prominent role in the process of collecting the folk literature of the Tajiks. As a result of their labors, works of Tajik oral literature have been published in newspapers, magazines and monographs. From the late 19th until the early 20th century, several Russian scholars were working in the field of Tajik popular literature.

As for Tajik researchers, in the 1920s Mahmudi and Zehni published samples of popular literature in collections, newspapers and magazines. In the 1930s interest in such activities increased; a number of scholars published such texts in periodicals, textbooks, and monographs. However, publications in the field tended to lose their academic quality in those years. Relatively few folklore texts were published in the 1940s. Tursunzoda (1940) published a collection in the Roman alphabet, which mostly contained samples of

1 Translated from the original Tajiki by Philip G. Kreyenbroek.

oral poetry. A relatively scholarly collection of Tajik fairytales was published in Russian translation by B. Niozmuhammadov (1945). However, the original Tajik version of this collection has not yet been published.

Thus, it was not until the late 1950s that Tajik researchers seriously began the task of collecting, publishing and studying popular Tajik literature. They eventually entrusted their collections to a "Folklore Archive" at the Rudaki Institute of Language and Literature. The Archive now holds more than 200,000 pages of popular literature. From 1966 onwards scholars began the process of ordering, codifying and classifying the archived material, under the direction of the Russian folklorist I. Levin. As a result, catalogues of "Proverbs," "Riddles," "*Robâ'is*," "Songs," and "Animal Fables," were produced. More than thirty volumes of scholarly works on Tajik folklore have so far been written. However, only two, those on "Animal Fables" (1 vol., *Kullioti Folklori Tojik* I, 1981) and "Proverbs" (2 vols., *Kullioti Folklori Tojik* IV, V, 1986, 1992), have found their way into print (see further below).

In the period 1970–90 the collecting of folklore material was relatively neglected. Still, short, popular collections appeared during this period and many folklore texts were published in schoolbooks and in the press. For one thing, researchers' time was occupied with bringing out the thirty-volume *Kullioti Folklori Tojik* (Comprehensive Collection of Tajik Folklore). Moreover, insufficient funds were available for travel. Thus, apart from a few haphazard recordings, popular literary works have not been collected in recent years. This is the more regrettable because it is still possible to collect and salvage folk literature that will disappear in the course of time.

In Philological Faculties of the Universities of Tajikistan, "Popular Creative Works" (i.e., folklore) forms part of the curriculum. During the second half of the 20th century two textbooks have been written: *Folklori Tojik* (Tajik Folklore) by N. Ma'sumi (1952), and *Ejodioti Dahanakiyi Tojik* (Tajik Oral Creative Works) by V. Asrori and R. Rahmonov (1980). A large number of scholars have contributed their publications on various genres of folk literature in the form of dissertations, learned articles in newspapers and magazines, or as introductions to monographs.

2. Proverbs and maxims

Tajik Folklorists distinguish between "proverbs" (*zarbulmasal*) and "maxims" (*maqol*). The term "proverb" is used for sayings containing wisdom based on common experience, expressed through metaphor, analogy, or allegory. For example, the saying *shokhi darakhti mevodor kham ast* (the branch of a fruit-bearing tree is bent) is a "proverb," for the image of the branch bowed down with fruit is used metaphorically for a wise, but modest and humble person (cf. the distich by Sa'adi: *nehad shâkh-e por-mive sar bar zamin*). A "maxim," on the other hand, is expressed directly and contains no such figures of speech, e.g. *pushaymonî sud nadorad* (regrets are useless). Nevertheless, proverbs and maxims are very similar in their goal and their brevity: both aim to instruct. Therefore the two are treated as one genre in most respects.

Although the study of Tajik proverbs and maxims began in the 1920s and '30s, the subject received far greater attention in the 1950s, '60s and '70s. In those decades both articles on, and collections of proverbs and maxims were published. Over 20,000 proverbs and maxims were recorded and are now preserved in the Tajik Folklore Archive.

Two volumes (IV, V) of *Kullioti Folklori Tojik* were published under Tilavov's direction; Hisomov and Murodov defended B.A. (Cand. Phil.) dissertations on the same subject. In *Kullioti Folklori Tojik* IV, 807 famous proverbs were published, with detailed studies in Tajiki, Russian, English, and Persian in Perso-Arabic script. The authors transcribed the texts in the *Kulliot* exactly as they were spoken, listing variants.

Tajik proverbs and maxims, are concerned, as expected, with various aspects of human experience, and reflect their good and bad facets in a concise manner. The following examples are taken from the *Kulliot*:

Odami bekor darakhti bebor	An idle man is a tree without fruit.
Devol mush dorad, mush gûsh dorad.	The wall has mice and mice have ears (i.e., beware what you say if you don't want it to be divulged).

Angura xûru boghasha napurs. Eat the grapes and don't ask (about) its vineyard.
Az yak dast sado namebaroyad. A single hand does not produce a (clapping) sound.

Many of these sayings are also found among Iranian and Afghan speakers of Persian, either in the same form or with slight variations.

3. Riddles

Riddles (*chiston*) were a source of much entertainment in the past. On winter evenings gatherings were organized, and children and young people often told riddles. In the Kulob area in particular, riddles were very popular among women and children during evening gatherings known as "*zochaboni*" (Asrori and Amonov 1980, p. 95). Riddles were also told by adults. The tradition of telling riddles has now all but disappeared; it is practiced only in a few rural areas.

In written sources riddles are also referred to as *muammo* or *lughuz*. Popularly they are called *matali meyoftaî* (Samarqand), *shugi meyoftagî* (Bukhara), *chiston* (Kulob, Hisor), or *chistun* (Gharm, Darvoz). A special form of the riddle is known as *chiston-bulbulon*. This is mainly heard among children. In *chiston-bulbulon* the real number of members of a family must be guessed; for example, the following question may be asked: "In whose house is *chiston-bulbulon* (or *chistobulbulakon*); three fathers, three mothers, eight daughters and nine sons?"[2] One only gets one guess; if it is wrong one has lost.

From the point of view of structure and content, riddles can be divided into two categories: simple and complex. Simple riddles are short and refer to some conspicuous qualities of the thing in question, e.g.,

---

2 i.e, one has to identify the house, three of whose inmates are fathers, etc.

Sanduqcha, puri mekhcha. (Gûgird)
A little box, full of pins. (Matches)

Osmon baroyad yalaqqî
Zamin faroyad taraqqî. (Kaland)
When it goes up to the sky, a flash
When it comes down to earth, a thud. (A pick)

Az sag past, az asp baland. (Zin)
Lower than a dog,[3] taller than a horse. (A saddle)

In complex riddles the object is alluded to by description, simile, or metaphor. As complex riddles consist of verse lines or metrical statements, they tend to offer better descriptions of the thing alluded to.

Gule didam, ki on bekhor boshad	I saw a rose that has no thorns
Na dar dasht-u na dar bozor boshad	It is found neither in the wilderness nor in the market.
Na ûro kas kharad, ne furûshad	One neither buys nor sells it,
Hamesha dar sarash bozor boshad. (Ilm)	There is always a (good) market for it. (Knowledge)

Riddles are now mostly heard in schools, although some people still make up new riddles for the young.

4. Bayt

Two half-lines or two distiches of poetry constitute a *bayt* (Persian: *beyt*). *Bayt*s are much used both in "high" and "popular" literature. A great many popular *bayt*s have been recorded. *Bayt*s are found in most parts of Tajikistan, but they are particularly popular in the areas of Maschoh, Ghonchi, Shahriston, Ayni, and Panjakent. One of the reasons for the popularity of the *bayt* may be the game of *bayt-barak*, traditionally played by two individuals or two groups. One would quote a line (*bayt*) and the other side replies by taking

---

3 When lying on the ground, a saddle is not as tall as a dog.

up the last letter of the *bayt* and begins a line with that letter. The game goes on until the participants get tired of it.

In some regions people recite several *bayt*s together; this is called *bayt-guzaronak* or *bayt-monî*. Mirsaidov (1964, p. 155) gives the following description of the game: "A young man and a group of girls recite some *bayt*s while working. For example:

| *Ey ghunchay gul, ba har sari kor marav* | Rose-bud, don't go along with just any work |
| *Ba guftay odamoni badkor marav* | Don't act upon the words of wicked people |

The girls listen eagerly to the *bayt*, and one of them—a high-spirited girl or the one at whom the poem was aimed—comes up with a 'reply' (*javob*). In this way the game of *bayt-guzaronak* can go on for some time. The young men and women do not just recite the *bayt*s from memory, but also extemporize *bayt*s about each other; this is known as *bayt-monî*.

This explains why new *bayt*s keep being composed. This writer has observed that in the region of Ghonchi, some youngsters regale their friends with half-lines (*mesrâ*) of the *bayt*s they have memorized, or with an altered version of some *bayt*s by a known poet. This helps to keep alive the knowledge of *bayt*s among the people.

In the Ghonchi region *bayt*s may either be sung or recited without accompaniment, or to the music of a tambourine or another instrument. While the singing is going on several *bayt*s may seem to form a song together, but listening closely one finds that each *bayt* is an independent unit with its own subject matter.

The sense which the author of the *bayt* wishes to convey is often made clear through a description set in a simple rural environment.

Most *bayt*s are about young people in love, but such themes as alienation and exile (*gharîbî*), parting and separation, affection and love for one's family, are also found in this genre.

Allusions, metaphors, repetitions, similes and dialogues are frequently found in *bayt*s. Even nowadays *bayt*s are recited as part of popular discourse in some regions; people may bolster their advice by inserting a *bayt* in it.

5. Dobayti

The *dobayti*, which consists of two lines of verse, is found in both "high" and "popular" literature. From the point of view of form and rhyme, the *dobayti* is similar to the quatrain (*robâ'i*): both consist of four hemistichs or *mesrâ*'s. According to R. Musulmoniyon the *dobayti* always has the same meter: the *hazaj-e mosaddas-e maqsur* (or *mahfuz*). This is true of the popular *dobayti* as well, except that those who compose popular *dobayti*s may arbitrarily lengthen or shorten a syllable, thus impairing the meter. The *dobayti* is considered one of the major genres of Persian poetry. Many *dobayti*s belonging to the popular traditions of Tajikistan, Afghanistan and Iran, are popularly attributed to Bâbâ Tâher-e Oryân, an 11th century mystical poet.

So far no separate monograph has been written on popular Tajik *dobayti*s. These poems are generally sung to the accompaniment of musical instruments, but they may also be recited. In Tajik *dobayti*s there is a strong emotional element, as they portray personal sensibilities and feelings. As is the case with *bayt*, love is the basic theme of Tajik *dobayti*s:

Du se rûz ast ki yoram nest paydo	It is two or three days that my beloved is absent.
Magar mohî shuday raftay ba daryo?	Has he become a fish and gone into the sea?
Bisozam changake az obi tillo	I'll make a hook of gold plating (lit., water of gold)
Bigiram yori xud az qa'ri daryo	And catch my beloved from the bottom of the sea.

Other topics, such as separation, alienation (*gharibî*), disappointment, poverty and death are also found in *dobayti*s, but compared to the *robâ'i* the philosophical and psychological contents of *dobayti*s are weak. The question of the formal distinctions between *dobayti* and *robâ'i* in folk literature has not yet been adequately resolved.

6. Robâ'i

Most Tajiks see the *robâ'i* as one of the foremost literary genres. Like the *dobayti* it consists of four *mesrâ*'s, and the two genres are similar in form and rhyme. In both *robâ'i* and *dobayti*, the first, second and fourth *mesrâ'* generally have the same rhyme, while the third *mesrâ'* does not. Occasionally, however, all four *mesrâ*'s rhyme, or the rhyme scheme is a a, b b. The typical meter of both *dobayti* and *robâ'i* is the *hazaj*. An important distinguishing feature is that the *robâ'i* always begins with a long syllable, and the *dobayti* with a short one.[4]

Amonov (1968) uses the term *robâ'i* for both, whereas others differentiate between *robâ'i* and *dobayti*. His main arguments are, (1) that the *dobayti* is much less current among Tajiks than the *robâ'i*, and (2) that the two are formally similar.

In the regions of Kulob and Gharm, and also in other areas, the *robâ'i* is sometimes called *falakî*, *kurtasurkhak*, *kurtasafedak*, *bayt*, or *chor-bayt*; in Bukhara it is known as *mukhammas* (lit. "quintet"). Similar local terms exist in Afghanistan.

The *robâ'i* can be sung with or without accompaniment of a musical instrument, or recited softly as poems. The genre can describe all aspects of life: exile and alienation, death and the impermanence of life, family and pure love, plaints about destitution, lamentations about fate, and similar topics. These have always been the subjects of *robâ'i*, whether composed in the past or today, e.g.,

Dar gushay bom tamburi diltang moyem	A sad-sounding lute in a corner of the roof, that's us
Chun jonvari ma'yusi sari sang moyem	Like a beast on a stone, despairing, that's us
Dege, ki ba jush oyad sarpûsh moyem	The lid on a pan coming to the boil, that's us
Oinay dukhtaroni rûpûsh moyem	Mirrors (reflecting the beauty) of veiled maidens, that's us.

---

4 See the Chapter on *Robâ'i* in Volume II/1 in this Series.

Sitora balandu moh balanday imshab	The stars are high and so is the moon tonight
Ay bakht-i badum, falak ba tangay imshab	My luck is out, fate is not kind tonight
Har shab ba bolini baland khob mekardum	Each night I slept on a well-filled pillow
Bolini mani gharib sangay imshab.	Poor me, my pillow is a stone tonight.
In moha bubin dar osmon kam budas	Look at the moon, there has seldom been such a one in the sky
Sad dardu alam bar sari odam budas	Hundreds of sorrows and pains have fallen on one
Sad dardu alam bar sari shakhse narasid	Hundreds of sorrows and pains have never fallen on anyone (till now)
In murdani odamî ba yak dam budas	This death of human kindness, it happened suddenly.

Typical features of the *robâ'i* include allusions, metaphors, similes, hyperbole, allegory, descriptions of nature, and flattering portraits of some individuals; for the audience these are a source of aesthetic delight. The *robâ'i* also reflects thoughts of a philosophical, spiritual or social nature. In southern Tajikistan many *robâ'is* are composed even today. As a result of recent upheavals and civil wars in Tajikistan, a number of Tajiks have fled to Afghanistan, where new *robâ'is* have been composed with such themes as patriotism, exile and alienation.

7. Songs

Fundamentally, all metrical texts that are sung, with or without music, are to be defined as songs. Typical genres include the following:

Tarona

A type of text is found in popular literature which has the formal characteristics of poetry, and which Amonov (1968, pp. 250–87) has termed *ashûla*. However, this type of metrical text, which usually consists of seven syllables (though sometimes of six or eight), is probably better defined as a *tarona*. Besides Tajikistan, the *tarona* is also found in the popular literatures of Afghanistan and Iran under various names.

The oldest *tarona* is found in the *Târikh-e Tabari*; it is said to have been sung by the children of Balkh when the conquering Muslim armies returned there after failing to penetrate further into Central Asia:

Az Khatlon omaziya	You came from Khatlon,[5]
Ba rû taboh omaziya	Having lost face
Obor boz omaziya	You came back as vagrants,
Khashang nizor omaziya.	You came looking furious.

A famous *tarona* is the following:

Raftem rohi durodur	We have traveled very far
Ovardem niholi gul	And brought back a rose bush.
In gula kujo monem	Where shall we plant this rose?
Dar havlii Mirzogul	In the house of Mirzogul.[6]

Other types of Tajik song have from four to fifty *mesrâ*'s, and sometimes even more. Amonov (1968) divides such songs into four categories according to content: joyful, satirical, historical, and songs for special occasions.

Joyful songs

The cheerful music of this type of song enhances people's joyful mood and may even make them want to dance. Certain aspects of life find reflection in cheerful songs. The structure of these songs varies.

---

5   A region in present-day Tajikistan.
6   I.e. 'thingamajig.'

Satirical songs

These songs depict certain realities of life in a humorous fashion so that they make the audience laugh. In such songs certain real-life occurrences and shortcomings of society are criticized with irony and wit.

Melancholy songs

Some songs reflect and express the pain and sorrow of human existence, allowing one to express feelings of grief.

Historical songs

Such songs describe occurrences and events that have actually taken place. The most famous example of this genre is *Shûrishi Vose'* (The great uprising), which describes the sad events of the uprising of 1885.

Songs for special occasions

Weddings, funerals and traditional festivals such as *Nowruz* and *Id al-Kabir* (the Feast of the Sacrifice) have their own popular songs. At all seasonal festivals, songs, narratives (*naql*), stories (*hikoyat*), witty stories (*latifa*), prayers (*duo*), and other folkloric genres are performed (see Akhmedov 1972). Ahmad (1987) and Qodirov (1998) have discussed the Navrûz (*Nowruz*) customs of various regions. Among various forms of entertainment during the *Nowruz* festival, young girls sing songs such as the following:

Boroni hamal	Rain of Aries
Ba mûyam amal	Do something to my hair
Mûyama daroz kun	Make my hair long
Darozu soz kun	Make it long and beautiful

THE POPULAR LITERATURE OF THE TAJIKS

When the rains failed, the people used to implore Nature for rain. In some regions this custom is called *Sus-khotun* (lit. 'slug'), in others *Ashaglon*; it was done by women. A woman wearing old and torn clothes, holding a clothes-horse (a frame for hanging clothes) in her hand, passed under the drainpipe while the others splashed her with water singing:

Sus-khotun, sus-khotun	Sus-khotun, Sus-khotun!
Alafakon tashna mondand	The grass is thirsty
Kampirakon gusna mondand	The old women are hungry

In the region of Khatlon and the Qarotegin valley the following song is popular:

Ashagloni rostina	Oh true Ashaglon
Osta bujunbon ostina	Master, shake your sleeves
Ghallai savzum qoq shud	My green grain has withered
Yak bor birez boruna.	Just once, pour out rain.

The people used to know many Navrûz songs, some of which have been recorded. The following song, for instance, can still be heard in various regions:

Navrûzu navbahoron	Nowruz and a new spring,
Fasli gul astu lola	The season of roses and tulips
Bulbul ba jûshi mastî	The nightingale in the heat of its passion;
Qumri ba ohu nola.	The turtle dove lamenting and complaining.

Harvesting songs

Formerly, at the time of collecting the harvest, the harvesters and helpers used folk songs to fight fatigue. The following song, *Man dogham* (I am hot), in which a group of people participate, is a good example. One of those present (A) sings one line and the others answer:

A: *He, allo, yore, man dogham, yo dust!*	A: Oh dear me, I am hot, my friend!
Chorus: *He, allo, yore, man dogham, yo dust!*	Chorus: Oh dear me, I am hot, my friend!

A: *Gandumaki khudrûî darav me-kardume, man dogham, yo dust!*
Chorus: *He, Allo, yore, man dogham, yo dust!*
A: *Ba kholi siyoy yor havaz mekar-dame, man dogham, yo dust.*

A: I've been harvesting wild wheat, I am hot, my friend!
Chorus: Oh dear me, I am hot, my friend!
A: I've been yearning for the black mole of my beloved's [cheek], I am hot, my friend!

Wedding songs

The Tajik cannot imagine the wedding ceremonies without songs. Merrymaking, dancing and singing begin as soon as the wedding proceedings start. Zehnieva (1978) gives a detailed account of Tajik wedding customs, and the songs belonging to them. She divides these songs into eight categories: (1) songs of invitation; (2) songs of preparation; (3) songs about separation; (4) festive songs; (5) songs of congratulation; (6) descriptive songs; (7) dancing songs; and (8) satirical songs.

A few examples of songs that are heard during the wedding ceremonies will be given below. When the bride is taken to the groom's house, a short ceremony is held in some regions which is known as *sar-shûyon* "washing the head," and during which songs are sung. These songs often reflect both joy and sadness at separation. For instance, the following song is heard at *sar-shûyon* ceremonies in Darvoz, Hisor, the area around Khatlon, and in the Qarotegin valley:

Zanho: *Gul-arûsak sar bishûy*

Paga ba'day raftanay
Arûs: *Sarma shusta chî kunum?*

Noshustagim behtaray.
Zanho: *Gul-arûsak kurta bipûsh*

Paga ba'day raftanay.
Arûs: *Kurta pûshida chî kunum?*
Nopushtanum behtraray.

Women: Beautiful little bride, wash your head
You are to leave tomorrow
Bride: Why should I wash my head?
It's better left unwashed.
Women: Beautiful little bride, put on your shirt
You are to leave tomorrow
Bride: why should I put on a shirt?
It is better if I don't put it on.

THE POPULAR LITERATURE OF THE TAJIKS

If the ceremony of *sar-shûyon* is performed in the bride's house, the traditional *sar-taroshon* is done at the groom's place. Formerly the groom's head was shaven before the wedding. The actual shaving is no longer done, but the ceremony is still performed in some villages. A few lines of the traditional song, which is sung to a cheerful tune, are given here:

Hama: *Ustoy langi sar-tarosh* / *Sara pokiza tarosh*	All: Lame master head-shaver, / Shave the head cleanly.
Sar-bayt-khon: *Khohari sha, ba to megum*	Soloist: Sister of the king, I tell you,
Dar sari sha rumol andoz.	Throw a handkerchief on the king's head.
Hama: *Ustoy langi sar-tarosh* / *Sara pokiza tarosh*	All: Lame master head-shaver, / Shave the head cleanly.
Sar-bayt-khon: *Dodarî sha, ba to megum*	Soloist: Oh daughter of the king, I tell you,
Dar sari sha toqî andoz	Throw a cap on the king's head
Hama: *Ustoy langi sar-tarosh* / *Sara pokiza tarosh.*	All: Lame master head-shaver, / Shave the head cleanly ...

In this way, the soloist addresses the groom's close relatives and asks them to give him presents.

One of the most interesting of these songs is *Salom-noma*, which is sung when the bride is sent to the groom's house, and when she enters it. This song is known in Bukhara, Samarqand, Khujand, Hisor, Uroteppa, Konibodom and other Tajiki-speaking regions. The performance of the *Salom-noma*, especially in Bukhara and Samarqand, reminds one of the theater. It should be sung by a person of good standing with a pleasant voice. After each verse, which ends with the words *salom megûyem* (we greet), a group of women standing opposite the singer reply with *hazor aleyk* (a thousand greetings in reply). The following example is from a *Salom-noma* text from Bukhara (many variants are known):

Salom-noma-khon:	Soloist:
Niholi qomati domod bahravar gardad	The groom's tree-like stature, May it become fruitful
Duo kunem ki û shokhi pursamar gardad	We pray that he may become a bough laden with fruit
Miyoni dûstu jamoat toji sar gardad	Distinguished among his friends and in the community.
Miyoni khalq sarfarozu mû'tabar gardad	And respected among the people
Miyon-basta ba khizmat salom megûyem!	Ready to serve, we greet him.
Gurûhi Zanho:	Women's group:
Hazor aleyk!	A thousand greetings in return.

Generally speaking, wedding songs can reflect joy, sorrow, sympathy, true love and similar aspects of the human condition.

Dirges (*marsia*)

After the death of a close friend or relative, the tradition of wailing and lamenting while describing the virtues of the deceased, is still alive among the Tajiks. The performance of dirges varies from area to area.

Dirges or odes of lamentation, whether in popular or in written literature, are generally regarded as belonging to a single genre, but each has its own characteristics. As to popular mourning songs, Muhammad Narshakhi's *Ta'rîkhi Bukhoro* (History of Bukhara) shows that as late as the tenth century, the people of Bukhara chanted lamentations on the occasion of the "burial" of the mythical hero Siyâvosh: "The people of Bukhara have remarkable songs about the death of Siyâvosh."

On the day of a death, in most Tajiki-speaking areas men and women separately lament and describe the good qualities of the deceased in a loud voice. If the deceased was young, the women's mourning may continue intermittently for up to a year after the burial. Persons who have a reputation for singing *marsia* are called *gûyanda* in some regions. In the north of Tajikistan, and among the

THE POPULAR LITERATURE OF THE TAJIKS

Tajiks of Uzbekistan, one of the women functions as *gûyanda* and loudly sings songs of mourning about the deceased, and after each *mesrâ'* or couplet the other women respond by yelling "*iiiiii.*" In the south there are also *gûyandas*, but the women do not yell.

In songs of mourning, the virtues of the deceased are usually described by the speakers. For example, when the deceased is an old man, his sons, daughters, wife, sisters, brothers and other relatives will each extemporize a song of mourning by recalling the qualities of the deceased in their own way. The following example is a couplet of the famous dirge called *Abdulmajidjonam, Balam* (My dear Abdulmajid, my child):

Az firoqat sûkhtam, ey nuri chashmonam, balam	I suffer burning, being separated from you, o light of my eyes, my child
Soya budî bar saram, sarvi khiromonam, balam	You were a shadow on my head, my cypress of elegant movement, my child
Chok-chok ast, in girebon to ba domonam, balam	My clothes are torn from the collar to the hem, my child
Nozaninam, qobilam, Adbulmajidjonam, balam.	My precious, well-mannered one, My dear Abdulmajid, my child.

As far as structure is concerned, the Tajik *marsia* may either conform to the rules of classical poetry (*she'r*), or transcend those boundaries. The entire text of *Abdulmajidjonam, Balam* appears to be metrical in the classical fashion. However, in most cases the people extemporize *marsias* about the qualities of the dead person, as was the custom of their ancestors, and some *mesrâ*'s are too long or too short, and some couplets have rhyme while others do not.

Improvisations (*badeha*)

This type of poetry is essentially sung by two people. The main theme of Tajik improvisations is love. In some ways the *badeha*, which is always sung by a man and a woman, is like a theatrical performance. Formerly, when women were not allowed to perform together with men, the woman's role was played by a man in women's clothes. The following is an example of such an exchange of improvised couplets, known as *Bobopirak* (from Nurjonov 1985). This *badeha* and some others have now become part of the repertoire of professional singers.

Bobopirak:
Holo ki nashistam dar boghi arab

Bolo ki nigar jam' shudan kulli ajab

Az mo tama'e zi lutfi khud nomi kun

Yak meva zi bogh bide, yak busa zi lab

Bobopirak (male partner):
Now I am sitting in the Arab garden

Looking upward one sees all miracles gathering

Please be kind and fulfill a wish of mine

Give me fruit from the garden, and a kiss from your lips!

Zan:
Ey dilbari dildor, salomoleykum
Ey munisi ghamkhor salomoleykum
Man dar talabi tasbehamu tu omadî
Tasbehro ba mo bide salomoleykum

Woman:
Oh lovely charmer, I greet you
Oh comforting friend, I greet you
I was looking for my rosary when you appeared
Give me your rosary, I greet you!

Bobopirak:
Ey dukhtari durdona aleykat vasalom
Ey oshiqi parvona aleykat vasalom
Man tasbehi khudro ba shumo bakhshidum
Yak busa ba mo bide aleykat vasalom.

Bobopirak:
Oh pearl-like maiden, I greet you

Oh lover like a butterfly, I greet you

I'll give you my rosary

Give me a kiss, I greet you.

8. Prose stories

Afsona

The question of the definition of oral prose genres is fraught with difficulty. On the one hand, the people themselves use a number of different terms for certain genres, or use one term for a number of different genres. On the other hand, no scholarly publications have so far been published on the subject of oral prose genres as a whole. The problem lies in the fact that all relevant terms are used more or less synonymously both by academics and by the people. Both in oral and written literature, various terms are used for what is here called *afsona*: e.g., *afsona*, *qissa*, *doston*, *rivoyat*, *sarguzasht* and *naql*. Still, the term *afsona* is most widely used for all the types of tales in most Tajiki-speaking areas, and is probably the most appropriate term.

On the basis of specialist works on the subject, one can divide Tajiki *afsona*s into the following categories: (1) tales about magic; (2) tales about animals; (3) tales about the realities of life; and (4) tales about love.

Tales about magic

As the name indicates, these tales have to do with sorcery and magic, i.e., problems described in the tale will be solved by means of magic and sorcery. These tales take one into a colorful, imaginary world and confront one with various fantastic realities, creatures and events, which are not found in the same way in other categories of *afsona*. In these tales the hero has to face difficult obstacles in order to achieve his goal, and he eventually overcomes these with the help of magic, witchcraft, and similar activities. Outstanding examples are the "mirror showing the world," "the speaking nightingale," and "the winged horse."

Tales that were studied during the last decades of the twentieth century may contain Russian expressions, or mention recently founded cities, or make other references to modern times. Moreover, a narrator may interweave a number of motifs from various tales into one *afsona*, or introduce a new topic into an existing tale. Nevertheless, their essential connection with sorcery is very strong.

The range of contents of tales connected with sorcery is wide and complex: they can assimilate a broad variety of topics. In the tale *Qilichpahlavon* (The Hero with the Sword), the hero attains his goal by burning the hair, wings, feathers, facial hair, or wool, of various creatures such as mice, ants and demons. In another tale, *Ahmad Davlat*, a faithful dog and cat obtain a magical knife, which was purloined by a treacherous, ignorant woman, and return it to its owner. The famous tale *Govi Zard* (The Yellow Cow), which describes how a stepmother torments her stepdaughter, is still popular. Magic plays a crucial role in all these tales.

Fables (tales about animals)

It is interesting to note that one often hears variants of such tales that have been influenced by such classical works as *Kalile o Demne*, the *Sendbâd-nâme*, and the *Thousand and One Nights* (cf. *Kullioti Folklori Tojik* I).

Tales about the realities of life

The characteristic feature of such tales is that they are concerned with the individual's private and social life. Such tales may be realistic (i.e., about actual events), or satirical.

"Realistic" tales often so closely reflect scenes from real life that one could easily forget that they are tales. Some such tales are well known throughout the Tajiki-speaking lands; others reflect the special conditions of certain regions.

As to "satirical" tales, these are generally about simple, deceived and misguided people.

Tales about love

In such tales the entire plot centers around the romantic love between two people. Love also plays a role in other tales, of course, but not as the central theme. The hero of such a tale has but one goal: to reach his beloved. These tales can also be divided into two categories: 1) the protagonists do not achieve their goal and their unhappy love causes them to depart from the world, i.e., the tale ends in tragedy; 2) the lovers reach their goal, and true love triumphs. Tales of love have their roots in a long and varied tradition. The people have known and loved such stories as *Leylâ and Majnun*, *Farhâd and Shirin*, *Bizhan and Manizhe*, *Vâmeq and Adhrâ*, *Yusof and Zoleykhâ*, and *Tâher and Zahrâ* for many centuries.

Edifying religious stories (*qissa*)

The terms *afsona*, *qissa*, *hikoyat*, and *rivoyat* are often used almost as synonyms. The most obvious characteristic of the *qissa* is that it contains edifying thoughts and reflections, or religious wisdom. The essential aim of the *qissa* is to guide society on the road to faith and consciousness, justice and true humanity, by means of religion.

The *qissa* does not have the same structure as the *afsona*; hardly any *qissa* begins with *bud*, *nabud* (there was, there was not). If a *qissa* does begin in this way, this is due to the influence of the *afsona*. Unlike the *afsona*, the *qissa* is not primarily a means of entertainment, but a vehicle for imparting moral advice.

The people have devout feelings about the *qissa*. Although, as in the *afsona*, events in a *qissa* may be described with a great deal of exaggeration, and indeed contain inventions no one could believe in, the people have a special respect for the *qissa* and perceive it as part of the religious tradition. Although they may not believe in some of the embellishments, they do accept that the essential events and miraculous deeds of the protagonists are true. This is because a majority of *qissa*s are about the Prophets of old, the Qor'an, Islam, traditions about the Prophet Mohammad, and other religious topics.

While *afsona*s are told by young and old, literate and illiterate, men and women, *qissa*s are mostly transmitted with faith and respect by people who have a certain standing and knowledge, and who are mostly literate. "Oral" transmitters tend to be professional storytellers or experienced older men and women.

Although saints, prophets, and other prominent religious figures do not usually play a major role in the *afsona*, the influence of the *qissa* on that genre is quite obvious; conversely, there are narrators of *afsona* who begin their performance with the religious formula *besme'llâh al-rahmân al-rahim*. Moreover, some figures, like Khizr, can be found coming to the hero's aid in either *qissa* or *afsona*.

The main heroes and protagonists of the oral *qissa* are: prophets, saints and figures directly associated with the Islamic faith, such as the Prophet Mohammad, Ali, Fâteme, and the Imams Hasan and Hoseyn. Other protagonists, such as Adam and Eve, Khizr, David, Solomon, Abraham, Moses, Jesus, Gabriel, Ezrâ'il, angels, and similar figures are also found there (see Rahmoni 1998).

Although most modern *qissa*s now exist in written form, changes still occur: they may become longer or shorter, and as a result new variants come into existence.

Rivoyat

The *rivoyat* is an essentially factual genre, based on events involving historical personages and the names of existing places. We can therefore use the term *rivoyat* for the type of tale that is based on historical reality. Obidov (1986) was the first to discuss the *rivoyat* as a separate folk genre.

Naql

A type of tale exists in folk literature which is similar to reminiscences and real life histories. Obidov (1984) argues that it is appropriate to define as *naql* those reminiscences, memoirs and other forms of oral literature that have greater literary value than ordinary stories. It is clear that this is a very well known genre among the people. Yarnevskiï (1969) has brought together all studies on the subject from the 1930s onwards, and shown on the basis of a wealth of material that it is correct to call such texts "oral stories." The *naql* resembles the ordinary story (*hikoya*) in many ways, but unlike the latter it deals with certain motifs drawn from daily life, which delight the audience.

Fabulous tales

This genre of oral prose has not only been insufficiently studied, but it has hardly been collected, let alone published. The term "fabulous tales" (*hikoyathoi asotirî*) was introduced by the present writer (Rahmoni 1994, p. 122) and was defined as follows: "This genre consists of tales whose protagonists are supernatural, they are short in form and fantastic in content, and are told by the people, who-believe in them even today when they are in difficulties, and in whose truth they have faith." These are popularly known under such titles as "stories" (*naql*), "fairy stories" (*naqli parî*), "tales about Khizr," "stories about Jinns," and the like. In our view the term "fabulous tale" is more suitable for this genre.

These are short, popular stories that describe both real events in people's lives and those produced by people's imagination, including tales about Khizr, fairies, disasters, jinn, ghosts, and other fantastic creatures. It is a characteristic feature of the "fabulous tales" that they portray events and motifs taken from daily life. Those who tell such stories aim at making the audience believe them.

Latifa

The *latifa* is very popular among Tajiks. Dehoti (1938) published a collection of Tajiki *latifa*s, and Mahdiev (1977) offers a detailed discussion of its origin and development, special characteristics, contents, structure, etc. Many *latifa*s have been published in periodicals and folklore collections, and even independently. A representative collection can be found also in Amonov (1994). A typical *latifa* is the following:

One day a young man asked a clever notable ('Efendi'): "My friend what should one do at times of hardship?" The Efendi answered: "It is simple: when you're young, steal, swindle and cheat; when you're old, become a Mullah or a Shaikh."

In the *latifa*, the events of everyday life are alluded to in a pithy and humorous way. The *latifa* is by definition short. There are always few characters, normally two but sometimes more. All subjects are treated by means of humorous dialogue. Some *latifa*s contain biting social satire; others treat some aspect of daily life with gentle humor and sparkling wit. The *latifa* always criticizes some fault, act of negligence, stupidity, or other human failings by means of simile, mockery, wordplay, or riddles.

Some Tajik *latifa*s make fun of simple people from certain areas. Thus, there are popular *latifa*s about "Shirinis" (Bukharans) and "Rumanis" (Khujandis).

In some respects the *latifa* is similar to the *afsona*, which is typically longer. Some people have made an *afsona* on the basis of several *latifa*s, and one *afsona* may seem to be composed of several *latifa*s.

The heroic epic

The heroic epics of the Tajiks have their origin in ancient times; the *Khwadây-nâmag* and the *Shahname* are the best examples of such ancient sources. *Afsona*s about Rostam are still told today. Professional public performances of episodes from the *Shahname* (somewhat like the *naqqâlî* tradition in Iran; see the chapter on *Naqqâlî*) used to be known in Tajikistan, but these no longer exist. In some villages, however, readings and retellings from epic texts like the *Shahname* and *Amîr Hamze*, the Uzbeg epics *Bobo Ravshan* and *Mashrab*, and Rumi's *Mathnavi-ye Ma'navi*, are held at a series of gatherings intended to console and divert the bereaved after a death.

Tajik researchers have recorded cycles from famous storytellers, of tales about Gurughlî (Gurgulî, Gurzod) and his family. They studied this material as a "heroic epic." *Gurughlî* is especially popular among Turkic-speaking peoples. While they recite *Gurughlî* as poetry or prose, accompanied by the *târ* (or the *târ* and the *doira*), the Tajiki text is always sung as poetry with music of the string-instrument known as *dambura*.

Heroism, courage and patriotism are key themes in the epic. The *Gurughlî* tradition has always been stronger in the south of Tajikistan (Qulob and Gharm), and is still alive there. Instead of *doston*, the singers usually call it *band* (stanza) and sometimes *shokha* (branch).

The singers of *Gurughlî* texts are known as *gurughlî-guy, gurughlî-saro*, or *guyanda*. Formerly the *gurughlî-saro* traveled from community to community accompanied by his pupils. He performed at community gatherings, feasts, weddings, and receptions. Although the higher social classes also enjoyed the skills of the *gurughlî-saro*, the audiences mainly consisted of small farmers and workers, since their hopes and aspirations were reflected in this work. The following is a typical stanza, about the birth and childhood of Gurughlî (from Braginskiï 1987, p. 51):

Gurughlî bubala shudu kalon	Gurughlî grew great and big
Ajab khushru pahlavon...	A wonderfully handsome hero...
Sahar khest Gurughlî vaqti azon	Gurughlî arose in the morning at the time of the call to prayer
Khabar nadoshtand Ahmad-u Yusufkhon	Ahmad and Yusufkhon did not know this.

9. Folk drama

Nurjonov (1985) has published 102 texts of folk dramas, recorded in many different places. He divides these texts into four categories: (1) plays; (2) puppet shows; (3) musical folk plays; (4) satirical plays.

10. Local poets

In the first half of the twentieth century there were Tajiks who, though illiterate, composed poetry orally. Clearly such people also existed in earlier times, but no one paid attention to their works.

Since the introduction of Folklore Studies the songs of such people have been recorded and studied. These popular poets included Karim Devona, Boboyunus Khudoidodzoda, Yusuf Bafo, Saidalî Valizoda, Homid Said, Hikmat Rizo, Said Kholzoda, and Qurbon Jalîl. In the Soviet period some of these men learned to read and write, and their poems were committed to writing.

The works of such poets can be divided into two categories: (1) folk texts that they have memorized and perform or interpret; (2) their personal creations.

11. Conclusion

It has not been possible in this chapter to analyze all existing genres in detail, so that the discussion has remained largely at the descriptive level. From this very brief account it can be seen that some genres of Tajik folklore have been studied by folklorists, while others have not even been seriously collected.

At the time of writing, works of popular literature are still being created or performed among the Tajiks but, with the spread of modern media, they are in the process of being forgotten. In any case, it will be possible for a few more years to record those works which the older generation still remembers, and thus to salvage at least part of the corpus of folklore from oblivion.

CHAPTER 13

ORAL AND POPULAR LITERATURE IN DARI PERSIAN OF AFGHANISTAN

Margaret A. Mills

1. Literacy and orality in Afghanistan

Until the initial spread of general public education starting in the mid-twentieth century, Afghan society was overwhelmingly non-literate, and it remains at the most perhaps twenty-five per cent functionally literate at time of writing (2004). This is a rough guess shared by various commentators, with no statistics available. The effect of wartime displacement on schooling was uneven: increased access for some refugees, especially rural emigrés who relocated in urban areas in Iran, Pakistan, and Afghanistan itself, but reduced or very limited access for many refugees in camps. School spaces for boys, though limited enough, vastly outnumbered those for girls. Post-secondary education was largely unavailable to refugees in Iran or Pakistan. Inside Afghanistan, there was systematic destruction of government schools outside those urban areas controlled by the Marxist government during the anti-Soviet period of warfare (1979–89). Yet a depletion of the male population formerly dominant in the teachers' colleges in the war years (due to draft vulnerability and/or service with the *mojâhedin* resistance), meant that more than half of those enrolled in teachers' colleges in the mid- to late 1980s were women, producing a large cadre of trained urban female teachers. A subset of male refugees in Pakistan had access to charity *madrese* education as part of the Islamic resistance effort. The closing of urban girls' schools during the Taliban period (1996–2001) is notorious, while the actual extent and effect of apparently widespread clandestine home-schooling of girls in urban areas is yet to be assessed. As recently as 1962, D. N. Wilber (1962, p. 84) cited estimates of six per cent overall literacy for men of all ethnic groups and two per cent for women. The figure of fifteen per cent literacy, which Elton Daniel (2001, p. 14) cites for Iran in 1956, was probably comparable to the overall literacy figure for Afghanistan in the mid-1970s, prior to the war years. Oral communications thus remain at the heart of the culture. Because women have had even less access to reading and writing than men, the percentage of literacy for women outside of cities is still in the single digits, with even primary schools often unavailable to them. There is thus a gendered aspect to the oral/literate distribution of expressive forms. Yet oral traditions and oral communication channels overlap and share content with traditional and post-traditional written media, through reading aloud at home and in public, and now, also, through post-literate mass media, especially radio and, to a lesser extent, television. It should also be mentioned that in terms of language, "Dari" designates standard and literary Persian throughout Afghanistan, while oral communication proceeds through at least ten other distinct languages as well as the many local dialects of Dari (Kâboli, Hazâragi, Tâjiki in several local forms, Herâti, Aymaq dialects, etc.). While the Afghan Persian dialects are generally mutually comprehensible, dialect features can act as markers for claims to cultural ownership of oral literary items (e.g. dialect words in a proverb or quatrain) and claiming of subgenres by region and/or ethnic subgroup, as in, for instance, the seven or more dialect- or region-specific terms for the shared genre of the lyric quatrain (*dobeyti/chahârbeyti*), and diverse terms for fictional folktale (*afsâne, owsâne, naql*, etc. See Rahmoni 2001). Recent folklorists and ethnomusicologists of Afghanistan (Rahmoni 1999; Sakata 2002, p. 58) have noted the phenomenon of distinctive region- or dialect-specific names for shared oral genres.

ORAL AND POPULAR LITERATURE IN DARI PERSIAN

2. Chapbooks and oral storytelling

The Afghan popular imagination was engaged well into the mid-twentieth century by both chapbook and oral narrative forms, such that knowledge of written literature, whether acquired by reading or orally, was admired. Though Afghan scholars of the 1970s and 1980s gave little analytic attention to the relationships of oral and written texts, written texts supported oral tradition. Indeed a substantial number of chapbook titles, even more than were immediately available for sale, found their way into oral performance. In this writer's experience in Herat in the mid-1970s, the following tales were identified by tellers as "having a book" (existing in written form), for the most part verifiably so in that copies of the works could be found for sale or in private collections. Furthermore, episodes from them were recorded in oral performance in Herat or Kabul (or in the case of one small body of *Shahname* stories, in Kholm/Tashqurghan). They are listed in the order first encountered in the field in 1974–76, some sources being cited or performed by more than one narrator: *Shâhzâde Ebrâhim*; *Shâhzâde Badi'-al-Molk*; *Habda Ghazâ*; short tales from the *Mathnavi* of Jalâl-al-Din Rumi and also from Nur-al-Din Abd-al-Rahmân Jâmi; episodes from the *Abu Moslem-nâme*; *Heydar Beg*; *Tavârikh-e Shâh Abbâs*; certain episodes of the Rostam cycle of the *Shahname* (as well as some Rostam stories not found in literary epics); *Salim-e Javâheri*; *Anvâr-e Soheyli*; *Najmâ-ye Shirâzi*; *Shâhzâde Bahrâm*; *Shâhzâde Sherbiya*; *Varghe o Golshâh*; *Amir Arsalân*; *Gol o Senoubar* (a title actually applied to a number of romantic folktales but also existing as a chapbook); *Siyâhmuy o Jalâli* (an oral romance based on an historical love affair of the mid-twentieth century that received brief written treatment by Mâyel Harawi); *Alf leyle fârsi*; *Hoseynâ*; *Falak Nâz*; *Amir Hamza*; *Mohammad Hanifa*; *Sabz pari*; *Tuti-nâme*; *Ketâb-e bâr-e dâneshi*; *Qesse-ye sang-tarâsh*, attributed to Âref; *Loqmân-e Hakim*; *Ketâb-e panj ganj*; *Leyli o Majnun*; *Momtâz*. More problematical were some anecdotes about Sa'di, deemed literary by the tellers, and *Ketâb-e Shâh Abbâs* (this from an entirely illiterate teller who may have been trying to impress his audience by claiming literary knowledge).

ORAL LITERATURE OF IRANIAN LANGUAGES

While there does not seem to have been any significant popular lithographic production in Afghanistan proper, a systematic history of publishing in Afghanistan remains to be written. Popular Persian literacy in Afghanistan was supported by book and chapbook production in Iran and the Subcontinent, however. In the mid-1970s, during this author's first research stay in Afghanistan, popular lithograph publications available for sale included those produced in Iran, of the sort detailed by Marzolph (1994), with some scattered volumes still for sale that dated back to the late nineteenth and early twentieth centuries, plus recent Tehran publications, together with publications from Peshawar, Lahore, and in one or two cases, older items from Delhi, all intended for a popular Persian-reading audience. These could be found in Afghan bazaar bookshops and also in private scholars' hands. Most of the chapbooks and larger lithographed volumes for entertainment reading were prose romances. Among those for sale in the mid-1970s were *Dâstân-e Amir Hamza, Amir Arsalân, Shâhzâde Momtâz, Habda Ghazawât, Jang-nâme-ye Bibi Deyghun, Falak Nâz, Shâhzâde Ebrâhim*, along with some literary story collections such as the mid-nineteenth century *Alf leyle fârsi*, or Vâ'ez Kâshefi's *Anvâr-e Soheyli*. More recent publications tended to be small format chapbooks of single romances (*Najmâ-ye shirâzi, Heydar Beg*), with the odd volume of Mollâ Nasreddin humorous stories thrown in. Dream-interpretation manuals also had a small but steady presence in the bazaar booksellers' inventories. One such was still for sale on a sidewalk bookseller's mat in Herat in 1995, in this author's observation, whereas the chapbook literature had all but disappeared at that point. Books and booksellers took a beating at times during the war years. Books looted from shops and private libraries, and anything else available, reportedly were sold for fuel in Kabul in the early 1990s, during the worst years of the civil war and a three-year drought. The popular literature available in Herat bookshops by the mid-1990s included Iranian authors and translations of European fiction.

ORAL AND POPULAR LITERATURE IN DARI PERSIAN

3. Research on oral culture in Afghanistan

Notwithstanding the apparent decline in popularity or availability of traditional chapbook literature, however, the 1980s were the high point of oral literature and culture research publication in Afghanistan. Afghan scholars produced a number of local or regional ethnographies containing examples of transcribed or described oral texts of various genres, as well as single-genre text anthologies, plus a few analytic presentations of certain genres (proverbs, riddles). Discussions in publications containing texts were and are overwhelmingly descriptive, rather than analytic, in nature. There was, however, an ongoing published discussion of the goals and methods of documenting oral literature as well as other popular cultural forms. These theoretical discussions, mostly programmatic and brief, are to be found in a few book-length genre studies, in the introductions to ethnographies and anthologies, and in the journal *Folklor,* which was later renamed first *Farhang-e khalq,* then *Farhang-e mardom* (both titles translate as 'People's culture'), according to the dominant Marxist party, Khalq or Parcham, respectively. Prior to the 1978 [Saur] revolution, the literary journal *Adab* also published occasional descriptive articles and calls for folk literature research in the 1960s and 1970s. Virtually all folklore and popular culture studies from the early 1960s through the 1980s were central government publications, produced in Kabul and sponsored first by the Ministry of Information and Culture, then in the Marxist period, by the Cultural Society of Kabul University and/or various ministries.

The Marxist government thus sponsored the accelerated production and publication of regional and local ethnographies and oral literature studies, all dedicated to the celebration, if not the creation, of Afghan national cultural identity through the recognition of its component local traditions. Judging by the presence or absence of analytic apparatuses, some of these books were obviously geared by their authors to a general-reader audience, and some to a more scholarly readership. Even when the subject matter is in another of Afghanistan's languages, the publications are in the two "national" languages, Dari or Pashto, e.g a study of Uzbeki proverbs published in Pashto (Othmân 1980), or a publication in Dari on Nuristani oral literature that begins with a short overview of oral literature genres in Afghanistan, then offers a sampling of Nuristani narratives in Arabic and Latin transcription with Dari translations (Jina 1991). The Marxist period also saw the first book-length publications by women (including Jina) on popular literature, though it is not clear when or whether women were able to do independent field research to procure their data. The logistics or circumstances of particular collecting projects are almost never discussed in the introduction or the analysis in any of the books this author was able to examine. One exception is the small folktale collection by Ahmad Ziyâ Siyâmak, *Morgh-e tokhm-e talâ'i* (The Bird with the Golden Egg). Siyâmak explains that he learned the thirty stories in the book from a single elderly man, an esteemed storyteller who claimed a repertoire of three hundred tales, during his own childhood in his home village in Herat Province. Another such small anthology, also published courtesy of *Farhang-e mardom* and very interesting for its attempt to preserve the Qandahar Persian dialect speech style of the storyteller, is Abd-al-Hoseyn Towfiq's *Owsâna si sâna* (The Tale of the Thirty Kinds), a collection of seventeen tales written down from Towfiq's memory of his own grandmother's performances of tales from her extensive repertoire.

Abdul Ali Ahrary, a colleague from Herat who was active in the resistance to Soviet occupation in the 1980s, opined that most of the research for these publications would have been done prior to the 1978 revolution, and that the authors, as intelligentsia, later became internal refugees in Kabul, where their earlier collected materials were published under government sponsorship (personal communication, 1996). The Tajik folklorist, Ravshan Rahmoni, however, was himself active in recording and analyzing oral texts in 1981–84, while performing an alternative service as a translator for Soviet advisors at Kabul University and elsewhere, and Asadollâh Sho'ur continued collecting activities even in the early 1980s while imprisoned in Kabul (Rahmoni, personal communication, 2004).

While the publication of Afghan oral literature dates to the 1920s (see below), the understood history and rationale for the vigorous publication movement of the 1980s in particular are indicated in the publishers' prefaces and the introductions by the author-compilers of these volumes. Almost formulaically, many prefaces to the works in Dari first invoke giants of classical Persian literature (especially Rudaki and Ferdowsi, then later authors) as the Afghan cultural legacy, quoting classical poets' discussion or use of the genre in question (proverbs, riddles, epic and romance) to demonstrate the antiquity and literary value of the form. The richness of Afghan culture down to the present is noted, and the materials in question are cited as valuable repositories of social-historical, psychological and ethnological insights on Afghan popular ideas and values, generally those supporting mutual responsibility and social solidarity. Thus the twin analytical modes of folklore study worldwide, aesthetic (literary) and sociological (ethnological/psychological), are duly invoked in the most general way, with reference to Afghan cultural history as a worthy and significant component of world culture, while the contentious and/or potentially antisocial or reactionary contents or effects of traditional cultural productions are not discussed. Little is offered in the way of close textual analysis. As in Soviet Central Asia, the ideological basis and rhetorical goal of the Marxist government's support for cultural organizations and publications were to create non-divisive, nontoxic forms of secular cultural nationalism, recognizing to a limited extent ethnic diversity and the religious or spiritual dimensions of popular culture through the ethnographic documentation of local ceremonies and rituals. This ignored the violent nationalist and internationalist opposition mounted by the Islamist *mojâhedin*, which had its own traditions, still mostly unstudied, in forms such as songs, poems, oral history and legends of encounters with the enemy; and martyrology narratives (Edwards 1996, 2002).

While by far the most extensive documentation of oral and popular literature attributable to Afghan sources is from the 1980s, a decade of officially sponsored publishing, the Marxist regime's support for popular culture publication continued and accelerated a trend of the 1970s. The following discussion is based unfortunately not on a complete sample of all publications, but only on impressions formed from the selection of materials accessible to the author, purchased in Afghanistan in 1974–76 and in Peshawar in 1994–95, and on extremely informative conversations with Tajik scholar, Ravshan Rahmoni, since 1999. It briefly sketches the history of Afghan scholarly attention to oral and popular literature and culture, before turning to a more detailed discussion of the contents of the literature as an imperfect reflection of the ambient oral culture of the mid- to late twentieth century (incomplete at base because research itself was hardly evenly distributed across genres and regions). The future of oral and popular culture and literature in the 21st century in Afghanistan is very unclear, dependent on future population displacement and repatriation, security and economic issues, as well as effects of planned and unplanned globalization both economic and ideological/informational, the development or non-development of popular and independent media as well as government media, education reform, intermittently but recurrently violent ethnic and regional tensions within the country, and other factors.

Asadollâh Sho'ur (1986), in his monograph on riddles, offers an introduction following the general format described above, beginning with the invocation of classical literary precedents establishing the antiquity of the genre. But beyond that, he goes on to provide a succinct history of Afghan scholarly interest in folklore. He traces the beginning of modern intellectual interest in the oral literature of Afghanistan back about 100 years, while the first publications of example texts date from the second decade of the 20th century, in the famous bi-monthly *Serâj al-akhbâr* (1910–19), with which the journalist Mahmud Tarzi, the premier Afghan modernist/nationalist of the period and father-in-law to the modernizing King Amânollâh, introduced modern journalism to Afghanistan. Sho'ur attributes the first call for scholarly research on folk and popular literature to the mid-1930s, when the term *mardom-shenâsi* (anthropology) first appeared in Dari, specifically credited to Sarwar Guyâ, who published his *Râhnâme-ye folklor* (Guide to Folklore), with the sponsorship of the Literary Society (*Anjoman-e Adab*) and *Paśto Tolǝna* (Pashto Academy) in Kabul in 1939.

By the late 1960s, the government's pictorial cultural journal *Lmar* (Sun) was publishing short descriptive articles illustrated

ORAL AND POPULAR LITERATURE IN DARI PERSIAN

with photos and drawings, and reports on folk literature and customs from various regions of Afghanistan as part of its mission to document and display for general readers, primarily Afghan, the country's cultural activities, portrayed as a worthy component of world cultural property alongside the folk culture being showcased by other nation states. Presentations described forms such as dance and music that, while greatly enjoyed by Afghans, were and are viewed as religiously suspect and not very respectable.

By the late 1960s and early '70s, the most active and intellectually ambitious folklore scholars in Afghanistan included Sho'ur himself; Abdul-Qayyum Qawim; Hafizullah Baghban (Hâfezollâh Bâghbân) and Enâyatollâh Shahrâni. Shahrâni was at work on Badakhshâni texts and lexicography from the 1960s and subsequently expanded his interests to the nationwide collection of proverbs, a book-length collection appearing in 1975 as *Amthâl o hekam* (Proverbs and Proverbial Sayings), almost 2500 proverbs, edited into standard Dari language and thus sacrificing potential information on dialect and local idiomatic expressions of interest. It was published in Kabul as a commemorative volume on the thousandth anniversary of the death of the poet Daqiqi. Shahrâni's choice of presentation in standard written language rather than local dialects, which he in some ways regretted (personal communication 1999), nonetheless served the purpose of making a wide variety of texts accessible to general readers, an appropriate goal of the cultural nationalism so prominent in folklorists' efforts to establish the value of the popular materials they studied. In his introduction to the 1975 book Shahrâni gives a brief history of prior proverb studies in Dari and Pashto, dating back to about 1925, by five other scholars. He continued his collecting activities and, in 1999 as an exile in Bloomington, Indiana, published *Zarbolmathalhâ-ye Dari-ye Afghânestân* (Dari Proverbs of Afghanistan) with a much expanded text collection. By 1995, Shahrâni estimated that he had amassed a collection of about 40,000 proverbs (personal communication). His own work has inspired some spirited recent debate (Barzin Mehr 2002).

Hafizullah Baghban began his folklore collecting activities, and published journal articles describing the folklore of his native

Herat province, while an education student in the late 1960s and early 1970s at Kabul University, and he later earned a doctorate in folklore from Indiana University with a theoretically ambitious, groundbreaking, and to-date unequaled dissertation on Herat's traditional folk theater (Baghban 1977). The dissertation includes English translations of texts and content analyses for a number of audio recordings of plays that Baghban made in the early 1970s in actual village performances at wedding and circumcision parties by itinerant comedy theater troupes based in and around Herat. The dissertation also includes a detailed study of the social composition and social interaction in performance of these professional troupes. Unfortunately, Baghban, trained in the premier graduate folklore program in the United States and teaching there in 1978 at the time of the Marxist coup, was not able to publish extensively or conduct further research on Afghan subjects. The published dissertation includes English translations of twenty entire plays as performed in Dari, but was subject to the American publishers' lack of interest in publishing extensive original-language oral texts.

Equally theoretically ambitious, but without the single-case focus that grounds and enriches Baghban's work, is Sho'ur's *Mofâheme-ye shafâhi va seyr-e târikhi-e ân dar Afghânestân* (Oral Communication and its Historical Developments in Afghanistan). He begins with a theoretical overview of European communications theory to establish the significance of the study of Afghan oral communications, follows with some essays on the history of newspaper publication as mass communication, and proceeds in the part of the book dedicated to oral communications to a series of case studies, including summary essays on song among different language groups (Hazâra, Balochi, Uzbek), as well as a detailed comparison of the historical changes in a Pashto song recorded by Darmesteter (1890) in the late nineteenth century and attested much later as recorded by and performed on Kabul Radio, in the 1980s. Sho'ur had previously published his major textual study of riddles (1986) with more than 600 riddles, distinguished according to variety and place of collection, with dialect features preserved. While Sho'ur's folklore publications are among the minority that endeavor to present dialect texts verbatim, some half dozen pub-

ORAL AND POPULAR LITERATURE IN DARI PERSIAN

lished dialect dictionaries or glossaries that have come to hand, bear witness to scholarly interest in local dialectology during this entire period (Afghâni Navis 1961; Fikrat 1976; Shahristâni 1982; Yamin 1983; Nabizâda Kâkar 1986; Asir Harawi 1989).

Theoretical inspiration was also derived during the Marxist period from collaboration and communication with Soviet-trained folklore scholars from Tajikistan. Soviet scholarly publication on Afghan oral literature actually began in 1927 in Russian (Andreev 1927),[1] while by the early 1960s studies in Tâjiki also appeared (Asadullaev 1964; Ma'sumi and Khalav 1965). The essay collection of R. Amonov, the dean of Tajik folklore studies, and V. Asrori entitled *Adabiyât-e shefâhi-e mardom-e Tâjik* (Oral Literature of the Tajik People) was edited and translated into Dari by Abd-al-Qayyum Qawim and Mohammad Afzal Banuwal in 1985, and published by the Kabul University Cultural Council. Included are essays entitled "Common Problems for Folklorists," "Movement for the Foundation of a Progressive Philosophy Concerning Folklore Study," and "Schools and Movements in Folklore Studies." The larger, second part of the book is a systematic series of chapters on different genres of Tajik folk expression and customs connected with rites of passage and calendrical rites.

The major Tajik contributor to the development of Afghan folk literature studies since the early 1980s has been Ravshan Rahmoni (Rahmâni, Rakhmonov) who, unlike the above-mentioned Tajik scholars, is still very active in documenting, publishing, and analyzing Persian-language texts from Afghanistan and Tajikistan. While performing alternative international-duty service in Kabul as a translator for Soviet advisors and faculty at Kabul University from 1981 to 1984, he conducted as much primary field recording and related research as time and private resources allowed. In 1984 he published *Nemunehâ-ye folklor-e Dari* (Specimens of Dari Folklore), texts selected from his own collecting activities, in three substantial volumes under the auspices of the Kabul University Cultural Council. Volume I is entitled *Afsânehâ-ye Dari* (Dari

---

1   I am indebted to Dr. Ravshan Rahmoni for discussion of the 1927, 1964 and 1965 references, to which I do not have access.

Folktales) with thirty-seven tales, some from dictation, some from field tape-recording. Vol. II, *Dobeytihâ va robâ'iyât* (Distiches and Quatrains) offers verses in both Perso-Arabic and Cyrillic scripts, and Vol. III, entitled *Sokhan-e bozorgân cheshme-ye aql ast* (The Speech of the Elders is the Wellspring of Wisdom) presents 2455 proverbs, also in both Perso-Arabic and Cyrillic scripts. Each volume includes an introductory essay. Rahmoni's dissertation, published in Russian in 1994, addresses the hitherto unstudied category of named Afghan oral poets and their poetry and performance styles in Dari, profiling several living and recently deceased poets from whom he gathered texts and biographical information in the early 1980s.[2] In 1995, Rahmoni published an expansion of Vol. I of *Nemunehâ-ye Folklor-e Dari,* a much-enlarged collection of ninety folktales transcribed in colloquial speech in Perso-Arabic script, again entitled *Afsânehâ-ye Dari.* The volume includes a substantial introductory essay and brief profiles of the storytellers from whom he recorded the tales in 1984. Rahmoni's work on folktales in particular has addressed the relative lack of attention that Afghan folklorists have so far given to systematic genre categorization of oral narrative, and in this large collection he organizes the texts according to analytic subcategories: magic tales, tales of experience, humorous tales, etc. Narrators of individual tales are identified in an appendix.

Recent Iranian interest in the folklore of greater Persia, both from scholars and the general public, has been of material help to Rahmoni and others (most recently, Sho'ur 2002) in publishing their scholarly work since the financial collapse of Afghan and Tajik cultural institutions resulting from the Afghan wars and the demise of the Soviet Union. Beginning in the early 1990s, Rahmoni has also edited and intermittently published, when financially possible, the bilingual Tâjiki-Dari folklore journal *Mardomgiyâh,* publishing among other topics sample texts in various genres from different locales (transcribed simultaneously in Dari, Tâjiki and sometimes in Latin as well), articles describing local customs, and articles regarding the relation between folk tradition and literary history

---

[2] I am indebted to Rahmoni himself for a summary description of this work.

(Rostam and *Shahname*, etc.) from Tajikistan and Afghanistan. Rahmoni, who was able to produce another issue of his journal in 2002, remains a highly active scholar of Persian-language folklore dedicated to the widest possible comparative scholarship on Persian-speaking Afghanistan and Tajikistan (see, e.g., Rakhmonov and Rakhimov 2006).

4. Collections of folk literature

Besides the theoretical writings and theoretically informed monographs mentioned above, the last decades of the twentieth century saw a number of other studies published, among which the following have reached this author:

Mâyel Harawi's small chapbook presentation of three prose romances, *Siyâhmuy, Litân, Maryam* (1967), named for three romances summarized in it, and noteworthy among other things for its frontispiece photo of the by-then aged romantic heroine, Siyâhmuy from Ghor. Her actual courtship by and marriage to her father's poor, but poetically inspired shepherd, Jalâli, in the first half of the twentieth century formed the stuff of a new romance, replete with lyric *dobeyti*s that became famous in Herat and were widely performed in the 1970s even by those who could not tell the story. The other two stories Harawi summarized in his small chapbook were more obscure by the mid-1970s. This author never heard them mentioned or performed in Herat. Like *Siyâhmuy*, they are briefly summarized by Harawi for the sake of publishing their numerous romantic *beyt*s, as *dobeyti*s (quatrains) are often called in Herat. More than one of the adept narrators that this author recorded in the 1970s, reiterated that people generally preferred to hear the stories with *beyt* (sung poetry) in them, supporting Harawi's focus on the verse in his publication of those three texts.

Mohammad Azam Sistâni's *Sistân, sarzamin-e mâsehâ va hamâsehâ* (Sistan, Land of Sands and Epics; Kabol 1985) includes an extended discussion of the geography of Sistân as represented in the epic stories of Rostam in the *Shahname*, well illustrating the powerful attachment to land and cultural identity sometimes mediated by this literature. Sistâni brought out a second book in 1989, *Mardom-shenâsi-ye Sistân* (Anthropology of Sistan), which includes a general discussion on oral literature, with sections on songs, proverbs, and folktales, with samples in standard Dari.

Asadollâh Sho'ur's *Tarâneha-ye Kuhsâr* (Songs of the Hill Country) is no less theoretically ambitious than his later work, previously mentioned, though at an earlier and different intellectual and ideological stage. It was published in 1974 by the Department of Folklore, Ministry of Information and Culture, in Kabul, which in 1972 had begun publishing the journal *Folklor*, in which Sho'ur and other folklorists also published articles. This book begins with a substantial analytic introduction to *dobeyti*, followed by 2005 quatrain texts, organized alphabetically in order of the *radif*.

Sho'ur's most recent publication, *Tarâneha-ye Gharjestân* (Songs of Gharjistan), dating in its original composition to the late 1980s, is an extensive collection of *dobeyti*s from the Hazâra region, supplemented with various appendices including a glossary, a comparison of variant lines, lists of dates and locales of recording keyed to each numbered quatrain, a list of the reciters, their age, occupation, and residence. The collection concludes with an example of a *marthiya* (elegy), a comic narrative poem about a bride and groom, and a prose folktale. All texts are in Hazâra dialect with standard Dari translations. The book was attractively calligraphed for lithographic reproduction, and has quite a saga of production. The over four hundred collected poems, organized in the book by *radif*, date from 1965 to 1976. According to information supplied by Rahmoni,[3] Sho'ur brought the calligraphed manuscript to Dushanbe during the Gorbachev period and deposited it at the Institute of Oriental Studies for expected publication, which became impossible due to political events. In 1992, the Institute was relocating in the midst of Tajikistan's civil war and many papers, including the manuscript, were discarded. Kamoluddin Aini rescued the manuscript literally from the fire, and word reached Rahmoni that he had it, though he was not willing to show it to others. Rah-

---

3   Personal communication, March 2004.

moni, visiting Columbus, Ohio, in 2000, met with Sho'ur, then a refugee resident in Toronto, Canada, and told him about the reported whereabouts of the manuscript, but Aini was still unwilling to acknowledge possession of the manuscript to Rahmoni, or even to Sho'ur when he arrived in Dushanbe and approached Aini. After some negotiations, assured by Sho'ur that he would be credited for rescuing the work, Aini returned the manuscript to Sho'ur, who was able to publish it under Iranian government sponsorship in 2002.

Mohammad Nâser Nasib, *Zemzemehâ-ye rustâ* (Rural Hummings), begins with a discussion of aspects of stylistics in *dobeyti*, then offers approximately 1600 examples (400 pages), unnumbered and unindexed, but with occasional lexical footnotes.

Nilâb Rahimi, *Sang-gardihâ-ye Panjshir* (Stone-strolling Verses of the Panjshir) offers a short introduction discussing the occasions for performance of Panjshiri *dobeyti* (while walking in the mountains, preferably in the moonlight, hence the romantic local term, *sang-gardi*, 'strolling [among] the stones'), and describing their imagery, meter, subject matter and language. Examples follow, alphabetized by first word, with fairly extensive footnotes explaining the texts, and further discussion keyed to page numbers, in an appendix.

Two small collections of proverbs published by the Marxist government seem more intended for popular readers than for scholars: Mowlânâ Khâl Mohammad Khaste's *Zarbolmathalhâ* (Proverbs), an alphabetized and numbered list of 1,152 un-annotated proverbs, was published as a memorial on the tenth anniversary of his death from a manuscript in the archives of the folklore journal *Farhang-e mardom* in 1983. In 1985, Aziz Ahmad Râbin prepared *Zarbolmathalhâ-ye âmiyâne* (Popular Proverbs), an alphabetized, but unnumbered, collection of approximately 800 proverbs published by the Ministry of Education in commemoration of the new cycle of the Loya Jirga (Legislative Assembly) of the Democratic Republic of Afghanistan. These two collections, composed perhaps two decades apart, illustrate the persistent tendency to treat proverbs as self-explanatory for readers and linguistically unproblematic, and to prize the collection or assemblage, large or small, in and of itself.

In the Marxist era and after, recognition of the emerging effect of media on oral texts and traditions is illustrated by two interesting small anthologies which endeavor to present and give background information for traditional songs sung or recorded by known artists, and broadcast by Radio Kabul. These are Pâ'iz Hanifi's *Âhanghâ-ye mahalli-ye mâ* (Our Local Tunes; 1986), which includes lyrics and a commentary for each named song, and Faqir Mohammad Nangiyâli's *Âhanghâ-ye mardomi-ye folklorik-e Afghâni* (Popular Afghan Folk Tunes), which includes along with its (typeset) commentary on songs indexed by title and singer, rather decoratively calligraphed lyrics. Some of the songs also include musical scores in western notation. Hanifi had previously published *Sorudhâ-ye mahalli* (Local Songs), a small collection of eleven traditional songs with background stories and commentary.

The Marxist period also saw folklore publications specifically addressing children's culture. One female-authored, government-sponsored genre collection intended for teaching nursery-school children was *Afsânehâ-ye kudakâne* (Tales for Children), compiled by Nafise Ayyub. Abd-al-Ghaffâr Gardizi compiled *Simâ-ye kudak dar farhang-e mardom: Majmu'e'i az tarânehâ-ye kudakân* (The Portrayal of Children in Popular Culture: a Collection of Children's Songs), including thirty-nine songs with some contextual descriptions of their occurrence, including designations as girls' or boys' songs, as sung in particular locales, etc. This undated publication commemorates the fifth anniversary of the Girl Scouts in Afghanistan. *Ketâb-e sorudhâ o bâzihâ-ye bâ angoshtân barâye atfâl-e senin-e 1 elâ 7-sâle* (A Book of Songs and Finger Games for Children Aged One to Seven Years) is a private publication produced by female refugee teachers for use in their preschool, a collection of children's songs and finger games with diagrammatic illustrations of the games. It was produced with very modest resources as a photocopied, A4-sized bound pamphlet by three teachers in a Montessori-type preschool for Afghan refugee children in Peshawar (Rahim et al. 1993). They explained in an interview about their teaching activities that they were afraid refugee children were being deprived of exposure to the traditional games and songs of childhood that were normal in Afghan children's informal culture before displacement, so they had tried to reconstruct the songs and games they knew, describe and illustrate them for school use by teachers who might not know them, and record them in a small book for future use.

An interesting small anthology organized around a theme rather than a genre, is Gholâm Heydar Yaqin's *Ayyârân o kâkâhâ ye Khorâsân* (Heroic Tricksters and Daredevils of Khorasan), that includes a general discussion of the concept of the *ayyâr* (a hero or hero's companion who is both warrior and trickster, a champion of justice who usually comes from a non-elite background), as reflected in the traditional history of Khorasan; discussion of the general character and practices of *ayyârs*; discussion of relevant books and tales in Dari and Pashto; of the Manâs and Goroghlu epics; and a chapter with profiles of eighteen historical or legendary *kâkâ* (daredevil, *bon vivant*) or *javânmard* (heroes of *noblesse oblige* or men of bravery, generosity and nobility of character who assist the underprivileged) characters from Afghanistan, including some samples of *marthiye* (elegy) and other verses composed for or about them. Yaqin concludes with a sampling of lines from literary poets, beginning with Ferdowsi, that mention *ayyâri*.

In the most recent generation of Afghan scholars, Shams-al-Haqq Âryânfar has published another thematically organized study, a summary of his doctoral dissertation (in Tajiki), *Simâ-ye Hazrat-e Ali r.z. dar farhang-e mardom-e fârsizabân* (The Character of His Eminence Ali, May God Be Pleased with Him, in the Culture of Persian-speaking People), including brief descriptions in Tâjiki of Dari oral poetry and prose genres dedicated to Hazrat-e Ali (including some samples of short verse forms) together with parallel descriptions of devotional genres from Tajikistan and Iran.

A few recent and not at all scholarly publications suggest that some private chapbook publishers now expect to find a market among general readers for newer varieties of folk literature anthologies (as opposed to the older chapbook romances now largely disappeared from the market). These small books include Mohsen Hasan Samangâni's *Yekdaste gol: behtarin dobeytihâ-ye mahalli* (A Bouquet of Blossoms: the Finest Local Quatrains); Mir Abd al-Qoddus Mirpur's *Zarbolmathalhâ, kalamât-e qesâr o goftârhâ barâ-ye dustdârân-e an'anân o rosumât-e melli-ye vatan-e aziz* (Proverbs, Aphorisms, and Sayings for the Friends of the Traditions and Customs of the Beloved Homeland); Farhâd Bakhshande's *Chistân* (Riddles); a small pirated collection of twenty of Ravshan Rahmoni's previously published folktales, entitled *Afsânehâ-ye nâder* (Rare Tales) and undated but published by Taj Mahal Company, Peshawar, perhaps in 2002 or later; a similarly undated, and anonymous, *Majmu'e'i az folklor-e âmiyâne-ye zabân-e Dari* (A Collection of Popular Folklore in Dari Language), published in Kabul, probably in the 1990s, by Ketâbkhâne-ye Kayumarth. The subtitle of this collection gives an idea of the popular press's inventory of folk genres: *Sorudhâ, robâ'iyât, dobeytihâ, meydabeytihâ, zarbolmathalhâ o chistânhâ, afsânehâ, revâyât o latifehâ* (Songs, Quatrains, Distiches, Short Verses, Proverbs and Riddles, Wonder Tales, Narratives and Jokes).

5. Studies by Western scholars

Among English-language scholars of Afghan oral traditions, David Edwards has published important books on oral history, primarily from Pashtun men, as the object of anthropological study and as a source for social and political history (1996, 2002), but he does not present original-language texts. He is currently (in 2004) undertaking, together with Maliha Zulfaqar and A.A. Musavi, a project to train and supervise Kabul University students in oral history field research, which promises a new generation of trained scholars and, in time, the publication of original-language texts in this very important genre, one not previously developed by Afghan folklorists. Isabelle Delloye's collection of Afghan women's personal narratives from the early 1980s, first published in French, then in English, (2002 and 2003, respectively) contributes to the under-researched topic of women's personal experience narratives, but the publication and study of personal experience narrative and oral history as genres in Dari language remains to be undertaken.

ORAL AND POPULAR LITERATURE IN DARI PERSIAN

Likewise, unfortunately devoid of original-language texts are this author's own publications on Herati folk narrative and related topics (Mills 1990, 1991). As is also illustrated by this author's series of publications on the theme of women's tricks (*makr-e zan*) in proverbs and tales (Mills 1999, 2000a, 2000b, 2001), the analytical approach entails a close reading of original, recorded oral performances. Even so, English-language scholarly publishing houses, while they encourage extended methodological, interpretive and theoretical discussion and tolerate whole-text translations to some extent, do not support the presentation of extended original-language transcripts, limiting the usefulness of the published studies of longer genres for comparison or reanalysis by subsequent researchers. In a computerized and Internet-accommodated future, it may be possible to publish verbatim transcriptions and original field recordings electronically, thus bypassing the growing economic constraints on paper publication and increasing to some extent the access to primary data for scholars who have the use of the Internet.

Whatever the fate of scholarly publications on oral and popular literature in Afghanistan in the future, this author's opportunities for conversations with Afghan scholars, in the mid-nineties and more recently, revealed their deep concern for the survival of traditional verbal arts in the far-from-normal social context of present-day Afghanistan, and their sense of the urgent need for cultural continuity and pride, and for the cultural research that can help to support that pride, in the face of the ongoing traumatized condition of Afghan society. Collaboration across borders with both Tajik and Iranian colleagues and institutions, including support for recent publications and scholarly training opportunities, has been a lifeline of sorts for Afghan scholars interested in Dari folk literature.

An ominous note was sounded by the Tajik literary scholar and publisher Munira Shohidi, editor of the journal *Fonus*, who convened a meeting of Afghan literary scholars in Dushanbe in March, 2004. The Pashto and Dari-speaking cultural researchers complained that cooperation and mutual interest, which were normal between the two languages' scholars in the past, are waning, an influence of the ethnic and regional divisiveness spawned by the civil wars following the Soviet withdrawal.

BIBLIOGRAPHIES

The study of popular literature in the Persian context

Benfey, T. *Pantschatantra. Fünf Bücher indischer Fabeln, Märchen und Erzählungen* (Pancatantra. Five books of Indian fables, fairytales, and narratives). Vols. 1–2. Leipzig, 1859.

Bolukbâshi, A. "Naẓari be adabiyyât-e âmme-ye Irân" (A look at the popular literature of Iran); in M.A. Emâm Ahvâzi, ed., *Chistânnâme-ye dezfuli*, Tehran, 2000, pp. 9–39.

Bruijn, J.T.P. de. "Die persische Volksliteratur im Mittelalter und ihr Verhältnis zur klassischen Literatur" (Persian popular literature and its relation to classical literature); in W. Heinrichs, ed., *Orientalisches Mittelalter* (Neues Handbuch der Literaturwissenschaft), Wiesbaden, 1990, pp. 465–74.

Cejpek, J. "Iranian Folk-Literature," in J. Rypka, ed., *History of Iranian Literature*, Dordrecht 1968, pp. 607–709.

Dow, J.R. "Naumann, Hans (1886–1951)," in M.A. Brown and B.A. Rosenberg, eds., *Encyclopaedia of Folklore and Literature*, Santa Barbara, Ca., Denver, Oxford, 1998, pp. 447–49.

Hanaway, W.L., Jr. "Popular literature in Iran," in P.J. Chelkowski, ed., *Iran: Continuity and Variety*, New York, 1971, pp. 59–75.

Heath, P. *The Thirsty Sword: Sîrat Antar and the Arabic Popular Epic*. Salt Lake City, 1996.

Maḥjub, M.J. "Dâstânhâ-ye âmiyâne-ye fârsi" (Persian popular stories). *Sokhan* 10.1 (1959), pp. 64–68 (continued in a total of 22 installments up to *Sokhan* 12 (1961), pp. 1013–25).

Marzolph, U. "Persian Popular Literature in the Qajar Period." *Asian Folklore Studies* 60/2 (2001), pp. 215–36.

Mills, M.A. "Folk tradition in the *Masnavî* and the *Masnavî* in folk tradition," in A. Banani, R. Hovannisian, and G. Sabagh, eds., *Poetry and Mysticism in Islam: The Heritage of Rûmî*, Cambridge, 1994, pp. 136–77.

ORAL LITERATURE OF IRANIAN LANGUAGES

Petráček, K. "Volkstümliche Literatur" (Popular literature), in H. Gätje, ed., *Gundriß der arabischen Philologie*. 2: *Literaturwissenschaft*, Wiesbaden, 1987, p. 241.

Pfeiffer, M. "Indische Theorie" (The Indian theory). *Enzyklopädie des Märchens* 7, Berlin and New York, 1993, cols. 151–57.

Chapter 1

Adivar, Adnan. *La science chez les Turcs ottomans*. Paris, 1939.

Âghâzâde, Alî Kamâl. *Pêshaki Diwâni Mahwi* (Pêşekî Dîwanî Meḥwî; introduction to the Diwan of Mahwî). Sulêmaniye, 1922.

Amêdî, Sadiq Beha'-el-Dîn, ed. *Dîwanî Melayê Cizîrî* (The diwan of Melayê Cizîrî). Baghdad, 1977. Transliterated into the Latin-Kurdish alphabet by Zeynelabidin Kaya and M. Emin Narozi, Stockholm, 1987.

Bedlisi (Bitlîsî), Sharaf-Khân Ebn-e Shams-al-Dîn. *Sharaf-nâma*. Russian trsl. by E.I. Vasil'eva. 2 vols. Moscow, 1967, 1976. See also Charmoy, Véliaminov.

Bennigsen, A. "Les Kurdes et la Kurdologie en Union Soviétique." *Cahiers du Monde Russe et Soviétique* 1 (1960), pp. 513–60.

Blau, J. *Le Kurde de 'Amâdiya et de Jabal Sindjâr*. Paris, 1975.

Idem, "Le kurde," in R. Schmitt ed., *Compendium Linguarum Iranicarum*, Wiesbaden, 1989, pp. 27–40.

Bruinessen, M. van, and H. Boeschoten, eds. *Seyahatname*. Leiden, 1988.

Cigerxwîn. *Dîwana 3, Kîme Ez* (The 3rd diwan: Who am I?). Stockholm, 1973.

Idem. *Dîwana 4-a Ronak* (The 4th Diwan: Light). Stockholm, 1980.

Idem. *Dîwana 5-a Zend-Avista* (The 5th diwan: Zend-Avesta). Stockholm, 1981.

Idem. *Dîwana 6-a Şifaq* (The 6th diwan: Dawn). Stockholm, 1982.

Idem. *Dîwana 7-a Hêvî* (The 7th diwan: Hope). Stockholm, 1983.

Charmoy, F. *Chèref-Nâmeh ou Fastes de la nation kourde*. 2 vols., 4 pts., St. Petersburg, 1868–75.

Chodzko, A. "Etudes philologiques sur la langue kurdes (dialecte de Suléimanié)." *Journal Asiatique*, April–Mai 1857, p. 298.

Cizîrî, A. *Dîwanî Şêx Ehmedî Cizîrî* (The diwan of Shaikh Ahmad Jizîrî). Hewlêr, 1964.

Edmonds, C.J. "Suggestions for the use of latin character in the writing of Kurdish." *JRAS* 17 (1931), pp. 27–46.

Idem. "Some developments in the use of Latin characters for the writing of Kurdish." *JRAS* 19 (1933), pp. 629–42.

Idem. "A Kurdish Lampoonist, Shaikh Riza Talebani." *Journal of the Royal Central Asian Society* 22 (1935), pp. 111–23.

Gem, M. *Hotay Serra Usifê Qurzkizi* (The seventy years of Yusif Qurzkizî). Stockholm, 1992.

Gorân, see under Kerîm.

Hartmann, M., ed. *Der kurdische Diwan des Schech Ahmed.* Berlin, 1904.

Helmi, see Hilmî.

Hilmî, Refîq. *Şi'r û edebiyatî kurdî*, (Kurdish poetry and literature). 2 vols., Baghdad, 1941, 1956.

Jizîrî, see Cizîrî.

Kerîm, Muḥemmed Mela Ebd-el-, ed. *Şîrîn u Khusrew, şakari şâ'irî nawdarî kurd Xanay Qubadi* (Shirin and Khosrow, the masterpiece of the famous Kurdish poet Khanay Qubadi). Baghdad, 1975.

Idem, ed. *Dîwanî Ḥacî Qadirî Koyî: hengawekî tir be rêgâda berew saxkirdinewe* (The diwan of Hâji Qâder Koyî, a fresh step on the path to study). Baghdad, 1976.

Idem, ed. *Sercemî berhemî Goran; bergê yekem: Dîwanî Goran* (The complete works of Goran, part 1: the *diwan* of Goran). Baghdad, 1980.

Idem. *Diwâni Mehwî, Melâ Mehmûd korrî Mela Uthmânî Balxî* (The diwan of Mehwî). Baghdad, 1397.

Idem. "Mewlewi: A great poet and *'alim* of southern Kurdistan," tr. by Homer Dizeyee and Michael L. Chyet. *Islam des Kurdes: Les Annales de l'Autre Islam* 5 (1998), pp. 59–82.

Khaznadâr, see Xeznedar.

Kurdo, Qanatê. *Tarîxa edebiyata kurdî* (History of Kurdish literature). vol 1. Stockholm, 1985.

Kurmancî, rojnama taybetî ya Enstîtuya kurdî ya Parîsê li ser pirsên zaravê kurmancî, hejmar 1–20, havîn 1987-havîn 1996 (Kurmanji, periodical of the Kurdish Institute of Paris, specializing in questions concerning the Kurdish language; nos. 1–20, Summer 1987–Summer 1996). Paris, 1999.

Jaba, A. A. *Recueil de notices et récits kourdes. Servant à la connaissance de la langue, de la littérature et des tribus du Kourdistan.* St. Petersburg, 1860.

Lescot, R. (ed. tr.). *Mamé Alan, Epopée kurde.* With a preface by Kendal Nezan. Paris, 1999.

Lewendî, Malmîsanij & Mahmûd. *Li Kurdistana Bakur û li Tirkiyê, Rojnamegeriya kurdî 1908–1981* (In Northern Kurdistan and Turkey, Kurdish Journalism1908–81). Uppsala, 1989.

MacKenzie, D. N. *Kurdish Dialect Studies.* 2 vols. Oxford, 1961, 1962.

Idem. "Malâ-ê Jizrî and Faqî Ṭayrân." In *Yâdnâme-ye Irâni-ye Minorsky*, Tehran, 1969, pp. 1–6.

Idem. "Some Gorânî Lyric verse." *BSOAS* 28.2 (1965), pp. 255–83.

Idem. "Kurds, Kurdistan: Language," in C.E. Bosworth *et al*, eds. *Encyclopaedia of Islam*, Leiden, 1986, pp. 479–80.

Idem. "Avroman," "Avromani." *EIr* III/1, London, 1987, pp. 110–11, 111–12.

Minorsky, V. "Remarks on the Romanized Kurdish Alphabet." *JRAS* 19 (1933), pp. 643–50.

Mokri, M. "Cinquante-deux versets de Cheikh Amîr en dialecte gurâni." *JA* 1956, pp. 391–422.

Idem, "Kurdologie et enseignement de la langue kurde en URSS." *L'Ethnographie, Revue de la Société d'Ethnographie de Paris* 1963, pp. 71–105.

Muḥemmed, Mes'ûd. *Hacî Qadir Koyi*. Baghdad, 1973.

Nazê, Bavê. *Stockholmê te chi dîtiye, bêje* (Stockholm, tell what you've seen). Stockholm, 1998.

Idem. *Giyayên bi xwînê avdayî* (Places watered with blood). Solna, 1989.

Paul-Margueritte, L. *Proverbes kurdes d'après les thèmes recueillis par l'Emir Kamuran Bedir Khan*. Paris, 1937.

Pirbal, Ferhad. "La situation de la littérature au Kurdistan d'Irak." *Études Kurdes* 2, Paris, 2000.

Qizilci, Hesen. *Pêkenînî geda* (The beggar's smile). Baghdad, 1985.

Qubadi, Xanay. See under Kerîm.

Resûl, 'Ezizedin Mistefa. *Şêx Riẓa Ṭalebanî* (Shaikh Riẓâ Tâlebânî). Baghdad, 1979.

Rondot, Pierre. "L'alphabet kurde en caractères latins d'Arménie soviétique." *Revue des Etudes Islamiques* III, Paris, 1933.

Rudenko, Margarita Borisovna. *Mam i Zin* (Mem and Zin). Moscow, 1962.

Idem. *Faki Teïran, Sheïkh San'an*. Moscow, 1965.

Idem. *Kharis Bitlisi, Leïli i Madjnun*, Moscow, 1965.

Sakisian, A. "'Abdal Khan, Seigneur kurde de Bitlis au XVIIème siècle et ses trésors." *JA* 229 (1957), pp. 253–76.

Se'id, Ebd-ul-Reḥman. *Komele Şi'rî Ḥacî Qadir Koyi* (Collected poems of Shaikh Hâji Qâder Kôyî). Baghdad, 1925.

Sejjadi, see Seccadî.

Seccadî, Ela'-el-Dîn (Alâ-al-Din Sejjâdi). *Mêjûy edebî kurdî* (History of Kurdish literature). Baghdad, 1956.

Şerefqendî, Hejar. *Dîwanî arifî rebbanî Şêx Eḥmedî Cizîrî*. Tehran, 1982.

Sharafqandi, see Şerefqendî.

BIBLIOGRAPHIES

Sloane, E. B. *Kurdish Grammar*. London, 1913.
Soltani, Anwar ed. *Anthology of Gorani Kurdish Poetry: compiled by A. M. Mardoukhi (1739 - 1797)*. London, 1998.
El-Ṭalibanî, Elî. *Diwanî Şêx Rizay Ṭalibanî* (The dîwan of Shaikh Rezâ Tâlebâni). Baghdad, 1946.
Uzun, Mehmet, ed. *Antolojiya Edebiyata Kurdî* (Anthology of Kurdish literature). 2 vols., Istanbul, 1995.
Idem. *Tu* (You). Stockholm, 1984.
Idem. *Mirina Kalekî Rind* (The beggar's smile). Stockholm, 1987.
Idem. *Siya evînê* (Chasing shadows). Stockholm, 1989.
Idem. *La poursuite de l'ombre*. With a preface by Yachar Kemal. Paris, 1999.
Idem. *Rojek li Rojên Evdalê Zeynikî* (A day in the life of Evdal Zeynik). Stockholm, 1991.
Idem. *Ronî mîna evînî, tarî mîna mirinê* (Light is like love, darkness is like death). Istanbul, 1998.
Vasilieva, E. I. *Mâx Sharaf-Khânum Kurdistânî, Khronika Doma Aradalân* (Chronicles of the house of Ardalan). Moscow, 1990.
Véliaminov-Zernof, V. *Scheref-Nameh ou Histoire des Kurdes, publiée pour la première fois, traduite et annotée*. Persian text 2 vols. St. Petersburg, 1860–62.
Wehbî, Tewfiq. *Xöndewariy Bâw* Baw (The traditional alphabetization). Baghdad, 1933.
Xeznedar, Cemal. *Râberî rojnâmegerî kurdî* (Guide to the Kurdish press). Baghdad, 1973.
Zaza, Noureddine. *Ma vie de Kurde*. Geneva, 1993.

Chapter 2

Kurdish periodicals

*Hawar*1–9. Various locations, 1932–43; repr. Stockholm, 1987.
Ronahî. Damascus 1942–44; repr. Uppsala, 1985.
Roja Nû. Beirut, 1943–45.

ORAL LITERATURE OF IRANIAN LANGUAGES

Primary literature: texts and translations

Amin, A. *Kurdish Proverbs.* New York, 1989.
Ayyubiyan, U. *Çirîkey Mem û Zîn: Kurdî Farsî* (The tale of Mem and Zin: Kurdish and Persian). Tabriz, 1962.
Bedir Xan, C. "Le folklore kurde." *Hawar* 3 (1932), pp. 9–11.
Idem. "La légende de Bingöl." *Hawar* 11 (1932), pp. 166–67.
Idem. "Le beau de la steppe." *Hawar* 24 (1933), pp. 376–77; 25 (1933), pp. 403–4.
Idem. "Herekol Azizan," "Besna." *Hawar* 22 (1933), p. 5.
Bedir Xan, K. and A. Falgairolle. *Le roi du Kurdistan.* Paris, 1938.
Blau, J. "Trois textes de folklore kurdes." *Études, Centre pour l'étude des problèmes du monde musulman contemporain* 7. Brussels, 1965.
Idem. *Le kurde de 'Amadiya et de Djabal Sindjar.* Paris, 1975.
Idem. *Mémoire du Kurdistan.* Paris, 1984.
Cambaz, T. *Tekstî heşt çîrokî efsaney kurdî* (Texts of eight Kurdish legends–Erbil region). Hewlêr (Erbil), 1986.
Celîl, C(elîl). *Zargotina K'urdê Suriaê* (The oral tradition of the Kurds of Syria). Yerevan, 1985.
Celîl, C(esim). *Kurdish National Popular Songs.* Yerevan, 1964.
Idem. *Kilamê Çiya* (Songs of the mountains). Yerevan, 1970.
Idem. *Emerê Celalî* (Omar the Jelali). Baghdad, 1982.
Celîl, C. and O. (Jalil, Dzhalilov). *Mesele û Metelokê K'urda bi Zimanê K'urdî û Rûsî: Kurdskie Poslovitsii i pogovorkii na Kurdskom i Russkom iazykakh* (Proverbs of the Kurds in Kurdish and Russian). Moscow, 1972.
Idem. *Zargotina K'urda (Kurdskiĭ fol'klor)* (The oral tradition of the Kurds). 2 vols., Moscow, 1978.
Celîl, O. *Kurdskiĭ Geroicheskiĭ èpos "Zlatorukiĭ Khan"* (The Kurdish heroic epic "Prince Goldenhand"). Moscow, 1967.
Idem. *Stranê Zargotina Kurdayê Tarixîyê* (Historical songs of Kurdish oral tradition), transliterated by Shakoor Mustafa and Anwar Kadir Muhammad. Baghdad, 1977.
Chaliand, G. *La poésie populaire kurde.* Paris, 1960.
Idem. *Poésie populaire des Turcs et des Kurdes.* Paris, 1961.
'Cigerxwîn' (Şêxmus Hisên). *Folklora Kurdî* (Kurdish folklore). Stockholm, 1988.
Cindî, H. and E. Evdal. *Folklora Kyrmanca* (Kurmanji folklore). Yerevan, 1936.
Cindî, H., ed. *Folklora Kurmanciyê: Berevok* (Kurmanji folklore: a collection). Yerevan, 1957.
Idem. *Kurdskie èpicheskie pesni-skazy* (Kurdish epic tales). Moscow, 1962.

BIBLIOGRAPHIES

Idem. *Meselok û xeberokêd cimaᵓeta Kᵓurda* (Proverbs and sayings of the Kurdish community). Yerevan, 1985.

Dufresne, M. "Un conte kurde de la région de Soᶜort." *JA* XV (1910), pp. 107-17.

Dzhalilov, see Celîl.

Dzhindi, see Cindî.

Fattaḥi-Qâzı, Q. *Manẓume-ye kordi* (Kurdish popular poetry). Tabriz, 1966-73.

Fellaḥ, K. *Pendekani Pîremêrd* (Pîremêrd's proverbs). Baghdad, 1980.

Hadank, K. *Untersuchungen zum Westkurdischen: Bōtī und Ēzādī*. Leipzig, 1938.

Ivanow, W. "Notes on Khorasani Kurdish." *Journal of the Asiatic Society of Bengal* 23 (1927), pp. 167-235.

Jaba, A.D. *Recueil de notices et de récits*. St. Petersburg, 1860.

Jardine, R.F. *Bahdinan Kurmancî: a Grammar of the Kurmanji of the Kurds of Mosul division and surrounding districts of Kurdistan*. Baghdad, 1922.

Jindi, see Cindî.

Kakeyî, H. *Helbijardeyek le honrawey folklorî kurdî nawçey germiyan* I (Selection of Kurdish folk poems from the Kirkuk region I). Baghdad, 1985.

Kerîm, M.S. *Şehîdanî qelay Dimdim: çîrok* (The martyrs of Castle Dimdim: a tale) Baghdad, 1958; repr 1983.

Le Coq, A. von. *Kurdische Texte, Kurmanji-Erzählungen und Lieder*. Berlin, 1903; repr. Amsterdam, 1979.

Lerch, P. *Forschungen über die Kurden und die iranischen Nordchaldäer* I-II. St. Petersburg, 1857-58; repr. Amsterdam, 1979.

Lescot, R. *Textes kurdes*. vol. I. Paris, 1940; vol. II. Beirut, 1942.

Idem (Tawûsparêz). "Xarabo." *Hawar* 38 (1942), pp. 604-8.

Idem. "Le mariage chez les Kurdes." *Hawar* 52 (1943), pp. 764-68.

Idem. "Chansons." *Hawar* 54 (1944), pp. 783-84.

MacKenzie, D.N. *Kurdish Dialect Studies*. 2 vols., London, 1961-62.

Makas, H. *Kurdische Texte im Kurmānjî-Dialekte aus der Gegend von Märdîn*. 3 vols., St. Petersburg/Leningrad, 1897-1926.

Mann, O. *Kurdische und Persische Forschungen IV.II.1-2: Die Mundart der Mukri-Kurden*. 2 vols., Berlin, 1906, 1909.

Mokri, M. "l'Arménie dans le folklore kurde." *Revue des Études Arméniennes* 1 (1964), pp. 347-76.

Idem. *La légende de Bīžan-u Manīja*. Paris, 1966.

Muermann, M. *Musto, Sahhe und Ousso. Eine Geschichte aus Kurdistan*. Bornheim-Merten, 1984.

ORAL LITERATURE OF IRANIAN LANGUAGES

Mukriani, G. *Zembîlfiroş* (The basket-seller). Hewlêr (Erbil), 1967.
Musaelian, Ê. S. *Zembîlfiroş: Kurdskaia poèma i eïo fol'klornie versii* (Zembilfirosh: a Kurdish poem and its folklore versions). Moscow, 1983.
Idem, ed., *Kurdskie narodnye pesni* (Kurdish popular songs). Moscow, 1985.
Nebez, J. *Kurdische Märchen und Volkserzählungen.* NUKSE (National Union of Kurdish Students in Europe), n.p., 1972.
Nikitine, B. "Kurdish Stories from my collection." *BSOS* 4 (1924), pp. 121–38.
Idem. "Quelques fables kurdes d'animaux." *Folklore* 40 (1929), pp. 228–44.
Noel, E. "The Character of the Kurds as Illustrated by their Proverbs and Popular Sayings." *BSOS* 1 (1920), pp. 79–90.
Nöldeke, Th. *Grammatik der neusyrischen Sprache.* Leipzig, 1868.
Paul-Margueritte, D. and K. Bedir Xan. *Proverbes kurdes.* Paris, 1938.
'Peresh' *Contes du Kurdistan.* 2 vols., Geneva, 1985, 1991.
Perwer, Ş. *Çîroka Newrozê* (The story of Newroz). Uppsala, 1990.
'Pîrêmerd' (Hecî Tewfiq). *Diwanzde sîwarî Meriwan* (The twelve horsemen of Meriwan). Suleymaniye, 1935.
Prampolini, G. *Proverbi kurdi*, Milan, 1963.
Prym, E. and A. Socin. *Kurdische Sammlungen, Erzählungen und Lieder in den Dialekten des Ṭûr 'Abdîn und von Bohtan.* 2 vols., St. Petersburg, 1887, 1890.
Rondot, P. "Trois chansons kurdes." *Cahiers du Sud* 274 (1945), pp. 817–24.
Sabar, Y. *The Folk Literature of the Kurdistani Jews*, New Haven and London, 1982.
Sajjâdi, see Seccadî.
Şarbajêrî, U. *Gencîney goranî kurdî* (Treasury of Kurdish songs). Baghdad, 1985.
Sebrî, O. "Gisîn (the Ploughshare)." *Hêviya Welêt* 1.2 (1964), pp. 14–15.
Idem. "Newroz." *ibid.*, pp. 4–5.
Seccadî, A. *Rishtey mirwarî* (A necklace of pearls). 8 vols., Baghdad, 1957–83.
Şemo, E. *Dimdim.* Yerevan, 1966; repr. Stockholm, 1983.
Idem. *Şivanê kurd/Le berger kurde.* Paris, 1989.
Silêman, X. *Gundiyatî* (Village life). Baghdad, 1985.
Idem and X. Cindî, *Êzdiyatî: liber Rojnaya Hindek Têkstêd Aînê Êzdiyan* (Yezidism: in the light of some religious texts of the Yezidis). Baghdad, 1979.
Smith, A. *National Identity.* London, 1991.
Soane, E. B. "A Southern Kurdish folksong in Kermanshahi dialect." *Journal of the Royal Asiatic Society* 1909, pp. 35–51.

Soane, E. B. and B. Nikitine. "The Tale of Suto and Tato." *BSOS* 3 (1923), pp. 69–106.
'Stranvan.' "Lawiqo! (O Young Man!)." *Hawar* 19 (1933), p. 3.
Wentzel, L.-Ch., ed. *Kurdische Märchen*. Köln, 1978.
Wikander, S. *Recueil de textes kourmandji*. Uppsala and Wiesbaden, 1959.
Idem. "Ein Fest bei den Kurden und im Avesta." *Orientalia Suecana* 9 (1960), pp. 7–10.
Xal, M. *Pend-î Pêşinan* (Wisdom of the ancestors). Baghdad, 1957.

Secondary literature

Allison, F. C. "Old and New Oral Traditions in Badinan," in P. G. Kreyenbroek and F. C. Allison, eds., *Kurdish Culture and Identity*. London, 1996, pp. 29–47.
Idem. "Kurden." *Enzyklopädie des Märchens* 8 (1995), pp. 635–47.
Idem. *The Yezidi Oral Tradition in Iraqi Kurdistan*. London, 2001.
Bedir Xan, C. "Le folklore kurde," *Hawar* 3 (1932), pp. 42–44.
Bedlisi (Bitlîsî), Sharaf-Khân ebn-e Shams-al-Dîn. *Sharafnâme*, ed. M. Abbâs. Tehran 1985.
Ben-Amos, D., ed. *Folklore Genres*. Austin, Texas, 1976.
Blau, J. and M. van Bruinessen, eds., "Islam des Kurdes." *Les annales de l'autre Islam* 5, Paris, 1998.
Bois, T. "L'âme des Kurdes à la lumière de leur folklore." *Cahiers de l'Est* 5 and 6, Beirut, 1946.
Idem. "Un coup d'œil sur la littérature kurde." *al-Machriq* 49 (1955), pp. 69–112.
Idem. "Poètes et troubadours au pays des Soviets." *al-Machriq* 53 (1959), pp. 266–99.
Idem. *Connaissance des Kurdes*. Beirut, 1965; trsl. as *The Kurds*. Beirut, 1966.
Idem, V. Minorsky, and D. N. MacKenzie. "Kurds, Kurdistan," in C. E. Bosworth *et al.*, eds., *Encyclopædia of Islam*, Leiden, 1986, pp. 438–86.
Bozarslan, M. E. *Mem û Zîn*. Istanbul, 1990.
Brauer, E. and R. Patai. *The Jews of Kurdistan*. Detroit, 1993.
Bruinessen, M. van. *Agha, Shaikh and State*. 2nd edition. London, 1992.
Idem. "Nationalisme kurde et ethnicité intra-kurdes," in H. Bozarslan, ed. *Les Kurdes et les Etats. Peuples Méditerranéens* 68/9 (1994), pp. 11–37.
Chalatianz, B. "Kurdische Sagen." *Zeitschrift für Volkskunde* 15 (1905), pp. 322–30; 16 (1906), pp. 35–46, 402–14; 17 (1907), pp. 76–80.

Chyet, M. "And a Thornbush Sprang Between them: Studies on Mem û Zîn, a Kurdish Romance." Ph.D. diss., University of California at Berkeley, 1991 [1991a].

Idem. "A Version of the Kurdish Romance Mem û Zîn with English Translation and Commentary," in R. E. Emmerick and D. Weber, eds., *Corolla Iranica: Papers in Honour of D. N. MacKenzie*, Frankfurt, etc., 1991 [1991b], pp. 27–48.

Cûtyar, X. et al. *Folklor, komele berhemekî folkloriye* (Folklore: a collection of folklore studies). 2 vols., Hewlêr (Erbil) and Baghdad, 1984, 1985.

Dankoff, R. *Evliya Çelebi in Bitlisi: the Relevant Section of the Seyahatname.* Leiden, 1990.

Driver, G. R. (British Government Publication). *Kurdistan and the Kurdish Tribes.* Mount Carmel, 1919.

Druzhinina, E. S. *Kurdskie skazki* (Kurdish stories). Moscow, 1959.

Dundes, A. "Texture, text and context." *Southern Folklore Quarterly* 28 (1964), pp. 251–65; repr. in A. Dundes, *Interpreting Folklore*, Bloomington, 1980, pp. 20–32.

Hassanpour, A. *EIr*, s.v. Bayt.

Idem. "The Creation of Kurdish Media Culture," in P. G. Kreyenbroek and F. C. Allison, 1996 [1996a], pp. 48–84.

Idem. *EIr*, s.v. Dimdim.

Kerîm, Muhemmed Mella. "Mewlewi: A great poet and '*alim* of southern Kurdistan." Translated by Homer Dizeyee and Michael L. Chyet. *Islam des Kurdes: Les Annales de l'Autre Islam* 5 (1998), pp. 59–82.

Kreyenbroek, P. G. and F. C. Allison, eds. *Kurdish Culture and Identity.* London, 1996.

Lescot, R. *Textes kurdes.* vol. 1, Paris, 1940; vol 2., Beirut, 1942.

Idem. "Littérature kurde." *Histoire des littératures* I, Paris, 1977, pp. 795–805.

Marzolph, U. *Typologie des persischen Volsmärchens.* Beirut, 1984.

Idem. "Der Weise Narr Buhlûl in den modernen Volksliteraturen der islamischen Länder." *Fabula* 28 (1987), pp. 72–89.

Middle East Watch. *Genocide in Iraq: the Anfal Campaign against the Kurds.* New York, 1993.

Mokri, M. "l'Arménie dans le folklore kurde." *Revue des Études Arméniennes* 1 (1964), pp. 226–42.

Nikitine, B. "La poésie lyrique kurde." *l'Ethnographie* 45 (1947–50), pp. 39–53.

Idem. *Les Kurdes: étude sociologique et historique.* Paris, 1956; repr., 1978.

BIBLIOGRAPHIES

Noel, E. "The Character of the Kurds as illustrated by their proverbs and popular sayings." *BSOS* 1 (1920), pp. 79–90.

Resûl, I.M. *Lêkolîne-y edeb-i folklor-i kurdî* (Kurdish folk literature). Baghdad, 1970.

Rudenko, M.B. "Kurdskie fol'klornye i literaturnyc versii poèmy *Leyli i Medzhnun* (The Kurdish folk and literary versions of *Leyli and Majnun*)." *Tezisy dokladov Vsesoiuznoï konferencii vostokovedov po Iranskoï filologii* (Papers of the All-Soviet Orientalists' Conference on Iranian Philology), Baku, 1963, pp. 19–30.

Idem. *Kurdskaia Obriadovaia Poèzia* (Kurdish Funerary Poetry). Moscow, 1982.

Idem. *Literaturnaia i Fol'klornye Versii Kurdskoï Poèmy "Iusuf i Zelikha"* (The literary and folk versions of the Kurdish poem "Yusof and Zoleykha"). Moscow, 1986.

Seccadî, A. *Mêjuy edebî kurdî* (A history of Kurdish literature). Baghdad, 1952.

Shakeli, F. *Kurdish Nationalism in Mem u Zin of Ehmedi Xani*. Uppsala, 1983.

Soane, E.B. *Grammar of the Kurmanji or Kurdish Language*. London, 1913.

Spies, O. "Kurdische Märchen im Rahmen der orientalisch vergleichenden Märchenkunde." *Fabula* 14.3 (1973), pp. 205–17.

Street, B.V. *Literacy in Theory and Practice*. Cambridge, 1984.

Uzun, M. *Rojekê ji rojên Evdalê Zeynik* (A day in the life of Evdalê Zeynik). Stockholm, 1991.

Idem. *Destpêka Edebiyata Kurdî* (The beginning of Kurdish literature). Ankara, 1992.

Virgil. *P. Vergili Maronis Opera.* ed. R.A.B. Mynors, Oxford, 1969.

Zimmerman, A. "Kurdish Broadcasting in Iraq." *Middle East Report*, July–August 1994, pp. 20–21.

Kurdish Music

Ahmad, W. *Amerekani musiqay kurdi* (Kurdish musical instruments). Erbil, 1989.

Barkhordâr, I. "Pazhuheshi dar musiqi-ye mahalli-ye Kordestân (An investigation of the folk music of Kurdistan)." *Majalle-ye Musiqi* 135 (1972), pp. 30–61.

Bayrak, M. *Kürt Halk Türküleri (Kilam û Stranên kurd): Önceleme – Antoloji* (Kurdish folk songs: an anthology). Ankara, 1991.

Blum, S. and A. Hassanpour. "The Morning of Freedom rose up: Kurdish popular song and the exigencies of cultural survival." *Popular Music* 5.3 (1996), pp. 325–43.

Celîl, C(emila) *K'ilamêd cima'eta K'urda* (Songs of the Kurdish community). Yerevan, 1964.
Idem. *Kurdskie Narodnye Pesni/K'ilamêd Cima'eta Kurda* (Kurdish folk songs). Moscow, 1965.
Idem. *K'ilam û Maqamêd Cima'eta K'urda/Kurdskie Narodnye Pesni i Instrumental'nye Melodii* (Kurdish traditional folk songs and instrumental melodies). 2 vols, Moscow, 1973, 1986. (vol. 1 repr. Stockholm, 1982).
Cewarî, N. *Kilamêd Cimaeta Kurdaya Govendê.* (Dance songs of the Kurdish community). Uppsala, 1983.
Cindî, H. *K'lamêd Cimaet'a K'ördaye Lîrîkîe* (Lyrical songs of the Kurdish community). Yerevan, 1972.
Christensen, D. "Kurdische Brautlieder aus dem Vilayet Hakkâri, Südost-Türkei."*Journal of the International Folk Music Congress* 8 (1961), pp. 70–72.
Idem. "Tanzlieder der Hakkari-Kurden." *Jahrbuch für musikalische Volks- und Völkerkunde* 1 (1963), pp. 1–47.
Idem. "Ein Tanzlied der Hakkari-Kurden und seine Varianten." *Baessler-Archiv* 23 (1975), pp. 195–215.
Idem. "Musical Style and Social Context in Kurdish songs." *Asian Music* 6 (1975), pp. 1–6.
Dzhindi, see Cindî.
Gerson-Kiwi, E. "The Music of Kurdistan Jews." *Yuval* 2 (1971), pp. 59–72.
Hassan, S. Q. "Les instruments de musique chez les Yézidi de l'Irak." *Yearbook of the International Folk Music Congress* 8 (1976), pp. 53–72.
Jindy, see Cindî.
Mokri, M. *Gurâni yâ tarânehâ-ye kordi/Kurdish songs in 11 Dialects with Transliteration, Persian Translation and Glossary.* Tehran, 1951.
Idem. "La musique sacrée des Kurdes 'Fidèles de vérité'." *Encyclopédie des musiques sacrées* 1 (1968), pp. 441–53.
Nezan, K. "Kurdish Music and Dance." *The World of Music* 21 (1979), pp. 19–32.
Tatsumura, A. "Music and Culture of the Kurds." *Senri Ethnological Studies* 5 (1980), pp. 75–93.

BIBLIOGRAPHIES

Chapter 3

Ahmed, S. S. *The Yazidis: their Life and Beliefs.* Ed. by H. Field. Miami, 1975.
Ainsworth, W.F. *Travels and Researches in Asia Minor, Mesopotamia and Armenia.* London, 1841.
Anastase, Marie de Saint-Elie. "al-Yazidiyya." *al-Machriq* 2 (1899), pp. 32–37, 151–56, 309–14, 395–99, 547–53, 651–55, 731–36, 830–36.
Idem. "La découverte récente des deux livres sacrées des Yézidis." *Anthropos* 6 (1911), pp. 1–39.
Asatrian, G.S. "O brate i sestre zagrobnoï zhizny" (On the brother and sister of the hereafter). *Strany i Narody Blizhnego i Srednego Vostoka (Kurdovedenie)* XIII (1985), pp. 262–71.
Awwad, G. "Bibliographie Yézidi." *al-Machriq* 63 (1969), pp. 709–32.
al-Azzawî, A. *Ta'rikh al-Yazidiyya va aṣl aqidatehem* (The history of Yezidism and the origin of its beliefs). Baghdad, 1935.
Badger, G.P. *Nestorians and their Rituals.* 2 vols., London, 1852.
Bedir Khan, Dj.A. "Quatre prières authentiques inédites des Kurdes Yézidis." *Kitêbxana Hawarê* V, Damascus, 1933.
Bittner, M. *Die Heiligen Bücher der Jeziden oder Teufelsanbeter (Kurdisch und Arabisch).* Vienna, 1913.
Bruinessen, M. van. "Haji Bektash, Sultan Sahak, Shah Mina Sahib and various avatars of a running wall." *Turcica* 21/3 (1992), pp. 55–69.
Idem. "Satan's psalmists: some heterodox beliefs and practices among the Ahl-e Ḥaqq of the Gurân district." n.p.
Bumke, P.J. "Kizilbash-Kurden in Derzim (Tunceli, Türkei); Marginalität und Häresie." *Anthropos* 74 (1979), pp. 530–48.
Bureke'i, see under Ṣafizâde.
Chabot, J.B. "Notices sur les Yézidis." *JA* 9/7 (1896), pp. 100–32.
Celîl, see Jalil.
Cindî, see Jindy.
Dâmluji, Ṣâdeq al-. *Al-Yazidiyya.* Mosul, 1949.
Dirr, A. "Einiges über die Jeziden." *Anthropos* 12/13 (1917–18), pp. 558–74.
Driver, G.R. "The Religion of the Kurds." *BSOS* 2 (1922), pp. 197–213.
Drower, E.S. *Peacock Angel.* London, 1941.
During, J. (1989), "The sacred music of the Ahl-i Haq as a means of mystical transmission," in G.M. Smith and C.W. Ernst, eds., *Manifestations of Sainthood in Islam,* pp. 27–41. Istanbul, 1989.
Edmonds, C.J. *Kurds, Turks and Arabs.* London, 1957.
Idem. *A Pilgrimage to Lalish.* London, 1967.

ORAL LITERATURE OF IRANIAN LANGUAGES

Empson, R. H. W. *The Cult of the Peacock Angel*. London, 1928.
Elahi, B. *The Path of Perfection: the Spiritual Teachings of Master Nur Ali*. London, etc., 1966.
Elahi, N. A. "*l'Esotérisme Kurde: Aperçu sur le secret gnostique des Fidèles de Vérité*." Paris, 1966.
Idem. *Borhân al-Haqq* (Proof of the Truth). Tehran, 1975.
Idem. *Ḥâshiye bar Ḥaqq al-ḥaqâyeq, yâ Shâhnâme-ye Ḥaqiqat* (Notes on the *Ḥaqq al-ḥaqâyeq*, or *Shâhnâme-ye Ḥaqiqat*). Tehran, n.d.
Frank, R. *Scheich ʿAdî, der grosse Heilige der Jezîdîs*. Berlin, 1911.
Frayha, A. "New Yezīdī Texts from Beled Sinjâr, 'Iraq.'" *JAOS* 66 (1946), pp. 18–43.
Furlani, G. *Testi Religiosi dei Yezidi*. Bologna, 1930.
Idem. "Sui Yezidi." *RSO* XIII (1932), pp. 97–132.
Idem. "Gli Interdetti dei Yezidi." *Der Islam* 24 (1937), pp. 51–57.
Idem. "Le Feste dei Yezidi." *WZKM* 45 (1937), pp. 65–97.
Giamil, S. *Monte Singar: Storia di un Popolo Ignoto*. Rome, 1900.
Guérinot, A. "Les Yézidis." *RMM* 5 (1908), pp. 581–630.
Guest, J. S. *The Yezidis: a Study in Survival*. London and New York, 1987.
Idem. *Survival among the Kurds: a History of the Yezidis*. London and New York, 1993.
Guidi, M. "Origine dei Yazidi e Storia Religiosa dell'Islam e del Dualismo." *RSO* XII (1932), pp. 266–300.
Idem. "Nuove Ricerche sui Yazidi." *RSO* XII (1932), pp. 377–427.
Hamzeh'ee, M. R. *The Yaresan: a Sociological, Historical and Religiohistorical Study of a Kurdish Community*. Berlin, 1990.
Ivanow, W. *The Truth-Worshippers of Kurdistan: Ahl-i Haqq Texts*. Leiden, 1953.
Jalil, O. and J. "Qewl û Beytê Êzdiya" (Religious verses of the Yezidis); in idem, *Kurdskij Folklor* II, Moscow, 1978, pp. 5–53.
Jendi, see Jindy.
Jindy, Kh. "al-Qawwâluna" (The *Qewwals*). *Roj* 4/5 (1998), pp. 28–40.
Joseph, I. "Yezidi texts." *American Journal of Semitic Languages and Literature* 25 (1909), pp. 111–56, 218–54.
Idem. *Devil Worship: the Sacred Books and Traditions of the Yezidiz*. Boston, 1919.
Kehl-Bodrogi, K. *Die Kizilbaş/Aleviten*. Berlin, 1988.
Kh^wâje al-Din, M. A. *Sar-sepordegân: târikh va sharḥ-e aqâyed-e dini va âdâb va rosum-e Ahl-e Ḥaqq* (Those who submit their heads: history and an account of the religious beliefs, and customs and traditions of the Ahl-e Haqq). Tehran, n.d.

BIBLIOGRAPHIES

Kreyenbroek, P. G. "Mithra and Ahreman, Binyamin and Malak Tâwûs: traces of an ancient myth in the cosmogonies of two modern sects," in Ph. Gignoux, ed., *Recurrent Patterns in Iranian Religions; from Mazdaism to Sufism*, Paris, 1992, pp. 57-79.

Idem. "Mithra and Ahreman in Iranian Cosmogonies," in J. R. Hinnells, ed., *Studies in Mithraism*, Rome, 1994, pp. 173-82.

Idem. *Yezidism: its Background, Observances and Textual Tradition.* Lewiston, 1995[a].

Idem. "Ahl-i Haqq," in J. R. Hinnells, ed., *A New Dictionary of Religions*, pp. 13-14. Oxford and Cambridge (Mass.), 1995[b].

Idem. "Yezidism," in J. R. Hinnells, ed., *A New Dictionary of Religions*, pp. 565-66. Oxford and Cambridge (Mass.), 1995[c].

Idem. "Religion and religions in Kurdistan," in P. G. Kreyenbroek and F. C. Allison, eds., *Kurdish Culture and Identity*, London, 1996, pp. 84-110.

Idem. "Morals and Society in Zoroastrian Philosophy," in I. Mahalingam and B. Carr, eds., *Companion Encyclopedia of Asian Philosophy*, London, 1997, pp. 46-63.

Idem. "On the Study of Some Heterodox Sects in Kurdistan," in J. Blau and M. van Bruinessen, eds., *Islam des Kurdes*, Paris, 1997, pp. 163-84.

Idem and S. Sperl, eds. *The Kurds: a Contemporary Overview.* London, 1992.

Idem and C. Allison, eds. *Kurdish Culture and Identity.* London and New Jersey, 1996.

Layard, A. H. *Nineveh and its Remains.* 2 vols, London, 1849.

Lidzbarski, M. "Ein Exposé der Yesiden." *ZDMG* 51 (1897), pp. 592-604.

Lescot, R. "Quelques Publications Récentes sur les Yézidis." *Bulletin d'Etudes Orientales* 6 (1936), pp. 103-8.

Idem. *Enquête sur les Yezidis de Syrie et du Djebel Sinjâr.* Beyrouth, 1938.

MacKenzie, D. N. "The origins of Kurdish." *TPS* 1961, pp. 68-86.

Meier, F. "Der Name der Yazīdī's," in idem, ed., *Westöstliche Abhandlungen*, Wiesbaden, 1954, pp. 244-57.

Menant, J. *Les Yéziniz: Episodes de l'Histoire des Adorateurs du Diable.* Paris, 1892.

Mingana, A. "Devil-worshippers: their Beliefs and their Sacred Books." *JRAS* 1916, pp. 505-26.

Idem. "Sacred Books of the Yezidis." *JRAS* 1921, pp. 117-19.

Minorsky, V. "Notes sur la secte des Ahlé Haqq." *RMM* 40-41 (1920), pp. 19-97.

Idem. "Notes sur la secte des Ahlé Haqq II." *RMM* 44-45 (1921), pp. 205-302.

Idem. "Etudes sur les Ahl-i Haqq." *RHR* 97 (1928), pp. 90-105.

Idem. "The Guran." *BSOAS* 11 (1943), pp. 75–103.
Idem. "Verses in Turkish," in Ivanow, 1953, pp. 199–202.
Idem. "Un Poème Ahl-i Haqq en Turc." In F. Meier, ed., *Westöstliche Abhandlungen.* pp. 258–62. Wiesbaden, 1954.
Idem. "Ahl-i Ḥaḵḵ." *EI.*, Leiden and London, 1960, pp. 260–63.
Mir-Hosseini, Z. "Inner truth and outer history: the two worlds of the Ahl-i Haqq of Kurdistan." *International Journal of Middle East Studies* 16 (1994), pp. 267–85.
Idem. "Redefining the truth: Ahl-e Haqq and the Islamic Republic." *British Journal of Middle Eastern Studies* 21.2 (1994), pp. 463–81 [b].
Idem. "Faith, ritual and culture among the Ahl-e Haqq." In P. G. Kreyenbroek and F. C. Allison, eds., 1996, pp. 111–34.
Mokri, M. "Le symbole de la perle dans le folklore persan et chez les Kurdes Fidèles de Vérité (Ahl-e Haqq)." *JA* CCXLVIII (1960), pp. 463–81.
Idem. *Shah-name-ye Haqiqat/Le Livre des Rois de Vérité: Histoire traditionelle des Ahl-e Haqq* I. Tehran and Paris, 1966.
Idem. *Le Chasseur de Dieu et le Mythe du Roi Aigle (Dawray Dâmyârî)* Wiesbaden, 1967.
Idem. "Le cavalier au coursier gris, le dompteur du vent: Etudes d'hérésiologie islamique et de thèmes mythiques iraniens." *JA* CCLXII (1974), pp. 47–93.
Idem. *La grande assemblée des Fidèles de Vérité: au tribunal sur le mont Zagros en Iran (Dawray-Dîwanay Gawra).* Paris, 1977.
Moosa, M. *Extremist Shiites: the Ghulat Sects.* Syracuse, 1988.
Murad, J. E. "The Sacred Poems of the Yazidis: an Anthropological Approach." Ph.D. diss. UCLA, Los Angeles, 1993.
Nau, F. "Note sur la Date et la Vie de Cheikh 'Adi, chef des Yézidis." *Revue de l'Orient Chrétien* 2/9 (1914), pp. 105–8.
Ṣafizâda, Ṣ. *Maâhir-e Ahl-e Ḥaqq* (Famous personalities of the Ahl-e Haqq). Tehran, 1981.
Idem. *Neveshtehâ-ye Parâkande dar bâre-ye Yâresân-e Ahl-e Ḥaqq* (Scattered writings about the Yaresan or Ahl-e Haqq). Tehran, 1982.
Idem. *Nâme-ye Saranjâm yâ Kalâm-e Khazâne* (The book of *Saranjâm* or the Kalâm of the Treasury). Tehran, 1996.
Idem. *Nâmâwarân-e Yâresân* (Famous people among the Yaresan). Tehran, 1997.
Schimmel, A. *Mystical Dimensions of Islam.* Chapel Hill, 1975.
Silêman, Kh. *Gundiyatî* (Village lore). Baghdad, 1985.
Silêman, Kh. and Kh. Jindy. *Êzdiyatî: liber Roṣnaya Hindek Têkstêd Aîniyê Êzdiyan* (Yezidism: in the light of some religious texts of the Yezidis). Baghdad, 1979.

Siouffi, N. "Notice sur la Secte des Yézidis." *JA* 7/18 (1880), pp. 78–83.
Idem. "Notice sur le Chéikh 'Adi et la Secte des Yézidis." *JA* 8/5 (1885), pp. 78–98.
Stead, F.M. "The Ali-Elahi Sect in Persian." *Moslem World* 1932, pp. 184–89.
Suri, M. *Sorudhâ-ye Dini-ye Yâresân* (Religious songs of the Yaresan). Tehran, 1965.
Weightman, S.C.R. "The Significance of the Kitâb Burhân ul-Ḥaqq: additional material for the study of the Ahl-i Ḥaqq." *Iran* 2 (1964), pp. 83–103.

Chapter 4

Andreyev, S. "Notes on the Ōrmur people." *Peterburgskoe Vostokovedenie* 4 (1993), pp. 230–38.
Idem. "British Indian views of the later followers of the Raushaniyya nineteenth and early twentieth centuries." *Iran* XXXII (1994), pp. 135–38.
Anṣâri, Bâyazid. *Kheyr al-Bayân*. Peshawar, 1967.
Idem. *Də resâle*. Kabul, 1986.
Arlinghaus, J.Th. "The Transformation of Afghan Tribal Society: Tribal Expansion, Mughal Imperialism and the Roshaniyya Insurrection, 1450–1600." Ph.D. diss., Duke University, 1988.
Arzani, Molla, *Diwân-e Arzâni*. The British Library, Shelf-mark Or. 4496.
Aslanov, M.G. "Narodnoe dvizhenie roshani i ego otrazhenie v afganskoi literature XVI–XVII vv." (The Rowshani popular movement and its reflection in the Afghan literature of 16–17th centuries.) *Sovetskoe Vostokovedenie* 5 (1955), pp. 121–32.
Bênawâ, Abd-al-Ra'uf. *Paśtunestân* (The Pashtun lands). Kabul, 1952.
Biddulph, C.E. *Afghan Poetry of the Seventeenth Century*. London, 1890.
Blumhardt, J.F. and D.N. MacKenzie. *Catalogue of the Pashto Manuscripts in the Libraries of the British Isles*. London, 1965.
Esfandiyar, see under Mowbad.
Darwêza, Âkhund. *Tadhkerat al-Abrâr wa'l-Ashrâr*. Delhi, 1892.
Dvoriankov, N.A. "Strofika poezii pashto" (The strophe structure of the Pashto poetry). *Problemy Vostochnogo Stikhoslozhenia*, Moscow, 1973. pp. 52–89
Efimov, V.A. *Iazyk Ormuri* (The Ormuri language). Moscow, 1986.

Elphinstone, M. *An Account of the Kingdom of Caubul and its Dependencies in Persia, Tartary and India.* 2 vols., London, 1839.
Gerasimova, A. S. and G. F. Girs. *Literatura Afganistana: Kratkiĭ ocherk* (The literature of Afghanistan: a short survey). Moscow, 1963.
Girs, G. F. *Istoricheskie pesni pushtunov* (Historical songs of the Pashtuns). Moscow, 1984.
Idem. "Pushtunskie versii traditsionnogo siuzheta o Bakhrame" (The Pashto versions of a traditional subject on Bahram). *Vostochoe istoricheskoe istochnikovedenie i spetsial'nye istoricheskie distsipliny* 2 (1994), pp. 64–83.
Idem. "Siuzhet o Saifulmuluke u pushtunov: istochnikovedcheskiĭ vzgliad na osobennosti vospriatia i adaptatsii traditsionnoĭ temy inoiazychnoĭ slovesnost'iu" (The topic of Sayf-al-Muluk among the Pashtuns: the source study perspective on the peculiarities of perception and adaptation of a traditional theme by a foreign language literature.) *Vostochnoe istoricheskoe istochnikovedenie i spetsial'nye istoricheskie distsipliny* 4 (1995), pp.5–49.
Ḥabibi, Abd-al-Ḥayy. *Paśtānə šo'arâ'* (Pashtun poets). Vol. I, Kabul, 1950.
Ḥayat Khan. *Afghanistan and its Inhabitants.* Translated by Henry Priestley. Lahore, 1874.
Hêwâdmal, Zalmay. "Də resâle də ta'lif pə bâb nażar" (A view on the authorship of the Epistle). *Kâbol* l, (1978).
Idem. *Catalogue of Pushtu Manuscripts in Indian Libraries.* Kabul, 1984.
Howell, E. and O. Caroe, trsls. *The Poems of Khushhal Khan Khattak.* Peshawar, 1963.
Ibbetson, D. C. J. *Outlines of Panjab Ethnography*: Being Extracts from the Panjab Census Report of l881, Treating of Religion, Language and Caste. Calcutta, 1883.
Inozemtsev, I. L. "Traktat o muzyke Khushkhal'-Khana Khattaka" (Treatise on the music by Khushhal Khan Khattak); in N. I. Prigarina, ed., *Sufizm v kontekste musul'manskoi kul'tury.* Moscow, 1989, pp. 302–18.
Kaleem. M. M. "Pushto Folk Songs." *Pakistan Quarterly* 6/3 (1954), pp. 20–62.
Keykhosrow, see under Mowbad.
Khâdem. Qeyâm-al-Din. *Bâyazid Rawśân.* Kabul, 1945.
Khaṭak. Khoṣ̌ḥâl Khân. *Koliyyât-e Khoṣ̌ḥâl Khân Khaṭak* (Complete works of Khoshhal Khan Khattak). With Introduction and notes by Dost Mohammad Khan Kamil Mohmand. Peshawar, 1960.
Kieffer, Ch. M. "Über das Volk der Pastunen und seinen Pastunwali" (About the Pashtun people and their Pashtunwali). *Mitteilungen des Instituts für Orientforschung* XVII (1971/72), pp. 614–24.

Kushev, V.V. "Ob uchasii syna Akhunda Darvezy v literaturnoï deiatel'nosti ottsa" (On the participation of Akhund Darwezahi's son in the literary activity of his father). *Pis'mennye pamiatniki i problemy istorii kul'tury narodov Vostoka* 5 (1969), pp. 94–99.

Idem. *Opisanie rukopiseï na iazyke pashto Instituta Vostokovedenia* (Description of the Pashto manuscripts in the Oriental Institute). Moscow, 1976.

Idem. *Afganskaia rukopisnaia kniga* (Handwritten Afghan book). Moscow, 1980.

Idem (Kushef). "Eqtebasât-e adabiyyât-e pashtu az zabân-e fârsi" (Borrowings from Persian in Pashto literature). *Faṣl-nâme-ye târikh-e ravâbet-e khâreji* 1 (2000), pp. 129–35.

Lahori, Gholâm Sarwâr Ṣâḥeb. *Khazinat al-Aṣfiyâ' men taṣnif va ta'lif* (The treasure of the chosen ones in composition and authorship). Lahore, 1902.

Leyden, J. "On the Roshaniah Sect and its founder Bayazid Ansari." *Asiatic Researches* XI (1810), pp. 363–428.

Livshits, V.A. "Poet-voin (Khushkhal'- Khan Khattak)" (The warrior-poet Khushhal-Khan Khattak). *Literaturnyï Tadzhikistan* 12 (1957), pp. 247–51.

MacKenzie, D.N. "Pashto Verse." *BOAS* XXI (1958), pp. 319–33.

Idem. "The Xayr al-bayan;" in *Indo-Iranica*: mélanges présentés à Georg Morgenstierne à l'occasion de son soixante-dixième anniversaire, Wiesbaden. 1964. pp. 134–40.

Idem. trsl. *Poems from the Diwan of Khushhal Khan Khattak*. London, 1965.

Idem. "The Qasida in Pashto": In S. Sperl and C. Shackle, eds., *Qasida Poetry in Islamic Asia and Africa*. Leiden, New York, Koln, 1996.

Majrouh (Majrooh), S.B. "Etude du Destar-nama de Khoshhal Khan Khattak." *Trudy XXV Mezhdunarodnogo Kongressa vostokovedov* II. Moscow, 1963, pp. 241–50.

Mannanov, A. "Sufiisko-panteisticheskoe napravienie afganskoi literature XVI–XV vv." (Sufi-pantheistic tendency in the Afghan literature of the sixteenth and seventeenth centuries). Cand.Phil. diss., Oriental Institute of Moscow. Moscow, 1970 (National Library of the Russian Federation, Shelf-mark DK/70–10/590).

Idem. "Ali Mukhammad Mukhis i ego divan iz Britanskogo Muzeia" (Ali Mohammad Mokhis and his diwan from the British Museum). *Pashto Quarterly* 7.1–2 (1983–84) pp. 76–91.

Masson, V.A. and V.M. Romodin, *Istoria Afganistana* (History of Afghanistan). Vol. 2, Moscow, 1965.

Mirzâ-Khân Anṣâri. *Diwân*. Kabul, 1970.
Idem. *Diwân*. Kabul, Pašto Ṭoləna, 1975.
Mokhleṣ, Ali Moḥammad, *Ḥâl-nâme-ye Bâyazid Rowshân*. Kabul, 1986.
Morgenstierne, G. "Notes on an Old Pashto Manuscript, Containing the Khair ul-Bayan of Bayazid Ansari." *New Indian Antiquary*, vol. II (1939–40), pp. 566–74.
Idem. "Khushhal Khan: the national poet of the Afghans." *Journal of the Royal Central Asian Society* XLVII (1960), pp. 49–57.
Idem. *EI²*, s.v. Afghan.
Mowbad Keykhosrow Esfandiyâr. *Dabestân-e Madhâheb*. Tehran, 1983.
Nurzai, Gul Mukhammad. "Istochniki osvoboditel'nykh motivov v tvorchestve Khushkhalia Khattaka" (The origin of liberation topoi in the art of Khushhal Khan Khattak). *Iranskaia filologia*. Moscow, 1971. pp. 138–46.
Gazetteer of the Peshawar District, 1897–98. Lahore, 1898.
Pelevin, M. S., "Khushkhal-khan Khattak (1613–1689): nachalo afganskoï poezii" (Khushhal Khan Khattak (1613–89): the beginning of Afghan poetry). *Peterburgskoe Vostokovedenie*, St Petersburg, 2001.
Plowden, H. M. *Translation of the Kalid-i-Afghani, the Text-book for the Pakkhto Examination*. Lahore, 1875.
Rafi', Ḥabib-Allah. *Də khalqo sanderi aw də folklor pə bâb landa tsəṙəna* (Short study of popular songs and folklore). Kabul, 1970.
Idem. *Rawśâni Likəni* (Rowshani writing); in idem, ed., *Roshan Memorial*. Kabul, 1976. pp. 155–204.
Raverty. H. G., ed. *The Gulshan-i-Roh*: Being Selections, Prose and Poetical, in the Pus'hto or Afghan Language. London, 1860.
Idem. *Selections from the Poetry of the Afghans, from the Sixteenth to the Nineteenth Century*: Literally Translated from the Original Pus'hto. London, 1862.
Idem. *A Grammar of the Puk'hto, Pus'hto or Language of the Afghans*. 3rd edition, London, 1867.
Idem. *Notes on Afghanistan and Part of Baluchistan*. London, 1888.
Reisner, I. M. *Razvitie feodalizma i obrazovanie gosudarstva u afgantsev* (The development of feudalism and the establishment of state among Afghans). Moscow, 1954.
Reshâd, Abd-al-Shokur. "Də Kheyr al-Bayan lik dawd" (The writing of Khayr al-Bayan). In Bâyazid Anṣâri, *Kheyr al-Bayân*. Kabul, 1975, pp. 55–80.
Rizvi, S. A. A. "Rawshaniyya movement." In *Abar-Nahrain* (Department of Middle Eastern Studies, University of Melbourne), VI (1966–67), pp. 63–91; VII (1967–68), pp. 62–98.

Rose, H. A. A. *Glossary of the Tribes and Castes of the Punjab and North-West Frontier Province*. Lahore, 1914.
Wâṣel, Rawśâni. *Tsə she'runa* (Some poems). Kabul, Paśto Ṭoləna, 1975.

Chapter 5

Adeleye, M. O. "Islam and Education." *Islamic Quarterly* 27/3(1983), pp. 140–47.
Afridi, Qabil Khan. "Amir Hamza Khan Shinwari: Life and Work." Ph.D. diss., Area Study Centre (Central Asia), University of Peshawar, 1990.
Ahmed, A. S. *Pukhtun Economy and Society: Traditional Structure and Economic Development in a Tribal Society*. London, 1980.
Anderson, B. *Imagined Communities: Reflections on the Origin and Spread of Nationalism*. London, 1991.
Anderson, J. W. "Doing Pakhtu: Social Organization of the Ghilzai Pakhtun." Ph.D. diss., The University of North Carolina at Chapel Hill, 1979.
Idem. "How Afghans Define Themselves in Relation to Islam;" in M. Nazif Sharani and Robert L. Canfield, eds., *Revolutions and Rebellions in Afghanistan: Anthropological Perspectives*, Berkeley, 1984, pp. 266–87.
Idem. "Sentimental Ambivalence and the Exegesis of 'Self' in Afghanistan." *Anthropological Quarterly* 58/4 (1985), pp. 203–11.
Asfar, G. "Amadou Hampate Ba and the Islamic Dimension of West African Oral Literature;" in Kenneth W. Harrow, ed., *Faces of Islam in African Literature*, London, 1991, pp. 141–50.
Bacha, Ali Hazrat. "Poets Urged to Play Their Role in Society." *Frontier Post (Peshawar)*, 29 September 1997.
Baily, John. "Music Censorship in Afghanistan before and after the Taliban;" in *Shoot the Singer*, New York and London, 2004, pp. 19–28.
Idem. *"Can you stop the birds singing?" The Censorship of Music in Afghanistan*. Copenhagen [2003 printing; 2001 copyright].
Banerjee, M. "A Study of the 'Khudai Khidmatgar' Movement 1930–1947, North West Frontier Province, British India." D.Phil. diss., Oxford University, 1994.
Barth, F. *Political Leadership among Swat Pathans*. London, 1959.
Idem. "Pathan Identity and Its Maintenance;" in *Features of Person and Society in Swat: Collected Essays on Pathans. Selected Essays of Fredrik Barth*, vol. II, London, 1981, pp. 103–20.

Idem. *The Last Wali of Swat: An Autobiography as told to Fredrik Barth.* Bangkok, 1985.
Bartlotti, Leonard. "Negotiating Pakhto: Proverbs, Islam and the Construction of Identity among Pashtuns." Ph.D. diss., University of Wales. 2000.
Idem and R.W.S. Khattak. *Rohi Mataluna (Pashto Proverbs).* Revised and Expanded Edition. Peshawar, 2006.
Bausani, A. and B. Blair. "Pashto Language and Literature." *Mahfil: A Quarterly of South Asian Literature* (Michigan State University, Asia Studies Center) 7(1971), pp. 55–69.
Bênawâ, Abd-al-Ra'uf. *Osani Likwal* (Modern writers). 3 vols., Kabul, 1961–68.
Bradsher, H.S. *Afghanistan and the Soviet Union.* Durham, 1985.
Caroe, O. *The Pathans: 550 B.C. – A.D. 1957.* Karachi, 1985.
Caron, James. "Poetry of the 1950s Pashtunistan." Unpublished paper presented at the American Institute of Afghanistan Studies, 2007.
Dani, A.H. *Peshawar: Historic City of the Frontier.* Lahore, 1995.
Dupree, L. *Afghanistan.* Princeton, 1980.
Dupree, N.H. "Afghan Literature;" in Leonard S. Klein, ed., *Encyclopedia of World Literature in the 20th Century*, vol. I/2, New York, 1981, pp. 18–20.
Idem "The Conscription of Afghan Writers: An Aborted Experiment in Social Realism." *Central Asian Survey* 4 (1985), pp. 69–87.
Dvoryankov, N.A. "The Development of Pushtu as the National and Literary Language of Afghanistan." *Central Asian Review*, 14 (1966), pp. 210–20.
Edwards, D.B. *Heroes of the Age: Moral Fault Lines on the Afghan Frontier.* Berkeley, 1996.
Enevoldsen, J. *The Nightingale of Peshawar: Selections from Rahman Baba.* Peshawar, 1993.
Evans-Von Krbek, J.H.P. "The Social Structure and Organization of a Pakhto Speaking Community in Afghanistan." Ph.D diss., University of Durham, 1977.
Farhadi, R. "Afghanistan: Literature." *EIr.* I, London, 1985, pp. 564–66.
Finnegan, R. *Literacy and Orality.* Oxford, 1988.
Idem. *Oral Traditions and the Verbal Arts: A Guide to Research Practices.* London, 1992.
Franck, D.S. "Pakhtunistan—Disputed Disposition of a Tribal Land." *Middle East Journal* 6 (1952), pp. 49–68.
Ghani, A. "The Persian Literature of Afghanistan, 1911–78, in the Context of Its Political and Intellectual History;" in E. Yarshater, ed., *Persian Literature,* New York, 1988, pp. 428–53.

Gregorian, V. "Mahmud Tarzi and Saraj-ol-Akhbar: Ideology of Nationalism and Modernization in Afghanistan." *Middle East Journal*, 21/3 (1967), pp. 345–68.
Habibi, Abd-al-Ḥayy. "Paxto Literature at a Glance." *Afghanistan* 20/3 (1967), pp. 45–54; 20/4 (1967), pp. 51–64; 21/1 (1968), pp. 53–57.
Hanaway, W. L. and M. Nasir. "Chapbook Publishing in Pakistan," in W. L. Hanaway and W. Heston, eds., *Studies in Pakistani Popular Culture*, Islamabad and Sang-e Meel, Lahore, 1996, pp. 339–61.
Hoti, Salim Shah. "Pakhto Academy: Victim of Constant Neglect." *Frontier Post (Peshawar)*, 8 December 1997.
Khalil, Mohammad Javed. "Pə Suba Sarḥad ke də makhtalifo Paśto Ṭoləno aw adabi jirgo tanżim aw də haghwi kâr" (The purpose and work of the various Pakhto Societies and cultural councils in the North West Frontier Province). M.Phil. diss., Pashto Academy, Peshawar University, 1994.
Khan, Gh. *The Pathans: A Sketch*. Peshawar, 1958.
Idem. "A Review of Pakhtun Cultural [sic] Society I." *Frontier Post (Peshawar)*, 1 December 1987.
Lindholm, Ch. *Generosity and Jealousy: The Swat Pukhtun of Northern Pakistan*. New York, 1982.
MacKenzie, D. N. "Pashto," in B. Comrie, ed., *The World's Major Languages*, London and Sydney, 1987, pp. 547–65.
Majrooh, Sayd Bahaouddin. "Afghan Intellectuals in Exile: Philosophical and Psychological Dimensions," in E. Anderson and N. H. Dupree, eds., *The Cultural Basis of Afghan Nationalism*, London and New York, 1990, pp. 71–83.
Miran, M. Alam. "Sociolinguistic Factors in Afghanistan." *Afghanistan Journal* 4 (1977), pp. 122–27.
Orakzai, M. Tanveer. "The Pakhtun's Legacy." *Frontier Post (Peshawar)*, 23 May 1999.
Poullada, L. B. "Political Modernization in Afghanistan: The Amanullah Reforms," in G. Grassmuck et al, eds., *Afghanistan: Some New Approaches*, Ann Arbor, 1969, pp. 99–148.
Idem. "Pushtunistan: Afghan Domestic Politics and Relations with Pakistan," in A. T. Embree, ed., *Pakistan's Western Borderlands: The Transformation of a Political Order*, Durham NC, 1977, pp. 126–51.
Rahman, T. *Language and Politics in Pakistan*. Karachi, 1996.
Idem. "The Teaching of Pashto: Identity versus Utility." *The News International (Islamabad)*, 6 June 1999.
Rittenberg, S. A. *Ethnicity, Nationalism and the Pakhtuns: the Independence Movement in India's North-West Frontier Province*. Durham, NC, 1988.

Roy, O. *Islam and Resistance in Afghanistan.* New York, 1986.
Shaheen, Selma. *Rôhi Sandare.* 2 vols, Peshawar, 1984, 1994.
Shams, Shams-al-Rahmân. "The Poets of Malakand." Peshawar, n.p., n.d.
Shinwari, Sher Alam. "Future of Pakhto Language and Literature Depends upon Pakhtuns." *Frontier Post (Peshawar)*, 24 November 1997.
Idem. "Pakhto Books Have Very Poor Market Value: Views of Dr. Iqbal Naseem Khattak." *Frontier Post (Peshawar)*, 19 January 1998.
Sirat, A.S. "Sharia and Islamic Education in Modern Afghanistan." *Middle East Journal*, 23/2 (1969), pp. 217–19.
Spain, J.W. *The Pathan Borderland.* Karachi, 1963.
Tendulkar, D.G. *Abdul Ghaffar Khan: Faith is a Battle.* Bombay, 1967.
Wakeel, Abdul. "The Lot of Today's Pathan Woman is not Different from that of Maimoonay's: Salma [Interview with Salma Shaheen]." *Frontier Post (Peshawar)*, 17 May 1998.
Wilson, D. "Afghan Literature: a Perspective," in G. Grassmuck *et al.*, eds., *Afghanistan: Some New Approaches*, Ann Arbor, 1969, pp. 81–98.

Chapter 6

Abd-al-Ra'uf, Naushahravi. *Pashto adab: ek ta'arof* (Pashto literature: an introduction). Peshawar, 1988.
Ahmad, Maulavi, of Tangiand and T.P. Hughes. *Ganj-i-Pukhto, or, Pukhto Treasury: being the government text-book for the lower standard of examination in Pukhto, the language of the Afghans.* London, 1882.
Ahmed, A.S. *Mataloona: Pukhto proverbs.* 2nd rev. ed., Karachi, 1975.
Akhtar, Akhtar Malik. *Mataluna pə Swât kśe* (*Matal*s in Swat). Mingora, 1995.
Baily, J. *The Making of Amir: An Afghan Refugee Musician's Life in Peshawar, Pakistan: A Study Guide to the Film.* Watertown, MA, 1990.
Idem, Director and ed. *Amir: An Afghan Refugee Musician's Life in Peshawar, Pakistan.* [Video-recording]. Royal Anthropological Institute, Beaconsfield (Buckinghamshire), and National Film and Television School, London, 1985.
Baltuck, N. *Apples from Heaven: Multicultural Folk Tales about Stories and Storytellers.* North Haven (Conn.), 1995.
Bartlotti, L.N. "Negotiating Pashto: Proverbs, Islam and the Construction of Identity among Pashtuns." Ph.D. diss. University of Wales, 2000.

BIBLIOGRAPHIES

Blumhardt, J.F. *Catalogues of the Hindi, Panjabi, Sindhi, and Pushtu Printed Books in the Library of the British Museum.* London, 1893 [Citations by Pushtu section's column numbers].

Idem. *Catalogue of the Library of the India Office* II. Part III: Hindi, Panjabi, Pushtu, and Sindhi Books. London, 1902 [Citations by Pushtu section's page numbers].

Idem and D. N. MacKenzie. *Catalogue of Pashto Manuscripts in the Libraries of the British Isles, Dublin.* London, 1965.

Boesen, I.W. "Conflicts of Solidarity in Pashtun Women's Lives," in B. Utas, ed., *Women in Islamic Societies: Social Attitudes and Historical Perspectives,* Copenhagen, 1983, pp. 104–27.

Bokhâri, Farigh. *Sar-ḥaddi ke Lok Git* (Folk songs of the frontier). Islamabad, 1974.

Idem and R. Hamdâni. *Pashto šâ'eri* I (Pashto poetry). Karachi, 1966.

Darmesteter, J. *Chants populaires des Afghans.* Paris, 1888–90.

Dhar, Asha. *Folk Tales of Afghanistan.* New Delhi, 1982.

Dupree, L. *Afghanistan.* Princeton, 1973.

Enevoldsen, J. *Sound the bells, O moon, arise and shine!* Peshawar, c. 1990.

Forest, H. *Wisdom Tales from Around the World.* Little Rock, 1996.

Gazdar, Mushtaq. *Pakistan Cinema, 1947–1997.* Karachi, 1997.

Ghazanvi, Khatir. *Sarḥaddi rumâni kahâniyân, Romantic Tales from Frontier.* Islamabad, 1978.

Grima, B. *The Performance of Emotion Among Paxtun Women: The Misfortunes Which Have Befallen Me.* Austin, 1992.

Idem. "Translating Pukhtun Romance: Sher Alam and Memuney," in E. Bashir, M.M. Deshpande and P.E. Hook, eds., *Select Papers from SALA 7,* Bloomington, 1987, pp. 141–62.

Idem. "Les contes legendaires pashtun: Analyse et traduction de cassettes commercialisèes." M.A. thesis, University of Paris, 1982. (Submitted as: Benedicte Johnson.)

Hanaway, W.L. "Chapbooks in Pakistan," in C.L. and M.J. Preston, eds., *The Other Print Tradition: essays on chapbooks, broadsides, and related ephemera,* New York, 1995, pp. 127–43.

Idem and M. Nasir. "Chapbook Publishing in Pakistan.' In W.L. Hanaway and W. Heston, eds., *Studies in Pakistani Popular Culture,* Islamabad and Sang-e Meel, Lahore, 1996, pp. 339–615. (Cited as H&N and entry number.)

Hamdâni, R. *Razmiya Dâstânen* (Epics). Islamabad, 1981.

Idem. *Chârbeyta.* Islamabad, 1978.

Hastings, E.G. *Report of the Regular Settlement of the Peshawar District.* Lahore, 1878.

Henderson, M.M.T. "Four Varieties of Pashto." *JAOS* 103.3 (1983), pp. 595–97.
Heston, W. "Rhyme and Repetition: Pashto Poetry as Song," in W.L. Hanaway and W. Heston, eds., *Studies in Pakistani Popular Culture*, Islamabad and Sang-e Meel, Lahore, 1996, pp. 289–338.
Idem. "Pashto Chapbooks, Gendered Imagery and Cross-cultural Contact," In C.L. Preston and M.J. Preston, eds., *The Other Print Tradition: essays on chapbooks, broadsides, and related ephemera*, New York, 1995, pp. 144–60.
Idem. "Footpath Poets of Peshawar," in A. Appadurai, F.J. Korom, and M.A. Mills, eds., *Gender, genre, and power in South Asian expressive traditions*. Philadelphia, 1991, pp. 305–43.
Idem. "Verse Narratives from the Bazaar of the Storytellers." *Asian Folklore Studies* 45–1 (1986), pp. 79–99.
Idem and M. Nasir. *The Bazaar of the Storytellers*. Islamabad, 1988.
Hughes, T.P., compiler and ed. *The Kalid-i-afghani, being selections of Pushto Prose and Poetry for the use of students*. 2nd edition. Lahore, 1893.
Jan, Ahmad. *Hagha dagha or "Odds and ends."* Peshawar, 1929; reissued with introduction by Qalandar Momand, Peshawar, 1986.
Jatoi, Iqbal Ali. *Bibliography of Folk Literature*. Islamabad, 1980.
Johnson, Benedicte: see Grima.
Kâkaŕ, Syal. *Čêghyân*. Quetta, 1970.
Lindholm, C. *Generosity and Jealousy: The Swat Pakhtun of Northern Pakistan*. New York, 1982.
Idem. *Frontier Perspectives: Essays in Comparative Anthropology*. Karachi, 1996.
MacKenzie, D.N. "Pashto Verse." *BSOAS* 21 (1958), pp. 319–33.
Magnus, R. and E. Naby. *Afghanistan: Mullah, Marx and Mujahid*. Boulder, 1998.
Mahmud, Sayyed Fayyâz. *There Was Once A King (Folk-Tales of Pakistan)*. Islamabad, 1980.
Malyon, F.D. *Some Current Pushto Folk Stories*. Memoirs of the Asiatic Society of Bengal 3. Calcutta, 1912. (English translation printed as *Pushto Folk Stories*. Islamabad, 1980.)
Manalai, Nadjib. "Metrique du pashto." *Cahiers de poétique comparée* 15 (1987), pp. 103–53.
Manuel, P. *Cassette culture: popular music and technology in North India*. Chicago, 1993.
Masson, C. *Legends of the Afghan Countries*. London, 1848.
Momand, Qalandar and Farid Ṣaḥrâ'i. *Daryâb: Paṣ́to Loghat* (Ocean: Pashto dictionary). Peshawar, 1994.

BIBLIOGRAPHIES

Nuri, Moḥammad Gol. *Mataluna* (Proverbs). Kabul, 1948.
Idem. *Melli Hendâra* (National mirror). Peshawar, n.d.
Idem. *Melli Sandəre* (National songs). Kabul, 1944.
Pakistan Statistical Yearbook 1995. Karachi, 1995.
Parker, B. and A. Javid. *A Collection of Afghan Legends.* Kabul, 1970.
"Pathan Folk Songs." *Pakistan Quarterly* 10.4 (1962), pp. 17–23.
Pishinvi, Ḥamid-Allâh. *Pashto ke romān* (The Pashto novel). Quetta, 1970.
Pourhadi, I.V. *Persian and Afghan Newspapers in the Library of Congress, 1871–1978.* Washington, 1979.
Idem. "Afghanistan's Newspapers, Magazines and Journals." *Afghanistan Journal* 3.2 (1976), pp. 75–77.
Pritchett, F.W. *Marvelous Encounters: Qissa Literature in Urdu and Hindi.* Delhi, 1985.
Qabil Khân Afridi. "Amir Hamza Khan Shinwari: Life and Works." Ph.D. diss., Peshawar University, 1990.
Quddus, Syed Abdul. *The Pathans.* Lahore, 1987.
Rafi', Ḥabib-Allâh. *Paśtô Pânga* (Pashto bibliography). Kabul, Vol. I: 1975; Vol. II: 1977. [HR[1]]
Idem. *Paśtô ketâb-śôd* (Pashto bibliographical guide). Kabul, 1978. [HR[2]]
Rahman, Tariq. *Language and Politics in Pakistan.* Karachi, 1996.
Raverty, H.G. *Selections from the Poetry of the Afghans.* Lahore, 1978. (Reprint of an 1880 edition as *Selections from Pushto Poetry of the Afghans.*)
Reśtin, Ṣeddiq-Allâh. *Də Paśtô də Adab Târix* (History of Pashto literature). Kabul, 1946.
Ṣabir, (Moḥammad) Ayyub. *Jadid Paśtô Adab* (Modern Pashto literature). Peshawar, 1974.
Salim, Ahmad. *Pashtun and Baloch History: Punjabi View.* Lahore, 1991.
Shah, Amina. *Tales of Afghanistan.* London, 1982.
Shaheen, Selma. *Rôhi sandəre (ṭapê)* (Pashto songs, *ṭapa*s). Peshawar, 1984.
Shpoon, Saduddin. "Paxto Folklore and the Landey." *Afghanistan Journal* 20.4 (1967), pp. 40–50.
Tair (Ṭâ'er), Moḥammad Nawâz. *Pə paśtô kśe də maśumânô sandəre aw ṣawtuna* (Children's songs and utterances in Pashto). Peshawar, 1988.
Idem. *Mataluna* (Proverbs). Peshawar, 1980.
Idem. *Ṭapa aw žwand* (The *Ṭapa* and life). Peshawar, 1980.
Idem and T.C. Edwards. *Rohi Mataluna* (Pashto proverbs). Peshawar, 1982.

Thorburn, S.S. *Bannu: or, Our Afghan Frontier*. London, 1876; repr. Lahore, 1978.
Vejdân, Moammad Shafiq. *Folklor-e Afghâni: Adabiyyât-e Mardom* (Afghan folklore: the people's literature). Kabul, 1969.
Żamir, Moḥammad Ḥasan, Sapi. *Paśtani sandəre* (Pashto songs) II. Kabul, 1956.
Żwâk, Moḥammad Din. *Paśtani sandəre* (Pashto songs) I. Kabul, 1955.

Chapter 7

Baloch, Bashîr Aḥmad. *Durr-čin* (Pearl Gatherer). Quetta, 1963.
Baluch, Mohammad Sardar Khan. *A Literary History of the Baluchis*. Quetta, 1977.
Barker, M.A. and A.K. Mengal. *A Course in Baluchi*. 2 vols., Montreal, 1969.
Dames, M.L. *Popular Poetry of the Baloches*. 2 vols., London, 1907.
Idem. *A Textbook of the Balochi Language*. 2nd ed., Lahore, 1909.
Elfenbein, J. *A Baluchi Miscellany of Erotica and Poetry, "Codex Or. Add. 24048 of the British Library*. Naples, 1983.
Idem. "Popular Poetry of the Baloches," in A.D.H. Bivar *et al* eds., *Papers in Honour of Professor Mary Boyce*. Acta Iranica 10, Leiden, 1985, pp. 159-78.
Idem. *EIr*, s.v. Baluchistan iii.
Idem. "Baločî," in R. Schmitt, ed., *Compendium Linguarum Iranicarum*, Wiesbaden, 1989, pp. 350-62.
Idem. "Batal." *Études Irano-Aryennes offertes à Gilbert Lazard. Studia Iranica 7*, Paris, 1989, pp. 87-94.
Idem. *An Anthology of Classical and Modern Balochi Literature*. 2 vols., Wiesbaden, 1990.
Idem. "Rahm Ali Mari," in P. Cipriano *et al* eds. *Misc. di Studi in Onore Walter Belardi*, vol .1, Rome, 1994, pp. 43-58.
Idem. "Baluchi," in G. Windfuhr, ed., *Iranian Languages*, London, 2003.
Geiger, W. "Baločische Texte mit Übersetzung" (Balochi texts with translation). *ZDMG* 43 (1889), p. 579ff; 47 (1893), p. 409ff.
Grierson, G.A., ed. *Linguistic Survey of India X: Eranian Family*. Delhi, 1921; repr., 1968. (LSI X)
Gul Khân Nasîr, *Hammal-i Jîhand*. Karachi, 1969.
Idem. *Balochî razmîna shâirî* (Balochi heroic poetry), Karachi, 1979.

BIBLIOGRAPHIES

Jahani, C. *Standardization and Orthography in the Balochi Language.* Uppsala, 1989.
Lewis, A. *Bilochi Stories as spoken by the Nomad Tribes of the Sulaiman Hills.* Allahabad, 1855.
Mâhtâk Balôčî. Karachi, 1956–58; Quetta, 1978–81, 1986-.
Mari, Sher Muhammad. *Balôčî kahnên šâhirî* (Classical Balochi poetry). Quetta, 1970. (ŠMM)
Nôkên Dawr. Quetta, 1961–71. (Quetta n.d.)
Ṣabir, Ghauth-Bakhsh. *Batal o Galwar* (Riddles and proverbs). Quetta, n.d. (1969)
Ulus, Quetta, 1961-.
Zarubin, I. I. "K izucheniu Beludzhskogo iazyka i fol'klora" (The study of Balochi language and folklore). *Zap. Koll. Vostokovedov* V, Leningrad, 1930, pp. 664–68.
Idem. *Beludzhkie Skazki* (Balochi tales) I. Leningrad, 1932; II, ibid., 1949.

Chapter 8

Dzhusoity Nafî. *Istoriya osetinskoi literatury* (History of Ossetic Literature). Vols. I–II, Tbilisi, 1980–85.
Kouznetsov, V. and I. Lebedynsky. *Les chrétiens disparu du Caucase* (The Christians of the Caucasus). Paris, 1999.
Schmidt, R., ed. *Compendium linguarum Iranicarum.* Wiesbaden, 1989.
Sjögren, A. J.: *Ossetische Sprachlehre* (Ossetic Grammar), St. Petersburg, 1844.
Thordarson, F. 'Ossetic literature'. In: *Encyclopedia of World Literature in the twentieth Century,* 2nd ed. vol. 3, pp. 444–45. New York, 1983.
Idem. *EIr*, s.v. Bäx Fäldisin.
Idem. "Ossetic," in R. Schmidt, ed., *Compendium linguarum Iranicarum*, Wiesbaden, 1989 (Thordarson 1989b), pp. 456–79.
Idem. "Notes on the religious vocabulary of the Alans," in: *Annual of Medieval Studies at CEU*, vol. 6, Budapest, 2000, pp. 213–24.
Idem. "Ossetic." *Encylopaedia Iranica Online*, 2006, available at www.iranica.com.
Zgusta, L. *The Old Ossetic inscription from the river Zelenchuk.* Vienna, 1987.

Select bibliography on the Nart Epic

Ossetic texts referred to

Narty kaddzhytæ. Dzæudzhyqæu, 1946.
Narty kaddzhytæ. Dzæudzhyqæu, 1949.

Secondary literature

Narty. Osetinskij geroicheskiĭ epos (The Narts, The Ossetian heroic Epic). Kniga 1–3, Moskva, 1989–91.
Abaev, V. I. *Nartovskiĭ epos Osetin* (The Nart Epic of the Ossetians). Cxinvali, 1982. (Repr. in: V. I. Abaev: *Izbrannye Trudy*, vol. I, Vladikavkaz, 1990, pp. 142–242.)
Dumézil, G. *Légendes sur les Nartes* (Legends on the Narts). Paris, 1930.
Idem. *Le livre des héros. Légendes sur les Nartes.* Traduit de l'ossète, avec une introduction et des notes de Georges Dumézil (The Book of Heroes. Legends about the Narts. Translated from Ossetic, with introduction and commentary by Georges Dumézil). Paris, 1965.
Idem. *Loki* (id.). Paris, 1948. (2nd ed., Paris, 1986.)
Idem. *Mythe et épopée. L'idéologie des trois fonctions dans les épopées des peuples indo-européens* (Myth and Epic. The tripartite ideology in the epics of the Indo-european Peoples). Paris, 1968, esp. pp. 441–575.
Idem: *Romans de Scythie et d'alentour* (Romances of Scythia and Surroundings). Paris, 1978.
Gippert, J. "Narten." *Enzyklopädie des Märchens* 9/3, Berlin and New York, 1999, pp. 1210–18.

Chapter 9

Aarne, A. and S. Thompson. *The Types of the Folktale.* Second Revision. Helsinki, 1961.
Abrishami, A. *Farhang-e panj-zabâne-ye amthâl va ḥekam* (A dictionary of proverbs and proverbial sayings in five languages). Tehran, 1996.
Idem. *Farhang-e novin-e gozide-ye mathalhâ-ye fârsi* (A new dictionary of selected Persian proverbs). Tehran, 1997.
Afifi, R. *Mathalhâ va ḥekmathâ dar âthâr-e shâ'erân* (Proverbs and proverbial wisdom in the works of the poets). Tehran, 1992.

BIBLIOGRAPHIES

Âl-e Aḥmad, J. *Dorr-e yatim-e Khalij. Jazire-ye Khârg* (A lonely pearl of the Gulf. The island of Khârg). Tehran, 1960.

Idem. *Owrazân. Vaz'-e maḥall, âdâb va rosum, folklor, lahje* (Ourâzân. Its locality, manners and customs, folklore, and dialect). Tehran, 1954.

Idem. *Tâtneshinhâ-ye Boluk-e Zahrâ* (The Tâti population of Boluk-e Zahrâ). Tehran, 1958.

Amanolahi, S. and W.M. Thackston. *Tales from Lurestan*. Cambridge, Mass., 1986.

Amini, A.-Q. *Dâstânhâ-ye amthâl* (The tales of the proverbs). Isfahan, 1945, 1954, 1972.

Idem. *Si afsâne az afsânehâ-ye maḥalli-ye Esfahân* (Thirty tales from the local tales of Isfahan). Isfahan, 1960.

Anwari-Alhosseyni, Sh. *Loghaz und Mo'ammâ: Eine Quellenstudie zur Kunstform des persischen Rätsels*. Berlin, 1986.

Arberry, A.J. *Poems of a Persian Sufi*. Cambridge, 1937.

Asadiyân-Khorramâbâdi, M. et. al. *Bâvarhâ va dânestehâ dar Lorestân va Deylam* (Popular beliefs and knowledge in Lorestân and Deylam). Tehran, 1979.

Asmussen, J.P. "Ein iranisches Wort, ein iranischer Spruch und eine iranische Märchenformel als Grundlage historischer Folgerungen." *Temenos* 1968, pp. 7–18.

Idem. "Remarks on some Iranian Folk-Tales Treating of Magic Objects, Especially A-T 564." *Acta Orientalia* 28 (1965), pp. 220–43.

Atâbak-zâdeh, S. *Jâygâh-e Dashtestân dar sar-zamin-e Irân* (The position of Dashtestân in the Iranian land). Shiraz, 1994.

AT = Aarne and Thompson 1961.

Âzâdeh, H. and A. Mokhabber. *Qeṣṣehâ-ye Fârs* (Tales from Fârs). Tehran, 2001.

Babay, R. *A Favor for a Favor. Ten Jewish-Persian Folktales*. Jerusalem, 1980 [in Hebrew].

Bani-Asadi, R. *She'r va mardom* (Poetry and the people). Tehran, 1980.

Baykal, Ö. "Animal Tales in the Mathnawi of Mevlana Jalalu'd-Din Rumi." *Erdem* 1 (1985), pp. 615–20.

Beeman, W.O. "Why Do They Laugh? An Interactional Approach to Humor in Traditional Iranian Improvisatory Theater." *Journal of American Folklore* 91 (1981), pp. 505–26.

Beyhaqi, H. *Pazhuhesh va bar-resi-ye farhang-e âmme-ye Irân* (A study and assessment of popular culture in Iran). Mashhad, 1986 (1365).

Idem. *Chehel afsâne-ye khorâsâni* (Forty tales from Khorâsân). Tehran, 2000.

Boldyrev, A. N., ed. *Skazki i legendy Sistana* (Tales and legends from Sistan). Moscow, 1981.
Bonelli. L. *Detti proverbiali persiani* (Persian proverbial sayings). Rome, 1941.
Boulvin, A. "Oslub-e elmi-ye tanẓim-e mavâdd-e qeṣṣehâ-ye âmiyâne" (A scientific method for the classification of popular tales). *Sokhan* 21 (1971), pp. 1159–70.
Idem. *Contes populaires persans du Khorasan* (Persian popular tales from Khorasan). 2 vols., Paris, 1975.
Boyle, J. A. "Popular Literature and Folklore in 'Attar's Mathnavis." *Colloquio italo-irano sul poeta mistico Fariduddin 'Attar*. Rome, 1978, pp. 57–70.
Braginskiĭ, L. *Iranskaia skazochnaia entsiklopedia* (Encyclopaedia of Persian tales). Moscow, 1977.
Bricteux, A. *Contes persans* (Persian tales). Paris, 1910.
Brockett, E. *Persian Fairy Tales*. Chicago and New York, 1962.
Bromberger, C. "Les blagues ethniques dans le nord de l'Iran" (Ethnic jokes in northern Iran). *Cahiers de littérature orale* 20 (1986), pp. 73–99.
Bruijn, J. T. P. de. "Die persische Volksliteratur im Mittelalter und ihr Verhältnis zur klassischen Literatur" (Persian popular literature in the Middle Ages and its relation to classical literature); in W. Heinrichs, ed., *Orientalisches Mittelalter (Neues Handbuch der Literaturwissenschaft)*, Wiesbaden, 1990, pp. 465–74.
Burnikel, E. *Beschreibungen von Iranreisen im Zeitalter des Barock* (Descriptions of travels to Iran in the Baroque period). M.A. Thesis, Saarbrücken, 1992.
Cejpek, J. "Iranian Folk-Literature," in J. Rypka, *History of Iranian Literature*, Dordrecht, 1968, pp. 607–709.
Chauvin, V. "Les contes populaires dans le livre de rois" (Popular tales in the Book of Kings). *Zeitschrift für Volkskunde* 21 (1911), pp. 85ff.
Chodzko, A. B. *Specimens of the Popular Poetry of Persia* ... London, 1842.
Christensen, A. *Contes persans en langue populaire*. Copenhagen, 1918.
Idem. "Les sots dans la tradition populaire des Persans" (Fools in Persian popular tradition). *AO* 1 (1923) pp. 43–75.
Idem. "La légende du sage Buzurjmihr" (The legend of the sage Burzurjmihr). *AO* 8 (1930), pp. 81–128.
Idem. "La princesse sur la feuille de myrte et le princesse sur le pois" (The princess on the myrtle-leaf and the princess on the pea). *AO* 14 (1936), pp. 241–57.

Idem. *Persische Märchen* (Persian tales.) [1939]. Düsseldorf/Köln, 1958 (partial English translation, London, 1971).
Clouston, W. A. *A Group of Eastern Romances and Stories from the Persian, Tamil, and Urdu.* London, 1889.
Idem. *Flowers from a Persian Garden and Other Papers.* London, 1890.
Idem. *Some Persian Tales from Various Sources.* Glasgow, 1892.
Darvishiyân, A. A. and R. Khandan. *Farhang-e afsânehâ-ye mardom-e Irân* (A dictionary of Persian folktales). Vols. 1–19, Tehran, 1998–2008.
Dehkhodâ, A.-A. *Amthâl va hekam* (Proverbs and proverbial wisdom). Vols. 1–4, Tehran, 1922–29.
Donaldson, B. A. *The Wild Rue: A Study of Muhammadan Magic and Folklore in Iran.* London, 1938.
Eilers, W. "Vierzeilerdichtung, persisch und außerpersisch" (Four-line poetry, Persian and non-Persian). *WZKM* 62 (1969), pp. 209–49.
Eliade, M. *Chashm-andâzhâ-ye osturi* (Mythical perspectives). Tehran, 1983.
Idem. *Osture, ro'yâ, râz* (Myths, dreams and mysteries). Tehran, 1995.
Elwell-Sutton, L. P. *Mashdi Galeen Khanom: The Wonderful Sea-Horse and Other Persian Tales.* London, 1950.
Idem. *Persian Proverbs.* London, 1954.
Idem. "Dâstânhâ-ye âmiyâne-ye Irân" (Persian popular tales). *Sepide-ye fardâ* 6 (1959), pp. 57–66.
Idem. "Scaldheads and Thinbeards in Persian Folk-tale Literature." *Laographia* 22 (1965), pp. 105–8.
Idem. "The Role of the Darvish in the Persian Folk-Tale." *Proceedings of the 26th International Congress of Orientalists* (1964), vol. 2, New Delhi, 1968, pp. 200–3.
Idem. "The Unfortunate Heroine in Persian Folk-literature." *Yâd-nâme-ye Irâni-ye Minorsky.* Tehran, 1969, pp. 37–50.
Idem. "Magic and the Supernatural in Persian Folk-literature." *Actes du Ve Congrès international d'arabisants et d'islamisants.* Bruxelles, 1970, pp. 189–96.
Idem. "The Influence of Folktale and Legend on Modern Persian Literature." *Iran and Islam.* Festschr. V. Minorsky. Edinburgh, 1971, pp. 247–54.
Idem. "Family Relationships in Persian Folk-Literature." *Folklore* 87 (1976), pp. 160–66.
Idem. "Mountain and Plain: Contrasts in Persian Folk-literature." *Studia Fennica* 20 (1976), pp. 331–37.
Idem. "A Narrator of Tales from Tehran." *Arv* 36 (1980), pp. 201–8.
Idem. "Collecting Folktales in Iran." *Folklore* 93 (1982), pp. 98–104.

ORAL LITERATURE OF IRANIAN LANGUAGES

Enjavi Shirâzi, A. *Ṭarz-e neveshtan-e farhang-e âmiyâne* (How to document popular culture). Tehran, 1967.
Idem. *Tamthil va mathal* (Proverbs and their tales). Vol. 1, Tehran, 1973[a]. [Enlarged version 1978.]
Idem. *Qeṣṣehâ-ye irâni* (Persian tales). 3 vols, Tehran, 1973[b], 1974, 1977, 1980.
Idem. *Ferdowsi-nâme* (The Ferdowsi book). Tehran, 1990.
Idem. *Godhari va naẓari dar farhang-e mardom* (Some thoughts about popular culture). Tehran, 1992.
Faqiri, A. *Tarânehâ-ye maḥalli* (Local songs). Shiraz, 1963.
Idem. *Qeṣṣehâ-ye mardom-e Fârs* (Folktales from Fârs). Tehran, 1970.
Idem. *Gushehâ'i az farhang-e mardom-e Fârs* (Some aspects of popular culture in Fârs). Shiraz, 1978.
Feinstein, A.S. *Folk Tales from Persia*. South Brunswick and New York and London, 1971.
Foruzânfar, B. *Ma'âkhedh-e qeṣaṣ va tamthilât-e Mathnavi* (Sources of the tales and allegories in the Mathnavi [of Rumi]). Tehran, 1954, 1991.
Friedl, E. "The Folktale as Cultural Comment." *Asian Folklore Studies* 34 (1975), pp. 127–44.
Friedl, E. "Women in Contemporary Persian Folktales," in L. Beck and N. Keddie, eds., *Women in the Muslim World*, Cambridge, Mass. and London, 1978, pp. 629–50.
Goldstein, J. "Iranian Jewish Women's Magical Narratives," in P.P. Chock and J.R. Wyman, eds., *Discourse and the Social Life of Meaning*, Washington, D.C., 1986, pp. 147–68.
Haag-Higuchi, R. *Untersuchungen zu einer Sammlung persischer Erzählungen* (A study of a collection of Persian tales). Berlin, 1984.
Ḥabibi Âzâd, N. *Ketâbshenâsi-ye âdâb va rosum-e Eṣfahân* (Bibliography of manners and customs of Isfahan). Tehran, 1993.
Ḥabibi Fahlyâbi, H. *Mamasani dar gozargâh-e târikh* (Mamasani in the course of time). Shiraz, 1992.
Ḥalabi, A.A. *The Development of Humour and Satire in Persia with Special Reference to 'Ubaid Zâkâni*. Ph.D. diss., University of Edinburgh, 1980.
Hanaway, W.L., "Formal Elements in the Persian Popular Romances." *Review of National Literatures* 2 (1971), pp. 139–61.
Hedâyat, S. *Neyrangestân* (A place of magic). Tehran, 1933, 1956, 1963.
Idem. "Folklor yâ farhang-e tude" (Folklore or popular culture) [1945]; in idem., ed., *Neveshtehâ-ye parâkande*, Tehran, 1965, pp. 447–83.
Homâyuni, S. *Yek hezâr va chahâr sad tarânehâ-ye maḥalli* (One thousand and four hundred local songs). n.p., 1969.

Idem. *Farhang-e mardom-e Sarvestân* (The folk-culture of Sarvestân.). Tehran, 1970, 1992.

Idem. *Gushehâ'i az âdâb va rosum-e mardom-e Shirâz* (Some aspects of popular manners and customs in Shirâz). Shiraz, 1974, 1992.

Idem. *Ḥoseyniye-ye Moshir* (The Hoseyniyye of Moshir). Tehran, 1976, 1992.

Idem. *Ta'ziye dar Iran* (Passion plays in Iran). Shiraz, 1989, 2001.

Idem. *Afsânehâ-ye Irâni* (Persian tales). Shiraz, 1972; Tehran, 1993.

Idem. *Tarânehâ-ye maḥalli-ye Fârs* (Local songs from Fârs). Shiraz, 2000.

Honari, M. *Owsungun: Afsânehâ-ye mardom-e Khur* (Owsungun. Folktales from Khur). Tehran, 1973.

Ivanow, W. "Rustic Poetry in the Dialect of Khorasan." *Journal of the Asiatic Society of Bengal* N.S. 21 (1925), pp. 233–313.

Izadpanâh, H. *Dâstânhâ va zabânzadhâ-ye Lori* (Tales and sayings of the Lori people). Tehran, 1983.

Jaktâji, M.T.A. *Afsânehâ-ye Gilân* (Tales from Gilân). Tehran, 2001.

Jamâlzâdeh, M.A. *Yeki bud, yeki nabud* (Once upon a time). Berlin, 1922.

Idem. *Farhang-e loghât-e âmiyâne* (A dictionary of colloquial terms). Edited by M.J. Maḥjub. Tehran, 1962.

Javâdi, S.K. *Hekâyât-e laṭif* (Charming tales). Tehran, 1996.

Jâvid, H. *Âvâhâ-ye ruḥ-navâz* (Mind-soothing melodies). Tehran, 2001.

Karbâschi, M.A. *Ketâbshenâsi-ye ketâbshenâsihâ-ye mardomshenâsi* (A bibliography of ethnographical bibliographies). Shiraz, 2001.

Karimzâde, M. *Chehel qeṣṣe. Gozide-ye qeṣṣehâ-ye âmiyâne-ye Irâni* (Forty tales. A selection of Persian popular tales). Tehran, 1997.

Katirâ'i, M., ed. *Aqâyed al-nesâ' va Mer'ât al-bolahâ'. Do resâle-ye enteqâdi dar farhang-e tude* (Women's beliefs and mirrors of fools. Two critical essays about popular culture). Tehran, 1970.

Idem. *Zabân va farhang-e mardom* (Language and popular culture). Tehran, 1978.

Khosravi, Kh. *Jazire-ye Khârg dar dowre-ye estilâ-ye naft* (The island of Khârg in the period of petrol exploitation). Tehran, 1963.

Kreyenbroek, P.G. *EIr*, s.v. Folk Poetry.

Kuhi Kermâni, H. *Chahârdah afsâne az afsânehâ-ye rustâ'i-ye Irân* (Fourteen tales from the tales of Persian peasants). Tehran, 1935. Later editions appeared as *Pânzdah afsâneh ...* (Fifteen tales ...). Tehran, 1954, 1969.

Idem. *Haftṣad tarâne az tarânehâ-ye rustâ'i-ye Irân* (Seven hundred songs from the songs of Persian peasants). Tehran, 1966.

Kuka, M. N. *The Wit and Humour of the Persians*. Bombay, 1894 (enlarged ed. entitled *Wit, Humour and Fancy of Persia*. Bombay, 1923, 1937).
Lâhsâ'izâdeh, A. and A. Salâmi. *Târikh va farhang-e mardom-e Davân* (The history and folklore of Davân). Tehran, 1991.
Lama'e, M. *Farhang-e âmiyâne-ye Boir Aḥmadi va Kohgiluye* (The popular culture of Boir Ahmadi and Kohgiluye). Tehran, 1970.
Lorimer, D. L. R. and E. O. Lorimer. *Persian Tales, Written down for the First Time in the Original Kermani and Bakhtiari*. London, 1919.
Lorimer, D. L. R. and E. O. Lorimer. *Farhang-e mardom-e Kermân* (The popular culture of Kermân). Translated by F. Vahman. Tehran, 1974.
Maḥjub, M. J. "Dâstânhâ-ye âmiyâne-ye fârsi" (Persian popular narratives). *Sokhan* 10/1, 1959, pp. 64–68 (continued in a total of 22 instalments up to *Sokhan* 12, 1961, pp. 1013–25).
Marzolph, U. *Die Vierzig Papageien. Das persische Volksbuch Chehel Tuti* (The forty parrots. The Persian chapbook *Chehel Tuti*). Walldorf, 1979.
Idem. *Der Weise Narr Buhlûl* (The wise fool Bohlul). Wiesbaden, 1983.
Idem. *Typologie des persischen Volksmärchens* (A typology of Persian folktales). Beirut, 1984 (*ṭabaqe-bandi-ye qeṣṣehâ-ye Irâni*. Tehran, 1992).
Idem. "Der Weise Narr Buhlûl in den modernen Volksliteraturen der islamischen Länder" (The wise fool Bohlul in the modern popular literatures of the Islamic lands). *Fabula* 28 (1987), pp. 72–89.
Idem. *Arabia ridens: Die humoristische Kurzprosa der frühen adab-Literatur im internationalen Traditionsgeflecht*. ("Laughing Arabia": jocular short prose narratives from works of early *adab*-literature in the context of international tradition). 2 vols, Frankfurt, 1992.
Idem. "Iran." *Enzyklopädie des Märchens* 7. Berlin/New York, 1993, cols. 248–70.
Idem. *Dâstânhâ-ye širin. Fünfzig persische Volksbüchlein aus der zweiten Hälfte des zwanzigsten Jahrhunderts* ("Sweet stories." Fifty Persian chapbooks from the second half of the twentieth century). Stuttgart, 1994[a].
Idem. "Folk Narrative and Folk Narrative Research in Post-Revolutionary Iran." *Middle East and South Asia Folklore Bulletin* 12/1, 1994[b], pp. 8–12.
Idem. "Die Revolution im Schulbuch. Die Grundschullehrbücher 'Persisch' vor und nach 1979." (The Revolution in schoolbooks. The primary readers "Persian" before and after the Revolution). *Spektrum Iran* 7/3–4 (1994), pp. 36–56.
Idem. "Popular Narratives in Jalâloddin Rumi's Masnavi." *The Arabist* 12–14, (1995) [a], pp. 275–87.

Idem. "Interkulturelles Erzählen. Der Transfer von Erzählgut in iranischen Grundschullehrbüchern." (The intercultural narrating of tales. The transfer of narratives in Persian primary schoolbooks); in C. Lipp, ed., *Medien populärer Kultur. Erzählung, Bild und Objekt in der volkskundlichen Forschung. Festschrift Rolf Wilhelm Brednich*, Frankfurt am Main, 1995[b], pp. 182–95.

Idem. "Pleasant Stories in an Easy Style: Gladwin's Persian Grammar as an Intermediary between Classical and Popular Literature," in B. Fragner et al., eds., *Proceedings of the Second European Conference of Iranian Studies*. Rome, 1995[c], pp. 445–75.

Idem. "Mollâ Nasroddin in Persia." *Iranian Studies* 28/3–4 (1995)[d], pp. 157–74.

Idem. "Illustrated Exemplary Tales: A Nineteenth Century Edition of the Classical Persian Proverb Collection Jâme' al-tamsil." *Proverbium* 16 (1999)[a], pp. 167–91.

Idem. "A Treasury of Formulaic Narrative: The Persian Popular Romance Hosein-e Kord." *Oral Tradition* 14/2 (1999)[b], pp. 279–303.

Idem. "Adab in Transition. Creative Compilation in Nineteenth Century Print Tradition." *Israel Oriental Studies* 19 (1999)[c], pp. 161–72.

Idem. "Variation, Stability, and the Constitution of Meaning in the Narratives of a Persian Storyteller," in L. Honko, ed., *Thick Corpus, Organic Variation and Textuality in Oral Tradition*, Helsinki, 2000, pp. 435–52.

Idem. *Narrative Illustration in Qajar Lithographed Books*. Leiden, Boston and Köln, 2001[a].

Idem. "Popular Literature in the Qajar Period." *Asian Folklore Studies* 40 (2001)[b], pp. 215–36.

Idem. "The *Persian Nights*. Links between the *Arabian Nights* and Persian Culture." *Fabula* 45 (2004) pp. 275–93.

Idem. "Regionale Stereotypen im Witz der Exil-Iraner." (Regional stereotypes in the jokes of expatriate Iranians). In: S. Hose, ed., *Minderheiten und Mehrheiten in der Erzählkultur*, Bautzen 2008, pp. 196–205

Idem. Amirhosseini-Nithammer, A. and A. Vakiliyân. *Qeṣṣehâ-ye Mashdi Galin Khânom* (The tales of Mashdi Galin Khânom). Tehran, 1995, 1997.

Massé, H. "Contes en persan populaire, recueillis et traduits." (Tales in colloquial Persian, collected and translated). *JA* 206 (1925) pp. 71–157.

Idem. *Croyances et coutumes persanes* (Persian beliefs and customs). 2 vols., Paris, 1938.

Mehdevi, A. S. *Persian Folk and Fairy Tales*. New York, 1965.

Meier, F. "Das Volk der Riemenbeinler." (The strap-legged people). In G. Wießner, ed., *Festschrift W. Eilers*. Wiesbaden, 1967, pp. 341–67.

Idem. "Orientalische Belege für das Motiv 'Nur einmal zuschlagen.'" (Oriental references for the motif "you only strike once"). *Mélanges d'Islamologie. Festschrift A. Abel*, Leiden, 1974, pp. 207–23.

Meisami, J. S. "Mixed Prose and Verse in Medieval Persian Literature," in J. Harris and K. Reichl, eds., *Prosimetrum. Crosscultural Perspectives on Narrative in Prose and Verse*, Cambridge, 1999, pp. 295–317.

Mihandust, M. *Samandar-e chel gis: Daftari az chand qeṣṣe ke dar Khorâsân shanide shode-ast* (Salamandar forty-locks. A booklet of some tales heard in Khorâsân). Tehran, 1973.

Idem. "Qeṣṣe dar qalamrow-e adabiyyât-e shafâhi." (In the realm of oral literature). *Mardomshenâsi va farhang-e âmme-ye Irân* 2, (1975), pp. 103–13.

Idem. "Puyâ-ye qeṣṣe dar farhang-e fekri-ye mardomân." (Of tales in popular intellectual culture). *Sokhanrânihâ-ye mohaqqeqân-e Markaz-e Mardomshenâsi-ye Irân dar haftomin kongere-ye taḥqiqât-e Irâni*. Tehran, 1977, pp. 45–52.

Idem. *Sib-e khandân va nâr-e geryân* (The laughing apple and the crying fire). Mashhad, 1991.

Idem. *Owsânehâ-ye âsheqi* (Popular tales of love). Tehran, 1999[a].

Idem. *Noh kelid. Daftari az owsânehâ-ye Khorâsâni* (Nine keys. A booklet of folktales from Khorâsân). Tehran, 1999[b].

Idem. *Sonnat-shekan. Daftari az owsânehâ-ye Khorâsâni* (The breaker of tradition. A booklet of folktales from Khorâsân). Tehran, 1999[c].

Idem. *Bâkerehâ-ye parizâd. Daftari az owsânehâ-ye Khorâsâni* (Fairy maidens. A booklet of folktales from Khorâsân). Tehran, 1999[d].

Idem. *Owsânehâ-ye kh^{w}âb* (Folktales of sleep). Tehran, 2001.

Mills, M. A. "Folk tradition in the *Masnavî* and the *Masnavî* in folk tradition," in A. Banani, R. Hovannisian, and G. Sabagh, eds., *Poetry and Mysticism in Islam: The Heritage of Rûmî*. Cambridge, 1994, pp. 136–77.

Mir-Kâẓemi, H. *Afsânehâ-ye mâ-zendegân* (Folktales of the [people who call themselves] "we are alive"). Tehran, 1988.

Idem. *Afsânehâ-ye shomâl* (Tales from the north). Tehran, 1994.

Idem. *Afsânehâ-ye diyâr-e hamishe bahâr* (Tales of the regions where spring rules forever). Tehran, 1995.

Mohammadi, M. H. and Z. Qâ'eni. *Târikh-e adabiyyât-e kudakân-e Irân*. Vol. 3–5: *Adabiyât-e kudakân-e dowre-ye Mashruṭiyyat* (A history of children's literature in Iran. Vol. 3–5: Children's literature during the Constitutional period). Tehran, 2001.

Moḥarrer, I. *Â'ine-ye â'inhâ va afsânehâ-ye Lorestân* (A mirror of customs and folktales of Lorestan). Tehran, 1986.

BIBLIOGRAPHIES

Morâdiyân-Garusi, A. A. *Qeṣṣehâ az Gilân* (Tales from Gilân). Tehran, 1977.

Motaref, K. *From the Land of Roses and Nightingales. A Collection and Study of Persian Folktales*, 2 vols., Ph.D. diss., Florida State University, Diss., Tallahassee, 1979.

Neubauer, E. *Tarânehâ-ye maḥallî. Volkstümliche persische Vierzeiler (do beytî), als Liedertexte gesammelt in Fârs und den angrenzenden Provinzen in den Jahren 1969–1971* (Local songs. Popular Persian four-line Poetry, collected as song-texts in Fârs and the neighbouring provinces in the years 1969–1971). unpubl. Ms., Frankfurt a. M, 1983.

Noṣeyri, P. "Afsânehâ-ye Lorestân." (Tales from Lorestân). *Nâme-ye farhang-e Irân* 1 (1985), pp. 59–72; 2 (1986), pp. 59–72.

Nurbakhsh, H. *Bohlul dar âthâr-e maktub va ḥekâyathâ-ye mardom* (Bohlul in written sources and folk stories). Tehran, 2003.

Omidsâlâr, M. "Storytellers in Classical Persian Texts." *Journal of American Folklore* 97 (1984), pp. 204–12.

Idem. "Eṣṭelâḥât-e farhang-e mardom dar zabân-e fârsi" (Expressions of popular culture in the Persian language). *Âyande* 12 (1986), pp. 543–56.

Idem. "Peri (Pari)." In *Enzyklopädie des Märchens* 10. Berlin and New York, 2002, pp. 743–46.

Idem and T. Omidsâlâr. "Narrating Epics in Iran," in M. R. MacDonald, ed., *Traditional Storytelling Today. An International Sourcebook*. Chicago/London, 1999, pp. 326–40.

Osmanov, N. *Persidskie skazki* (Persian tales). Moscow, 1958.

Osmanov, M.-H. *Persidskie narodnye skazki* (Persian popular tales). Moscow, 1987.

Osterhammel, J. *Die Entzauberung Asiens: Europa und die asiatischen Reiche im 18. Jahrhundert* (The demystification of Asia: Europe and the Asiatic empires in the eighteenth century). München, 1998.

Pak, G. *A Study of the Animal Folk-Tales in Iran*. M.A. diss., Edinburgh, 1979.

Panâhi Semnâni, M. *Âdâb va rosum-e mardom-e Semnân* (Manners and customs of the people of Semnân). Tehran, 1985.

Idem. *Tarâne va tarâne-sarâ'i dar Irân: Seyri dar tarânehâ-ye melli-ye Irân* (Songs and singing in Iran: A study of national songs in Iran). Tehran, 1997.

Idem. *Do-beytihâ-ye bumi-sarâyân-e Irân* (Four-line poetry of the Iranian regional population). Tehran, 2000.

Partovi Âmoli, M. *Rishehâ-ye târikhi-ye amthâl va ḥekam* (The historical roots of proverbs and proverbial sayings). 2 vols., Tehran, 1990.

Pâyande, M. *Mathalhâ va eṣṭelâḥât-e Gil va Deylam* (Proverbs and proverbial expressions from Gilân and Deylam). Tehran, 1973.
Idem. *Â'inhâ va bâvardâshthâ-ye Gil va Deylam* (Customs and popular beliefs from Gilân and Deylam). Tehran, 1976.
Phillot, D. C. "Some Current Persian Tales, Collected in the South of Persia from Professional Story-Tellers." *Memoirs of the Asiatic Society of Bengal* 1.18 (1905–07), pp. 375–412.
Idem. "Some Persian Riddles Collected from Dervishes in the South of Persia." *JRAS* 2.4 (1906), pp. 88–93.
Idem. "A Note on Sign-, Gesture-, Code- and Street-language, etc., among the Persians." *JRAS* 3.9 (1907), pp. 619–22.
Pishdâdfar, F. *Afsânehâ-ye mardom-e Irân-zamin dar farhang-e mardom-e Dartujân* (Iranian folktales in the popular culture of Dartujân). Vol. 5, Bandar Abbâs, 2001.
Radhayrapetian, J. *Iranian Folk Narrative: A Survey of Scholarship.* New York and London, 1990.
Rahgozar, R. *Fażl[-Allâh] Mohtadi (Ṣobhi).* Tehran, 1994.
Rahmâniyân, D. *Afsânehâ-ye Lori: Afsânehâ-ye Lori, Bakhtiyâri va Shushtari* (Lori tales. Tales of the Lori, Bakhtiyâri and Shushtari peoples). Tehran, 2000.
Rahmoni, R. *Târikh-e gerd-âvarî, nashr va pazhûhesh-e afsânehâ-ye mardom-e fârsizabân: Irân, Tâjikestân, Afghânestân* (The history of the collections, publication and study of folktales in the Persian language: Iran, Tajikistan, and Afghanestan). Dushanbe, 2001.
Ravânipur, R. *Afsânehâ va bâvarhâ-ye jonub* (Tales and popular beliefs of the south). Tehran, 1990.
Romaskevich, A. A. *Persidskie narodnye skazki* (Persian popular tales). Moscow, 1934.
Rozenfel'd, A. Z. *Persidskie narodnye skazki* (Persian popular tales). Tashkent, 1958.
Idem. *Persidskie skazki* (Persian tales). Moscow, 1956.
Ruḥolamini, M. *Bâvarhâ-ye âmiyâne dar bâre-ye fâl-e Ḥâfeẓ* (Popular beliefs about the oracle of Hâfez). Tehran, 1990.
Rypka, J., ed. *History of Iranian Literature.* Dordrecht, 1968.
Sâdât-e Eshkevari, K. *Afsânehâ-ye Eshkevar-e bâlâ* (Tales from Eshkevar-e bâlâ). Tehran, 1973.
Sajjâdpur, F. *Fosun-e afsâne: Taḥlil va bar-rasi-ye afsânehâ-ye âmiyâne-ye Irâni* (The charm of tales: a study and assessment of Persian popular tales). Tehran, 1999.
Salimi, M. *Qeṣṣehâ-ye âmiyâne-ye mardom-e Irân* (Popular Persian folktales). Tehran, 1993.

Ṣan'atiniyâ, F. *Ma'âkhez-e qeṣaṣ va tamthilât-e mathnavihâ-ye Aṭṭâr-e Neyshâburi* (The sources of the tales and allegories in the Mathnavis of Attâr of Neyshâbur). Tehran, 1990.

Sattâri, J. *Dar qalamrow-e farhang-e mardom* (In the realm of popular culture). Tehran, 1987.

Idem. *Zamine-ye farhang-e mardom* (The field of popular culture). Tehran, 1991.

Scott, C. T. *Persian and Arabic Riddles.* The Hague, 1965.

Shahidi, E. *Pazhuheshi dar ta'ziye va ta'ziye-khʷâni az âghâz tâ pâyân-e dowre-ye Qâjâr dar Tehrân* (A study of Ta'ziye and its performance from the beginning to the end of the Qâjâr period in Tehran). Tehran, 2001.

Shahri, J. *Qand va namak żarbolmathalhâ-ye Tehrâni be-zabân-e moḥâvere* (Sugar and salt. Tehran proverbs in colloquial language). Tehran, 1991.

Shakurzâdeh, E. *Aqâyed va rosum-e âmme-ye mardom-e Khorâsân* (Popular beliefs and customs in Khorâsân). Tehran, 1967, 1984.

Idem. *Dah hezâr mathal-e fârsi va bist-o-panj hezâr mo'âdel-e ânhâ* (Ten thousand Persian proverbs and twenty-five thousand corresponding versions). Mashhad, 1993 (new edition entitled *Davâzdah hezâr mathal-e Fârsi va si hezâr mo'âdel-e ânhâ* [Twelve thousand Persian proverbs and thirty thousand corresponding versions], Mashhad, 2001).

Shâmlu, A. *Qeṣṣehâ-ye Ketâb-e Kuche* (The tales from the "Book of the Streets"). Tehran, 2000.

Shari'atzâde, A. *Farhang-e mardom-e Shâhrud* (The popular culture of Shâhrud). Tehran, 1992.

Shvarts, E. A. *K istorii izucheniya fol'klora Irana* (On the history of the study of Iranian folklore). Dushanbe, 1974.

Idem. Ne'matov, T. *Namunahoi folklori Eron* (Specimens of Iranian folklore). Dushanbe, 1963.

Ṣobhi, F. *Ketâb-e Ṣobhi* (Sobhi's book). Tehran, 1933.

Idem. *Afsânehâ* (Tales). 2 vols., Tehran, 1945–46.

Idem. *Afsânehâ-ye Bu Ali Sinâ* (Tales about Bu Ali Sinâ). Tehran, 1954.

Idem. *Afsânehâ-ye kohan* (Old tales) 1–2. Tehran, 1944–46.

Idem. *Afsâneha-ye bâstani* (Ancient tales). Tehran, 1953.

Idem. *Dâstânhâ-ye melal* (Tales of the nations). Tehran, n.d.

Idem. "Ta'thir-e afsânehâ-ye Irân dar afsânehâ-ye khâreji" (The influence of Persian tales on foreign tales). *Mardomshenâsi* 2 (1958), pp. 119–21.

Ṭâhbâz, S. *Yush.* Tehran, 1964, 1996.

Tâkehârâ Sh. and A. Vakiliyân. *Afsânehâ-ye Irâni be-revâyat-e emruz va diruz* (Persian tales in versions of today and yesterday). Tehran, 2002.

Taqvâ, M. *Ḥekâyathâ-ye ḥeyvânât dar adab-e fârsi* (Animal tales in Persian literature). Tehran, 1997.
Tazhibi, S. and Sh. Shojâ'atdust. *Lâlâ, lâlâ, gol-e lâle: Barâ-ye owliyâ-ye tarbiyati* (Hushaby, baby, tulip: for teachers). Tehran, 1978, 2000.
Vahman, F. "Dâstânhâ-ye ablahân." (Stories of fools). *Sokhan* 9 (1969), pp. 755–65, 897–911.
Idem. "Jam'-âvari-ye afsânehâ-ye Irâni" (The collection of Persian tales). *Sokhan* 18.2 (1968), pp. 171–77.
Vakiliyân, A. *Tamthil va mathal* (Allegories and proverbs). Vol. 2, Tehran, 1987.
Idem. *Ramażân dar farhang-e mardom* (The month of Ramazân in popular culture). Tehran, 1991.
Idem. *Chistânhâ-ye kh^{w}ândani* (Riddles worth reading). Tehran, 1996, 1998.
Idem. *Mathalhâ va owsânehâ-ye Irâni* (Popular Persian tales and stories). Tehran, 1999.
Idem. *Qeṣṣehâ-ye mardom. Gerd-âvarde-ye pazhuheshgarân-e pazhuheshkade-ye mardom-shenâsi-ye Sâzmân-e Mirâth-e Farhangi* (Folktales. Collected by the students of the Department of Ethnography at the Organisation for the Cultural Heritage). Tehran, 2000.
Idem and Kh. Ṣâleḥi. *Hażrat-e Ali dar qeṣṣehâ-ye âmiyâne* (Our Lord Ali in popular tales). Tehran, 2001.
Weryho, J.W. "Sîstânî-Persian Folklore." *Indo-Iranian Journal* 5 (1961–62), pp. 276–307.
Wilson, B.K. *Fairytales of Persia*. New York, 1961.
Yamamoto, K. *From Storytelling to Poetry: The Oral Background of the Persian Epics*. (Ph.D. diss., University of London, 2000) Leiden, 2003.
Zamâni, M. *Ketâbshenâsi-ye farhang-e âmme va mardomshenâsi-ye Irân* (A bibliography of popular culture and ethnography of Iran). Tehran, 1971.
Zhukovski, V. *Obraztsy persidskogo narodnogo tvorchestva* (Examples of Persian popular creative works). St Petersburg, 1902.
Zhukovski, V.A. *Materiali dlia izuchenia persidskikh narechiï* (Materials for the study of Persian dialects). 3 vols., St. Petersburg, 1888, Petrograd, 1922 (repr. Tehran, 1976).

BIBLIOGRAPHIES

Chapter 10

Abd-al-Jalil Naṣir-al-Din Qazvini, *Naqż, ma'ruf be ba'ż mathâleb al-navâṣeb fi naqż: ba'ż fażâ'eḥ al-ravâfeż* (Annihilation, known as some faults of the enemies of Ali: annihilation of "Some Faults of the Forsakers"). Edited by Mir Jalâl-al-Din Moḥaddeth. Tehran, 1979.

Âl-e Dawûd, A. *EIr*, s.v. Coffee House.

Afshâr, I. ed. *Eskandar-nâme* (The Book of Alexander). Tehran, 1964.

Eskandar-nâma. Translated by Minoo S. Southgate as *Iskandarnamah: A Persian Medieval Alexander-Romance.* New York, 1978.

Afshâri, M. "Javânmardi va qalandari va farhang-e âmme-ye Irân" (Javânmardi and Qalandari: Iranian popular culture). *Chistâ* 6/7–8 (1989), pp. 493–507.

Idem. "Haft lashkar yâ Shâhnâme-ye naqqâlân" (The seven armies or storytellers' *Shâhnâme*). *Farhang* 7(1990), pp. 475–93.

Idem and Mehdi Madâyeni, eds., *Haft Lashkar* (Ṭumâr-e jâme'e-ye naqqâlân) az Kayumarth tâ Bahman (The seven armies: storytellers' Ṭumâr from Kayumars to Bahman). Tehran, 1998.

Anonymous. *Qeṣṣe-ye Ḥoseyn-e Kord-e Shabestari, bar asâs-e ravâyat-e nâshenâkhte-ye mowsum be Ḥoseyn-name.* Edited by Iraj Afshar and Mehrân Afshari, Tehran, 2006.

Asadi Ṭusi, Abu-Naṣr Ali. *Garshâsp-nâme* (The Book of Garshâsp). Edited by Ḥabib Yaghmâ'i. Tehran, 1938.

Idem. *Garshâsp-nâme.* Translated by Clément Huart and Henri Massé as *Le Livre de Gerchâsp: Poème persan d'Asadî* (junior) *de Ṭoûs.* 2 vols., Paris, 1926–51.

Aubin, E. *La Perse d'aujourd'hui.* Paris, 1908.

Bahâr, Moḥammad-Taqi, ed. *Mojmal al-tavârikh va'l-qeṣaṣ* (A compendium of chronicles and stories). Tehran, 1940.

Idem. *Sabkshenâsi* (Typology of Persian poetry). 3 vols, 2nd ed., Tehran, 1958.

Beyhaqi, Abu'l-Fażl Moḥammad. *Târikh-e Beyhaqi* (The History of Beyhaqi). Edited by Ali-Akbar Fayyâż. Mashhad, 1971.

Bighami, Moḥammad. *Dârâb-nâme-ye Bighami* (The book of Dârâb by Bighami). Edited by Dhabih-Allâh Ṣafâ. 2 vols, Tehran, 1960–62.

Idem. *Dârâb-nâme-ye Bighami.* Translated by W. L. Hanaway as *Love and War: Adventures from the Firuz Shâh Nâma of Sheikh Bighami*, New York, 1974.

Beyżâ'i, B. "Namâyesh dar Irân (4), naqqâli" (Theater in Iran (4), storytelling). *Majalle-ye Musiqi* 3/66 (1962), pp. 15–33.

Boyce, M. "Some Remarks on the Transmission of the Kayanian Heroic Cycle." *Serta Cantabrigiensia* (1954), pp. 49–51.
Idem. "Zariadrès and Zarêr." *BSOAS* XVII/IV (1955), pp. 463–77.
Idem. "The Parthian Gôsân and Iranian Minstrel Tradition." *JRAS* (1957), pp. 10–45.
Bruijn, J.T.P. de. "Poets and Minstrels in Early Persian Literature." In *Transition Periods in Iranian History*: Actes du Symposium de Fribourg-en-Brisgau (22–24 Mai 1985): *Studia Iranica* Cahier 5 (1987), pp. 15–23.
Clinton, J.W. *The Divan of Manûchihrî Dâmghânî: A Critical Study.* Chicago, 1972.
Darmesteter, J. *Le Zend-Avesta*: traduction nouvelle avec commentaire historique et philologique. 3 vols., Paris, 1892–93 (repr. 1960).
Davidson, O.M. "The Crown-Bestower in the Iranian Book of Kings." *Acta Iranica* 24 (1985), pp. 61–148.
Idem. *Poet and Hero in the Persian Book of Kings*. Ithaca and London, 1994.
Idem. "The Text of Ferdowsi's *Shâhnâma* and the Burden of the Past." *Journal of the American Oriental Society* 118 (1998), pp. 63–68.
Idem. *Comparative Literature and Classical Persian Poetics*. Costa Mesa, CA, 2000.
Davis, Dick. "The Problem of Ferdowsî's Sources." *Journal of the American Oriental Society* 116/1 (1996), pp. 48–57.
Dodge, B. *The Fihrist of al-Nadim*. 2 vols., New York, 1970.
Dustkhʷâh, J. "Naqqâli, honar-e dâstânsarâ'i-ye melli" (Naqqâli, the art of national storytelling). *Jong-e Eṣfahân* 4 (1966), pp. 73–88.
Idem. "Dâstân-e Garshâsp" (The story of Garshâsp). *Jong-e Eṣfahân* 5 (1967), pp. 99–106.
Idem. "Kâve-ye âhangar be revâyat-e naqqâlân" (Kâve the blacksmith as transmitted by the storytellers). *Irân-Nâme* 10/1 (1992), pp. 122–44.
Falsafi, N. "Târikh-e qahve va qahve-khâne dar Irân" (History of coffee and coffee houses in Iran). *Sokhan* 5/4 (1954), pp. 258–68.
Farâmarz ebn-e Khodâdâd Arrajâni, *Samak-e Ayyâr*. Edited by Parviz-Nâtel Khânlari. 5 vols., Tehran, 1968–74.
Idem. *Samak-e Ayyâr*. Translated by Frédérique Razavi as *Samak-e Ayyar*, Paris, 1972.
Ferdowsi, Abu-'l-Qâsem, *Shahname* (The Book of Kings). Edited by Djalal Khaleghi-Motlagh. 8 vols., New York, 1988–2007.
Idem. *Firdousi, Shakh-name: Kriticheskiĭ tekst*. Edited by E.Z. Bertels et al., 9 vols., Moscow, 1960–71.
Idem. *Le Livre des Rois*. Edited and translated by J. Mohl. 7 vols., Paris, 1838–68.

BIBLIOGRAPHIES

Gaillard, M. *Le Livre de Samak-e Ayyâr: Structure et idéologie du roman persan médiéval.* Paris, 1987

Hanaway, W.L. "Persian Popular Romances before the Safavid Period." Ph.D. diss., Columbia University, 1970.

Idem. "Formal Elements in the Persian Popular Romances." *Review of National Literature* II/1(1971)[a], pp. 139–60.

Idem. "Popular Literature in Iran," in P.J. Chelkowski, ed., *Iran: Continuity and Variety,* New York, 1971[b], pp. 59–75.

Idem. "Introduction," in idem, ed., *Love and War,* New York, 1974, pp. 1–24.

Idem. *EIr,* s.v. Amir Arsalân.

Idem. *EIr,* s.v. Dârâb-nâma.

Idem. *EIr,* s.v. Dâstân-sarâ'i.

Ḥâfeẓ, Shams-al-Din Moḥammad. *Divân-e Ḥâfeẓ* (Poetical works of Hâfeẓ). Edited by Parviz-Nâtel Khânlari. 2 vols, Tehran, 1980.

Irânshâh ebn-e Abi-'l-Kheyr, *Bahman-nâme* (The Book of Bahman). Edited by Raḥim Afifi. Tehran, 1991.

Kâshefi-Sabzevâri, Mowlânâ Ḥoseyn-Vâ'eż. *Fotovvat-nâme-ye solṭâni.* Edited by M.-J. Maḥjub. Tehran, 1971.

Idem. *Fotovvat-nâme-ye solṭâni.* Translated by Jay R. Crook as *The Royal Book of Spiritual Chivalry.* Chicago, 2000.

Key-Kâvus ebn-e Eskandar. *Qâbus-nâme.* Edited by Gholâm-Ḥoseyn Yusefi Tehran, 1966.

Idem. *Qâbus-nâme.* Translated by R. Levy as *A Mirror for Princes.* London, 1951.

Keyvani, M. *Artisans and Guild Life in the Later Safavid Period.* Berlin, 1982.

Khaleghi-Motlagh, Djalal. "Dar pirâmun-e manâbe'-e Ferdowsi" (On Ferdowsi's Sources). *Iranshenasi* 10/2 (1998), pp. 512–39.

Idem. "Takrâr dar Shâh-nâme" (Repetition in the *Shahname*). *Iranshenasi* 13 (2002), pp. 526–51, 814–38.

Lesân, Ḥ. "*Shâhnâme*-khᵂâni" (Recitation of *Shahname*). *Honar va Mardom* 159–160 (1976), pp. 2–16.

Loghat-nâme. Edited by Ali-Akbar Dehkhodâ. Tehran, 1959–73.

Lord, A.B. *The Singer of Tales.* Cambridge, Mass., 1960.

Maḥjub, M.-J. "Sokhanvari" (Poetic competition). *Sokhan* 9/7 (1958), pp. 530–35; 9/8 (1958), pp. 631–37; 9/9 (1958), pp. 779–86.

Idem. "Sokhanvari." Translated by F. Meier and annotated by R. Gramlich as "Drei moderne Texte zum persischen 'Wettreden'." *ZDMG* 114 (1964), pp. 289–327.

Idem. "Moqaddame" (Introduction); in Naqib al-Mamâlek, *Amir Arsalân,* Tehran, 1961–62, pp. I–LXVIII.

Idem. "Taḥavvol-e naqqâli va qeṣṣe-khʷâni, tarbiyat-e qeṣṣe-khʷânân va ṭumârhâ-ye naqqâli" (Transformation of *naqqâli* and storytelling: training of storytellers and Tumârs of *naqqâli*). *Nashriyye-ye Anjoman-e Farhang-e Irân-e Bâstân* 8/1 (1970), pp. 39–66.

Marzolph, U. *Dâstânhâ-ye shirin: Fünfzig persische Volksbüchlein aus der zweiten Hälfte des zwanzigsten Jahrhunderts.* Stuttgart, 1994.

Idem. "A Treasury of Formulaic Narrative: The Persian Popular Romance Ḥosein-e Kord." *Oral Tradition* (2000).

Idem. *EIr*, s.v. Ḥosayn-e Kord-e Šabestari.

Massé, H. *Firdousi et l'épopée nationale.* Paris, 1935.

Matini, Jalal. "Dar bâre-ye mas'ale-ye manâbeʿ-e Ferdowsi." (On the Article "The Problem of Ferdowsi's Sources"). *Iranshenasi* 10/2(1998), pp. 401–30.

Mélikoff, I. *Abû Muslim: Le 'Porte-Hache' du Khorassan dans la tradition épique turco-iranienne.* Paris, 1962.

Minovi, M. *Ferdowsi va sheʾr-e u* (Ferdowsi and his poetry). Tehran, 1976.

Molé, M. "Garshâsp et les Sagsâr." *La Nouvelle Clio* 3 (1951), pp. 128–38.

Idem. "Un poème persan du comte de Gobineau." *La Nouvelle Clio* 4 (1952), pp. 116–30.

Idem. "L'épopée iranienne après Firdôsî." *La Nouvelle Clio* 5 (1953), pp. 377–93.

Naqib al-Mamâlek, M.-A. *Amir Arsalân.* Edited by Moḥammad-Jaʾfar Maḥjub. Tehran, 1961.

Naṣrâbâdi, Mirzâ Moḥammad-Ṭâher. *Tadhkere-ye Naṣrâbâdi* (The history of the poets by Naṣrâbâdi). Edited by Vaḥid Dastgerdi. Tehran, 1939.

Omidsalar, M. "Olga M. Davidson. *Poet and Hero in the Persian Book of Kings.*" *Irânshenâsi* 2/2 (1995), pp. 436–57.

Idem. "Unburdening Ferdowsi: *Poet and Hero in the Persian Book of Kings.*" *Journal of the American Oriental Society* 116/2 (1996), pp. 235–42.

Idem. "Taʾammolâti-ye pirâmun-e sâde-engâri" (Reflections on Misconceptions about the Orality of the *Shahname*). *Iranshenasi* 11/1(1999), pp. 146–57.

Omidsalar, M. and T. "Narrating Epics in Iran," in M. R. MacDonald, ed., *Traditional Storytelling Today: An International Sourcebook*, Chicago and London, 1999, pp. 326–40.

Ong, W. J. *Orality and Literacy The Technologizing of the Word.* London and New York, 1982.

Page, M. E. "Naqqâli and Ferdowsi: Creativity in the Iranian National Tradition." Ph.D. diss., University of Pennsylvania, 1977.

BIBLIOGRAPHIES

Idem. "Professional Storytelling in Iran: Transmission and Practice." *Iranian Studies* XII/3–4 (1979), pp. 195–215.

Parry, M. *The Making of Homeric Verse: The Collected Papers of Milman Parry*. Edited by A. Parry. Oxford, 1971.

Sâdât-e-Eshkevari, K. "Naqqâli va Shâhnâme-khʷâni" (Naqqâli and recitation of Shâh-nama). *Honar va Mardom* 153/154 (1973), pp. 142–48.

Ṣadâqat-Nezhâd, J. *Ṭumâr-e kohan-e Shâhnâme-ye Ferdowsi* (Ancient Tumâr of Ferdowsi's *Shahname*). Tehran, 1995.

Ṣafâ, Dhabiḥ-Allâh. *Ḥamâse-sarâ'i dar Iran* (Composing epics in Iran). 5th printing. Tehran, 1970–71.

She'âr, J., ed. *Qeṣṣe-ye Amir-al-Mo'menin Ḥamze: moshtamel bar 69 dâstân* (The tales of Hamze the leader of the faithful: containing 69 tales). Tehran, 1347.

Shirazi, Forud Ismail-Beigi. "A Study of the Evolutionary Trend and the Current Atmosphere and Condition of Shâhnâmikhâni in Iran." Ph.D. diss., Wayne State University, 1973.

Soroudi, S. "Islamization of the Iranian National Hero Rustam as Reflected in Persian Folktales." *Jerusalem Studies in Arabic and Islam* 2 (1980), pp. 365–83.

Ṭarsusi, Abu Ṭâher Moḥammad. *Dârâb-nâme-ye Ṭarsusi* (The book of Dârâb by Ṭarsusi). Edited by Dhabiḥ-Allâh Ṣafâ. 2 vols, Tehran, 1965–67.

Idem. *Abu-Moslem-nâme: Ḥamâse-ye Abu-Moslem-e Khorâsâni* (The book of Abu-Moslem of Khorasani). Edited by E. Yaghmâ'i. Tehran, n.d.

Tauer, F. "Persian Learned Literature from its Beginnings up to the End of the 18th Century," in J. Rypka, ed., *History of Iranian Literature*, Dordrecht, 1968, pp. 419–82.

Torâbi, Vali-Allâh. "Mard mikhʷâham ke bâr-e gham keshad" (I want a man who carries the burden of sorrow). *Keyhân-e Varzeshi* 36 (1990), pp. 14–17.

Waldman, M. R. *Toward a Theory of Historical Narrative: A Case Study in Perso-Islamicate Historiography*. Columbus, 1980.

Wallenbourg, J. von. *Notice sur le Schàh'-Namé de Ferdoussì, et traduction de plusieurs pièces relatives à ce poème*. Vienna, 1810.

Yamamoto, K. *The Oral Background of Persian Epics: Storytelling and Poetry*. Leiden, 2003.

Zariri, Morshed Abbâs. *Dâstân-e Rostam va Sohrâb: revâyat-e naqqâlân* (The story of Rostam and Sohrâb: storytellers' narrative). Edited by Jalil Dustkhʷâh. Tehran, 1990.

Zâkâni, Obeyd. *Kolliyyât-e Obeyd-e Zâkâni* (The collected works of Obeyd-e Zâkâni). 2nd printing. Edited and annotated by Parviz Atâbaki. Tehran, 1964–65.

Chapter 11

Behzâdi-Anduhjerdi, H., ed. *Gozide-ye Ḥamle-ye Ḥeydari* (A selection from the *Ḥamle-ye Ḥeydari*). Tehran, 1991.

Brook, P. "Leaning on the Moment: A Conversation with Peter Brook." *Parabola* 4, May/June 1979.

Browne, E.G. *A Literary History of Persia*. 4 vols., Cambridge reprint, 1969.

Canetti, Elias. *Crowds and Power*. New York, 1978.

Chelkowski, P.J., ed. *Ta'ziye: Ritual and Drama in Iran*. New York, 1979.

Idem. "Iran: Mourning becomes Revolution." *Asia*, May/June 1980, pp. 30–45.

Idem. "Popular Shi'i Mourning Rituals." *Alserat* 12, Spring/Autumn 1986.

Idem. "In Ritual and Revolution: The Image in the Transformation of Iranian Culture." *Views: The Journal of Photography in New England* 10/3, 1989[a].

Idem. "Narrative Painting and Painting Recitation in Qajar Iran." *Muqarnas* 6, 1989[b], pp. 98–111.

Idem. "Popular Arts, Patronage and Piety." In L.S. Diba and M. Ekhtiar, eds., *Royal Persian Paintings: the Qajar Epoch 1785–1925*. London, 1998, pp. 90–97.

Idem and H. Dabashi. *Staging a Revolution: the Art of Persuasion in the Islamic Republic of Iran*. New York, 1999.

Grunebaum, G.E. von. *Muhammadan Festivals*. London and New York, 1958.

Homâyuni, Ṣâdeq. *Ta'ziye dar Irân* (*Ta'ziye* in Iran). Shirâz, 1989.

Kâshefi, Mollâ Ḥoseyn Vâ'eẓ. *Rowżat al-Shohadâ'* (The garden of martyrs). Edited by M. Ramażâni. Tehran, 1962.

Maḥjub, Moḥammad-Ja'far. "Az fażâ'el- va manâqeb-khʷâni tâ rowze-khʷâni" (From the praising of virtues to *rowze-khʷâni*). *Irân-Nâme* 2/3 (Spring 1984), pp. 402–31.

Majalle-ye Sorush 166, October/November 1982 (Âbân 1361).

Mamnoun, P. *Ta'zija: schi'itisch-persisches Passionsspiel*. Vienna, 1967.

Membré, M. *Mission to the Lord Sophy of Persia (1539–1542)*. London, 1993.

Nâẓerzâde-Kermâni, Farhâd. "Ḥamle-khʷâni gune-ye mohemmi az naqqâli-ye madhhabi dar Irân" (*Ḥamle-khʷâni*, an important form of religious storytelling in Iran). *Faṣl-nâme-ye honar* 1999, pp. 65–74.

Oxford Encyclopedia of the Modern Islamic World. 4 vols., New York, 1995.

BIBLIOGRAPHIES

Pelly, L. *The Miracle Play of Hasan and Husain*. 2 vols., London, 1879.
Peterson, S. R. "Shi'ism and Late Iranian Arts." Ph.D. diss., New York University, 1981.
Riggio, M. C., ed. *Ta'ziyeh: Ritual and Popular Beliefs in Iran*. Hartford, Conn., 1988.
Rossi, E. and A. Bombaci. *Elenco di Drammi Religiosi Persiani* (A list of Persian religious dramas). Citta del Vaticano, 1969.

Chapter 12

Ahmad, R. *Navrûzi olamafrûz* (Nouwruz illuminating the world). Dushanbe, 1978.
Akhmedov, R. *Vesenniï Kalendarno-obriadovyï fol'klor Tadzhikov* (Tajik folklore about spring, the calendar, and ceremonies). Cand. Phil. Dissertation. Dushanbe, 1972.
Amonov, R. *Folklori sokinoni sargahi Zarafshon* (The folklore of the inhabitants of the Upper Zarafshan area). Stalinabad, 1960.
Idem. *Ejodioti dahanakii aholii Kûlob* (Oral creative works of the people of Kulob). With additions by F. Murodov. 2nd ed., Dushanbe, 1963.
Idem. *Lirikai khalqii Tojik* (Tajik folk lyrics). Dushanbe, 1968.
Idem. *Ruboioti khalqii va ramzhoi badeî* (Popular *robâ'i*s and poetic symbols). Dushanbe, 1987.
Idem. *Latîfaho* (Witty stories). Dushanbe, 1994.
Idem. "Qissai diori chashmasor" (A tale from the land of the many springs). *Adib*, 1995, p. 150.
Idem, ed. *Dasturulamal oid ba jam' kardani èjodiyoti dahanakiyi khalq* (Guidelines for collecting popular creative works). Stalinabad, 1960.
Idem, and I. Kalontarov. *Chistonho*, (Riddles). Stalinabad, 1956.
Idem, and K. Ulughzoda. *Afsonahoi Khalqii Tojikî* (Tajik folktales). Stalinabad, 1957.
Idem, and S. Normatov. *Taronahoi Navrûzî*, (Nowruz songs). Stalinabad, 1960.
Idem, and M. Shukurov. *Namunahoy folklori diori Rûdakî*, (Examples of the folklore of Rudaki's homeland). Revised edition. 2 vols., Dushanbe, 1963.
Andreev, M. S. "Darvazskaia Skazka" (Stories from Darvaz). *Zhivaia Starina* 2–4, 1912, pp. 485–88.
Idem, and A. A. Polovtsev. "Materiali po etnografii Iranskikh plemion Sredneï Azii. (Ishkashim i Vakhan)" (Materials for the ethnography of

the Iranian peoples of Central Asia. Ishkashim and Vakhan). *Muzeia Antropologii i Etnografii. Imper. Ak. Nauk, Etnografia,* I. 9. St. Petersburg, 1911.

Idem, and E. M. Peshereva. *Iagnobskie Teksty* (Yaghnobi texts). Moscow and Leningrad, 1957.

Arandarenko, G. A. "Darvaz i Karaterin: Etnograficheskiĭ Ocherk" (Darvaz and Karaterin: an ethnographic essay). St. Petersburg, 1889.

Asrorî, V. *Ejodioti Iusuf Bafo* (The creative works of Yusuf Bafo). Stalinabad, 1956.

Asrorî, V. *Zarbulmasal va maqolhoi Tojikî* (Tajik proverbs and maxims). Stalinabad, 1956.

Idem. *Zhanrhoi khurdi folklorî* (The genres of folklore). Dushanbe, 1987.

Idem, and R. Amonov. *Ejodioti dahanakii khalqî Tojik,* (Oral creative works of the Tajik people). Dushanbe, 1980.

Bartol'd, V. V. "Nauruz v Samarkande" (Nowruz in Samarkand). *Turkestanskie Vedemosti* 14, 1897.

Braginskiĭ, A. S. *Iz Istorii Tadzhikskoĭ Narodnoĭ Poezii: Elementy Narodnogo-poeticheskogo Tvorchestva v Pamiatnikakh Drevneĭ i Srednevekovoĭ Pis'mennosti* (On the history of Tajik folk poetry: elements of folk poetry in ancient and medieval literary texts). Moscow, 1956.

Idem. *Gurugli: Tadzhikskiĭ Narodnyĭ Epos* (Gurughli: the Tajik national epic). Moscow, 1987.

Boldirev (Boldyrev), A. N. "Eposi dahanakii Tojikiston" (The oral epic of Tajikistan). *Adabioti Sotsialisti* 11–12, 1934, pp. 37–39.

Idem. *Namunai folklori tojik* (A sample of Tajik folkore). Vol 1. Under the supervision of E. Bertels. Leningrad and Stalinabad, 1938.

Boldyrev, A. N. "Ustnyĭ Epos Tadzhikistana" (The oral epic of Tajikistan). *Druzhba Narodov* 1, 1939, pp. 299–304.

Idem. "Tadzhikskie Chorbaity" (Tajik *chorbaytis*). *Druzhba Narodov* 7, 1941, pp. 261–64. Translated from Tajiki by N. Lebedev.

Idem. "Voprosy Izucheniia Tadzhidskogo Narodnogo Tvorchestva" (Questions about the study of Tajik national folklore). *Trudy Tadzhikskogo Filiala Akademii Nauka SSSR* 29, 1951, pp. 99–108. Stalinabad.

Chalishev, S. *Zhinzn' i Tvorchestvo Saidali Vali-zade* (The life and creative work of Said-Ali Valizade). Cand. Phil. thesis. Dushanbe, 1972.

Idem. *Folklori diori Vose'* (The folklore of the Vose' area). Dushanbe, 1990.

Dehoti, A. *Latifaho. Majmu'a* (Witty sayings: a collection). Stalinabad, 1938.

Fathulloev, S. *Gûrûghlî: dostoni bahoduroni Chambuli Maston* (Gurughli: a tale of the heroes of Chambuli Maston). Vol. 3. Recited by Haqnazar Kabud. Dushanbe, 1963.

BIBLIOGRAPHIES

Fozilov, M. *Farhangi zarbulmasal, maqol va aforizmhoi Tojikiu Forsi* (Thesaurus of Tajik and Persian proverbs, maxims and aphorisms). Vols. 1-3, Dushanbe, 1975-78.

Gulrukhsor. *Folklori vodii Qaroterin* (The folklore of the Qaroterin valley). Dushanbe, 1986.

Gûrûghlî, see under Fathulloev; Kholov and Hisomov.

Habibov, A., ed. *Chistonho* (Riddles). Dushanbe, 1962.

Iarnevskiï, I.Z. *Ustnyï Rasskaz kak Zhanr Fol'klora* (Oral stories as a folklore genre). Ulan-Ude, 1969.

Iavich, M.M. *Tadzhikskie Skazki o Zhivotnykh: Opyt Kolichestvennogo Analyza Tadzhikskogo Fol'klora* (Tajik stories about animals: an experiment in the quantitative analysis of Tajik folklore). Vol. 1, Dushanbe, 1986.

Karimzoda, H. *Zarbulmasal va chistonhoi Tojiki* (Tajik proverbs and riddles). Moscow and Leningrad, 1931.

Kholov, M and Q. Hisomov. *Gûrûghlî: eposi khalqii Tojiki* (Gurughli: a Tajik folk epic I). Vol. 1. Recited by Qurbonali Rajabov. Dushanbe, 1963.

Kholov, M and Q. Hisomov. *Gûrûghlî: dostoni bahoduroni Chambuli Maston* (Gurughli: the tale of the heroes of Chambuli Maston). Vol. 2. Recited by Qurbonali Rajabov. Dushanbe, 1963.

Kodirov, R. *Folklori marosimii torevoliutsionii Tojikoni vodii Qashqadario* (The folklore of pre-revolutionary customs of the Tajiks of the Qashqadaryo Valley). Dushanbe, 1963.

Kullioti Folklori Tojik I: Masalho va Afsonaho dar borai Hayvanot (Comprehensive collection of folklore, vol. I: parables and fables about animals). Edited by I. Levin, J. Rabiev, and M. Iavich. Moscow, 1981. (In Tajiki and Russian).

Kullioti Folklori Tojik IV, V: Zarbulmasalho (Comprehensive collection of folklore, vols. IV, V: proverbs). Edited by B. Tilavov, F. Murodov and Q. Hisomov. Dushanbe, 1986, 1992.

Mahdiev, S. *Folklori Norak* (The folklore of Norak). Dushanbe, 1963.

Idem. "Problemai zhanri latifa" (The problem of the genre "witty sayings"). *Donish*, 1977.

Mahmudî and Zehnî. *Omuzesh: Qiroat baroi sinfi 3* (Learning: reading for the third grade). Samarkand and Leningrad, 1926. (In Persian script.)

Ma'sûmî, N. *Foklori Tojik. Kursi konspektivî baroi ghoibkhonai Inst. Pedagogî* (Tajik folklore. A course of lectures for the Dept. of Extramural Studies of the Pedagogical Institute). Stalinabad, 1952.

Mirsaidov, S. "Baït hamchûn zhanri folklorî" (The *beyt* as a genre in folklore). *Sharqi Surkh* 11, 1964.

Mirzoev, A. "Dar borai dostoni 'Gurugli'" (On the tale of Gurughli). *Sharqi Surx* 1 (1940), pp. 35–36.
Musulmonion, R. *Nazariai adabiot* (A theory of literature). Dushanbe, 1990.
N. N. *Ash'ori hamasroni Rûdakî* (Poems of Rudaki's contemporaries). Stalinabad, 1958.
Nal'skiï, Ia. I. *Narodnyï Poèt 'Bobo Iunus Khudoidod-zade'* (The folk poet Bobo Yunus Khudoydodzade). Stalinabad, 1955.
Narshahi, Abûbakr Muhammad binni Ja'far. *Ta'rikhi Bukhoro* (History of Bukhara). Dushanbe, 1979.
Nazarov, H. *Dar justujûi Karim Devona* (In search of Karim the Mad). 3rd reprint, Dushanbe, 1968.
Niazmuhammedov, B., ed. *Tadzhikskie Skazki* (Tajik stories). Under the supervision of E. N. Pavlovskiï. Stalinabad, 1945.
Nurjonov, N. *Dramai Khalqii Tojik* (Tajik folk drama). Dushanbe, 1985.
Obidov, D. *Afsonahoi hajvî-maishii Tojikî* (Tajik satirical tales and tales about life). Dushanbe, 1978.
Idem. "Naql" (Oral stories). *Entsiklopediai Sovietii Tojik* 5, Dushanbe, 1984, p. 125.
Idem. "Rivoiat" (The revâyat). *Entsiklopediai Sovietii Tojik* 6, Dushanbe, 1986, p. 359.
Pisarchik, A., S. Tojiddinov and Homidjonova. *Zarbulmasal va Maqolhoi Tojiki* (Tajik proverbs and maxims). Stalinabad, 1960.
Qodirov, R. *Folklori Tojikoni Qashqadario* (The folklore of the Tajiks of Qashqadaryo). 3 vols.: Vol. I: *Afsonahoi Sehromez* (Tales concerned with magic). Under the supervision of R. Ahmad and Ia. Rajabî, Dushanbe, 1998. Vol. II: *Afsonaho, dostonho, hikoiot, naql, rivoiot va latifaho* (Afsânes, dâstâns, ḥekâyats, revâyats and witty stories). Under the supervision of R. Ahmad and Ia. Rajabî. Dushanbe, 1998.
Rabiev, Dzh. *Klassifikatsionnoe Znachenie Povestvovate'lnykh Sredstv Tadzhikskoï Narodnoï Prozy: Opyt Kolichestvennogo Analiza Tadzhikskogo Fol'klora* (A classified survey of the importance of the narrative assets of Tajik folk prose: An experiment in the quantitative analysis of Tajik folklore). Vol. 1, Dushanbe, 1986.
Rabiev, J. *Afsonahoi Ûroteppa* (Tales from Uroteppa). Dushanbe, 1992.
Rahmatov, H. "Naqlu rivoyatho" (Oral stories and *revâyats*); in R. Amonov, ed., *Dasturulamal oid ba jam' kardani èjodiyoti dahanakii khalq*, Stalinabad, 1960, pp. 90–91.
Rahmonî, R. "Hikoiathoi asotiri hamchun zhanri folklor" (Mythological tales as a folklore genre); in no ed., *Tezishoi Konferensiai Apreli ilmî-nazariavii professoronu muallimon*. Dushanbe, 1994.

BIBLIOGRAPHIES

Rahmonî, R. *Shughoi Bukhoro dar sabti Ravshan Rahmonî* (Tales from Bokhârâ recorded by Ravshan Rahmonî). Moscow, 1997.

Idem. *Qissaho, rivoiatho va duohoi Bukhoro dar sabti Ravshan Rahmonî* (Moral stories, *revâyat*s and prayers from Bokhârâ recorded by Ravshan Rahmonî). Dushanbe, 1998.

Rozenfel'd, A.Z. "Zoloto Kishlak: Predanie" (The golden village: a legend). *Kommunist Tadzhikistana* 7, 1957.

Idem. *Namunahoi folklori Darvoz* (Samples of the folkore of Darvaz). Stalinabad, 1955.

Idem, and N.P. Rychkova. *Skazki i Legendy Gornykh Tadzhikov* (Fairy-tales and legends from the Tajik mountains). Moscow, 1990.

Semionov, A.A. *Etnograficheskie Ocherki Zarafshanskikh Gor i Darvaza* (Ethnographical essays on the mountains of Zarafshan and Darvaz). Moscow, 1903.

Idem. *Materialy dlia Izuchenia Narechia Gornykh Tadzhikov Tsentral'noï Azii: Gramaticheskiï i Pamiatniki Narodnogo Tvorchestva* (Material for the study of the dialect of the mountain Tajiks of Central Asia: aspects of grammar and folklore texts). Moscow, 1900.

Shakarmamadov, B. *Surudhoi Tûi Pamir* (Wedding songs from the Pamirs). Khorug, Pamir, 1993.

Shermuhammadion, B. and D. Obidzova, eds. *Haft Alloma* (Seven scholars). Dushanbe, 1994.

Shermuhammadion, B. and D. Obidzova, eds. *Qissaho az rûzgori Firdavsî*, (Tales from the time of Ferdowsi). Dushanbe, 1994.

Shermuhammadov, B., ed. *Afsonahoi Samarqand* (Tales of Samarkand). Vol. I, Dushanbe, 1966.

Sirojiddin, B. and R. Qahhor. "Nuskhai khattii Salomnoma" (Manuscripts of the *Salâm-nâme*). *Mardumgioh* 1–2, 1994.

Sufiev, A. *Cîstonhoy khalqii Tojikî* (Tajik folk stories). Dushanbe, 1972.

Idem. *In'ikosi voqeiati Sovietî dar folklori Tojik* (The reflection of Soviet reality in Tajik folklore). Dushanbe, 1977.

Idem. *Folklor: afkori èstetikî va ijtimo'ii khalq* (Folkore: the people's aesthetic and social thoughts). Dushanbe, 1982.

Idem. *Hazoru yak chîston*, (A thousand and one riddles). Dushanbe, 1994.

Suhaïlî, J. and H. Homidî. *Gurughlî: Eposi khalqii Tojikî* I (Gurughli: the Tajik folk epic). Recited by Qurbon Jalil. Stalinabad and Leningrad, 1941.

Sukhareva, L.A. and O.A. "Zagadki. Vosem' Variantov Tadzhidskoï Versii Skazki 'Koza i Semero Kozliat'" (Riddles. Eight variants of the Tajik version of the tale "The goat and the seven kids"). *Materialy po Tadzhikskomu Fol'kloru*, Samarkand, 1934.

Sukhareva, O. A. "Brodiachie Siuzhety v Tadzhidskikh Skazakh. Soobshchenie o Doklade" (Vagabonds in Tajik stories. Communication). *Biuleten Samarkandskogo Gosudarstvennogo Universiteta* 8 (1925), p. 145.
Sumane az har Samane (A Flower from every meadow). Dushanbe, 1966.
Tilavov, B. *Sukhanhoi Dilafrûz* (Words to gladden the heart). Dushanbe, 1973.
Idem. *Poètika Tadzhikskikh Narodnykh Poslovits i Pogovorki* (The poetics of Tajik popular proverbs and sayings). Dushanbe, 1967.
Idem. *Tadzhikskie Poslovitsy i Pogovorki: Opyt Kolichestvennogo Analiza Tadzhikskogo Fol'klora* (Tajik proverbs and sayings: an experiment in the quantitative analysis of Tajik folklore). Vol 2: A study of the modern oral repertoire. Dushanbe, 1989.
Tursunzoda, M. *Namunai Folklori Tojik* (A sample of Tajik folklore). Stalinabad/ Leningrad, 1940.
Idem, and A. N. Boldyrev. *Folklori Tojik* (Tajik folklore). Stalinabad, 1957.
Zehnieva, F. *Surudhoi marosimi tûi Tojikon* (Wedding songs of the Tajiks). Dushanbe, 1978.

Chapter 13

Afghâni-Navis, Abdollah. *Loghât-e âmiyâne-ye fârsi-ye Afghânestân* (Colloquial vocabulary of the Persian of Afghanistan). Kabul, 1961 (2nd printing, 1985).
Amânov, R. and V. Asrâri. *Adabiyât-e shafâhi-ye mardom-e tajik* (Oral literature of the Tajik people). Dari ed. and trsl. Abd-al-Qayyum Qawim and Moḥammad Afżal Banuwal. Kabul, 1985.
Andreev, M. S. *Po etnologii Afganistana. Dolina Pandshir* (On the ethnography of Afghanistan: the Panjshir valley). Tashkent, 1927.
Anon. *Majmu'e'i az folklor-e âmiyâne-ye zabân-e dari: sorudhâ, robâ'iyât, dobeytihâ, meydabeytihâ, żarbolmathalhâ o chistânhâ, afsânahâ, revâyât o laṭifehâ* (A collection of the popular folklore in the Dari language: songs, quatrains, distiches, short verses, proverbs and riddles, wonder tales, narratives and jokes). Kabul, n.d. (1990s?)
Âryânfar, Shams-al-Ḥaqq. *Simâ-ye ḥażrat-e Ali "r. z." dar Farhang-e Mardom-e Fârsizabân* (The character of his eminence Ali, peace be upon him, in the culture of Persian-speaking peoples). Dushanbe (privately printed), 2001.
Asadullaev, S. *Namuneho-ye zarb ol-masal va maqolho-ye tojikon va uzbekon-e viloyat-e Qataghan-e Afghoniston* (Examples of the proverbs

and sayings of the Tajiks and Uzbeks of the province of Qataghan, Afghanistan). Dushanbe, 1964. [In Tajiki.]

Asir Harawi, Gholâm Ḥeydar. *Anbânche-ye gap-i Harât* (A skin-bag of Herat speech). Peshawar, 1989.

Ayub, Nafisa. *Afsânahâ-ye kudakâne dar kudakistân-e sanin-e 3–7 sâla* (Children's folktales in the kindergartens for ages 3–7 years). Kabul, 1983.

Baghban, Hafizullah. *The Context and Concept of Humor in Magadi Theater.* 4 vols., Ann Arbor (UMI), 1977.

Bakhshanda, Farhâd. *Chistân* (Riddles). [Place of publication effaced], 1997.

Barzinmehr, Abd-al-Ghani. *Naqdi bar ketâb-e "Żarbolmathalhâ-ye Dari"-ye Enâyâtollâh Shahrâni* (Critique of the book *Dari Proverbs*, by Enâyâtollâh Shahrâni). Peshawar, 2002.

Daniel, E. *The History of Iran.* Westport, Conn., 2001.

Delloye, I. *Femmes d'Afghanistan* (Women of Afghanistan). Paris, 2002.

Idem. *Women of Afghanistan.* Translated by M. de Jager. Saint Paul, Minn., 2003.

Edwards, D. *Heroes of the Age: Moral Fault Lines on the Afghan Frontier.* Berkeley, 1996.

Idem. *Before Taliban: Genealogies of the Afghan Jihad.* Berkeley, 2002.

Fekrat, Moḥammad Âsef. *Loghât-e zabân-e goftâri-ye Harât* (Vocabulary of colloquial language of Herat). Kabul, 1976.

Gardizi, Abd-al-Ghaffâr. *Simâ-ye kudak dar farhang-e mardom: majmu'a-i az tarânahâ-ye kudakân* (The expressions of children in popular culture: a collection of children's songs). n.p.

Guyâ, Sarwar. *Râhnamâ-ye folklor* (Guide to folklore). Kabul, 1939.

Ḥanifi, Pâ'iz. *Sorudhâ-ye maḥalli-ye mâ* (Our local songs). Kabul, 1967.

Idem. *Âhanghâ-ye maḥalli-ye mâ* (Our local tunes). Kabul, 1986.

Jina, Yâsmin Akmal. *Afsânahâ-ye Nuristâni* (Nuristani folktales). Kabul, 1991.

Khasta, Mowlânâ Khâl Moḥammad. *Żarbomathalhâ* (Proverbs). Kabul, 1983.

Ma'somi, N. and M. Khalav. *Namunahâ-ye folklor-e khalqhâ-ye Afghânestân* (Examples of the folklore of the peoples of Afghanistan). Dushanbe, 1965.

Mills, M. A. *Oral Narrative in Afghanistan: The Individual in Tradition.* New York, London, 1978 (repr. 1990).

Idem. *Rhetorics and Politics in Afghan Traditional Storytelling.* Philadelphia, 1991.

Idem. "Whose Best Tricks? *Makr-i Zan* as a Topos in Persian Oral Literature," *Iranian Studies* 32/3 (1990), pp. 261–70.

Idem. "Seven Steps Ahead of the Devil: A Misogynist Proverb in Context," in P. Enges, ed., *Telling, Remembering, Interpreting, Guessing: A Festschrift for Prof. Anniki Kaivola-Bregenhøj on her 60th Birthday*, Joensuu, 2000[a], pp. 449–58.

Idem. "Women's Tricks: Subordination and Subversion in Afghan Folktales," in L. Honko, ed., *Thick Corpus, Organic Variation and Textuality in Oral Tradition*. Studia Fennica Folkloristica 7. Helsinki, 2000[b], pp. 453–87.

Idem. "The Gender of the Trick: Female Tricksters and Male Narrators." *Asian Folklore Studies* 60/2 (2001), pp. 238–58.

Mirpur, Mir Abd-al-Qoddus. *Żarbolmathalhâ, kalamât-e qeṣâr o goftârhâ barâ-ye dustdârân-e an'anân o rosumât-e melli-ye vaṭan-e aziz* (Proverbs, aphorisms, and sayings for the friends of the traditions and customs of the beloved home country). Peshawar, 1995.

Nabizâda "Kâkar," Moḥammad Avaâ. *Lahjehâ-ye moravvaj-e mardom-e Hazâra, Deyzangi, Behsud va Jâghori* (Current dialects of the people of Hazara, Daizangi, Behsud and Jaghuri). Kabul, 1986.

Nangiyâli, Faqir Moḥammad. *Âhanghâ-ye mardomi-ye folklorik-e afghâni* (Afghan folk tunes). Peshawar, 1997.

Naṣib, Mohammad Nâṣer. *Zemzemahâ-ye rustâ* (Rural hummings). Kabul, 1991.

Othmân, Âref, trsl., *Də xalqo taffakor: də Afghânistân də Uzbêkâno mataluna aw maqulê* (Popular reflections: proverbs and sayings of the Uzbeks of Afghanistan). Kabul, 1980.

Râbin, Aziz Aḥmad. *Żarbolmathalhâ-ye âmiyâne* (Popular proverbs). Kabul, 1985.

Raḥim, Khadija, Turpikey Shahâbzâda and Ḥekmat Mohmand. *Ketâb-e sorudhâ o bâzihâ-ye bâ angoshtân barâ-yi aṭfâl-e sanin-i 1 elâ-ye 7 sâla* (A book of songs and finger games for children aged one to seven years). Peshawar, 1993.

Raḥimi, Nilâb. *Sangardihâ-ye Panjshir* (Stone-strolling verses of the Panjshir). Kabul, 1986.

Rahmoni, Ravshan. *Afsânehâ-ye Dari* (Dari folktales). Tehran, 1995.

Idem. *Afsânehâ-ye nâder* (Rare folktales). Peshawar, n.d. (2002?)

Idem. *Namunehâ-ye folklor-e Dari* (Specimens of Dari folklore). Vol. 1: *Afsânehâ-ye Dari* (Dari folktales). Vol. 2: *Dobeytihâ va robâ'iyyât* (Quatrains and distichs). Vol. 3: *Sokhan-e bozorgân chashm-e aql ast* (The speech of the elders is the essence of wisdom). Kabul, 1984.

Idem. *Prostonarodnaia Literatura Sovremennogo Afghanistana: Ustnaia Avtorskaia Poezia na Yazike Dari* (Popular literature of contemporary Afghanistan: oral poetry by named authors in the Dari language). 2 vols., Moscow, 1994.

Idem. *Afsona va zhenrho-yi digar-i nasri-i shafohi*, (Folktales and other oral prose genres). Dushanbe, 1999. [In Tajiki.]
Idem. *Târikh-e gerdâvari, nashr va pazhuhesh-e afsânehâ-ye mardom-e fârsizabân: Irân, Tâjikestân, Afghânestân* (History of collection, publication and research on the folktales of Persian-speaking peoples: Iran, Tajikistan, and Afghanistan). Tehran, 2001.
Sakata, L. *Music in the Mind*. 2nd ed. Washington, D.C., 2002.
Samangâni, Mohsen Hasan. *Yak daste gol: behtarin dobeytihâ-ye mahalli* (A bouquet of flowers: the finest local quatrains). Peshawar, 1998.
Shahrâni, Enâyatollâh. *Amthâl va hekam* (Proverbs and wise sayings). Kabul, 1975.
Idem. *Żarbolmathalhâ-ye dari-e Afghânistân* (Dari proverbs of Afghanistan). Union City, CA., 1999.
Shahrestâni, Shâh Ali-Akbar. *Qâmus-e lahja-ye dari-ye Hazâragi* (Dictionary of the Hazaragi Dari dialect). Kabul, 1982.
Sho'ur, Asadollah. *Chistânhâ-ye shafâhi-e Dari* (Oral riddles in Dari). Kabul, 1986.
Idem. *Mofâheme-ye shafâhi wa seyr-e târikhi-e ân dar Afghânistân* (Oral communication and its historical characteristics in Afghanistan). Kabul, 1988.
Idem. *Tarânehâ-ye Gharjestân* (Songs of Gharjistan). Tehran, 2002.
Idem. *Tarânehâ-ye Kohsâr* (Songs of the hill country). Kabul, 1974.
Sistâni, Mohammad A. *Sîstân, Sarzamîn-e mâsehâ wa hamâsehâ* (Sistan: land of sand and epics). Kabul, 1985.
Idem. *Mardomshenâsi-ye Sistân* (Anthropology of Sistan). Kabul, 1989.
Siyâmak, Ahmad Ziyâ. *Morgh-e tokhmṭalâ'i* (The bird with the golden eggs). Kabul, n.d.
Towfiq, Abd-al-Hoseyn. "Owsâne si sâne" (The tale of thirty kinds). *Farhang-e mardom*, Kabul, n.d.
Wilber, D.N. *Afghanistan: Its People, Its Society, Its Culture*. New Haven, 1962.
Yamin, Mohammad Hoseyn. *Farhang-e talaffoz-e loghât bâ bayân-e ma'âni-ye ân: moshtamel bar alfâẓ-e motadâwel-e diruzi va emruzi-ye zabân-e Dari* (Pronouncing dictionary with definitions; including fashionable expressions of yesterday and today in the Dari language). Kabul, 1983.
Yaqin, Gholâm Heydar. *Ayyârân o kâkâhâ-ye Khorâsân dar gostare-ye târikh* (Heroic tricksters and daredevils of Khorasan in the span of history). Kabul, 1986.